Welcome

Free software always sets off alarm bells. Will it be as good as paid-for packages? Will it try and sneak other unwanted apps onto your PC? Will it constantly nag you to update to a premium version? In this guide, we've scoured the web to find hundreds of free applications that deliver high-quality features and no nasty surprises.

This guide doesn't just provide a bland directory of free software – it shows you exactly how you can get the most out of the hundreds of packages we recommend. These pages are packed with step-by-step tutorials and workshops that show you precisely how to use the software we've tested thoroughly ourselves.

The free apps we've found can perform a wide variety of tasks, from helping to make Windows work the way you want it to, to making sure your PC is properly backed up and protected from viruses, to building a family tree. We've got software that can sort out your finances, put you in the cockpit of a flight simulator, or record classic TV programmes streamed over the internet.

There's genuinely something for everyone in this guide, and the only thing you'll need to spend after you've bought this guide is the hours of time enjoying your new software.

Editor: | Barry Collins

EDITORIAL

Editor: Barry Collins

Art Editor: Ian Jackson

Consulting Editor: Robert Irvine

Group Editor: Daniel Booth

Digital Production Manager: Nicky Baker

MANAGEMENT

MagBook Publisher: Dharmesh Mistry

Operations Director: Robin Ryan

MD of Advertising: Julian Lloyd-Evans

Newstrade Director: David Barker

MD of Enterprise: Martin Belson

Chief Operating Officer: Brett Reynolds

Group Finance Director: Ian Leggett

Chief Executive: James Tye

The Definitive Guide To Free Software ISBN 1-78106-455-5

LICENSING AND SYNDICATION

To license this product please contact Carlotta Serantoni on +44 (0) 20 7907 6550 or email carlotta_serantoni@dennis.co.uk

To syndicate content from this product please contact Anj Dosaj-Halai on +44 (0) 20 7907 6132 or email anj_dosaj-halai@dennis.co.uk

The paper used within this MagBook is produced from sustainable fibre, manufactured by mills with a valid chain of custody.

Printed at Southernprint

Contents

8
Andy\Pictures\2013-08 - XYplorerFree 14.50.0200 - XYplorer Free Edition

45

53
SAMSUNG
Solid State Drive

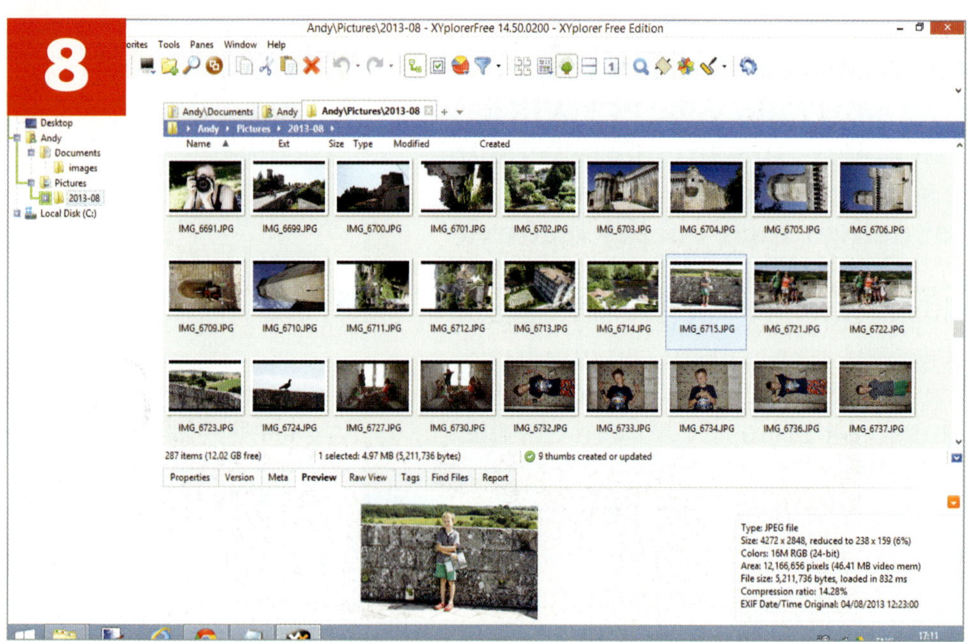

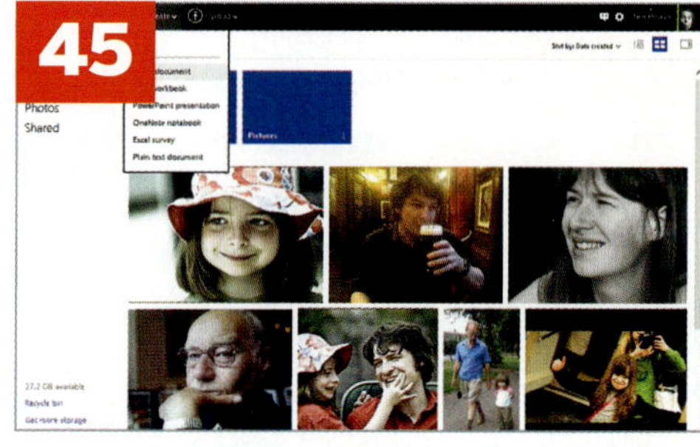

Free Software / Contents

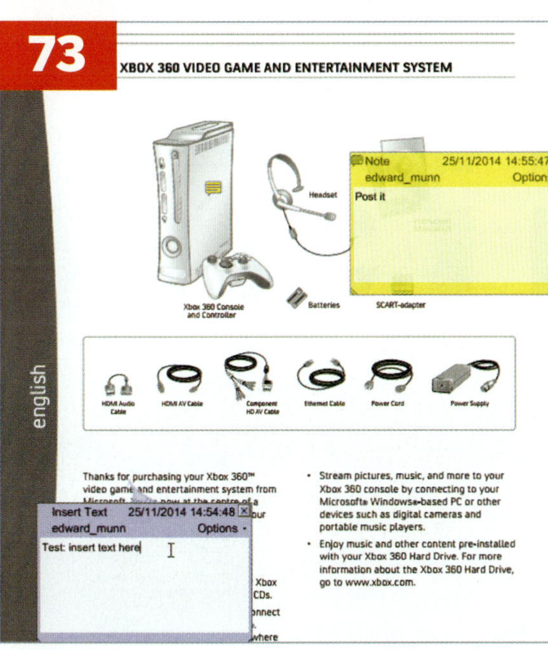

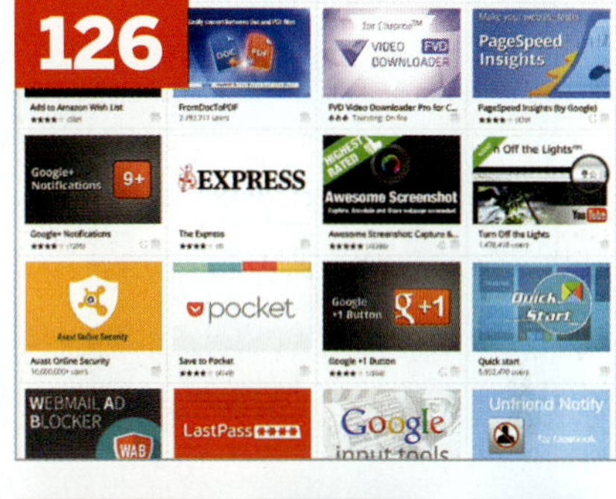

Chapter 1

Brilliant Windows tools

Customise Windows and add powerful new features to your operating system, with our guide to the very best Windows add-ons and tweaks

Windows is a massively powerful operating system that has hundreds of features that most people will never touch. However, it's far from perfect, especially Windows 8! In this chapter, we'll open your eyes to dozens of different tools and tweaks that will allow you to get more from your operating system. We'll show you how you can replace core features, such as Windows Explorer and Task Manager, with more powerful alternatives. We'll reveal how to automate different Windows tasks, how to improve upon the built-in search engine, and how you can get past common problems with the troublesome Windows Update.

CONTENT

Better than Explorer

There are lots of free alternatives to Windows Explorer that provide more tools and options than Microsoft's file-management software. We put six of the best to the test

XYplorerFree | www.xyplorer.com | ★★★★★

FEATURES ★★★★★ **PERFORMANCE** ★★★★★ **EASE OF USE** ★★★★☆

What we liked:

XYplorer doesn't stray far from the familiar interface used by Windows Explorer (File Explorer in Windows 8), showing a standard tree-like window on the left-hand side and an expanded folder view on the right. The great thing about XYplorer is that it feels like everything has been analysed and refined, so while it still looks familiar, it's also a lot better.

In the tree window, for example, the current path you're using is highlighted with a thick green line, which makes it very easy to see. You can also click the Mini Tree button, which takes out all the branches of the tree that you're not using, making it even clearer.

Each time you click a folder, it opens in a new tab. This means you don't have to keep hitting the Back button, but just switch to the tab you want instead. The only downside is that the tabs can get cluttered if you've opened a lot of folders. Each tab has a crumb trail at the top of the window so you can see where you have been and where you can go, though there are still browser-like Back, Forward, Up and History buttons, too.

The comprehensive file-search function splits different types of searches into different tabs, depending on whether you're looking for files by size, date, attributes or content. There's a simple duplicate finder, too.

Some files can be previewed by selecting the option from the tabs in the bottom half of the screen and there are many more views available than the standard Explorer selection.

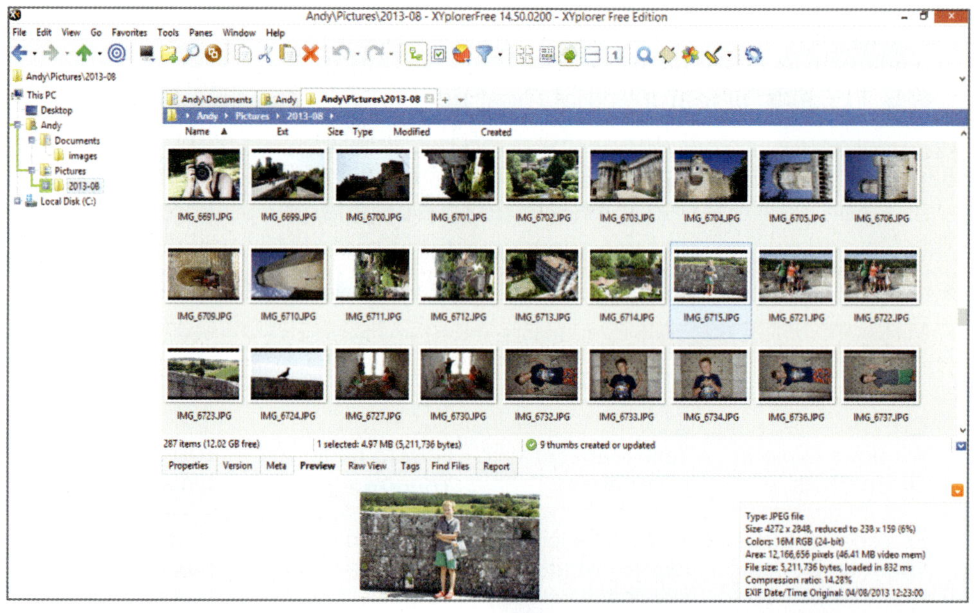

You also get a phenomenal selection of configuration options that let you change default views, colours and almost anything else you can think of. Best of all – and despite its amazing range of features – XYplorer is portable, so you don't even need to install it.

How it can be improved:

The version we reviewed is the free version of a commercial tool, so there are some features that free users are missing out on. We don't think you'll need them, but if you really want custom columns and custom keyboard shortcuts, they're yours for $29.95 (around £19).

OUR VERDICT

XYplorerFree is a near-perfect Explorer replacement that provides a familiar interface and a solid refinement of the basic tools included in Microsoft's file manager. It's the free version of a paid-for program, but we don't think you'll miss the Pro version's more advanced features.

Q-Dir | bit.ly/qdir358 | ★★★★☆

FEATURES ★★★★☆ **PERFORMANCE** ★★★★☆ **EASE OF USE** ★★★☆☆

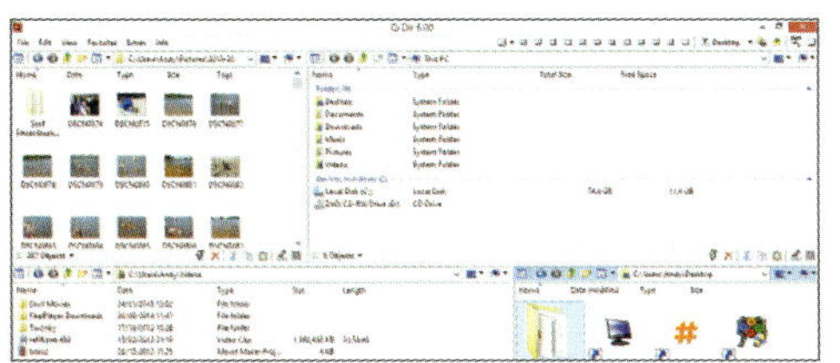

What we liked:

Some Explorer alternatives use dual windows, so you can easily drag and drop files from one folder to another. Q-Dir takes this a giant leap further, defaulting to four Windows that splits your screen into quarters. If this is too much for your liking, you can drop the number of windows to three, two or one, using the window-arrangement icons across the top of the screen.

The software appears fairly standard beyond this split-screen interface, but it has a lot of extra tools tucked away that you can access via its icons.

You can create shortcuts to favourite views and folders; print a contents list of a folder; get a handy tree view in one or more of your windows; and use the colour filter to make files of different types easier to recognise.

How it can be improved:

Most of the Explorer replacements don't exactly look spectacular but Q-Dir is particularly plain. If you have a small screen, the four-screen view is cramped and although four windows are handy every now and then, most of the time you'll probably only use two.
Still, it's good to have the option to use mutliple windows for when you need to copy files all over the place.

OUR VERDICT
Having four windows to cut and paste between isn't something you need every day, but it can come in handy, and it's easy to reduce the number in Q-Dir if you don't need them. The software has a lot of extra tools you won't find in Microsoft's Explorer, though they are tucked away under icons and menus.

Explorer++ | explorerplusplus.com | ★★★★☆

FEATURES ★★★☆☆ **PERFORMANCE** ★★★★☆ **EASE OF USE** ★★★★☆

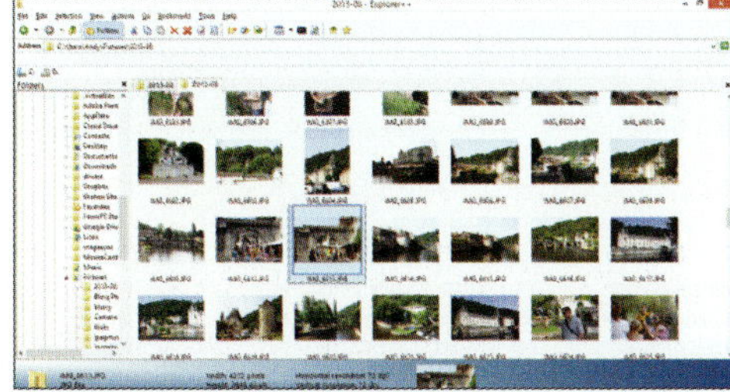

What we liked:

Explorer++ has some handy selection tools that let you choose files automatically, without having to use the usual Shift+left-click combination. For example, you can select them by file type or by using a wildcard of your own, such as one that picks out any files that start with a particular letter or word.

There are a number of optional toolbars you can choose to display or hide.
The bookmarks toolbar lets you save a particular view, then easily return to it in one click. Other toolbars let you show the address bar or provide buttons for your various drives.

There's a tabbed view, so you can have several windows open at the same time, but there isn't as wide a range of views available as with XYplorer. However, like our five-star winner, Explorer++ is completely portable.

How it can be improved:

Explorer++ has a few extra tools and options, but it doesn't look that different from Windows. The blue bar at the bottom is a bit of a waste of space, too.

OUR VERDICT
This program doesn't have all the new and unique tools of XYplorer and Q-Dir, but it still improves on Windows Explorer and is a safe bet if you want a familiar interface without too many changes.

BEST OF THE REST

Cubic Explorer

www.cubicreality.com/ce

Cubic Explorer can be run as a portable program or installed on your PC to improve its performance. Its slightly dated, blue-hued interface devotes more space to files than the other software, and it uses a tabbed interface to make more than one window available at a time. However XYplorer has more options.

NexusFile

www.xiles.net/nexusfile

For an Explorer alternative with a different look, try NexusFile. Its black interface looks like a throwback to the Command Prompt, and it uses colour coding to give an at-a-glance view of the types of file you have in each folder. However, we found the dark background wasn't very clear and was further hampered by tiny icons. On the plus side, the software is powerful and defaults to a dual-screen view, which is great for managing files – you simply drag them from one view to the other.

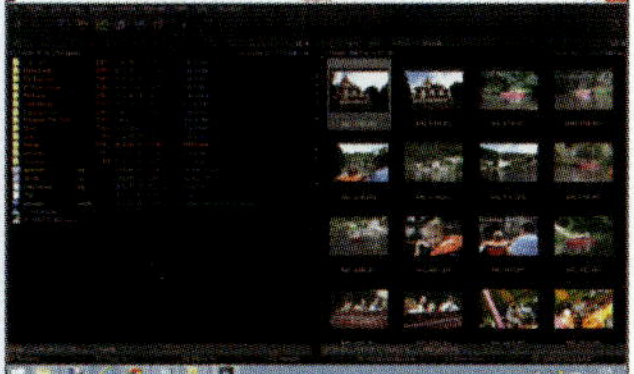

Multi Commander

multicommander.com

Multi Commander uses a versatile dual-screen interface and has a lot of built-in tools. There's a bank of buttons at the bottom providing links to frequently used shortcuts to drives, which can also be used to perform functions such as Copy and Paste. A tip of the day and a number of hints around the screen will keep you learning, but there's a lot to find out about this software, which might be too much to take in for casual users. There's also a lot going on, so the screen can look a bit fussy.

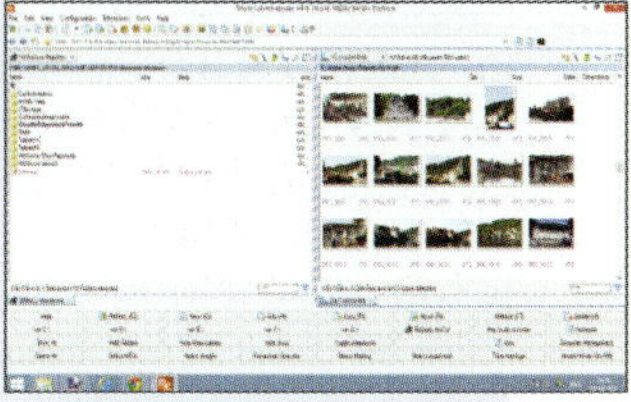

Make Windows run better with a superior Task Manager

Windows comes with a built-in tool that monitors your PC and kills misbehaving programs and processes. We rate six free alternatives that do an even better job

Process Explorer | bit.ly/process361 | ★★★★★

FEATURES ★★★★★ **PERFORMANCE** ★★★★★ **EASE OF USE** ★★★★☆

What we liked:

Process Explorer doesn't require installation, which means you can run it directly from a USB flash drive when it's needed. It displays a list of running processes and colour codes them to make them easier to distinguish, often adding icons so you can tell which programs they belong to.

The list of items can be sorted to make resource-hogging applications easier to find, and you can right-click an item to set its priority from one of seven levels on offer, ranging from Real-Time to Idle. The same right-click menu will also let you kill a process, kill a process tree (including all the other items related to a process) and scan suspicious entries using the VirusTotal online virus checker (www.virustotal.com).

If you're unable to identify a running process, you can choose to 'Search Online' to find out what it is and where it comes from. Double-clicking an item will also bring up a very comprehensive Properties window.

If you come across a file or folder that can't be deleted because Windows claims it's being used, Process Explorer can help you find out which process is responsible so you can remove the lock.

Process Explorer is a great tool and if you want to set it as your default task manager, simply go into Options and select 'Replace Task Manager'.

How it can be improved:

The processes are colour-coded to help you understand them, but it's not immediately clear what each colour means. You can find out by going to Options, Configure Colours, but this could be more clearly presented.

Also, you can only find out what the hardware graphs at the top represent by hovering your mouse over them. We would prefer to have permanent labels to make them easier to read at a glance.

OUR VERDICT

Process Explorer is hugely useful and comes jam-packed with features. You might need to spend some time browsing the Help files to understand its more advanced tools, but it's a great program nonetheless.

System Explorer | systemexplorer.net | ★★★★☆

FEATURES ★★★★★ PERFORMANCE ★★★★☆ EASE OF USE ★★★★☆

What we liked:

System Explorer tells you everything you could possibly want to know about everything that happens on your PC, both in the past and right now. The tabs along the top provide access to information relating to Processes, Performance, Connections and History. Under Processes, you can filter the list of running processes by users; grey out Windows system entries; show or hide services; and switch to a tree-view mode. As well as showing the resources being used by your PC's processes, the software can run a security check on them and identify potential malware using its online security database.

When installing the program, you can choose between two view modes: Task Manager Mode (which uses tabs and is optimised for performance) and Explorer Mode (which has a vertical menu with all its tools listed).

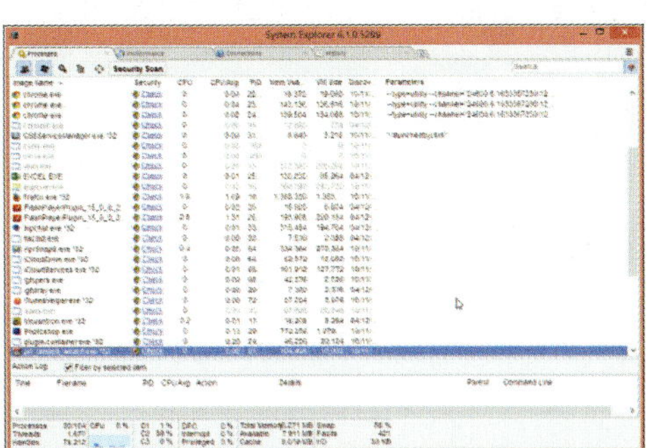

How it can be improved:

System Explorer is packed with features but they are crammed into a very cramped design, which can make it confusing to understand and navigate.

OUR VERDICT
A complex system tool that helps you troubleshoot problems and identify possible malware infections.

Process Lasso | bit.ly/lasso361 | ★★★★☆

FEATURES ★★★★☆ PERFORMANCE ★★★★☆ EASE OF USE ★★★★☆

What we liked:

When a process starts to misbehave or consume too many system resources, the simplest solution is to terminate it. However, by this time your PC may have already slowed to a crawl. Process Lasso takes a pre-emptive approach and automatically stops programs hogging resources in the first place. It lets you adjust the priority of programs and switch between two power modes: ProBalance (the default) and EnergySaver Enabled, which conserves energy when your PC is idle. There are also four Power Profiles available: Balanced, Bitsum Highest Performance (great for gaming), High Performance and Powersaver.

The best thing about Process Lasso is that you don't need any great technical knowledge to use it and it can be left to manage things automatically.

How it can be improved:

Certain features, such as the Process Watchdog (which monitors memory and CPU limits), are only available for a set period before you're pushed to upgrade to the paid-for Pro edition. Also, some of the more advanced options could be easier to understand.

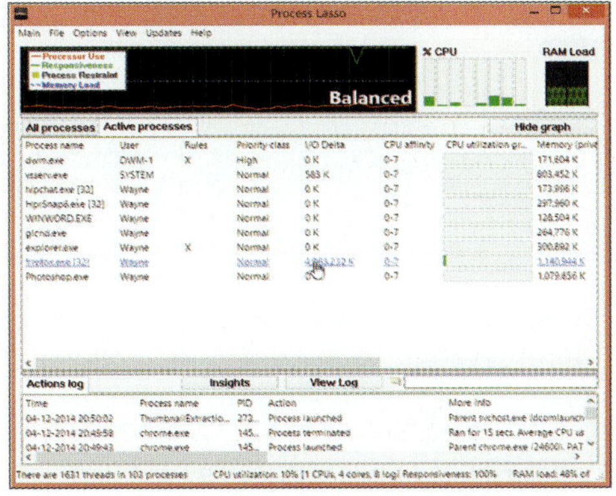

OUR VERDICT
If your PC has limited resources such as a slow processor and not much memory, Process Lasso will ensure it runs as efficiently as possible.

BEST OF THE REST

Chameleon Task Manager Lite

bit.ly/cham361

The 'Lite' part of this program's name tells you this is a cut-down version of a more powerful paid-for product, but don't let that put you off. The software displays all running processes and has columns showing processor and memory usage, drive activity and more. Simply right-click a process to kill it or adjust its priority. You can also set what the program should do when you double-click an entry (stop it, restart it, switch to it or open Settings).

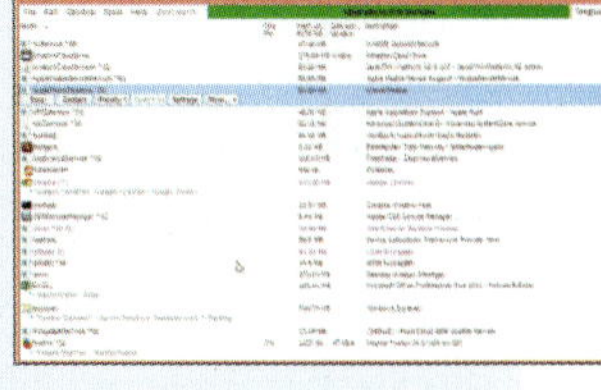

Process Hacker

processhacker.sourceforge.net

This is an excellent open-source task manager that offers much of the same functionality found in Process Explorer. Processes are colour-coded and you can terminate individual ones or entire trees. It's also easy to identify and kill any programs that are accessing the internet without your knowledge. However, it hasn't been updated in a year, which is a big negative.

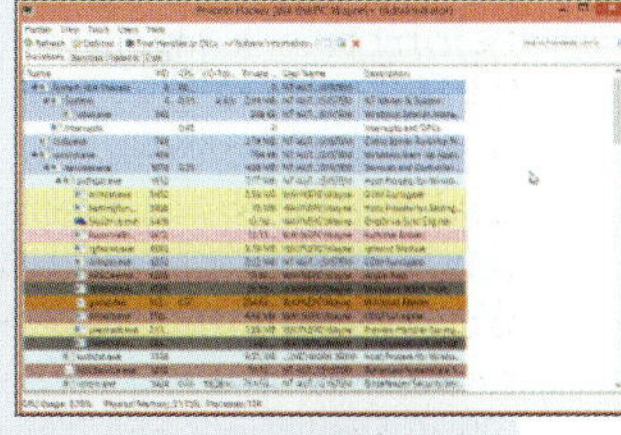

DBC Task Manager

bit.ly/task361

DBC is an attempt to replicate Windows 8's superior Task Manager in Windows 7. It's a decent effort, although lacking in features compared to the others included in this round-up. It's fully portable, so you can run it from a USB flash drive, and has tabs for Processes, Performance, Users, Details and Services.

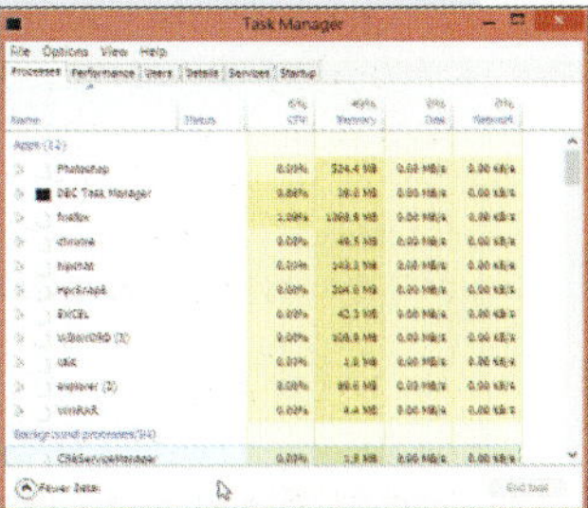

Hack Windows to Beat Microsoft's Restrictions

Don't let Windows tell you what you can and can't do. Over the next five pages, we reveal how to bypass Microsoft's constraints so you can make your PC run the way you want it to

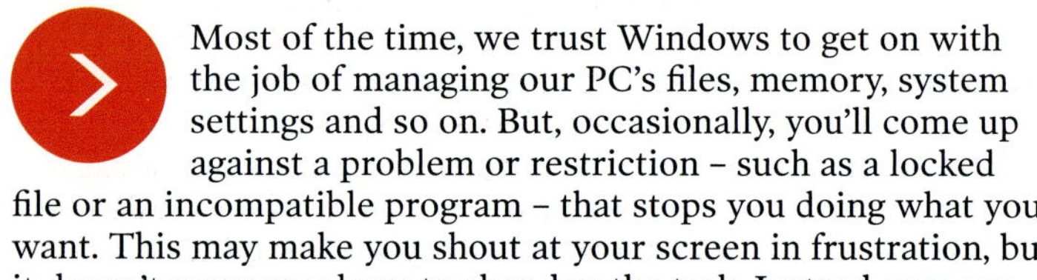

Most of the time, we trust Windows to get on with the job of managing our PC's files, memory, system settings and so on. But, occasionally, you'll come up against a problem or restriction – such as a locked file or an incompatible program – that stops you doing what you want. This may make you shout at your screen in frustration, but it doesn't mean you have to abandon the task. Instead, you can try 'hacking' Windows to get around the constraint.

In this feature, we round up our favourite tweaks for solving common Windows frustrations without messing up your computer's system. We'll show you how to take ownership of locked files and folders; recover a lost Windows licence key; activate various 'God modes' to access hidden settings; and much, much more. In short, we will put you back in control of your operating system.

WARNING: Some of the hacks in this feature require editing the Windows Registry. Make sure you create a backup of the key you're going to edit by going to File, Export. Several tips also require you to be the administrator of your PC, which you can set up by following the instructions in our three-step walkthrough on page 16.

Hack your files and folders

Give your drives a different letter

Windows automatically assigns a letter to each drive on your PC, whether it's a fixed one, such as a hard drive, or a temporary one, such as a USB memory stick. However, its choice of letters can sometimes make no sense: for example, if you have a lot of drives, they might be labelled C, E, G, I and Y.

You can change the drive letters to something more logical by using the built-in Computer Management tool. Click the Start button and open the Control Panel.

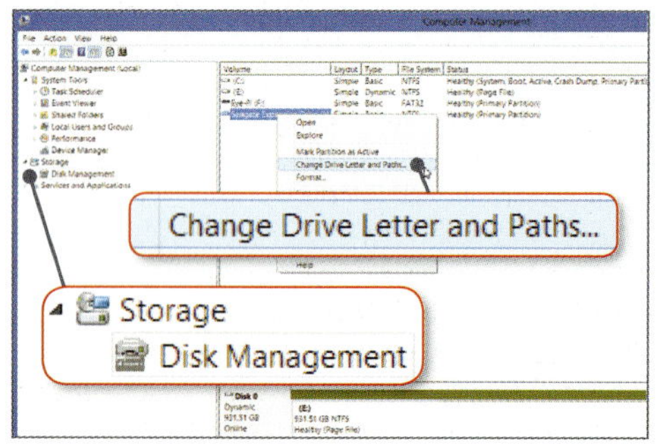

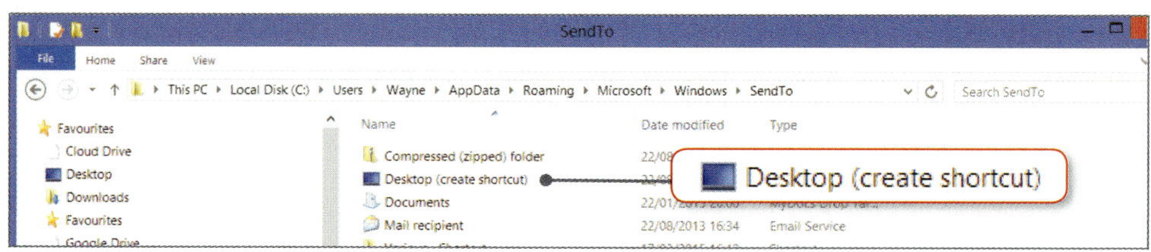

Click 'System and Security', then Administrative Tools, and double-click Computer Management (in Windows 8+, you just need to search for 'Computer Management'). Select Disk Management in the left-hand pane to bring up a list of drives on the right. Right-click a drive and select 'Change drive letter and paths'. Click Change, pick an unassigned drive letter from the list, and click OK.

Add new locations to the Send To menu

You can send files on your PC to locations you regularly access, such as a USB flash drive, by right-clicking them and opening the Send To menu. If the right-click menu doesn't list the folder you need, just go to the folder you want to add, right-click it and go to Send To, 'Desktop (create shortcut)'. A new shortcut to that folder will appear on your Desktop.

Now open Windows Explorer, type shell:sendto in the location bar at the top and hit Enter. The available Send To options will be displayed. Drag and drop the new shortcut to this folder. You can also remove unwanted locations to make your Send To menu more tidy.

Always open files in your chosen program

Some programs take ownership of certain file formats; for example, a photo editor

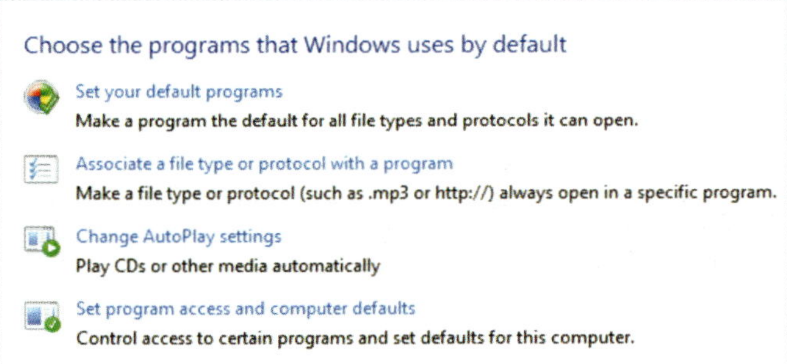

might set itself to open every type of image file. If you'd rather designate a different program to open certain file types, you can set the default options yourself using the Default Programs feature.

In Windows 7, click the Start button and select 'Default Programs'. In Windows 8+, you can simply search for 'Default Programs' and launch it. You can then choose the program you want as your default choice for opening a particular file type.

Add tick boxes to select multiple items

The quickest way to pick more than one file in Windows is to hold down Shift or Ctrl while you click the files you want. However, you can also add tick boxes next to your files and select them by ticking these boxes.

In Windows 7, click Start and type 'Folder options' into the search box. Open the View tab and tick 'Use check boxes to select items'. In Windows 8, open File Explorer, click the 'View' tab, and tick 'Item check boxes'.

Take ownership of locked files and folders

Windows prevents you from deleting or modifying files or folders that are being used by a program or by the system itself. However, it can sometimes tell you that an item is in use by another person or process when it clearly isn't. The easiest way to unlock a file is to reboot your PC, but you can also use a program such as NoVirusThanks File Governor (bit.ly/filegov368) to free the locked item without having to restart. It lets you unlock files with a single click, scan folders for locked items and quickly terminate restrictive processes. You should only unlock/delete a file if you are sure it's safe to do so.

Help Windows open unknown file formats

If Windows doesn't know how to open a particular file, you can use Open With from the right-click menu to select a program yourself. OpenWith Enhanced (bit.ly/openwith368) is a more sophisticated version of this built-in tool that can suggest an appropriate program. Right-click the file you want to open and select Open With, then Choose Default Program. OpenWith Enhanced will display a selection of possible choices, so you can set your preferred program as the default.

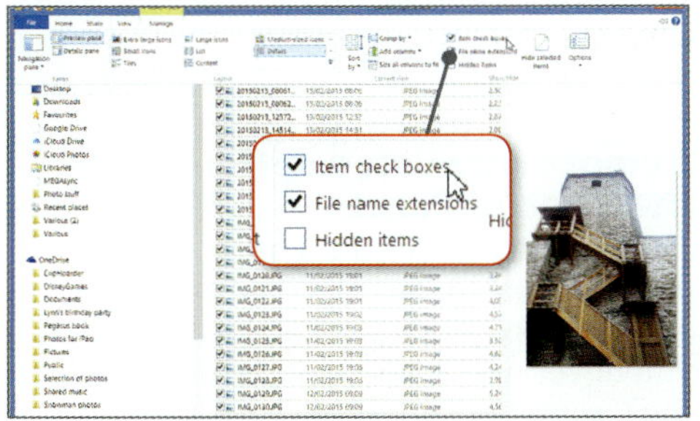

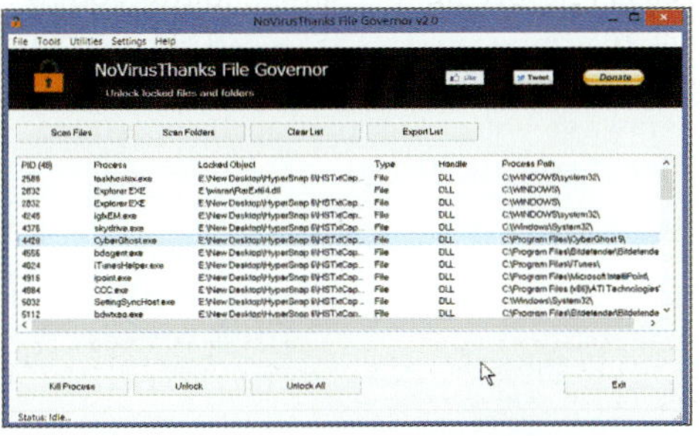

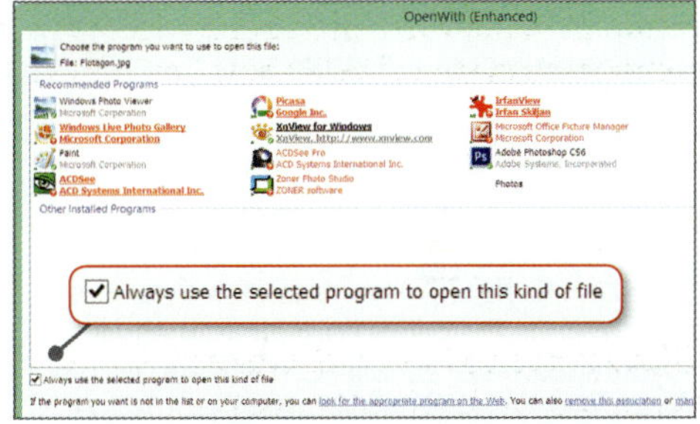

Change your system settings

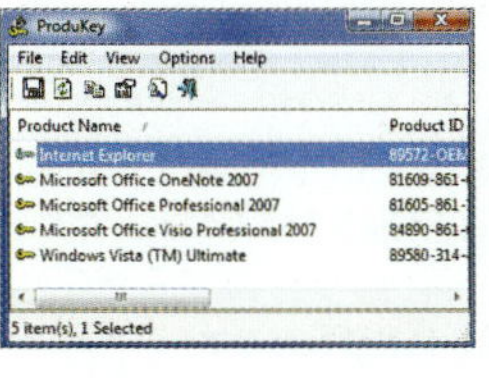

Recover a lost Windows licence key

If you want to reinstall Windows from scratch, you'll need to enter your original licence key during the installation process. If you can't remember what you've done with it, don't worry, it's easy to track this down. Just run ProduKey from Nirsoft (www.nirsoft.net) – it's a tiny program that lists the CD key for Windows, along with any keys for Microsoft Office, if you have the suite installed. Note that due to the hacking nature of the program, your anti-virus software may flag it as a threat, but it's perfectly safe to use.

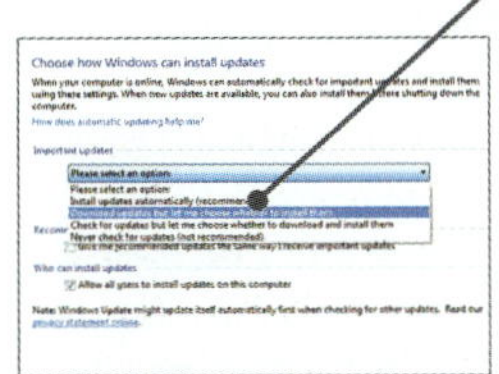

Stop Windows restarting after an update

If your PC is set to automatically download and install updates, there's a good chance Windows will restart your system as soon as the process is complete. To stop this happening, open the Control Panel, click 'System and Security', then click Windows Update. On the left, click 'Change settings', then change the updates option to either 'Download updates but let me choose whether to install them', or 'Check for updates but let me choose whether to download and install them'.

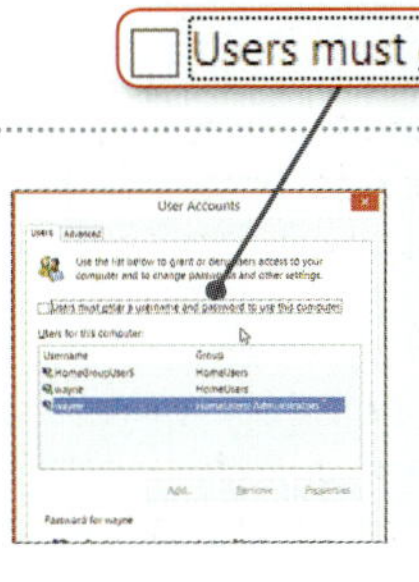

Log into Windows 8+ automatically

Windows 8+ is designed with security in mind, so it forces you to enter a password and log into your Microsoft account before you can start using it. If you don't share your computer with other people, and are confident that no one has access to your PC, you can configure the operating system to bypass this stage.

From the Start screen, press Windows+X, click Run and type netplwiz. Click OK and highlight your account. Untick 'Users must enter a username and password to use this computer'. Click

MINI WORKSHOP
Create keyboard shortcuts for your favourite programs

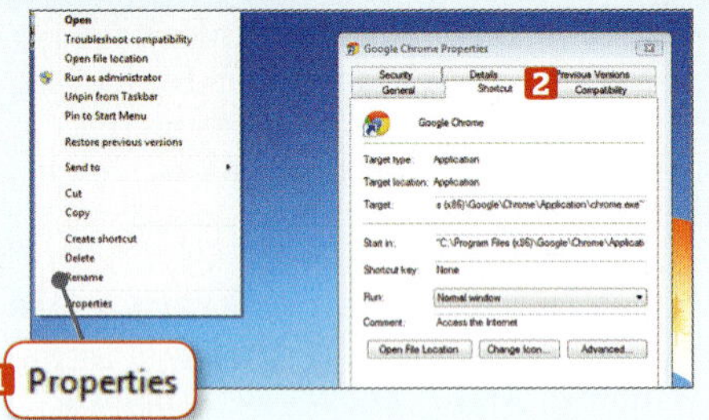

1 Windows lets you assign hotkeys to your favourite programs (as well as folders and web pages), so you can launch them directly from the keyboard. If you have a shortcut to the program on your Desktop, right click this and select Properties. **1** A window will open showing the Shortcut tab. **2**

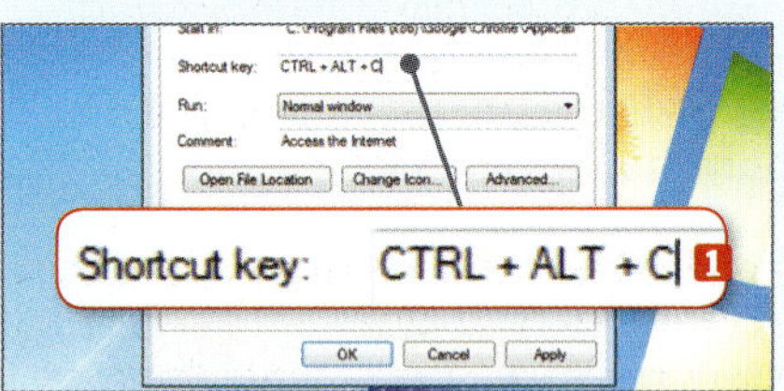

2 Click inside the Shortcut Key box **1** and press any letter or combination of letters on the keyboard. It should be something easy to remember – 'C' for Chrome, for example. Additional keys, such as Ctrl and Alt will be added automatically to avoid potential conflicts with existing shortcuts.

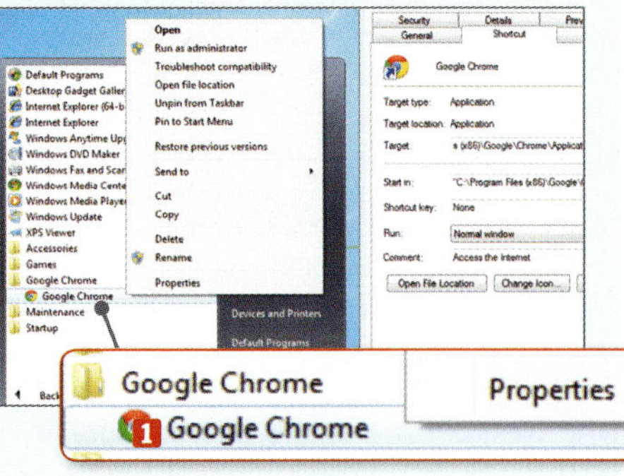

3 Click Apply, then OK. In future, pressing this keyboard combination will start the program. You can also assign hotkeys to programs pinned to the taskbar or the Start menu. Just right-click the shortcut for the program you want to assign a hotkey to **1** and repeat the process described above.

Apply. Enter your password and confirm it, then click OK. Restart your PC and, when Windows loads, it will automatically log you in.

To go straight to the Desktop, type Navigation on the Start or Apps screen, open Navigation Properties, and tick 'When I sign in or close all applications on a screen, go to the desktop instead of Start'.

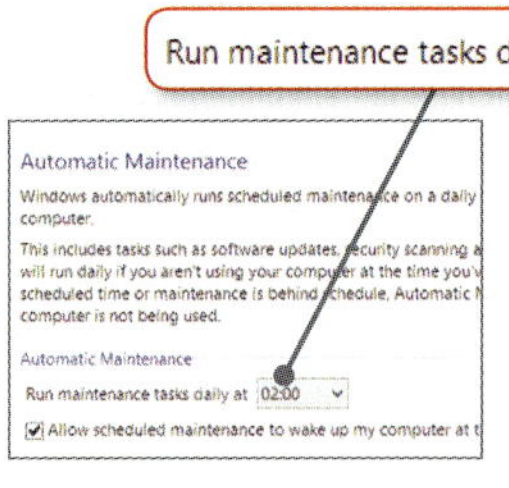

Change when scheduled maintenance runs

In Windows 8+, common maintenance tasks such as software updates, security scanning and system diagnostics run daily, usually in the early hours of the morning. If you want to change this to a different time, open the Control Panel and select 'System and Security', Action Centre, Maintenance. Under Automatic Maintenance, click 'Change maintenance settings' and use the drop-down menu to select a new time. Scheduled maintenance can wake your computer at the arranged time if you allow it to.

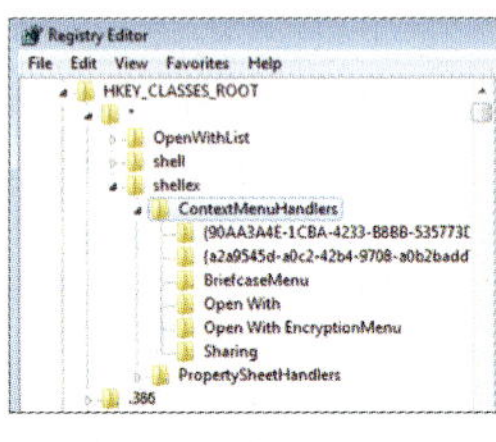

Customise your right-click menu

The right-click context menu gives you easy access to all sorts of options, which change depending on where you are (in a program, on the Desktop) and what software you have installed. The menu can become quite crowded, and will often offer lots of entries you don't need or never use. You can remove the clutter by editing the Registry. Click Start and type regedit into the box, then hit Enter to launch the Registry editor (Regedit). Navigate to:

HKEY_CLASSES_ROOT*\shellex\ContextMenuHandlers

The name of installed programs that have added themselves to the context menu will be listed, and you can select and delete them.

To avoid delving into the Registry manually, you can also edit the right-click menu using the free program Easy Context Menu (www.sordum.org).

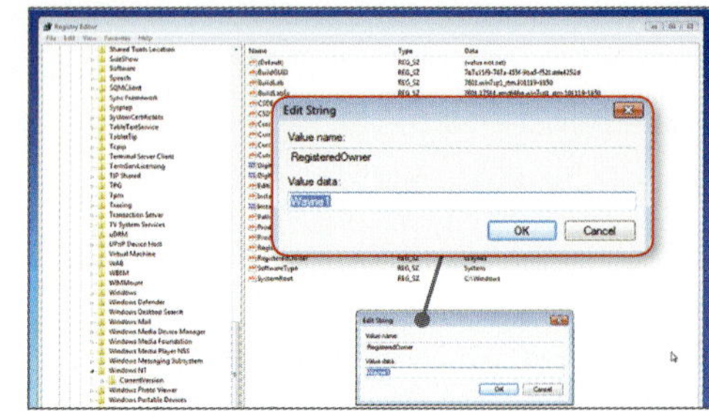

Change the registered owner of your PC

If you've bought or inherited a second-hand PC, you might want to change the name of the previous owner to something else (or, if the registered owner is just "Windows User", to something more personal). This can be done using a simple Registry tweak. Launch Regedit and navigate to:

HKEY_LOCAL_MACHINE\SOFTWARE\Microsoft\Windows NT\CurrentVersion

Double-click 'RegisteredOwner' (and, optionally, 'RegisteredOrganization') and change the Value Data to something else.

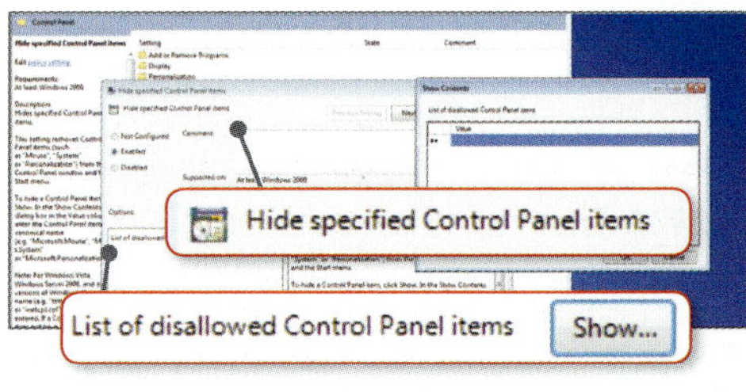

Remove unwanted options from the Control Panel

If you view the Control Panel contents by 'Large icons' or 'Small icons', there's a good chance you'll see entries listed that you never use. These can be hidden using the Group Policy Editor.

Type GPEdit.msc on the Start screen in Windows 8+, or in the Search box in Windows 7, and launch it. Go to User Configuration, Administrative Templates, then Control Panel, and double-click 'Hide specified Control Panel items'. Enable the feature and view the 'List of disallowed Control Panel items' to choose any more you want to hide.

Uninstall Internet Explorer

Internet Explorer is an integral part of Windows, but you can get rid of it if. Click the Start button, open the Control Panel, click Programs, then click 'Programs and Features'. In the left pane, click 'Turn Windows features on or off' and deselect Internet Explorer.

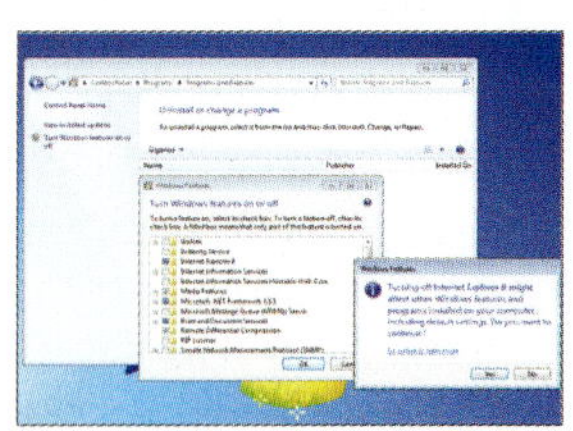

Unlock hidden PC power

Activate God Mode to access hidden settings

There's a special God Mode tucked away in Windows that displays all your PC's admin tools and control options on a single screen. To activate it in Windows 7, go to Start, Computer and select the C: drive; in Windows 8+, open File Explorer and select the C: drive. Right-click inside the window and select New, Folder. Highlight this folder, press F2, name it `GodMode.{ED7BA470-8E54-465E-825C-99712043E01C}` and press Enter.

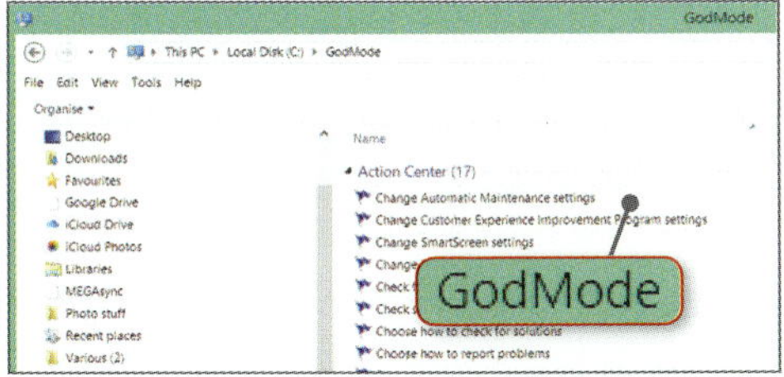

Activate alternative God Modes

There are several alternative modes to the God Mode (described above) that bring all the settings for specific Windows features together in one place to save you searching around for them. This means you can choose only to display the settings you need most often, rather than the all-encompassing God Mode in the previous tip. They are all activated in the same way, but each one uses a different string. Try any of these:

My Computer: `{20D04FE0-3AEA-1069-A2D8-08002B30309D}`
Default Programs: `{17cd9488-1228-4b2f-88ce-4298e93e0966}`
Performance: `{78F3955E-3B90-4184-BD14-5397C15F1EFC}`
Power Settings: `{025A5937-A6BE-4686-A844-36FE4BEC8B6D}`
Network: `{208D2C60-3AEA-1069-A2D7-08002B30309D}`
Programs and Features: `{15eae92e-f17a-4431-9f28-805e482dafd4}`
Location Settings: `{00C6D95F-329C-409a-81D7-C46C66EA7F33}`
Printers: `{2227A280-3AEA-1069-A2DE-08002B30309D}`
Icons And Notifications: `{05d7b0f4-2121-4eff-bf6b-ed3f69b894d9}`
Firewall and Security: `{4026492F-2F69-46B8-B9BF-5654FC07E423}`
Application Connections: `{241D7C96-F8BF-4F85-B01F-E2B043341A4B}`
Credentials and Logins: `{1206F5F1-0569-412C-8FEC-3204630DFB70}`

Give important programs extra power

You can prioritise your favourite applications so they receive more of the available processing power on your PC. Right-click the taskbar and launch Task Manager. Right-click an Application and select 'Go To process' (or 'Go to details' in Windows 8+). Right-click the process you want to prioritise and select Set Priority. This can be Realtime, High, Above Normal, Normal, Below Normal or Low.

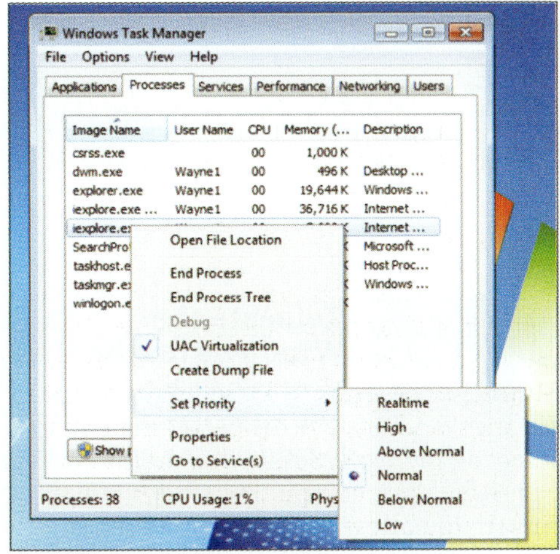

Access hidden emoji icons in Windows 8+

If you're running Windows 8.x on a tablet, such as Microsoft Surface Pro 3, you can access a wealth of emoji via the touchscreen keyboard. You can still access them on on a regular Windows 8+ PC, but it takes a little work. Right-click the taskbar, go to Toolbars and select Touch Keyboard. A virtual keyboard will open (with a button for it in the taskbar); just click the emoji key and select the characters you want. As well as the usual smileys, there are hand signs, hearts, cartoon characters, vehicles, food, weather symbols, and many more.

Run Windows XP in Windows 8.1

Windows 8+ comes with Hyper-V, Microsoft's replacement for Windows

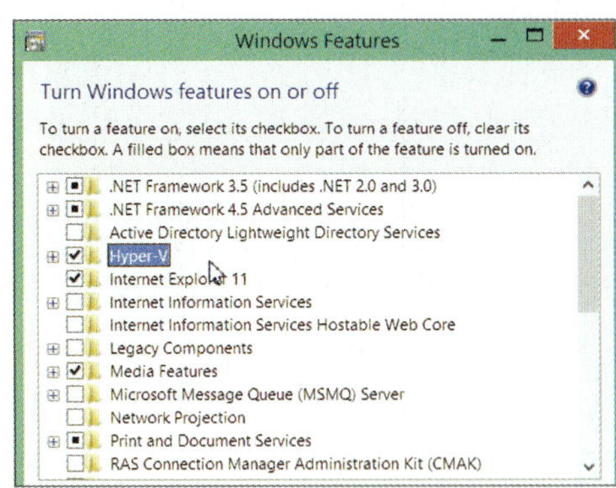

Virtual PC (the app that lets you run a version of XP under Windows 7). To use it, type `OptionalFeatures` from the Start screen to launch the 'Turn Windows features on or off' box. Select Hyper-V in the list and click OK. Once the requested changes have been made, reboot your PC. When Windows loads, go to the Start screen, scroll to the right and click the Hyper-V Manager tile to launch the feature and access XP.

Use the XP task switcher in newer versions of Windows

Okay, so this isn't really 'unlocking hidden power' but it's still a cool feature. If you've used Windows for any length of time, you'll know you can switch between running programs by pressing Alt+Tab. In Windows 7 and 8+, this displays thumbnails of open windows. But hidden away in the newer versions of Windows is the old XP task switcher. To activate it, hold down Alt (and keep it held down), then tap the other Alt button, and press Tab.

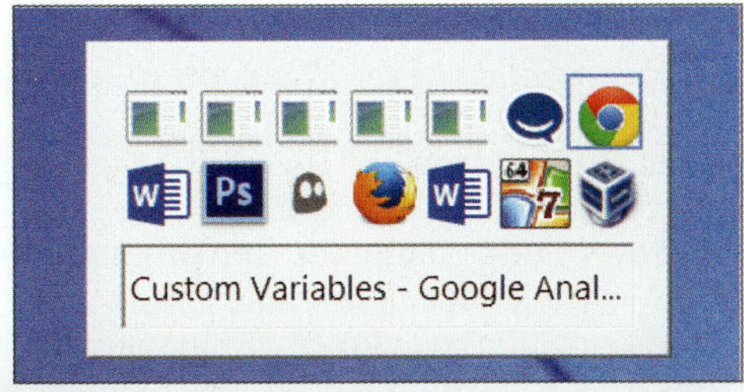

MINI WORKSHOP | Get administrator rights on any Windows 7 PC

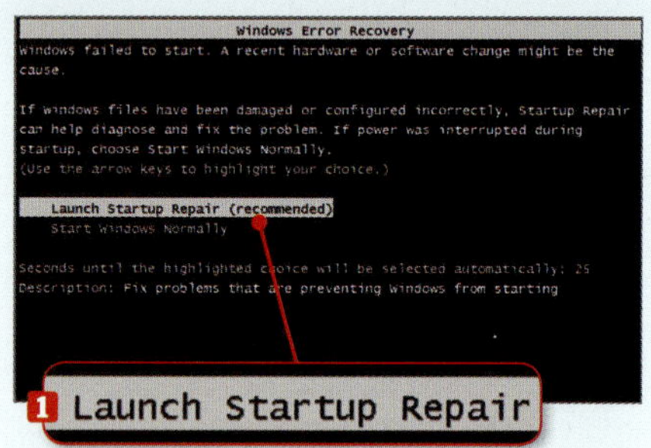

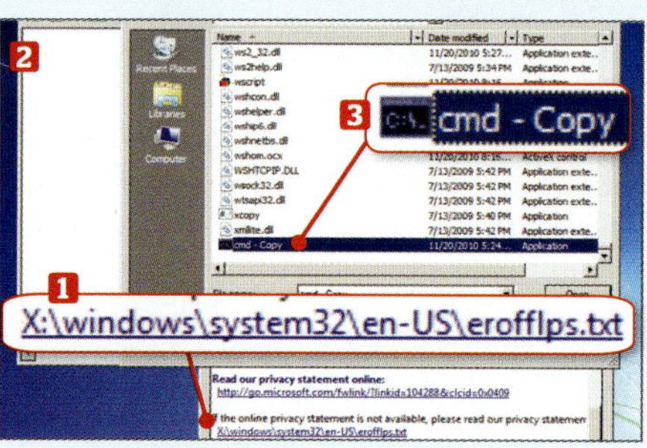

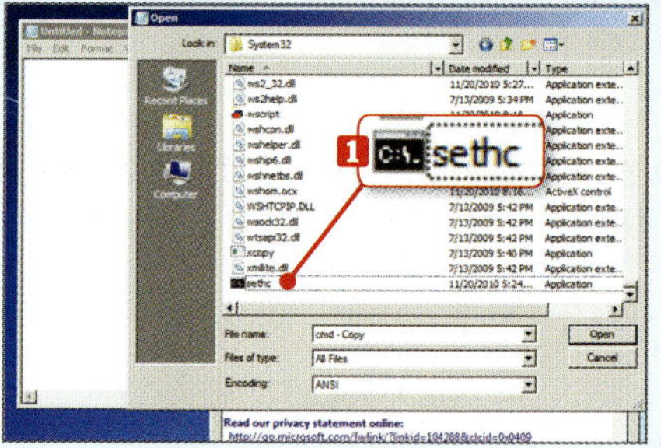

1 To become the administrator of any Windows 7 PC, hold down the power button when the Starting Windows screen shows, so your computer turns off. Restart your PC and you should see the Windows Error Recovery screen. Select 'Launch Startup Repair (recommended)'. **1** Click Cancel when asked if you want to restore your computer using System Restore.

2 You'll see the message 'Startup Repair cannot repair this computer automatically'. Click 'View problem details' and click the privacy statement text link at the bottom. **1** Notepad will open. **2** Go to File, Open and double-click your system drive. Go to Windows/System32. Select 'All files' for the type, and then find and select 'Cmd'. Press Ctrl+C, then Ctrl+V to create a copy. **3**

3 Locate 'sethc' and rename it 'sethc1'. Rename the copy of Cmd to 'sethc' **1** and close Notepad. Restart your PC. At the login screen, tap Shift five times. Type `net localgroup Administrators` into the command window, and find an administrator name to use. Type `net user <admin name> *` (using the actual name). Enter a new password. You can now log in as that administrator.

Customise how Windows looks

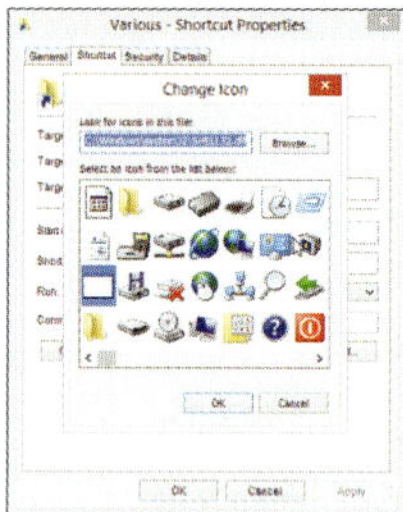

Change the icons for folders

It's easy to change the default icons offered by Windows, and doing so will make it easier to find your favourite folders. Right-click a folder and select 'Properties'. In Windows 7, select the 'Customize' tab, go to the 'Folder icons' section and click 'Change icon'. In Windows 8+, select the Shortcut tab and click 'Change icon'. Pick one of the icons on offer and click OK. There are different designs to be found in C:\Windows\system32\imageres.dll and C:\Windows\system32\SHELL32.dll

Get Windows 10 icons in older versions of Windows

The latest builds of the Windows 10 Technical Preview have a new and rather striking icon set. If you like them, you can install the new icons in Windows 7 or 8+ using the free program New Win10 Iconpack Installer (bit.ly/win10icon368). You can easily change the icons back to normal if you decide you don't like them.

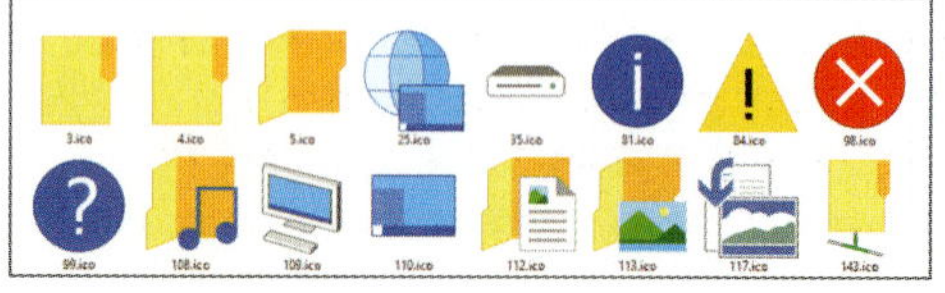

Relocate the Windows taskbar

Most people have the taskbar in its default location at the bottom of the screen, but if you have a widescreen monitor, move the taskbar to the left-hand side of the Desktop to make better use of the available space. Right-click the taskbar and untick 'Lock the taskbar'. Click and drag the bar up to the left (or right) side. Once it's in place, right-click it and select 'Lock the taskbar' again.

Customise the Windows 7 login

You can change the look of the login screen via the Windows registry. Launch Regedit and navigate to: HKEY_LOCAL_MACHINE\Software\Microsoft\Windows\CurrentVersion\Authentication\LogonUI\Background

Double-click the DWORD (32 bit) Value called OEMBackground (if it's not there you will need to create it via the right-click context menu). Set its value to 1. Next go to:

HKEY_LOCAL_MACHINE\Software\Policies\Microsoft\Windows\System

Double-click UseOEMBackground and set the value to 1. If it isn't there, create a new DWORD (32 bit) Value.

Copy the image you want to use into the %windir%\system32\oobe\info\backgrounds folder (create the info and

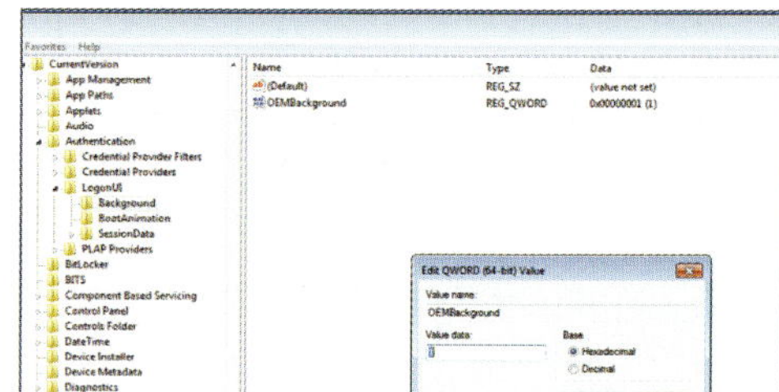

backgrounds folders if they don't exist). The file will need to be the same shape (aspect ratio) as your monitor, and be less than 256KB in size. Rename the image to 'backgroundDefault.jpg'. When you're done, log off and on again; the new image should appear on the login screen.

Remove the ribbon in File Explorer

The File Explorer in Windows 8.1 uses Microsoft Office's ribbon design. You can hide or display it by clicking the tiny arrow next to the Help icon, but if you want to hide it permanently, there's a tweak you can use. Type GPEdit.msc on the Start screen, launch it and navigate to Computer Configuration, Administrative Templates, Windows Components, File Explorer. Double-click 'Start File Explorer with Ribbon Minimized' and click Enabled. Click OK and, when you restart Explorer, the ribbon will be gone.

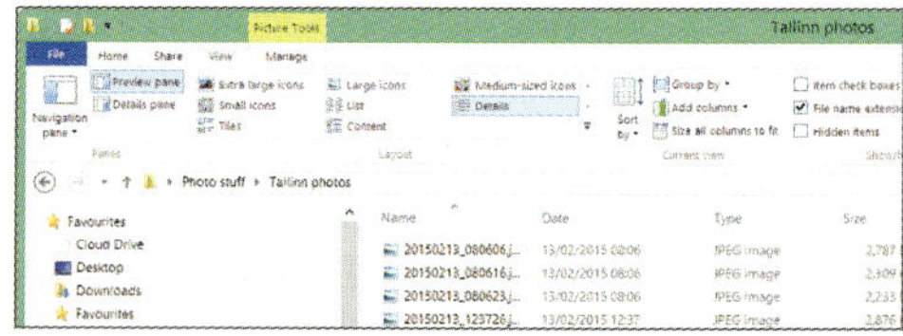

100 Windows tweaks in one program

The Windows Tweaker is a well-designed, easy-to-use program that offers a wide range of one-click Windows hacks. It's compatible with all versions of Windows from Vista onwards and you can use it to perform a range of handy functions such as setting Windows Explorer to restore your previous session and scheduling a shutdown for a specific time in the future. Here are our favourites.

Windows Tweaker: www.thewindowstweaker.com | 10 mins | Vista, 7, 8.1+

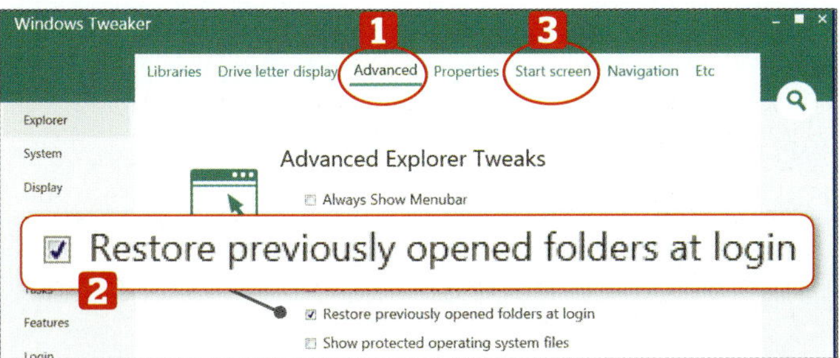

1 Download and run Windows Tweaker. If you want Windows Explorer to remember your previous session, click the Advanced tab 1 and select 'Restore previously opened folders at log in'. 2 Click 'Start screen' 3 to view options for Windows 8's Start menu.

2 You can set Windows 8 to go straight to the Desktop on start-up. 1 There are also options to automatically show the Apps screen when you click Start 2 and to list Desktop apps first in this view when your apps are sorted by category. 3

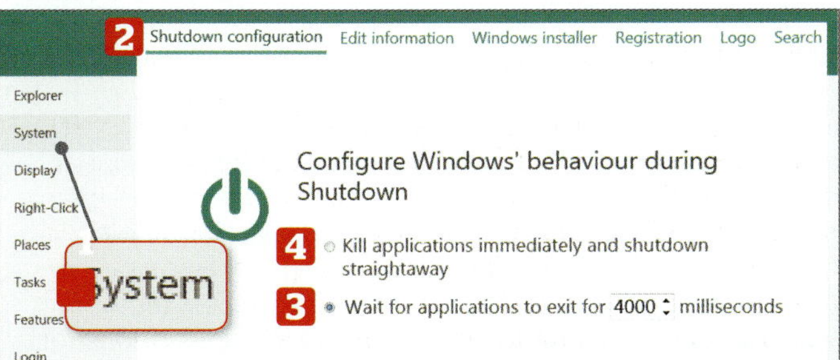

3 When you shut down your PC, it waits for running applications to close. Click System 1 and, under 'Shutdown configuration', 2 you can set the length of this delay 3 or choose to 'Kill applications immediately and shutdown straightaway'. 4

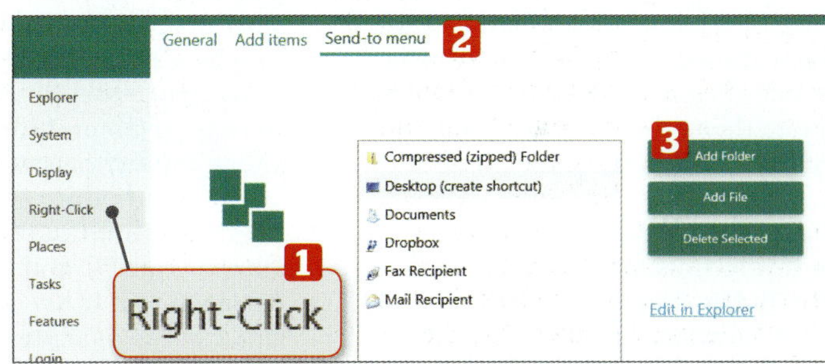

4 Select Right-Click. 1 On the General tab, you can set the Control Panel to appear in the Desktop's right-click menu. If you frequently send files to the same location, click 'Send-to menu' 2 and Add Folder 3 to add a new directory to Windows' send-to dialogue.

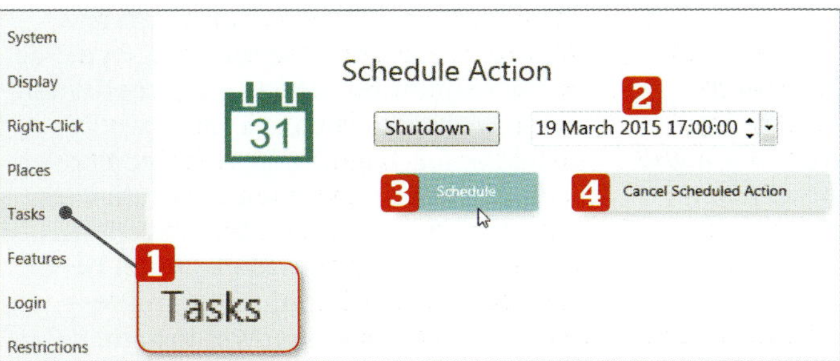

5 If you prefer to run security scans and other tasks after you've gone to bed, you can set your PC to shut down automatically. Click Tasks, 1 choose a date and time 2 from the 'Schedule shutdown' tab and click Schedule. 3 You can cancel this by clicking Cancel Scheduled Action. 4

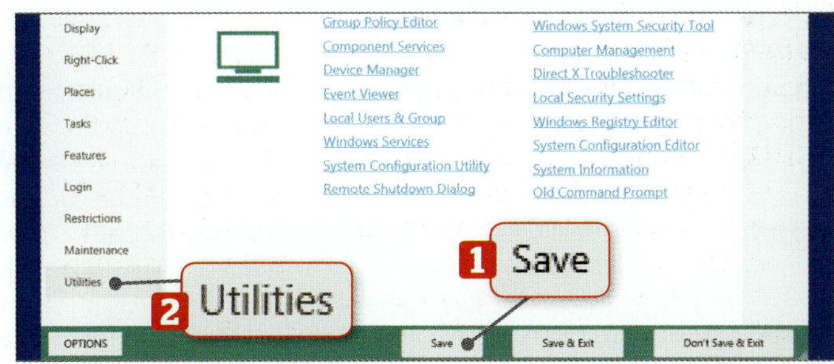

6 It's important that you remember to click Save in Windows Tweaker 1 to store any changes you've made. You will usually need to restart your PC before your changes will take effect. For a range of handy shortcuts to Windows' system, disk and network tools, click Utilities. 2

Remove pointless Windows files & folders

Your PC is littered with files and folders you never asked for and don't need. Find out what all this junk is – and how to get rid of it for good

Open your Documents folder, and what do you see? More folders, with obscure names such as CrashDump and NativeFus_Log, and files with weird extensions, such as Thumbs.db and desktop.ini. Oh, and maybe a few documents.

With the exception of at least some of the documents, you didn't create these items, and you may have no idea what they are or who put them there. You're probably not keen to touch them either, given that they look like viruses. If you do delete them, they usually regenerate, which doesn't exactly make them endearing.

In this section, we'll take a closer look at the mysterious files and folders that turn up in Documents or on your Desktop. We'll reveal what they are, why they're there and how to get rid of them for good – or even hack them into something useful.

Thumbs.db

What is it?

Thumbs.db is a database file containing a cache of photo thumbnails, and it's created automatically when you open a folder of photos or videos. Thumbs.db supposedly makes thumbnails load more quickly, but you won't see much difference unless your PC is particularly old or slow.

Thumbs.db files may be hidden by default on your PC, so you may not realise how many you've got and how much hard drive space they're taking up. To un-hide them, follow the steps in the box, below.

Find a Thumbs.db file on your PC and hover over it to see how big it is. We're not talking gigabytes, but these files can easily run to hundreds of megabytes, and you may have lots of them, accounting for a big chunk of hard drive space. They also clog up your cloud storage service (where they're totally useless) if you've set up automatic syncing.

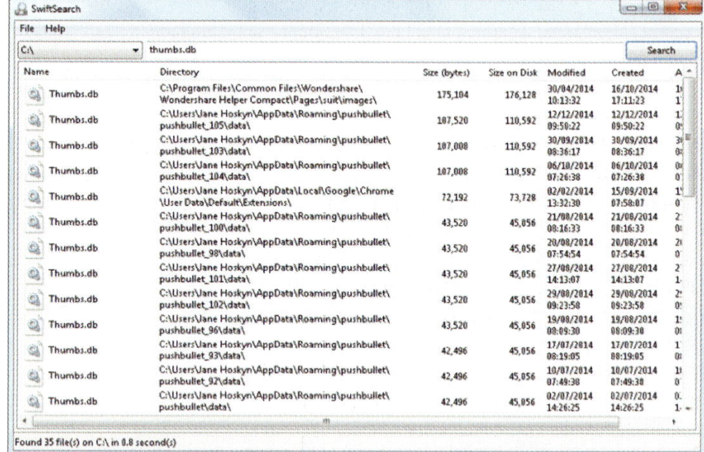

Use Swiftsearch to see how many .db files are clogging up your PC

Can you delete it?

Yes. First, track down all your Thumbs.db files using the free, portable tool SwiftSearch, which you can download from the open-source site Sourceforge (www.snipca.com/14709). Run the program, select 'C:\' (your main hard drive) from the dropdown menu at the top-left, type <type>thumbs.db</type>, then press Enter. The results appear instantly. Our PC contained 35 Thumbs.db files, including four bigger than 100MB (see screenshot).

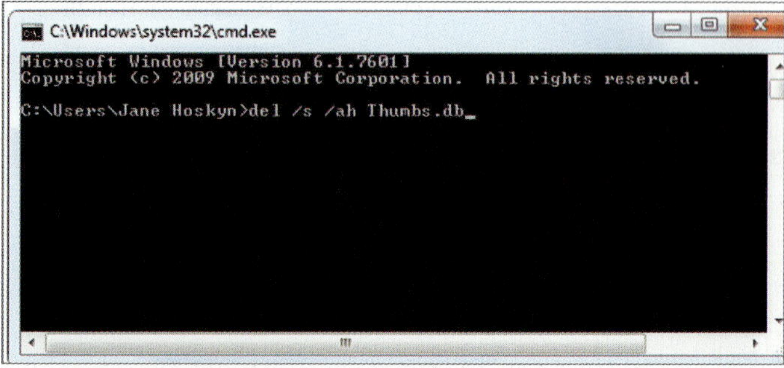

You can delete all Thumbs.db files in one go using Command prompt

Remove it for good:

Deleting all your Thumbs.db files using SwiftSearch and/or Windows Explorer (File Explorer in Windows 8/8.1) would take a while, so use the Command Prompt. Type <type>cmd</type> into Start and press Enter to open it, then type <type>del /s /ah Thumbs.db</type> and press Enter.

If you use thumbnails a lot, it won't take long for Thumbs.db files to creep back into your system and start chewing up space again, but you can prevent this with a quick Windows hack. You'll need to be logged in as administrator. Press Win+R to open the Run window, then type <type>gpedit.msc</type> and click OK. In the window that opens, navigate through these folders: User Configuration, Administrative Templates, Windows Components and then Windows Explorer (Windows 7) or File Explorer (Windows 8/8.1). In the right-hand pane, double-click

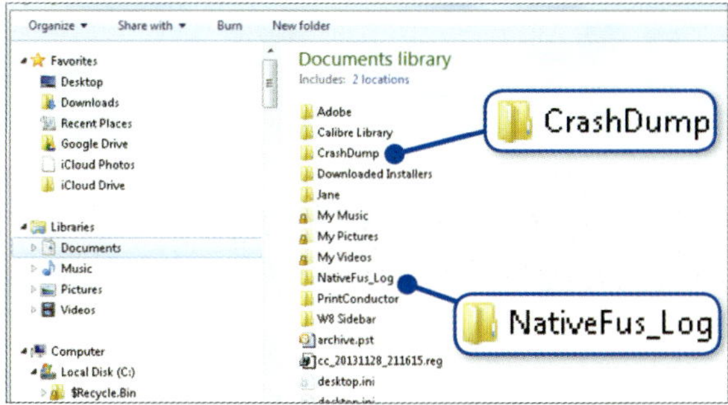

CrashDumps and NativeFUS_ Log contain crash log files, which wastes lots of space

'Turn off the caching of thumbnails in hidden thumbs.db files' and click Enabled, then OK. You'll never be bothered by Thumbs.db again.

CrashDump and NativeFus_Log

What are they?

These two are the Tweedledum and Tweedledee of folders, usually turning up together and always getting in the way. Double-click to open either, and you'll find more junk (crash log files, which can be huge) or nothing at all. They usually appear in Documents and were created by software, such as Nero DVD software or Kies (Android file-management) software (www.snipca.com/14724), and they store information about CPU usage and crashes. Its usefulness is limited, especially if you've removed the original software.

We've seen lots of questions about these folders on malware forums. Be assured, they're not malware, but they do act like it – they have odd names, they appeared out of nowhere and they regenerate when deleted.

Can you delete them?

Yes. If the folders are empty, they're an annoyance rather than a problem. If there are huge crash log files inside them, then they're definitely a problem and should be removed.

Using SwiftSearch, look for files with the extensions LOG or MDMP ('minidump') and delete them if they're hogging space. To weed out pointlessly large folders, use the free program WinDirStat (https://windirstat.info; best download link is Sourceforge, www.snipca.com/14726). WinDirStat is great for managing your hard drive space, because (unlike Explorer) is reveals folders' exact sizes and which software created them. However it takes a while to gather its detailed 'tree' of folders and their sizes, so you might prefer the free new tool SpaceSniffer (www.snipca.com/14727). Its findings aren't as detailed as WinDirStat but it's much faster, revealing massive folders at a glance. It's also rather beautiful.

Remove them for good:

Windows' built-in tool Disk Cleanup can automatically clear out crash logs and other space hogs. It's easy to use, but it can be a bit gung-ho – it doesn't give you much control, and we've seen it removing useful program files. Instead, use CCleaner (www.piriform.com/ccleaner). Its default Windows Cleaner tool includes Memory Dumps and Windows Log Files, and if you click Applications you can add Crash Reports and many more file types to the clean. To add even more options to CCleaner, install the new tool CCEnhancer (www.snipca.com/14728).

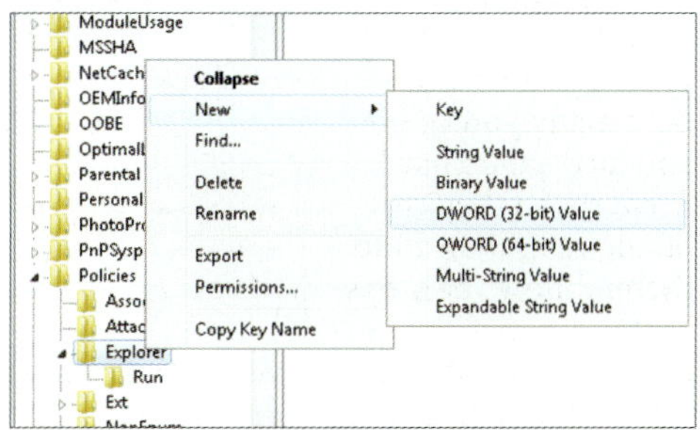

You can remove all desktop.ini files from your PC by creating a new Registry value

Desktop.ini

What is it?

Desktop.ini files contain display settings for whichever folder they're stored in. This includes the folder's icon and the 'info tip' text that pops up when you hover your mouse over it. Like Thumbs.db, desktop.ini files are created automatically (and repeatedly) by Windows all over your PC. They're always hidden by default, so you'll need to un-hide them before you can track them down.

We found no fewer than 401 desktop.ini files on our PC – nearly 12 times as many as Thumbs.db – but they didn't take up much space. Our biggest desktop.ini file was 3MB, and most were a few kilobytes.

The Mac equivalent of desktop.ini is DS_Store. You may see these files popping up in Explorer if you've ever connected an iPad or iPhone to your PC.

Incidentally, after un-hiding your system files you'll see two desktop.ini files on your Desktop. This is because your PC has two Desktop folders – one for the administrator (normally stored at C:\Users\YourName\Desktop) and one in Users\Public.

Can you delete it

Yes, but there's not much point. Windows will replace it automatically with a new desktop.ini file, and the folder's settings will return to default.

In fact, desktop.ini files can be very useful. You can customise a folder by creating a desktop.ini file using just Notepad and the Command Prompt. For example, to customise a folder's info tip to say 'This folder is for cat photos', create a <jb>Unicode</jb> text file in Notepad and include the line 'InfoTip=This folder is for cat photos'. Save the file as 'desktop.ini' inside the relevant folder, then use the command line to apply the customisations. Microsoft has full instructions (www.snipca.com/14714).

Remove it for good:

If you really want to remove all instances of desktop.ini, try this Registry hack. Type <type>regedit</type> into Start, click 'regedit.exe', then click Yes to open the Registry Editor, and go to the HKEY_LOCAL_MACHINE root key. Now follow the folder path: Software\Microsoft\Windows\CurrentVersion\Policies\Explorer. Right-click the Explorer folder, click New and click DWORD to create a new value. Call it UseDesktopIniCache and set its value to '0'.

Find out what any system file is and does by typing it into FileInfo.com

Never lose another file

Windows hasn't included a decent search tool since XP's Search Assistant. If you miss the helpful cartoon hound, there's plenty of free software to help you out. We compare six tools for locating lost files

Agent Ransack | bit.ly/agent368 | ★★★★★

FEATURES ★★★★★ **PERFORMANCE** ★★★★☆ **EASE OF USE** ★★★★★

What we liked:

There's nothing modern about Agent Ransack's interface, which uses a classic Windows look rather than adding design elements of its own. This makes it functional but familiar, and its classic icons and pop-out tool-tips make finding your way around very simple.

To search for something, just type what you're looking for into the 'File name' or 'Containing text' boxes (or both), choose the folder to start from (it defaults to your entire hard drive if you don't refine it) and press Start.

It's a good idea to put your own filters in place where you can, such as limiting the search to particular file types or locations, because the software will look for the files in every nook and cranny of your hard drive.

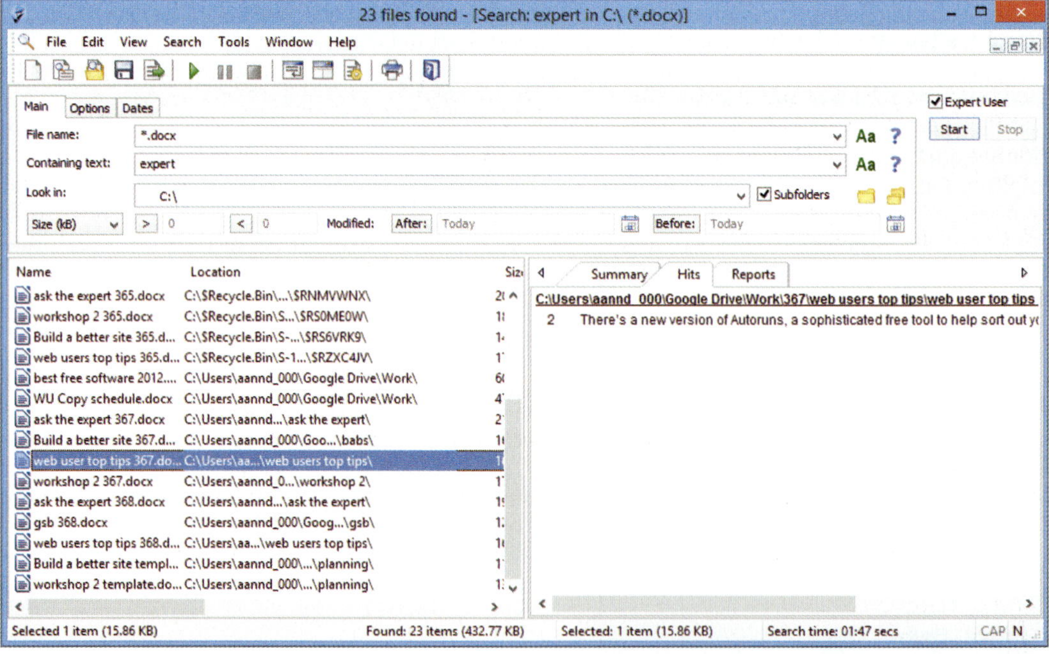

Once you get your results, the Summary and Hits tabs are particularly useful. Summary gives an overview of the number of files Agent Ransack has searched and the matches found. Hits goes a step further: if you're looking for text in a document, for example, it tells you which lines of the document the text appears on and displays the context.

When you install the software, it's set up to run in Expert User mode, but you can untick this option if you prefer a simpler interface. This removes less commonly used features, including the file size and date-filtering options.

How it can be improved:

Because Agent Ransack scans everything each time it's set to look for an item, the search is slow but thorough. It took the software nearly two minutes to scan our entire hard drive for files ending in '.docx' that contained a certain word. The onus is on you to refine your search as much as possible.

Also, results aren't shown in any sensible order - in our test searches, we found things showing up in temp folders and the Recycle Bin before we got to the actual files we were looking for. In other words, it could be more efficient.

OUR VERDICT

While it's not the prettiest or the fastest search tool we tested, it is the most thorough. As long as you're happy to wait for your results, Agent Ransack will always find your file.

Copernic Desktop Search Lite | www.copernic.com | ★★★★★

FEATURES ★★★★★ PERFORMANCE ★★★★★ EASE OF USE ★★★★☆

What we liked:

Copernic Desktop Search Lite is a great-looking search tool, but because it's a trimmed-back version of paid-for software, you have to tolerate an 'upgrade today' advert every time you run the software.

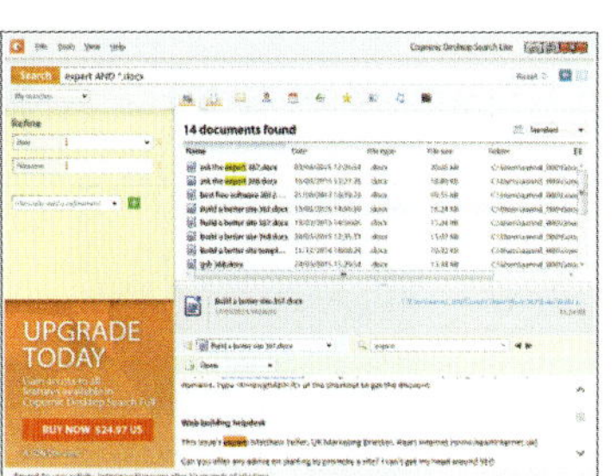

When you first install Copernic, it creates an index of your hard drive's contents. To save time, it limits this to a section of your hard drive where your searched-for files are most likely to be located, which includes the Documents folder.

This only took a few minutes on our test PC, but when we searched for our test file, Copernic didn't find it, because it was outside the default index. It's easy to add more folders and re-index the files, but this means you have to anticipate where those lost files might be. However, if a file is in the index, it will be discovered very quickly, and there's a handy preview window that highlights words in documents to show you where they appear.

How it can be improved:

The free version of the software has a few limitations but they're easily worked around. The most significant restriction is that you can't use it to search for files on external or network drives.

OUR VERDICT

Copernic does the same job as Agent Ransack, but faster. You have to index your files first, though, because it won't find anything that hasn't been catalogued.

Everything | voidtools.com | ★★★★☆

FEATURES ★★★☆☆ PERFORMANCE ★★★★★ EASE OF USE ★★★★☆

What we liked:

Everything is a different type of search tool. Instead of waiting for you to type a search term before it starts looking for the results, it lists every file on your hard drive and filters out the irrelevant ones as you type.

The great thing about this is that it's totally inclusive. You know the file you're looking for is there, it's just a case of weeding out all the wrong ones until you get to it. You can do this by adding your own filter controls. At the most basic level, this means using the drop-down menu on the right of the search bar to pick specific types of files, such as audio, video or document. If you want to take this a step further, you can type in wildcards, such as *.docx (which filters out any file that isn't a Word document) and use logical operators such as 'and' and 'not'. If there are specific searches that you perform a lot, you can bookmark them for future reference.

How it can be improved:

Everything doesn't search the content of files. This is a huge gap in your search arsenal and will probably mean you'll need another search tool installed alongside this one.

OUR VERDICT

Everything's reverse approach to search is refreshing but while it's excellent for sifting out files from the chaos of your hard drive, it can't search a file's contents.

BEST OF THE REST

LookDisk

bit.ly/lookd368

LookDisk isn't quite as sophisticated as Agent Ransack, but it's completely portable and we found it a little faster. It makes it easier to set up searches but it doesn't offer a preview of any files that are found. This isn't helpful if you're looking to find something like text in a file, where the context of a particular word can help you find what you're looking for.

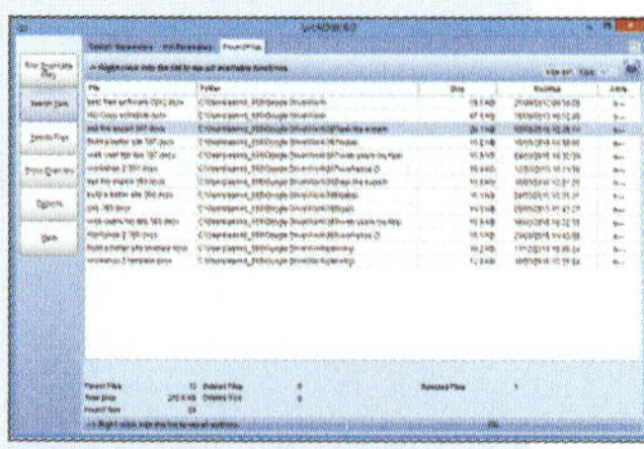

DocFetcher

docfetcher.sourceforge.net

DocFetcher is an open source alternative to Copernic, which indexes some or all of your hard drive to perform super-speedy searches. Although it looks promising, its main drawback is that you must have Java installed in order to run it, which is a bit old fashioned and will put a lot of people off.

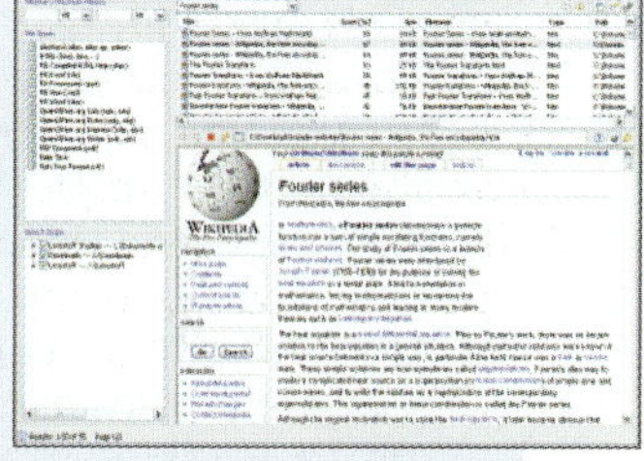

UltraSearch

bit.ly/ultra368

Instead of indexing your files, UltraSearch uses the Master File Table (MFT) to find what you're looking for. While this makes it fast at tracking down files, it can't search their content. If you don't need a file finder that can search content, we'd still recommend Everything over UltraSearch because it's just as fast and we preferred the way Everything works by weeding out the files you don't want rather than searching for the one you do

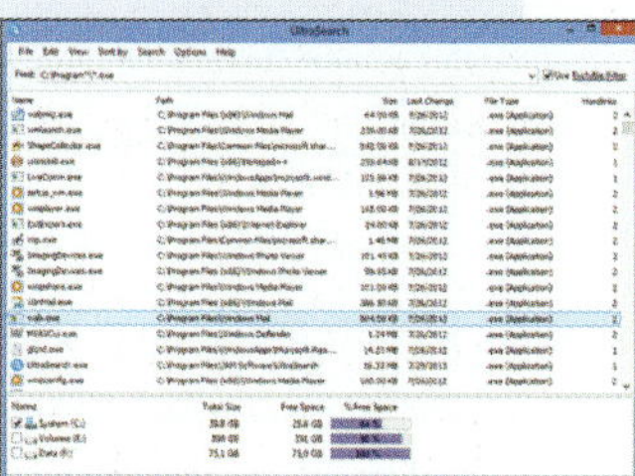

TOP TIPS for automating tasks in windows

Record tasks to replay later with one click

TinyTask (bit.ly/tiny364) is an amazing tool that can automate a wide range of tasks by saving your key strokes and mouse movements so you can repeat the actions in one click. As it's name suggests, it is tiny, at just 33KB, and makes no changes to your system folders or Registry. In fact, it doesn't have to be installed at all, and can be run from a USB drive instead.

Double-click it to display a tiny toolbar with six icons. When you click the blue orb, it will turn red and record every action you perform until you click the button again to stop it. You can then replay the recording by clicking the green Play button. For example, if you recorded yourself opening a browser and typing a URL, the software would recreate the task every time you play it back. It's a handy way of automating short, repetitive tasks.

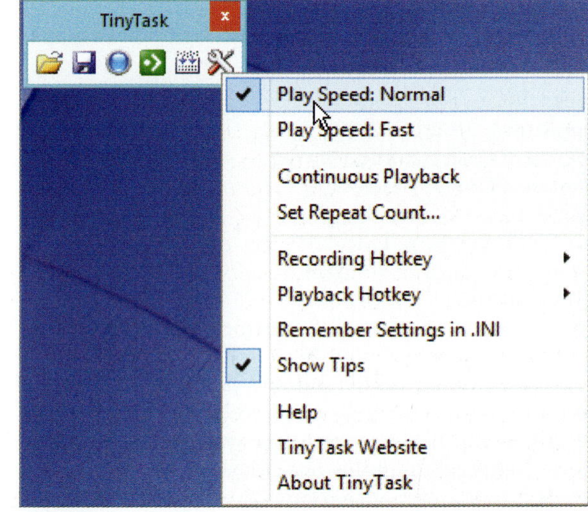

Record simple tasks using TinyTask and then replay them to perform the action automatically

Start programs with hotkeys

Instead of searching the Start menu or Start screen for programs, you can create keyboard shortcuts for them. Open Explorer, find a program in 'C:\Program Files', right-click it and select Send To, 'Desktop (create shortcut)'. Right-click the icon on the Desktop and select Properties. On the Shortcut tab, click inside the 'Shortcut key' box and press any combination of keys, such as Ctrl+Shift+P. Click OK. Now, whenever you use that key combination, the program will run. Just make sure you don't use a shortcut key combination that's already being used elsewhere.

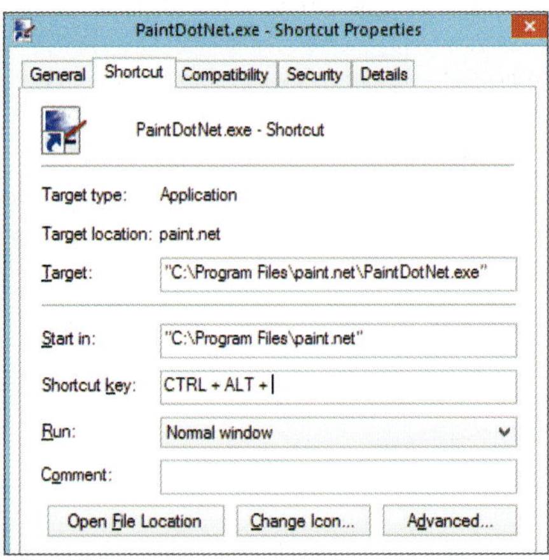

Create shortcuts to programs and then define hotkeys to start them

Start several programs simultaneously

Free program Splat (bit.ly/splat364) lets you perform several actions with a single mouse-click or key-press, which is particularly useful when you want to start several programs at once. Download it, unzip the file, open the folder and double-click 'splat.exe' to run it. In Windows 8, you'll then need to click the 'More info' link and then 'Run anyway' to bypass Microsoft's program blockers.

Splat saves your commands in lists that it calls 'profiles'. Click the first toolbar button to create a new profile and name it. Select it in the profiles list and double-click an empty line in the Action column on the right. A window opens and, at the top, you can select an action to perform. Choose Audio and you can pick an MP3 music file to play; select Run and a program in the 'C:\Program Files' folder can be launched.

Creating music playlists and running groups of programs is very straightforward. Any number of entries can be added to a profile, so you could start your favourite music and programs simultaneously. Delays and pauses can be added to a profile, to allow programs time to start or music to play, for example.

You can also make advanced functions start and stop, close applications and kill processes in the Task Manager. However, it's best to avoid these unless you're sure of what you are doing. But if you know your way around Windows, you could use

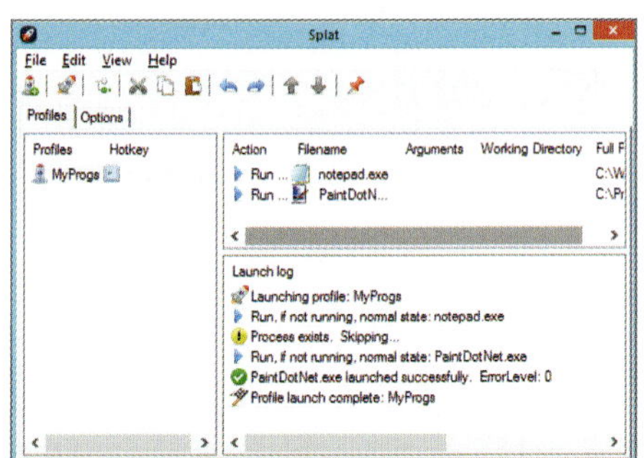

Create profiles in Splat to run programs, play music and perform other commands

this to create profiles that shut down unnecessary services when you want to play a game or watch a movie without interruptions. You could then create another profile to start them again afterwards.

Create triggers for actions

Shutter Lite (free from bit.ly/shut364) lets you set events that will automatically trigger certain actions. Run it and you'll see two lists: one for events and the other for actions. Click the Add button and choose one of the 13 events from the list. These include Countdown, which counts down hours, minutes and seconds; On Time, which triggers at a certain time; and CPU Usage, which lets you define a maximum or minimum processor usage. Shutter Lite can also recognise when a window title appears on the screen, or a laptop's lid is opened or closed. You can group together combinations of events as triggers, such as the CPU level falling below 5 per cent after 6pm.

Click the Add button above the Actions list to choose an action you want the event to trigger, such as shutting down the computer, opening files, running programs, playing a message, controlling the volume, running the screensaver and many more. As with the events, actions can be combined so you could, for example, make Shutter Lite turn off your computer and sound an alarm when the CPU usage falls below 5 per cent after 6pm, meaning that your computer will let you know that it's shutting down for the evening if it is not being used. Click the Start button after defining the events and actions to minimise the program to an icon in the notification area.

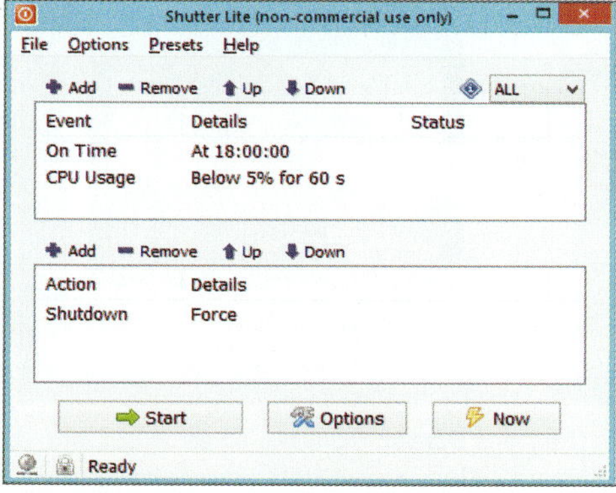

Use Shutter Lite to define actions you want performed when certain events occur

TAKE IT TO THE NEXT LEVEL

More advanced tips for when you're feeling brave

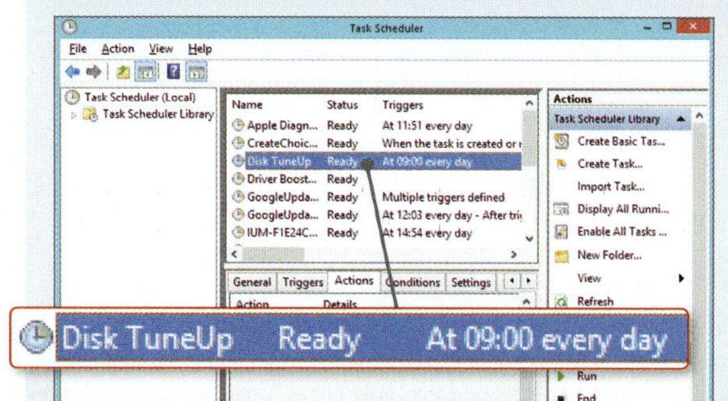

Task Scheduler can be used to automatically start programs when certain events occur

Use the Task Scheduler

Windows has a built-in tool called Task Scheduler which you can use to automate tasks in the OS or on any program that's running on it. Most people aren't aware of it and it's been particularly well hidden in Windows 8. However, it's extremely useful for certain tasks, such as running the Disk Defragmenter every day to optimise your hard drive and maintain performance.

Click Start or go to the Start screen and type schedule, then click Task Scheduler or 'Schedule tasks'. Open the Action menu and select Create Task. Enter a name for the task on the General tab, such as Drive Tune-up. Tick the option to 'Run with highest privileges' (in other words, as an administrator).

You now need to set a trigger that determines when the task is run, so select the Triggers tab and click New. The 'Begin the task' menu has several options, such as 'At log on' and 'At startup', but the one we want is 'On a schedule'. You can then select Daily and set a start time, such as 09:00. To ensure that the defrag takes place, even if your computer isn't yet switched on at 9am, select the Settings tab and tick 'Run task as soon as possible after a scheduled start is missed'.

Select the Actions tab and click New. Set the Action to 'Start a program' and click the Browse button, then select Defrag.exe from the C:\Windows\System32 folder. Type c: in the 'Add arguments' box, so the program will defragment drive C:, and click OK. Select the Conditions tab and tick 'Start the task only if the computer is idle for'. Here you can set a time, such as 10 minutes, and there is an option to stop the task if the computer ceases to be idle. You can also specify that it shouldn't run when a laptop is on battery power, so that defragmentation doesn't run it down. Click OK to finish.

Disk Defragmenter will now automatically run every day to tune up your hard drive.

Control applications with AutoIt

AutoIt (www.autoitscript.com) is a powerful programming language that can automate just about anything in Windows. It not only lets you start applications, but also control them. It does this by sending mouse-clicks, key-presses and menu selections directly to the application. For example, you could set it to start WordPad or Notepad, and then send key presses to access the file menu and then open a document, such as a standard letter. You could then continue to edit it yourself or send more key presses and commands, such as printing it and closing it when you've finished.

If you fancy a challenge and want to automate some of the applications on your PC, install AutoIt. Right-click in an Explorer window and select New, AutoIt Script to create a new program script. Right-click it afterwards and select Edit Script. There isn't space here to explore this automation tool in detail, but there are some useful step-by-step tutorials at bit.ly/auto364.

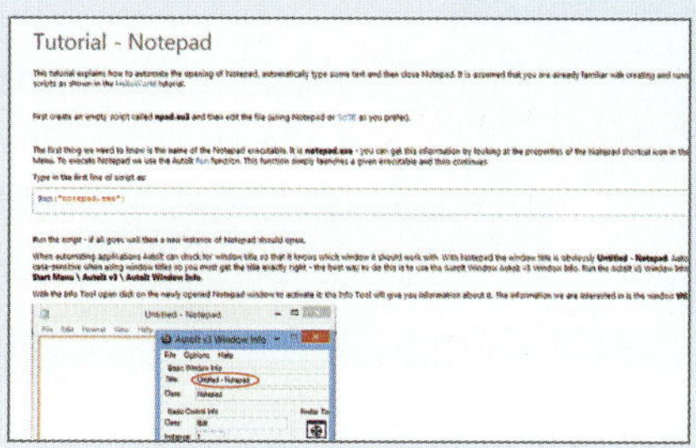

Work through AutoIt's tutorials to find out how to use the scripting tool

Customise Windows 8.1's built-in tools

EXPERT TIP
Changing the boot screen logo is surprisingly complicated. It's embedded in the operating system and you need to make changes to several different settings to make it work. The Windows 8.1 Boot Screen Logo Changer (bit.ly/bootlogo362) will help you do this, but follow the instructions carefully. You'll also find some useful notes on using it at bit.ly/bootnotes362.

Windows 8.1 fixed a lot of the things that were annoying about Windows 8, and its built-in tools let you configure it further. However, some elements still can't be changed, such as the list on the Windows+X menu and the way the Start screen operates.

Luckily, there are developers creating tools you can use to change these and many other elements in Windows 8.1. Winaero (winaero.com) has around 60 freeware programs listed on its homepage, many of which use a quick tweak to target a specific problem, and we've included several in this Workshop, along with a few from elsewhere.

As with all downloads, make sure you click the correct button because the pages these programs appear on are often peppered with similar buttons that are installers for ads for other programs. Also, make sure your PC is fully backed-up and you've created a restore point before you start making changes.

Winaero: winaero.com | 30 mins | Windows 8.1

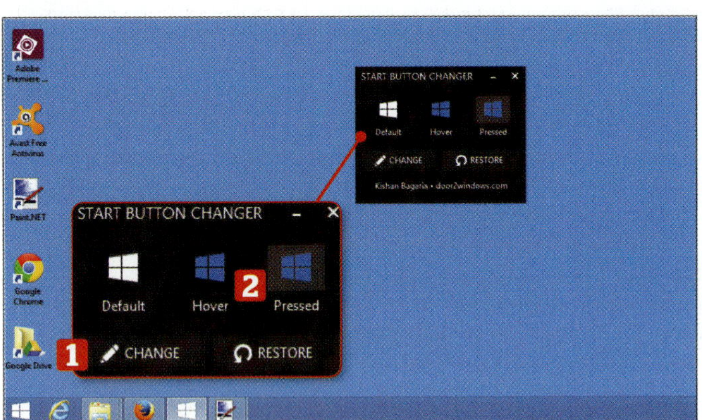

1 Download and install Start Button Changer from bit.ly/change362. Click the Change button **1** to swap the main icon for another (use GIF, JPEG or PNG images). To change the Hover and Pressed images, **2** right-click and choose Change Mask Image.

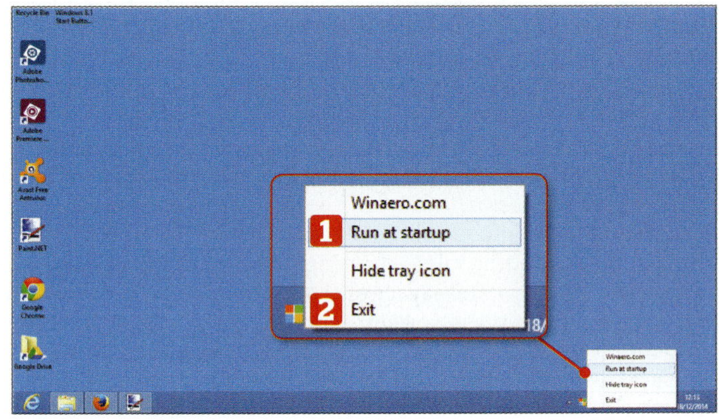

2 To remove the Start button, install and run StartIsGone from bit.ly/gone362. An icon appears in the notification area. Right-click it, then click 'Run at startup' **1** to keep the Start button hidden when you restart, or click Exit **2** to bring it back.

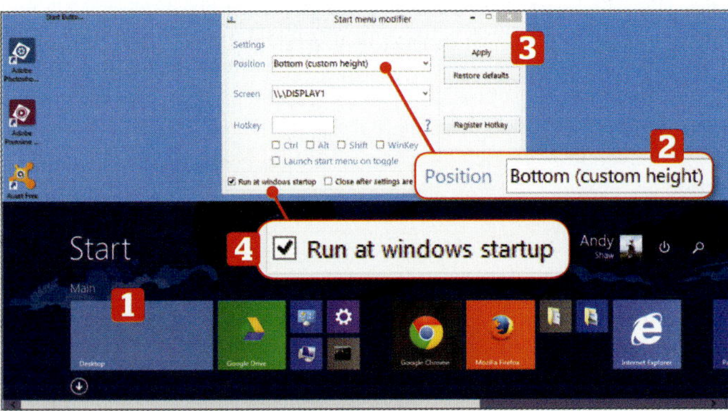

3 Start Menu Modifier (bit.ly/menumod362) makes the Start screen act more like a Start menu by opening it within the Desktop. **1** Choose the location where you want it to open **2** and click Apply. **3** Tick the box to run it when Windows starts. **4**

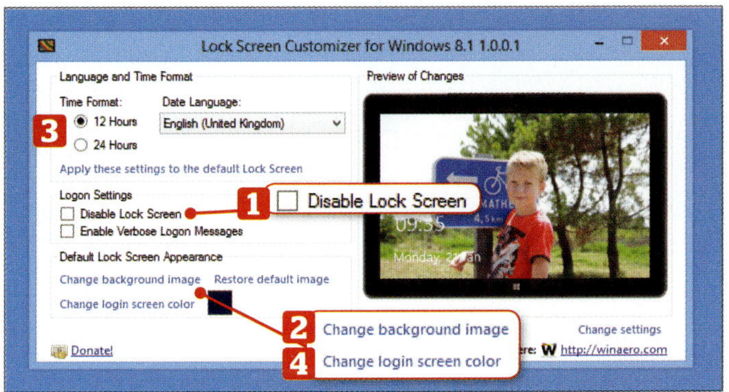

4 You can tinker with the Lock Screen from the Charms bar, but Lock Screen Customizer (bit.ly/lock362) lets you make further tweaks. You can disable it, **1** change the background, **2** switch the type of clock **3** and change the colour of the login screen. **4**

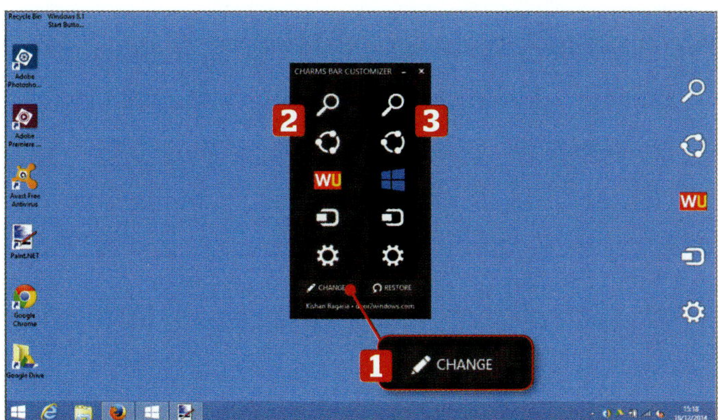

5 Charms Bar Customizer (bit.ly/charms362) changes the Charms icons. Double-click an icon to replace and click Change. **1** The left-hand icons **2** appear when your mouse moves to a corner of the Desktop; the right-hand ones **3** appear when you hover over a charm.

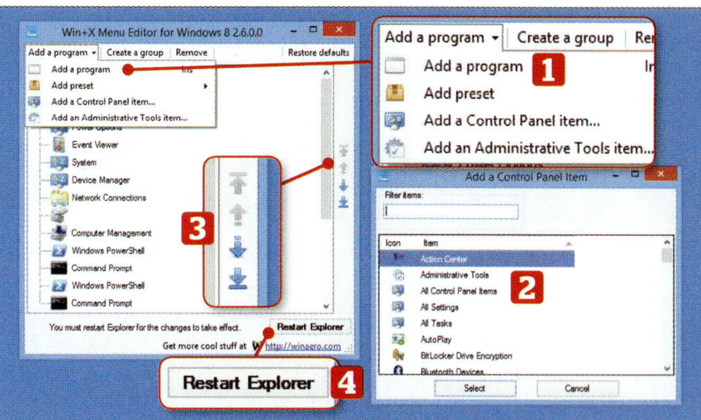

6 Win+X Menu Editor (bit.ly/menu362) customises the Windows+X menu. Click 'Add a program' **1** to choose from programs or other items, then make a selection from the pop-out Window. **2** Use the arrows to change the order, **3** then Restart Explorer. **4**

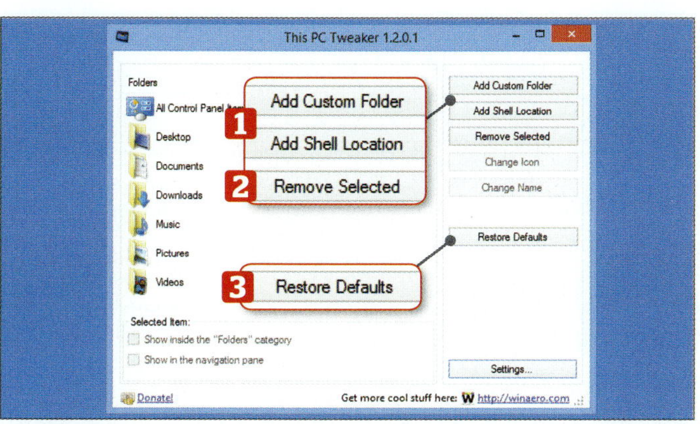

7 This PC Tweaker (bit.ly/this362) lets you add folders and Shell Locations **1** (such as the Control Panel) to the This PC window. You can also remove elements that are already there. **2** If you change your mind, click Restore Defaults **3** to reset everything.

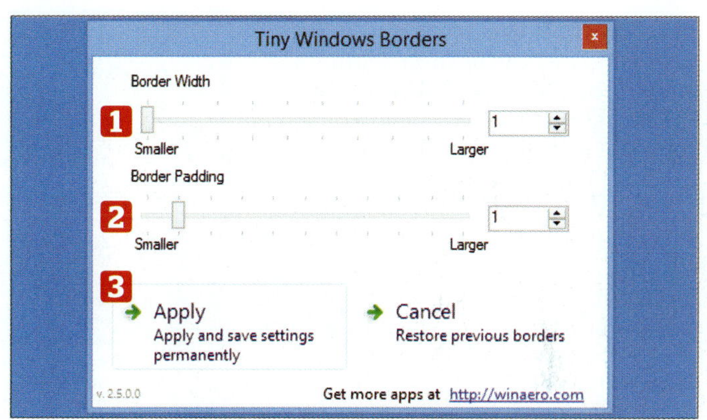

8 The borders of windows are quite thick by default in Windows 8.1. Tiny Windows Borders (bit.ly/tinyb362) lets you reduce the border width **1** and the padding around it. **2** Click Apply **3** to see the effect of your changes.

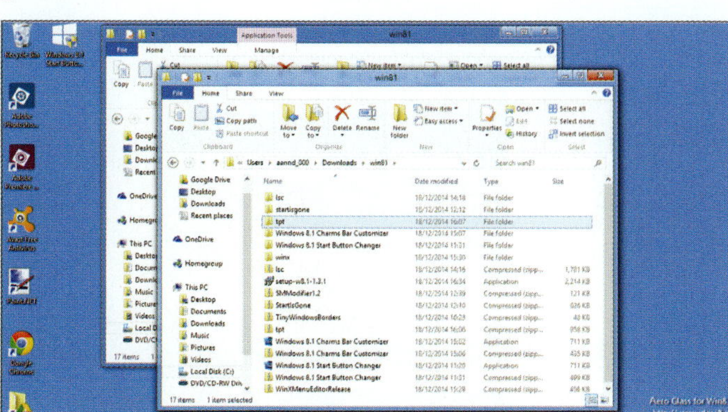

9 Microsoft's translucent Aero theme was dropped because it harmed performance, but if you have a powerful PC, you can bring it back with Aero Glass for Win8.1+ (bit.ly/aero362). Installing the software immediately launches the theme onto your PC.

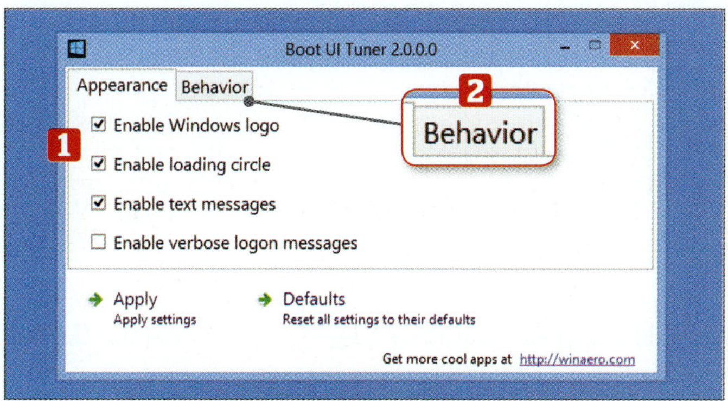

10 Boot UI Tuner (bit.ly/boot362) lets you remove start-up elements, such as the logo and revolving-circle icon. **1** The Behavior tab **2** hides advanced options, including 'Always display advanced boot options', which helps you enter Safe Mode.

Supercharged alternatives to the Windows Clipboard

The Windows Clipboard is OK for basic tasks but there are much better alternatives available. We round up the best free contenders

Ditto | ditto-cp.sourceforge.net | ★★★★★

FEATURES ★★★★☆ **PERFORMANCE** ★★★★★ **EASE OF USE** ★★★★☆

What we liked:

When downloading Ditto, you can choose between the standard 64-bit version or a portable one. The latter runs from a USB stick and means you can carry around your clipboard manager and plug it into whatever computer you happen to be using.

Like our other top picks, Save.Me and Shapeshifter, Ditto runs alongside the Windows Clipboard and uses the same Ctrl+C (cut) and Ctrl +V (paste) key combinations. This means you can start using it right away and only dabble with Ditto's extra tools when you want to.

The program captures and stores text, images and web addresses, and you can set the number of items it stores (the default is 500), after which the oldest item will be deleted as you add new ones. Alternatively, you can mark individual clips as 'Never Delete' and they'll always stay in the Ditto database.

The amount of storage space for your clippings is similar to Save.Me, and it works better with large clip collections than Shapeshifter. Clipped items are searchable and easily inserted into the document of your choice.

The Ditto window is much smaller than that of our other award-winning clipboards, but it has options galore for combining clips into Groups (such as salutations, sign-offs and signatures for writing letters and emails), and lets you edit existing text clips or create new ones from scratch. You can also have Ditto sit on top of other programs and keep it rolled up next to the menu bar to save space on small screens. Like Save.Me, everything is stored in a database, so you can switch off the PC knowing that your clips will be saved.

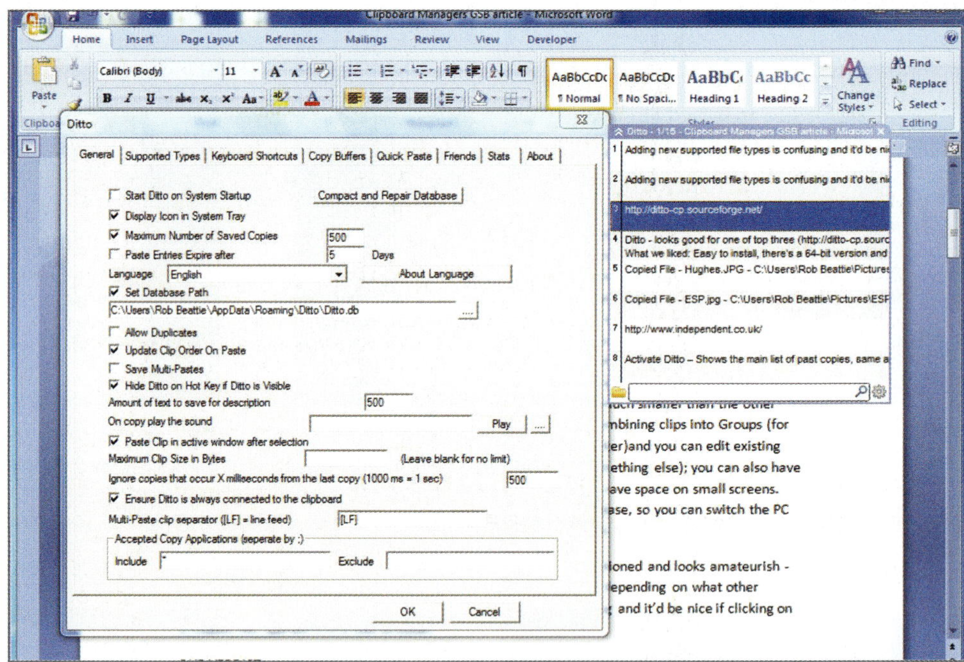

How it can be improved:

Ditto's interface looks amateurish and unloved, and could do with some care and attention. Its always-on-top mode doesn't always work, depending on what other programs are running. Adding new supported file types is confusing and it would be helpful if clicking a clipped URL opened it in a web browser.

OUR VERDICT

Despite its dated look, Ditto does the business. It works alongside the existing Windows Clipboard and hides away when you don't need it, but it still packs plenty of power when you do.

Save.Me | www.aiclipboard.com/save.me | ★★★★☆

FEATURES ★★★★☆ **PERFORMANCE** ★★★☆☆ **EASE OF USE** ★★★★☆

What we liked:

Save.Me comes as a single executable file, so you don't need to install it on your PC. Its interface is better looking than Ditto's and it has a good Default View, which lists commands on the left, clips in the middle and a preview of the currently selected clip on the right.

Save.Me's window takes up more space than Ditto's, but is better suited to storing photos and website URLs, because it previews them live and in full. Like the other clipboard managers here, it can clip text, graphics and web addresses, and you can also create new text snippets and save them for later. Save.Me also has a unique Logbook View, which organises clips by date, as well as a useful Research View with customisable columns displaying headings such as Topic, Date, Content and more. Like Ditto, it stores clips even after you turn off your PC.

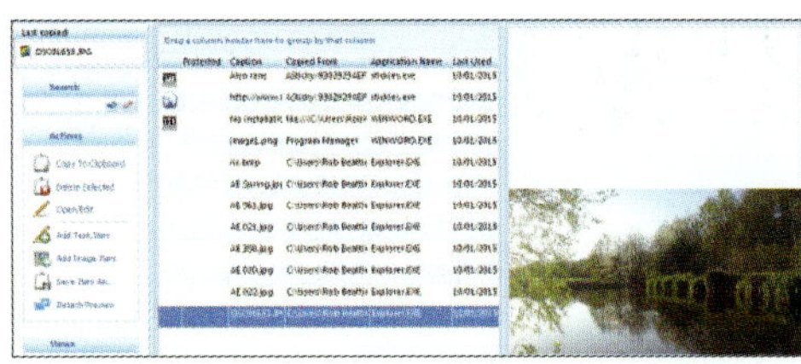

How it can be improved:

It's easy to miss some of Save.Me's best features, such as the ability to customise the columns in Research View. The Search facility sometimes produces inconsistent results, finding words in some text clips but not others.

OUR VERDICT

Save.Me is better than Ditto at storing visual information, but there's no documentation to guide you around its features and its web previews can slow things down.

Shapeshifter | bit.ly/shape363 | ★★★☆☆

FEATURES ★★★☆☆ **PERFORMANCE** ★★★★☆ **EASE OF USE** ★★★★☆

What we liked:

At last, a clipboard manager that doesn't look like it was designed in 1995. Shapeshifter's clean interface is more edgy than the others and although that's due in part to having fewer features, it's noticeably more refreshing than its staid rivals.

Like the other clipboard managers in this round-up, it uses the same Copy and Paste commands as Windows, but holding down Ctrl+V displays its main window in Integrated Mode, so you can select the item you want to paste. Shapeshifter is the easiest of our top picks to master because there are so few options and its use of large thumbnails makes it well suited to working with graphics.

How it can be improved:

We would have liked Shapeshifter to provide a better explanation about how the three different modes work and the advantages of each, rather than having to work it out for ourselves. In Integrated Mode, you can't open the viewer and close it again if you don't paste

OUR VERDICT

Shapeshifter is a good choice if you want more power than the standard Windows Clipboard, but don't need to store items permanently or use Ditto and Save.Me's more complex tools.

BEST OF THE REST

OrangeNote
www.orangenote.littlesoftware.ca

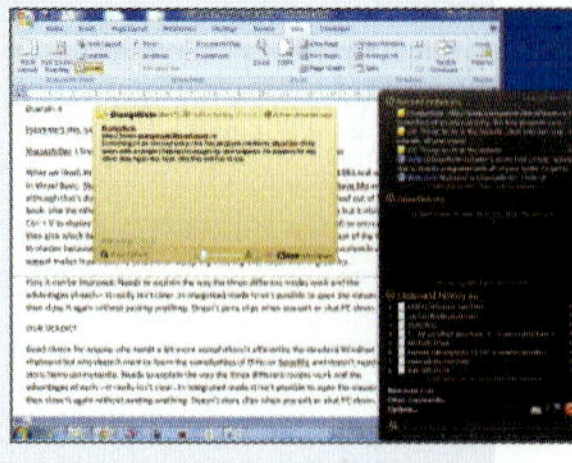

Something of an unusual entry, this free program combines attractive sticky notes with a simple clipboard manager for text snippets. It has an appealing interface; plenty of hotkeys for fast access; and taggable and searchable notes. Although there's no support for any other data types, the program is neat, effective and fun to use.

xNeat
www.xneat.com/clipboard-manager

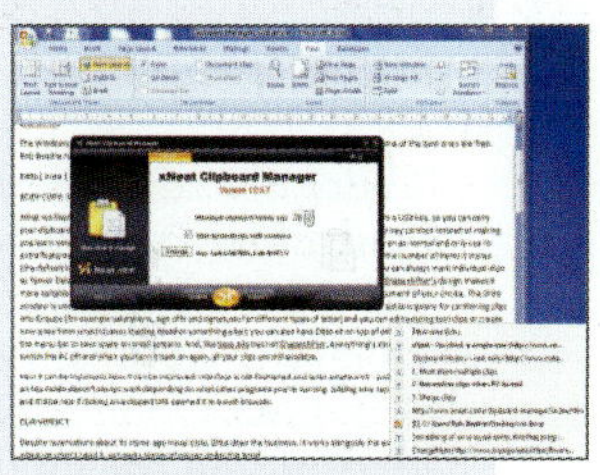

This unobtrusive, low-powered clipboard manager hasn't been updated for a while and lacks any database-style features. However, if all you want is access to a simple pop-up list of recently clipped items (text, URLs and images) that you can access via a hotkey and paste into an open application, it's definitely worth a look. You can also choose the number of items stored in the clipboard at any one time.

Clipboard History
bit.ly/clip363

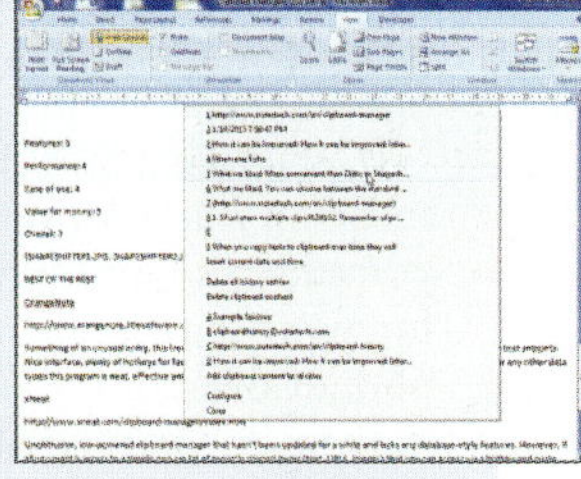

Clipboard History is another text-only clipboard manager that uses the same simple approach as xNeat but adds some extra features. These include inserting the date and time at the current cursor position; the ability to delete all clipboard entries from a pop-up menu; and a clever tool to set exclusions, so that text containing specific keywords will never be copied to the clipboard. It also lets you edit items and set them as 'sticky', so they won't be deleted.

TOP TIPS for Solving Windows update problems

Windows Update troubleshooting

If you're having problems updating Windows, there is is a useful built-in Windows Update Troubleshooter that can help. You access it the same way in Windows 7 and 8, although it works slightly differently in the two operating systems.

Go to the Control Panel and open Windows Update in one of the 'icons' views. Click the 'View update history' link on the left and find the link near the top of the window that says 'Troubleshoot problems with installing updates'. Both Windows 7 and 8 provide tips and answers to common questions, but Windows 7 goes further and has a 'Fix it' button that downloads a troubleshooter. Click the button, then click Run in the next window. When it's finished, restart your PC and Windows Update should be as good as new.

Troubleshoot problems with installing updates

An automatic troubleshooter is available that fixes some problems with Windows Update, and it might resolve this error for you.

To run a Windows Update troubleshooter

1. Click this button:

Fix this problem

2. In the **File Download** dialog box, click **Run**, and then follow the steps in the wizard.
3. Open Windows Update, and try to install the update again.

If that didn't work, here are solutions to some common problems with installing updates.

▸ I tried to install updates but one or more didn't get installed.

You can fix most update problems using Windows' troubleshooting Fix It tool

Install updates when you want

There are settings you can adjust to control how and when Windows checks for updates and installs them. Open the Control Panel, then open Windows Update. Click 'Change settings' on the left and, under 'Important updates', choose one of the options. Select 'Install updates automatically' if you want to leave everything to Windows.

If you find that Windows installs updates at inconvenient times and wants to reboot the computer or run updates when you'd rather shutdown and pack away, choose 'Download updates but let me choose whether to install them'.

If you use a laptop with a mobile internet connection or metered Wi-Fi, you may be paying by the megabyte for your bandwidth, and if you use a budget broadband connection, you may suffer bandwidth restrictions where your data usage is limited at specific times of the day. In such cases, you should tick 'Check for updates but let me choose whether to download and install them', so you can prevent large updates from downloading during peak times.

Selecting 'Never check for updates' only turns off automatic updates; you can still get the updates you need by clicking the 'Check for updates' button. The advantage of this is that you can download updates at a time that's convenient for you; the drawback is that it's up to you to remember to do so! Stick a note in your diary to remind yourself to carry out updates at a quiet time of the week, or schedule the update to run at a specific time (see 'Take it to the next level', opposite).

Install optional updates

Most Windows updates are necessary, but a few are optional. They are easy to miss because you'll only know about them if you go into your Update settings. Every now and again, it's worth manually checking for optional updates and installing them. Open Windows Update to see your update status, such as 'You're set to automatically install updates'. If there are any optional updates, you will see a link below. Click it to see a list and select each one in turn to see a description on the right: they could be anything from video driver updates to fixes for specific problems. It's not compulsory to install them but Windows usually works better if you do.

Update problem? Fix it!

Microsoft has 'Fix it' tools at bit.ly/msfix361 that solve a variety of problems. These reset the components used by the service and there are separate 'Fix it' tools for Windows 7 and 8, and XP and Vista. Select the appropriate one for your operating system.

Stop malware blocking automatic updates

Adware and malware have been known to block updates and they can also prevent you from selecting

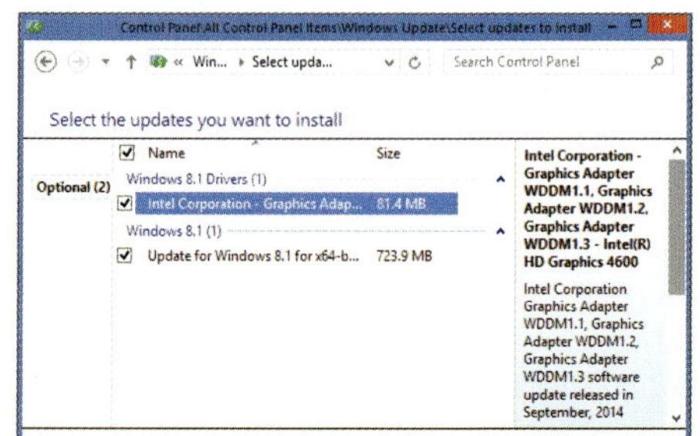

Don't miss out on optional updates; they can be very useful

automatic updates in Windows Update in the Control Panel. If you're having problems with Windows Update and have security software installed, run a full scan of the computer. Download the free version of Malwarebytes Anti-Malware (www.malwarebytes.org) and run it. If it cleans up any infections, reboot the PC and try setting Windows Update to automatic again.

Update your anti-virus

Security software needs to be as up-to-date as possible to detect the latest viruses, Trojans, rootkits and other types of malware on a computer, so make sure your anti-virus program is updating itself when it needs to. Check its status in case a fault is stopping updates from downloading or installing. Normally, updates are only provided for a year after purchase, so check whether you are still receiving them.

Every security program will have a different way to check this, but if you look around the software's main screen, it should tell you when your licence expires (if it's paid-for software) and when the last virus-definition update occurred.

Anti-virus programs let you change the frequency of updates. Some will update every hour, with options to change this to longer periods, such as once a day. Hourly updates aren't essential, so set this to a less frequent period if you want.

Many anti-virus programs have a Game mode, in which all notifications, scans and updates are put off while you play games. This could be useful for delaying updates if you are busy doing something that puts a lot of strain on your processor and hard drive, such as video editing.

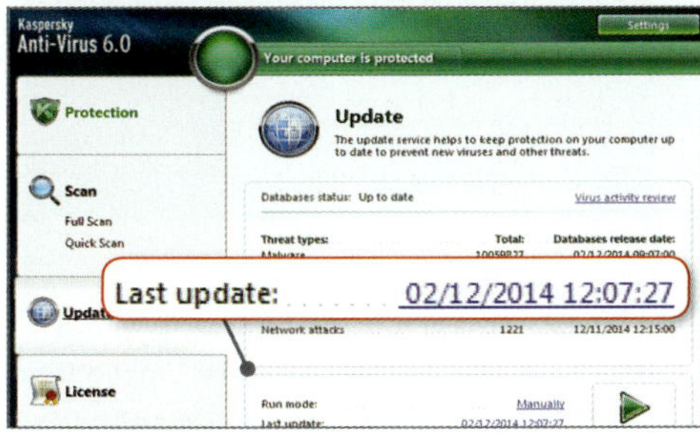

It's vital that your security software is as up-to-date as possible

TAKE IT TO THE NEXT LEVEL

More advanced tips for when you're feeling brave

Check for failures

Windows Update sometimes fails and you should keep an eye out for when this happens. Open Windows Update in the Control Panel and click 'View update history'. In the Status column, you may find a few items marked as Failed. This is not unusual and isn't a big problem as long as the update was tried again and successfully downloaded. You should see an identical, more recent entry in the list of successful updates. Try the troubleshooter if problems persist.

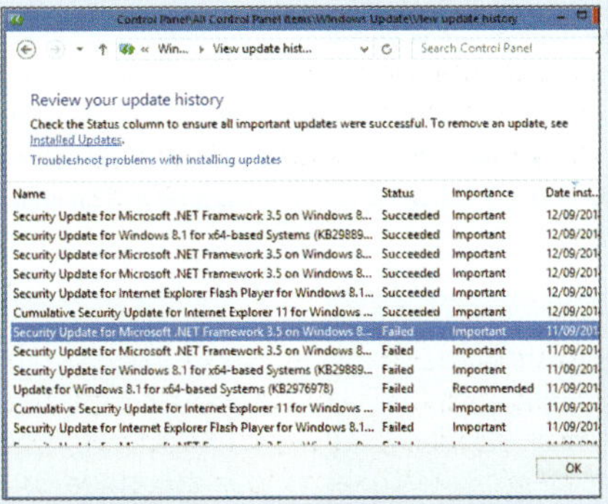

Find any failed updates and check that a later attempt was successful

Schedule updates

Windows 7 has a useful update scheduler that lets you choose when to install updates so Windows Update doesn't bother you with install and restart requests when you're busy. Open Windows Update and set it to install updates automatically. Below you can choose 'Every day' or just one specific day of the week when you want the updates to be installed. If your computer isn't switched on at the set time, the updates will occur the next time you power up.

In Windows 8, you can click a link that says 'Updates will be automatically installed during the maintenance window'. It is set to run at 03:00 every day, but if your PC is normally switched off at night, the update will install as soon as it is left idle after switching it on, whatever time of the day that is.

Unfortunately there's no way to choose a day of the week to install updates in Windows 8, although if a reboot is necessary, Windows 8.1 usually asks whether or not to install updates when you shut down or restart. There is also an option to allow scheduled maintenance (which includes updates) to wake the computer from sleep. So instead of switching off completely at night, just put the computer into Sleep mode (this option is available when you shut down your PC). The computer will power up at 3am, check for updates and install them, then go back to sleep. You can also use the Power Options in the Control Panel to set the PC to go into Sleep mode when it's been idle for a certain length of time.

Check the service

Automatic Windows updates are driven by a service running in the background; if it's not running, the updates won't occur, and you might not even be able to select automatic updates. To check the service, press Windows+R, type services.msc and press Enter. Scroll down to the bottom of the list and double-click Windows Update. Make sure that the 'Startup type' is set to Automatic or 'Automatic (Delayed start)'.

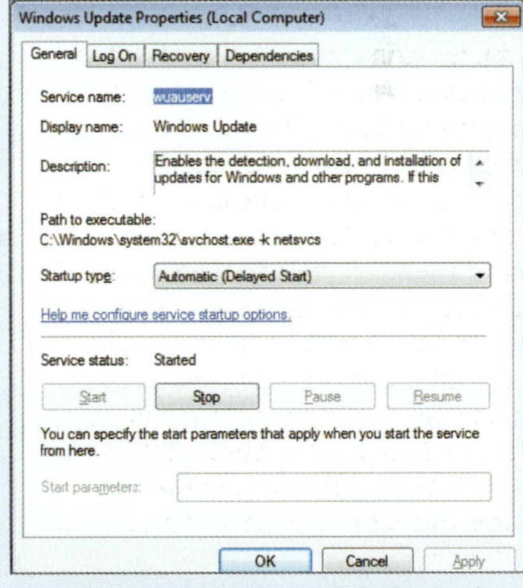

If Windows Update doesn't work, check that the service is running properly

Updates rely on three other services, too. Double-click Background Intelligent Transfer Service and set the 'Startup type' to Manual. Application Identity should be set to Manual and Cryptographic Services should be set to Automatic.

Get a better Command Prompt

You can manage your files and folders much more quickly if you use your keyboard instead of your mouse, but the basic Windows Command Prompt is woefully short on useful tools. PyCmd fixes this with extra shortcuts and features to streamline your command-line work. For a full list of the standard Windows commands, which also work in PyCmd, visit dosprompt.info/commands.

PyCmd: pycmd.sourceforge.net | 10 mins | XP, Vista, 7, 8+

1 It's easy to make a mistake when laboriously typing directory names using the cd command. PyCmd remembers every folder you've ever been to, even from previous sessions. Hold down Alt and use the left/right cursor keys to jump to previously visited folders. 1

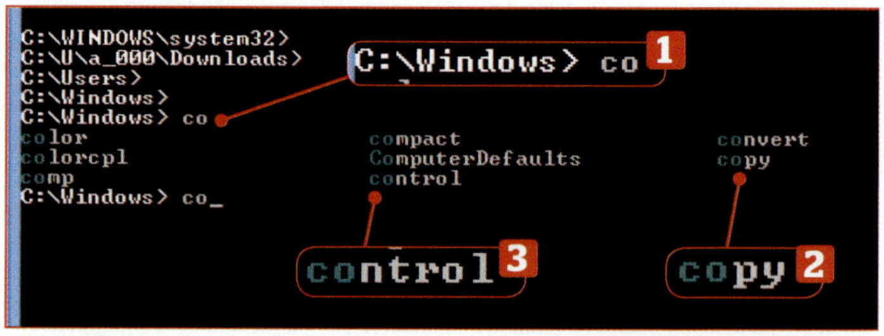

2 Start typing a letter or two, then press Tab. 1 The screen shows all the options for those letters, including commands such as 'copy' 2 or executable files such as 'control' 3 (which, because we're in the Windows directory, would launch the Control Panel).

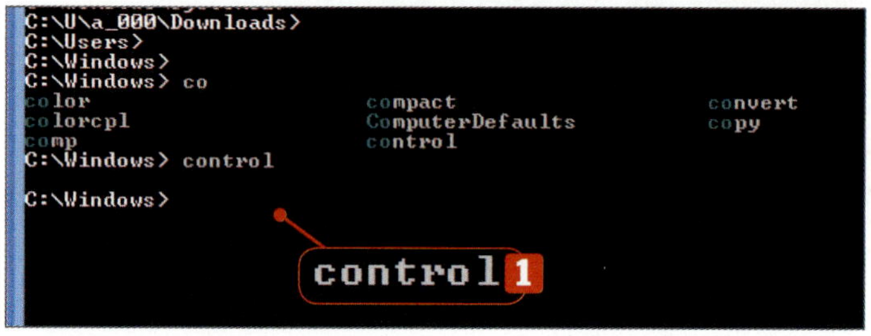

3 The letters appear again on the line below, so you don't need to retype them. If only one option exists for the folder you're in, it will be typed in full when you press Tab, 1 so you can just press Enter to execute it.

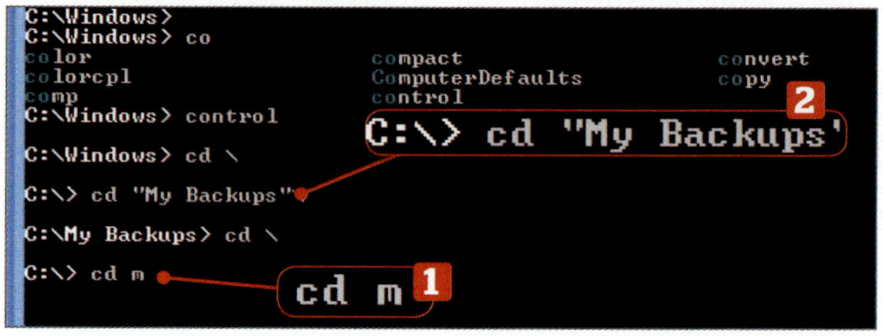

4 You can use the same trick to quickly move to folders, even those with tricky spaces in their names. This folder only has one folder beginning with 'm' called 'My backup'. Here we've typed `cd m` 1 and pressed Tab; PyCmd fills in the rest automatically. 2

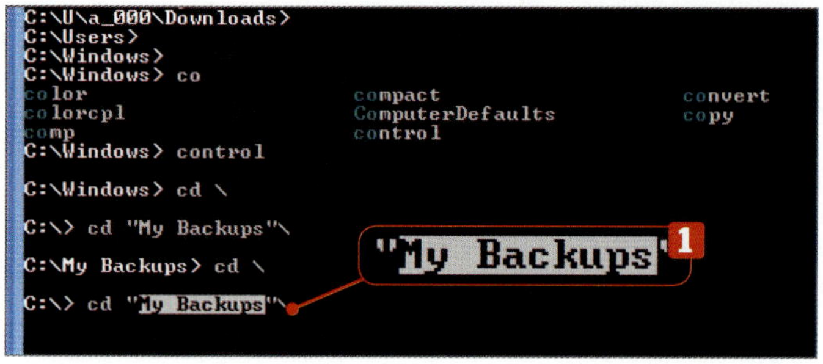

5 Unlike the Windows Command Prompt, you can use Ctrl+X, Ctrl+C and Ctrl+V to cut, copy and paste. To highlight something you've typed, use the cursor keys to move through the letters and hold down Shift at the same time to highlight them. 1

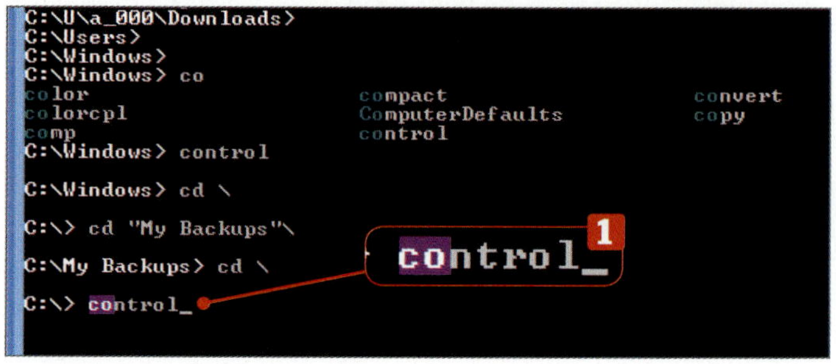

6 Press the up arrow to show previously used commands. To search history, type a letter or two and press the up arrow. It will scroll through commands that contain those letters, highlighting them in purple. 1 Press up or down to rotate through the options.

Chapter 2

Security and backup

Keeping your PC protected is vital. Our advice will show you how to get the most from security and backup software

Viruses are more prevalent than ever and can wreck a perfectly good PC with the click of a mouse button. If you haven't got an up-to-date, reliable backup of your PC's personal data, you really could lose everything if a virus forces you to wipe everything clean or a hard disk fails. In this chapter, we'll show you how to set up free anti-virus software and adware cleaners, how to avoid being plagued by false alarms from your chosen security software, how to keep your personal data safe, and how to make sure everything is backed up properly with apps that won't cost you a penny.

CONTENT

Protect your PC with 360 Internet Security

Entrusting your PC's safety to a program (and a company) you've never heard of sounds risky, but Qihu 360's 360 Internet Security has performed very well in recent anti-virus tests from a variety of specialists, including our own Dennis Technology Labs (www.dennistechnologylabs.com). 360 Internet Security comes with three anti-virus engines – 360 Cloud Engine, QVM II Engine and Bitdefender – and offers real-time and on-demand protection, which makes it a viable alternative to the likes AVG and Avast.

The software can also protect you from other threats including potentially malicious downloads, phishing websites, keyloggers and infected USB drives. There's even a cleaner tool that helps free up space and safeguard your privacy.

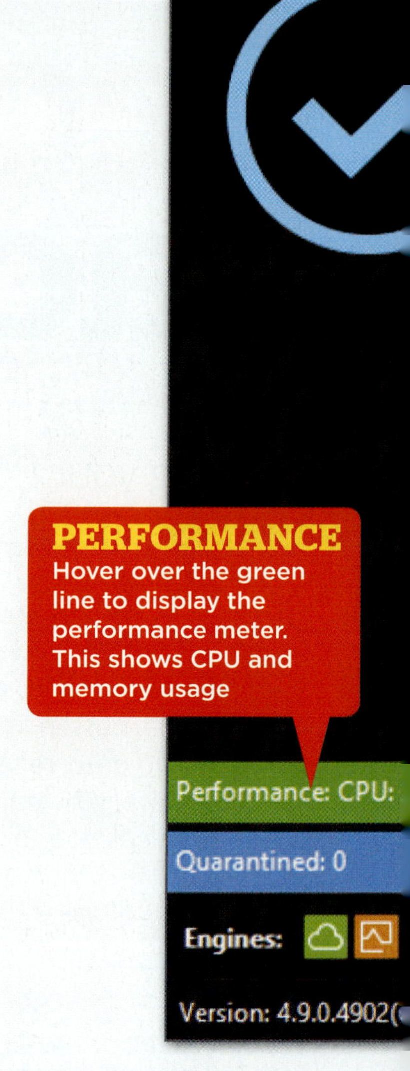

PERFORMANCE
Hover over the green line to display the performance meter. This shows CPU and memory usage

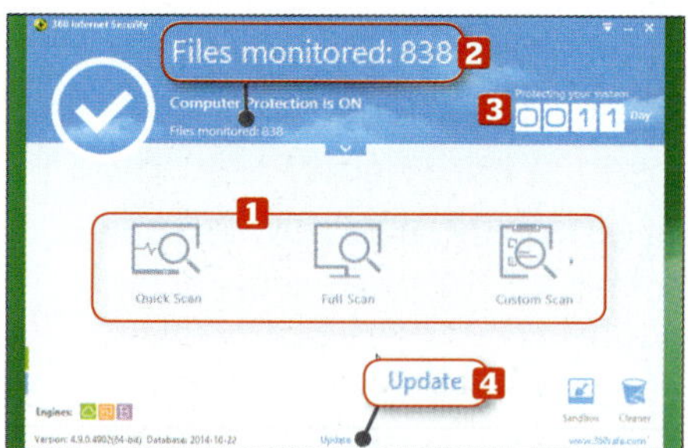

1 360 Internet Security's interface is clean and intuitive with large buttons that let you run Quick, Full and Custom scans. **1** It also shows you the number of files it is monitoring **2** and how long it's been protecting you for. **3** To manually update the software, click the link **4** at the bottom of the page.

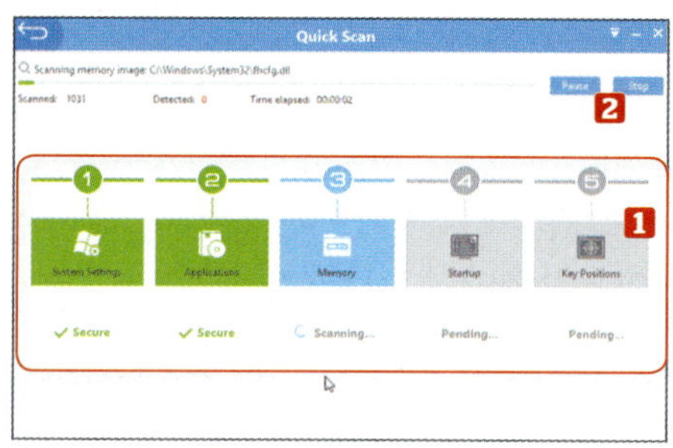

2 Start by running a quick scan to check your PC's settings, applications, memory, start-up and key positions (places most likely to harbour viruses). **1** Hover your mouse over any of the entries to find out more about what the program is scanning for. You can pause or stop **2** the scan at any time.

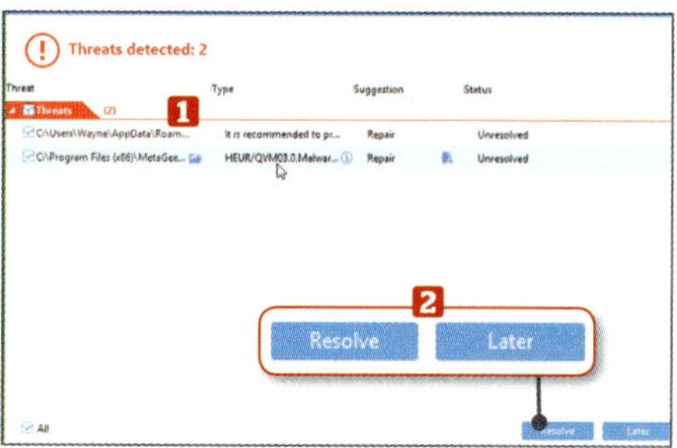

3 When the scan has completed, you're presented with results **1** displaying the location, type, suggested action and status of any threats found. Hover over an item to show buttons that let you open its containing folder, view details and add it to a whitelist. You can resolve the problems or leave them until later. **2**

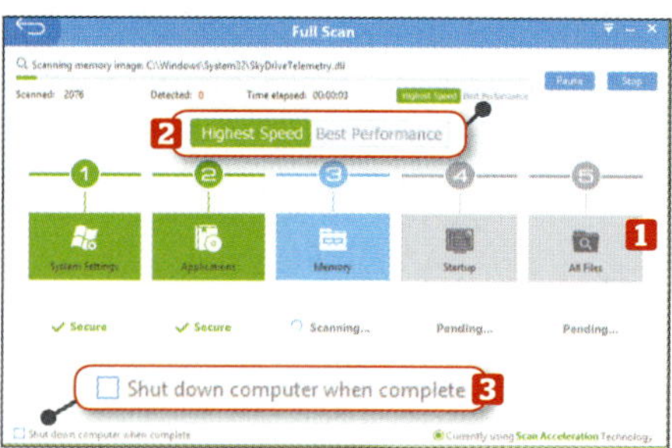

4 A full scan is similar to a quick one, but instead of scanning key positions it will check all files. **1** Because it's more thorough, scans take a lot longer to complete but you can choose between highest speed and best performance. **2** You can also set the computer to shut down once the scan has completed. **3**

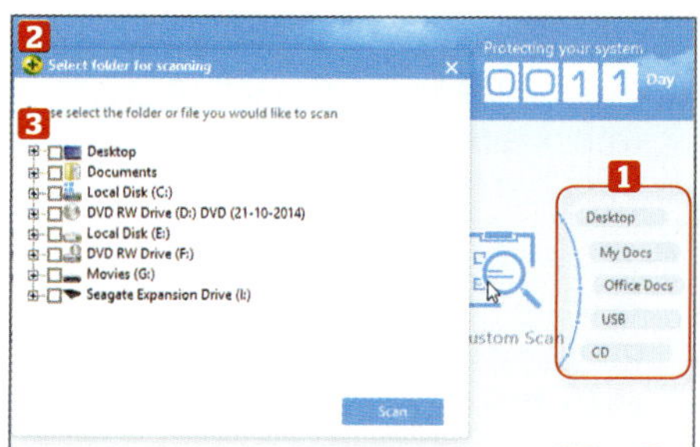

5 A custom scan lets you target specific areas. Hover your mouse over the button and choose an option from the selection, which includes the Desktop, My Docs, USB and CD drives. **1** Click the button to choose a file or folder to scan. **2** Navigate through the drives and folders by clicking the plus signs. **3**

MENU
Click the Menu button to access the program settings, pick a different theme and view the log file

QUARANTINE
Access quarantined files by clicking the blue line, then clicking the View link

ENGINES
Click any of the buttons to view details about the three anti-virus protection engines. QVM II Engine and BitDefender can be disabled here, if you wish

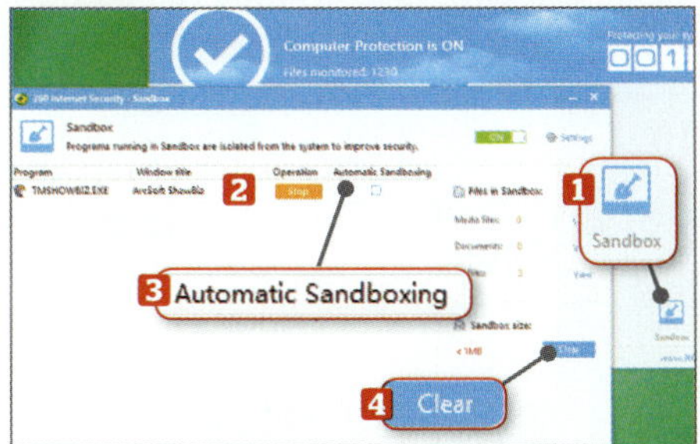

6 The Sandbox **1** isolates potentially dangerous programs (such as those downloaded from dubious sites) so they can't interfere with the rest of your PC. Drag an application onto the Sandbox interface to run it. **2** You can choose to automatically sandbox a file; **3** and clear the sandbox, **4** erasing all files in it.

7 The Cleaner tool **1** removes all traces of your browsing, Windows and Office history. **2** Click a down arrow **3** to choose the areas to target, then click the green 'Start scan' button **4** to begin a sweep. When it's finished, click the 'Clean up' button to remove all the junk and free up space.

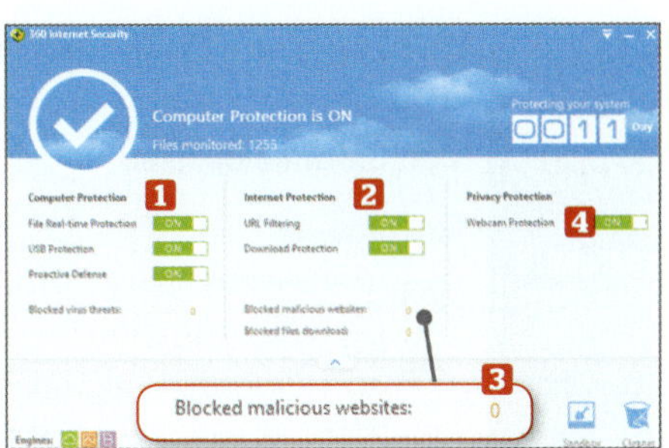

8 To configure the software, click the arrow under the top banner. You can choose the type of protection for your computer **1** and internet. **2** Click the number by a blocked threat **3** for more info in the program log. You can toggle Webcam Protection on or off. **4** This feature prevents unauthorised access.

Explore Avast Free 2015's new features

Avast Free Antivirus was an award winner in Web User magazine's 2015 antivirus test (bit.ly/webuser363), outperforming all the other free programs that were put through their paces. The 2015 version of the software received a major overhaul and introduced a range of new tools. In this Workshop, we show you how to make the most of its best new features.

Avast Free Antivirus 2015: www.avast.com | 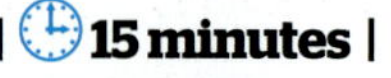 15 minutes |  XP, Vista, 7, 8.1+

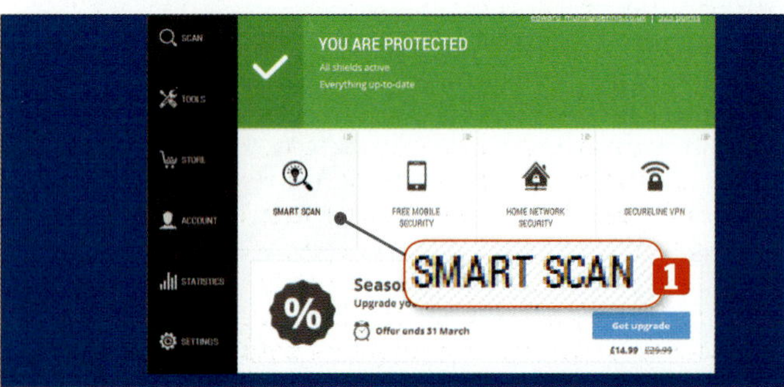

1 Download, install and run Avast Free Antivirus 2015. Smart Scan is a new feature that integrates all Avast's on-demand scans. Click its button **1** to runs Virus & Malware, Browser Cleanup, Home Network Security and GrimeFighter scans.

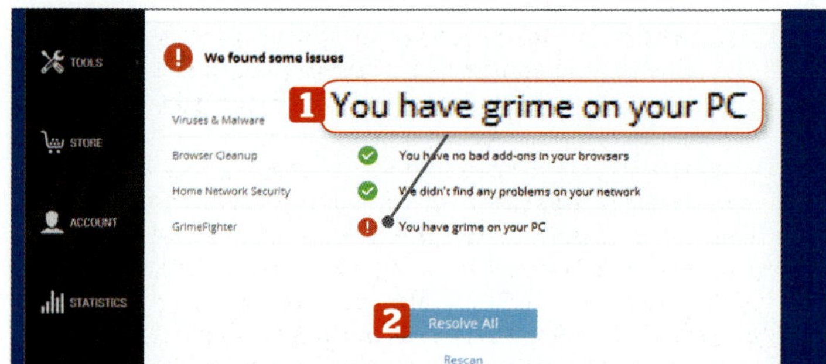

2 If Avast finds anything suspect, a screen appears after the scans are completed showing the location of the problem. **1** Click the blue Resolve All button **2** to have the program take you through the necessary steps to fix the the problems.

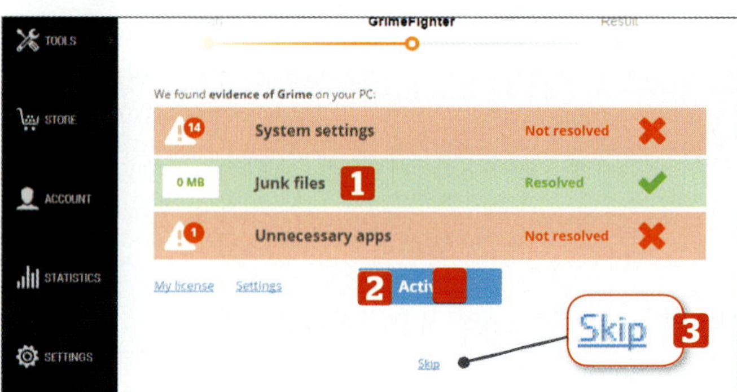

3 By default, GrimeFighter clears your junk files, **1** but you'll need to buy a licence for the tool (for £29.99) if you want it to delete unnecessary apps and optimise your System settings. To do this, click the blue Activate button; **2** otherwise, select Skip. **3**

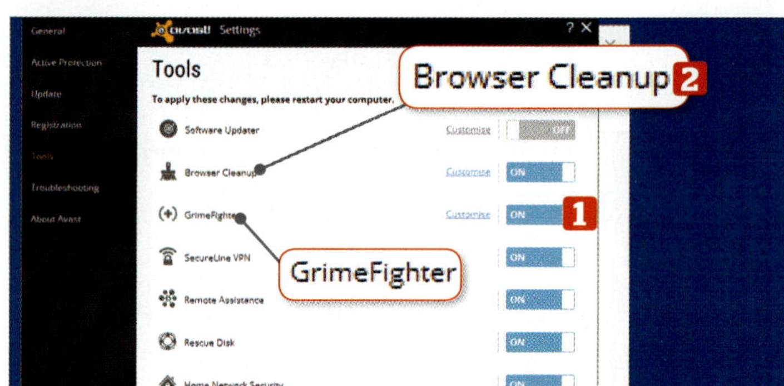

4 A screen appears showing that Smart Scan has finished. To exclude GrimeFighter from future scans, click Settings, Tools and turn GrimeFighter's switch to off. **1** From this screen, you can also disable Browser Cleanup, **2** which looks for bad browser add-ons.

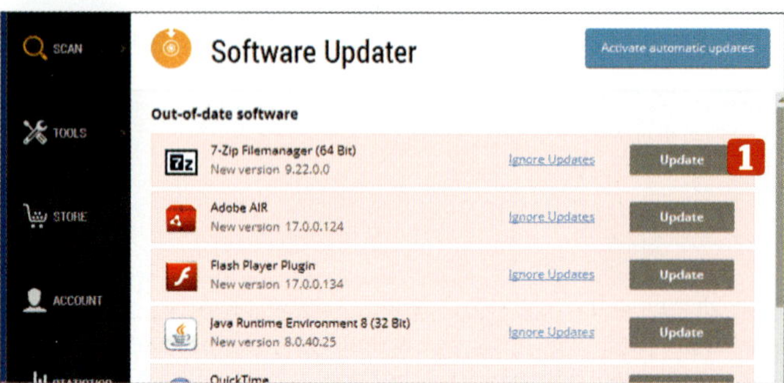

5 To enable Avast's tool for updating outdated software on your PC, turn on Software Updater from this menu. To run it, select Scan, then 'Scan for outdated software'. A list of out-of-date software is displayed; just click the Update button **1** for any you want to update.

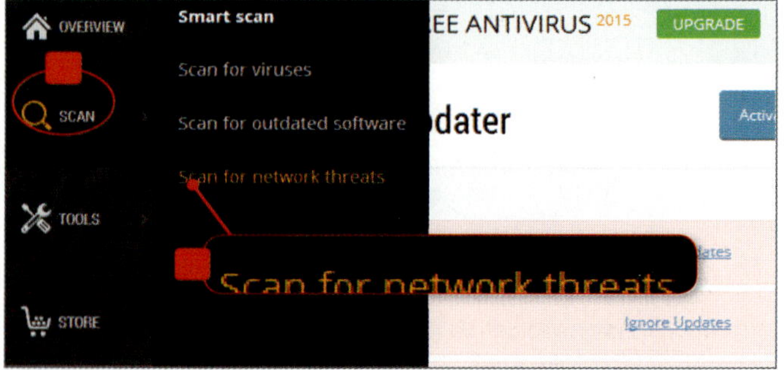

6 New to Avast Free Antivirus 2015, the Home Security Network scan checks for security problems on your home network that are not necessarily isolated to your device. To run only this type of scan, select Scan **1** and choose 'Scan for network threats'. **2**

AdwCleaner 4.200

www.snipca.com/16022 What you need: Windows XP, Vista, 7 or 8/8.1

Our favourite tool for getting rid of unwanted toolbars, browser hijackers and other adware is now even better. The new version of AdwCleaner doesn't add loads of fancy functions; instead it's been updated to work faster and remove more junk.

We wouldn't normally recommend a program that's only had performance updates. But we're making an exception for AdwCleaner because it's one of the most useful tools on our PC and we wanted to show you, click by click, how to use it.

AdwCleaner scans your PC's files, processes and browsers for evidence of adware and malware, including toolbars and other PUPs (potentially unwanted programs). It then lists the malicious files and lets you delete them all with one click.

This new version is faster than its predecessor, especially in the scanning stage, and uses more powerful technology to kill infected processes. It can now detect infected preferences in Chrome, making it more effective against browser hijackers such as the horrendous Binkiland (www.snipca.com/16025).

AdwCleaner is a portable tool, so you don't have to install it, and you can copy its program file ('adwcleaner_4.200.exe') to a USB stick for running on any PC. To run it, click the EXE file, click Yes, and then click 'I agree' to open the program window.

The downside of portable software is that it isn't updated automatically, so you'll have to check for new versions and install them manually. Only use the link above to download AdwCleaner; don't click any pop-ups claiming to contain an update. Scammers have used this trick to sneak a fake version of AdwCleaner on to PCs, which is more likely to leave malware, not remove it.

1 Click the Scan button to update AdwCleaner's database (this takes about two seconds, compared with up to half a minute in the previous version) and begin scanning your PC.

2 When the scan is finished, click the tabs, such as Registry and Internet Explorer, to see the infected files AdwCleaner found there. Untick anything you're sure is a false positive.

3 To see all the infected files in one list, click Tools, then 'Quarantine manager'. Also, click Logfile to open the list in Notepad and save it for your records.

4 Click Cleaning to remove all the files discovered by AdwCleaner, then restart your PC to complete the process. Run AdwCleaner again to make sure everything's been removed.

Stop your anti-virus blocking safe software

Over-vigilant security software sometimes flags harmless files as malware. Here we explain what you can do to identify, prevent and report these so-called false positives

Scan the suspicious file using VirusTotal

No security software is 100-per-cent foolproof, so a second opinion is always useful, particularly if you're not sure whether a download is genuinely malicious or not. VirusTotal (www.virustotal.com) doesn't just give you a second opinion, it gives you more than 50, by running your file through multiple anti-virus engines, including big names such as Symantec, Bitdefender, Sophos, McAfee and Kaspersky. Best of all, this simple but powerful online tool is completely free and you don't need to register with VirusTotal to use it.

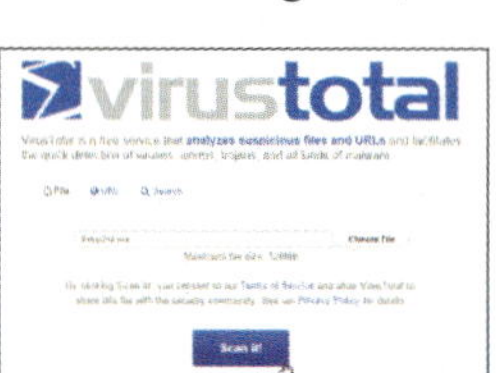

Click the Choose File button to upload a suspicious file from your PC, then click 'Scan it' to see the results. Currently, the only limitation on a file is its size, which needs to be smaller than 128MB.

If you use Firefox, you can install VirusTotal's add-on VTzilla (bit.ly/vtzilla365) to analyse downloads from your browser before they get anywhere near your PC. Just right-click a download link and choose 'Scan with VirusTotal' or click the toolbar button to scan the current page for malware.

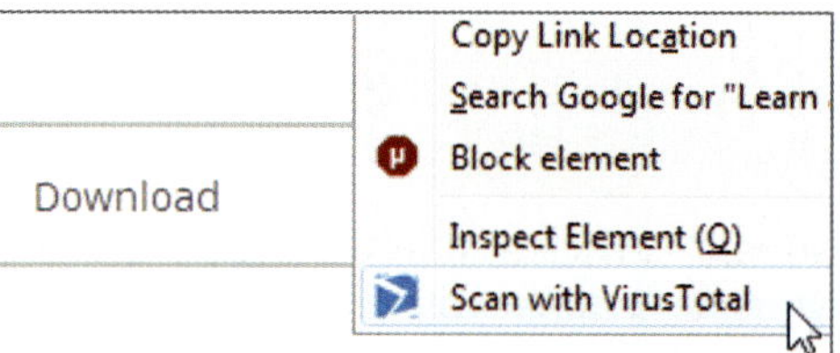

Chrome users can install VTchromizer (bit.ly/vtchromizer365), which works in the same way.

Check a program using Should I Remove It

If a program you've already installed is causing problems with your security software – for example, because your firewall is blocking its access to the internet – you can check it for malware using Should I Remove It (www.shouldiremoveit.com). This handy free tool scans all your installed programs and ranks them in order of how dangerous they are. Any programs flagged red represent a potential security risk and should be removed immediately.

Click a program to see information about it, including its install size. The 'What is it?' button takes you to the Should I Remove It website where you'll find a full description of the program and the number of other users who have removed it. The Uninstall button lets you remove the program from within Should I Remove It, rather than via the Windows Control Panel, which can often be very slow.

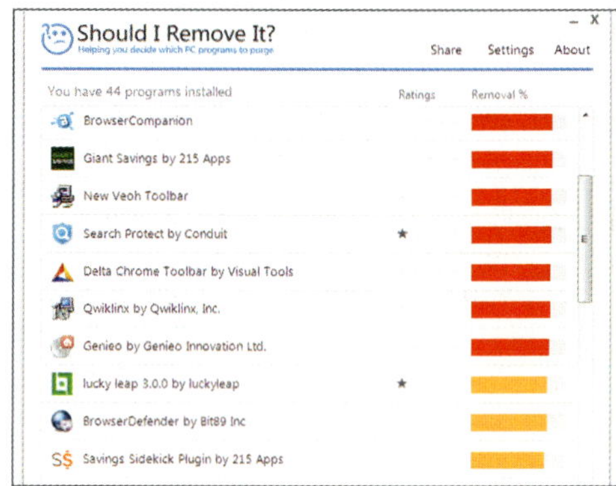

Search online threat databases

Many of the bigger security companies publish comprehensive databases of known malware that let you check your suspicious program against an up-to-date list of genuine threats. Of these, Symantec's Security Response (www.symantec.com/security_response) is one of the biggest and easiest to

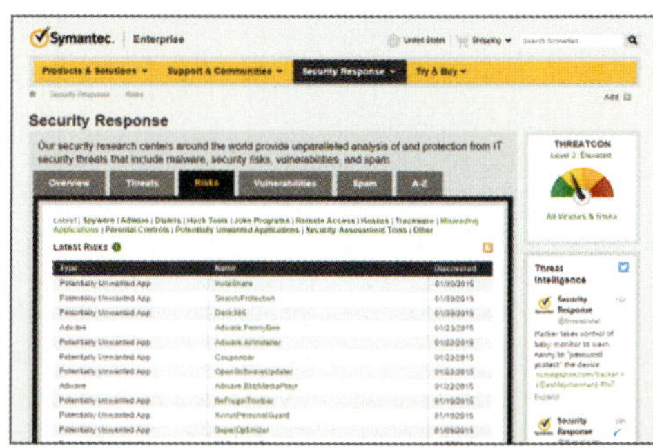

browse. The page splits findings into Threats, Risks and Vulnerabilities – the Risks tab is where you'll find potentially unwanted programs (PUPs), adware and misleading applications, while Threats covers the latest Trojans, ransomware and other nasties. Each category lists entries by date, with the most recently identified at the top, but you can also browse risks and threats by clicking the A-Z tab or by typing the name of your suspicious file into the search box.

Run the suspicious download in a sandbox

A great way to test a program you're not sure about is to run it in a sandbox, which is a ring-fenced section of your hard drive where you can safely install and run applications in isolation without affecting the rest of your PC. Sandboxie (www.sandboxie.com) has been around for ages but remains the best tool of this type. It's still free, too, though you'll have to put up with a nagging message after 30 days unless you pay £14 for a licence.

Once you've installed Sandboxie, when you want to run a program you've downloaded, right-click the installation

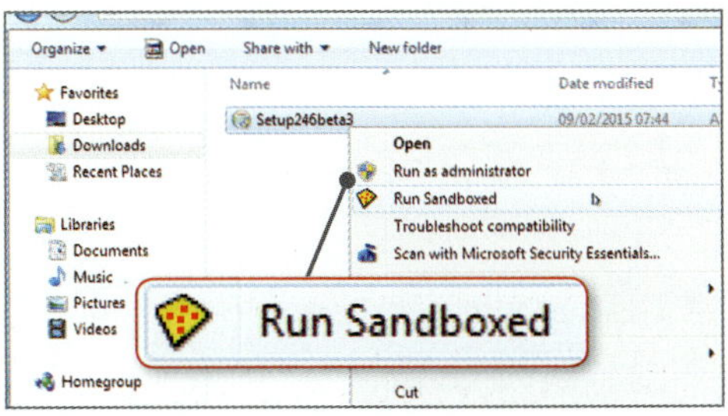

file, select Run Sandboxed and choose DefaultBox. If you decide you no longer want the program – or anything else – in your sandbox, right-click the Sandboxie icon in the notification area and select DefaultBox, then Delete Contents to wipe the slate clean.

Tweak your security settings

If your anti-virus software has quarantined a program you've downloaded, rather than merely provided a warning, it's usually possible to unblock it. However, we wouldn't recommend doing so because if there's even a shred of doubt, you should leave the 'infected' file where it is and follow your security software provider's official procedure for querying a potential false positive (see next tip). That way, you'll know that the file has been verified by experts before you run it.

If, on the other hand, a program has installed without being flagged as unsafe by your anti-virus program but is now being blocked by your firewall, it may be safe to unblock it. First, get a second opinion on the software's safety (see 'Should I Remove It' tip). The procedure for unblocking it will depend on the firewall you're using. With Windows Firewall, for example, you need to open the Control Panel, click 'System and Security', then click 'Allow a program through Windows Firewall'. On the next screen, click 'Change settings' and put a tick by the program you want to unblock. If the program isn't listed, click 'Allow another program', then highlight the application and click Add.

Report the false positive to the security company

Security companies realise that falsely identifying malware is a pain for users and an even bigger pain for the legitimate software developers, so it's in everyone's interests to make sure wrongly blocked programs are identified and corrected as soon as possible. The best way to do this is to let your security software provider know about any programs you think have been incorrectly blocked. Some anti-virus programs allow you to do this from within the program itself – look for a 'false positive' or 'send sample' option when a program is blocked or quarantined.

Each security software company has its own reporting process. In Avira's Free Antivirus, for example, you open the management console, click Quarantine on the left, then highlight the suspicious program in the list and click the envelope icon in the top toolbar. Fill in the form and click OK to send the file to the company for analysis.

Alternatively, you can simply email the company or see if there's a form to report false positives on its website. Symantec has a form at bit.ly/symantec365, for example, while for Kaspersky, you should visit newvirus.kaspersky.com, select False Alarm and upload the file.

WHY DO FALSE POSITIVES OCCUR?

Most security software works by checking files and programs against a regularly updated list of known malware. The best programs also look for 'virus-like' behaviour, to protect you against malware that has not yet been officially identified. However, this can occasionally result in the security program falsely identifying a legitimate application as malware, based on behaviour that the anti-virus application deems as suspicious. A pattern of code may, for example, match the same pattern contained in a known virus signature. But however annoying or worrying false positives might be, it's worth remembering that it's better to be safe than sorry and a legitimate program blocked is preferable to malware being let through.

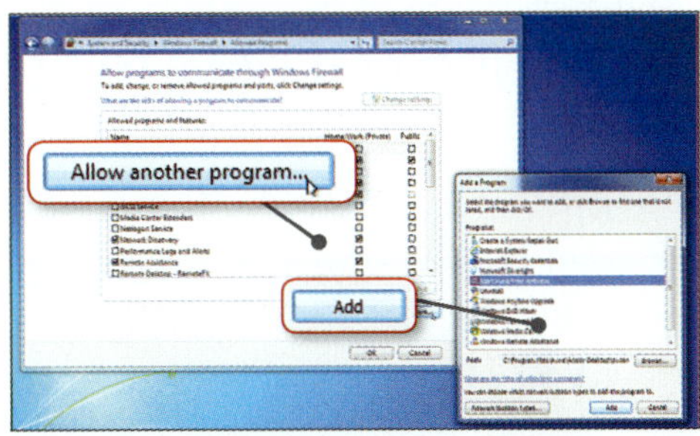

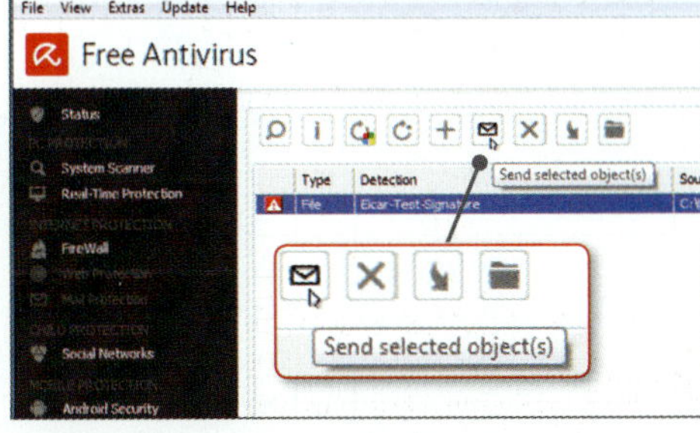

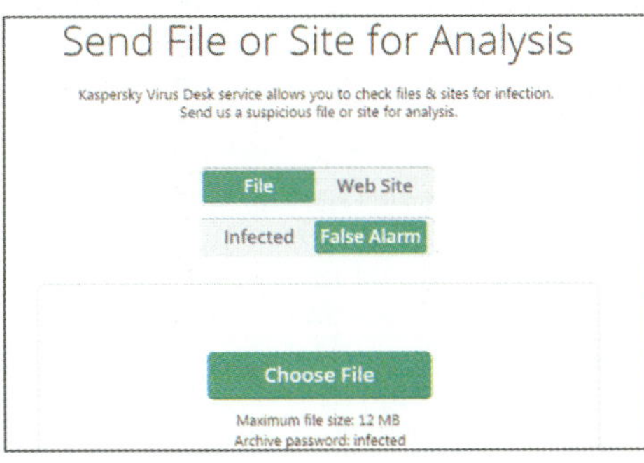

Remove your personal data from files

When you share files online, you could be giving away more information about yourself than you realise. Find out how to strip sensitive data from files before sharing them

The next time you share a photo on Facebook or send a Word document as an attachment, stop for a second and consider the hidden information these files may contain: who you are, who you work for, where you were when you took a particular photo, and all sorts of other details.

Individually, these small pieces of data may not amount to much, but combined with other information, it could allow someone to build a picture that compromises your privacy. In this feature, we explain some free and easy ways to strip this data from the files you share, to stop your private information falling into the wrong hands.

Strip EXIF data from your photos

Every time you take a photo, your camera stores information about it in the Exchangeable Image File Format (EXIF) including when and where the photo was taken, and details of your camera's settings. You can stop your camera or mobile device logging location information by turning off geo-tagging (this is usually in your camera settings on an Android phone or tablet, and under Privacy, Location Services, Camera on iOS), but to keep the rest of your data private, you'll either have to remove it before you share the photo or tweak your PC so the data isn't recorded.

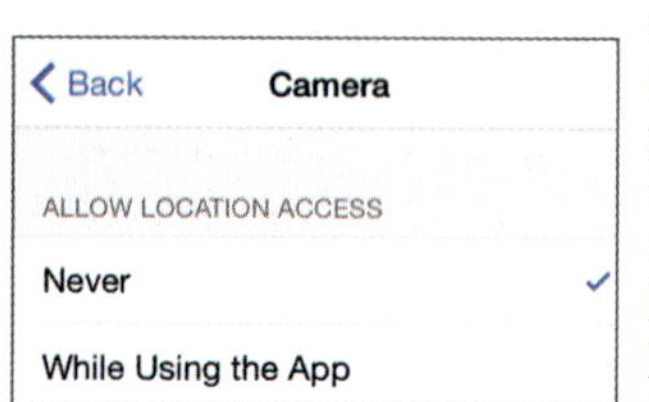

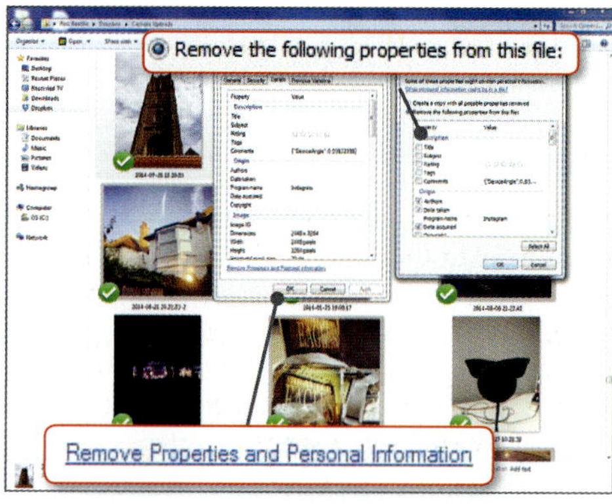

To do this in Windows, right-click a photo and choose Properties from the menu. When the dialogue box opens, click the Details tab. At the bottom, click the 'Remove Properties and Personal Information' link and, when the next dialogue box opens, make sure 'Remove the following properties from this file' is selected and put a tick next to any EXIF data you want to remove. Then click OK.

Alternatively, you can choose 'Create a copy with all possible Properties removed' and click OK. Windows will create a new copy of the image with no EXIF information so you can share the 'clean' copy and keep the original separate. Usefully, if you select more than one photo, Windows will apply your changes to all of them.

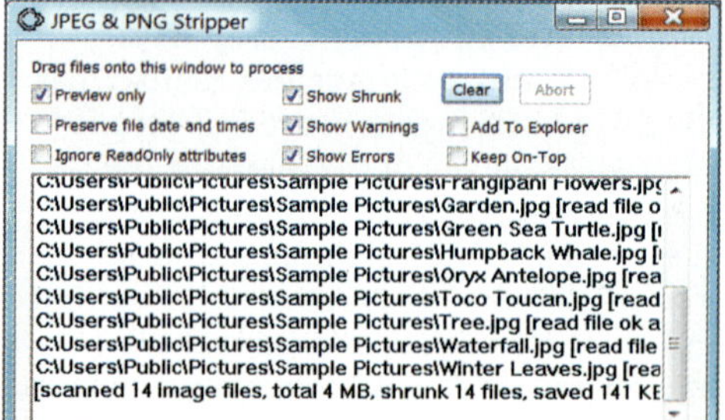

If you don't want the hassle of deleting data manually, try the handy free program JPEG and PNG Stripper (bit.ly/jpeg362). This targets entire folders of images and, as the name suggests, strips all EXIF information from any JPEG and PNG files it finds.

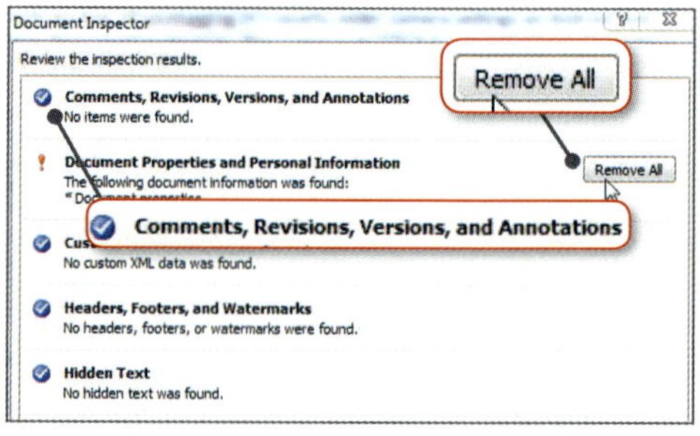

Remove personal info from Office files

Private data in Office documents comes in two varieties: metadata (details such as author name, subject and title) and your own additions that you might not want other people to see, such as comments and revisions that you later toned down or rough preliminary notes you knocked up to get started with a PowerPoint presentation.

If you're using Office 2007, open the file you want to check, click the Office button, choose Prepare from the menu and click Inspect Document. Tick the items you want to check (for example, Comments,

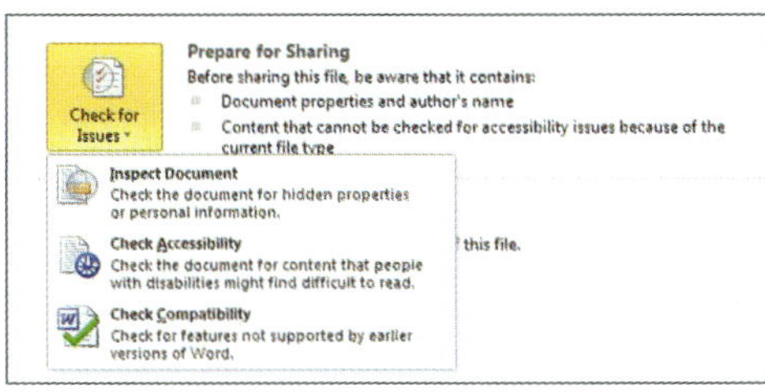

Revisions, Versions and Annotations), then click the Inspect button. This will flag any relevant information, which you can delete by clicking Remove All next to an item.

In later versions of Office, open the File menu and click 'Check for Issues' in the panel next to 'Prepare for Sharing'. From there, choose Inspect Document, then follow the same process as before.

If you're using a version of Office from before 2007, it's worth checking out a free program called Document Metadata Cleaner (bit.ly/metadata362). This scans Word, Excel and PowerPoint files and lets you remove any hidden metadata in one fell swoop. It works with all versions of Windows and is very easy to use.

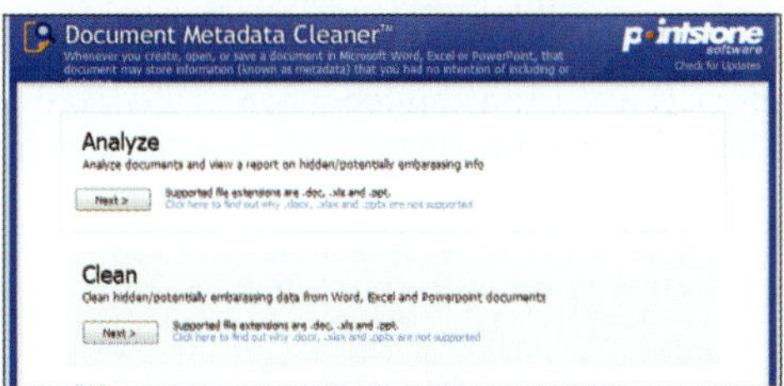

Delete metadata from PDF files

Like Office documents, PDFs sometimes contain information that you might not want people to see without your permission. If you own one of Adobe's paid-for products, it's easy to get rid of metadata, but if you don't, then it's more problematic.

The free version of Adobe Reader will torment you by displaying metadata, but not letting you edit it. Instead, you'll need to use a tool such as BeCyPDFMetaEdit. Download and install it from bit.ly/becy362, accepting all the defaults. Launch the program, then right-click the PDF you want to edit and you'll see a new option – 'Edit metadata' – in the right-click menu. Select this to open the program with the PDF already loaded. Make sure the Metadata tab is selected and from there you can individually remove fields – such as the author, date created and date modified – or just click the Clear All Fields button to get rid of the lot. Click Save and you're done.

Remove information from MP3 files

Although audio files contain less sensitive data than images, you might still want to remove the star ratings from an album, details of when it was created or its audio bitrate, all of which are likely to be included with the file. And if you've downloaded the song illegally, there

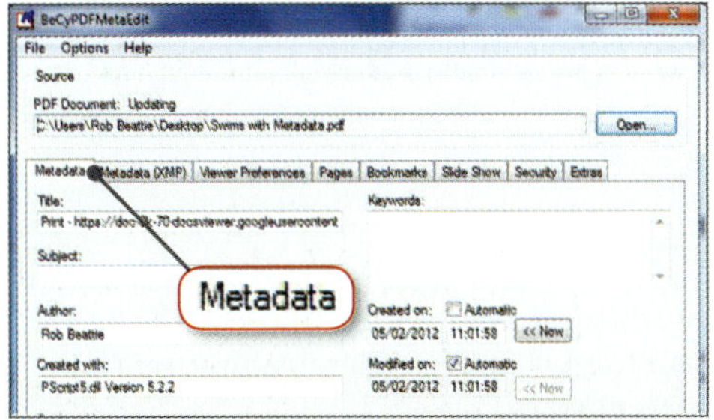

might be evidence of your shameful behaviour embedded in the file. You can remove this information from MP3s by using exactly the same technique applied to EXIF data in our first tip: right-click the file, choose Properties, select Details and follow the same steps.

For more control, the free audio editor Audacity (audacity.sourceforge.net) has a

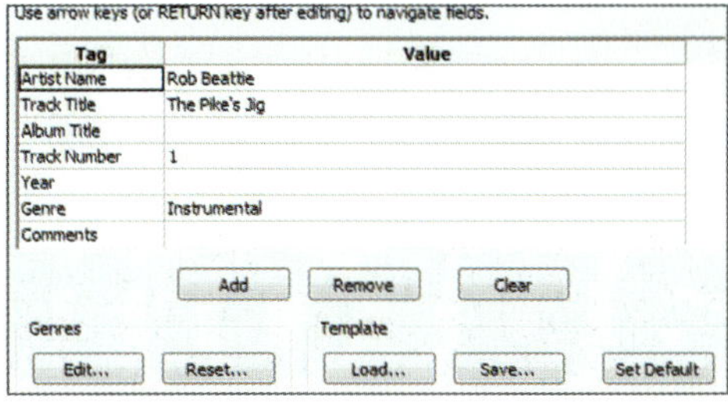

good ID3 tag editor under Files, Open Metadata Editor. Or if carrying this out one file at a time seems too tedious, try the excellent all-in-one ID3 tag editor MP3tag (www.mp3tag.de/en), which can remove tags from multiple files and folders simultaneously. Handy if an entire album has the wrong listings.

Be careful how you use this program because you'll have to painstakingly re-enter the deleted data if you want it back again.

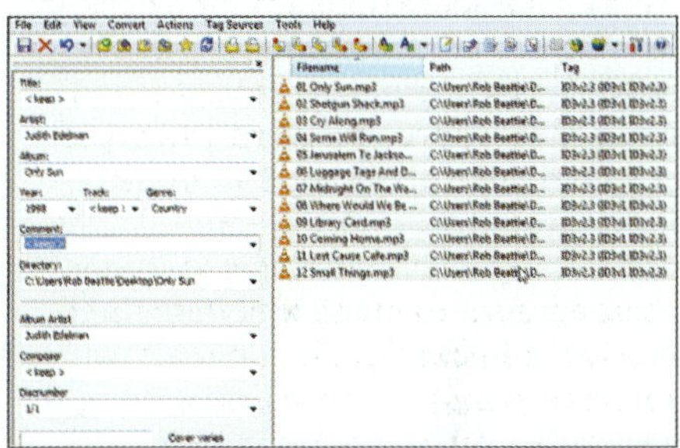

WHAT'S THE PROBLEM WITH METADATA?

It's a reasonable question and one that most people will answer with an "I've-got-nothing-to-hide" shrug. Even if that's true, information about what you do and where you go in both the real and virtual world is valuable, and even the tiniest snippet of information (your name on a document, your location on a photo) can be used to piece together a picture of who you are and what you're up to. That's why services such as Facebook and Google Mail are free, and it's why they're able to target you with ads based on things you like and topics you talk about.

Mobile devices and their built-in location services take this to a more intimate extreme. While they are fantastically useful for finding the nearest pub or fast-food joint, they also allow companies to track where you go, as well as providing clues about what you like to eat and drink. Snap a photo and it'll be easy to discover where the picture was taken and what shutter speed you used, together with the make and model of the camera.

In a few years time, as you stroll into town wearing your Google glasses, advertisers will be able to tell when you're approaching a place where you like to eat, at which point they can display personalised ads - perhaps with money-off incentives - as you walk past the door.

Delete old files automatically

Regularly removing unwanted files from your PC and phone helps to save space and protect your privacy. Our guide explains how to make items self-destruct automatically

Delete files from a specific folder

A popular Christmas gift idea is to create calendars and photobooks using images from a personal collection. This usually involves selecting pictures and copying them to a new folder to work with, but when the calendar or book is complete, that folder often remains undeleted, leaving unnecessary, space-hogging duplicate images on your hard drive.

One way to stop this happening, and to prevent other old items from taking up room, is to install Cyber-D Autodelete (bit.ly/cyber361). This useful free program keeps watch on any folders you add to its main monitoring window and then removes them at a specific point in time. Files can be moved to the Recycle Bin, deleted completely or sent to a different folder, such as one on a back-up drive. The program will even remove empty sub-folders when it's finished.

You should practise this a few times using the software's Recycle or 'Move to folder' options before trusting it to delete anything permanently, and check the logs to make sure you're removing the correct files.

Delete your downloads after 60 days

Once you've installed a program (and uninstalled it, if you didn't like it), there's no point in hanging onto the installation file, so it's a good idea to clear items from your Downloads folder after a set time – say, 60 days. You can use an old-school batch-command trick that requires a simple piece of programming.

First, open Notepad in Windows from the Programs, Accessories menu and type

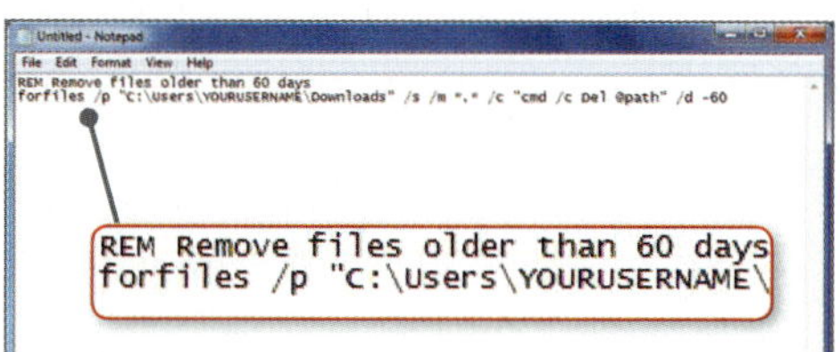

the following, taking care to keep the same formatting:

REM Remove files older than 60 days
forfiles /p "C:\Users\YOURUSERNAME\Downloads" /s /m *.* /c "cmd /c Del @path" /d -60

Make sure you change the folder path to one that matches your own Downloads folder (if you're not using the default one set by your browser) and replace YOURUSERNAME with your own username. The example we've given finds files more than 60 days old and moves them to the Recycle Bin – that's what the '60' at the end of the line is for – but you can change the number to 30, 90, 72 or whatever works best for you. Save the file as a text document but make sure you add '.bat' on the end to mark it as a batch file. When opened, this runs the program.

Next, open the Start menu, type Task Scheduler and press Enter. In the Actions list on the right, select Create Basic Task, give the deletion task a name and a description, then choose when you'd like it to run. In the Action section, select 'Start a program', then navigate to where you stored the batch file you created and select it. Review your task, then click Finish.

Delete old emails you no longer need

Some emails are important enough to keep forever but most will have served their purpose after a matter of days. You can use your webmail service's built-in tools to keep things neat and tidy. In Outlook.com, for example, open an email and click the Sweep button at the top. From here, you can set Outlook .com to delete all emails more than 10 days old from that sender; keep the latest

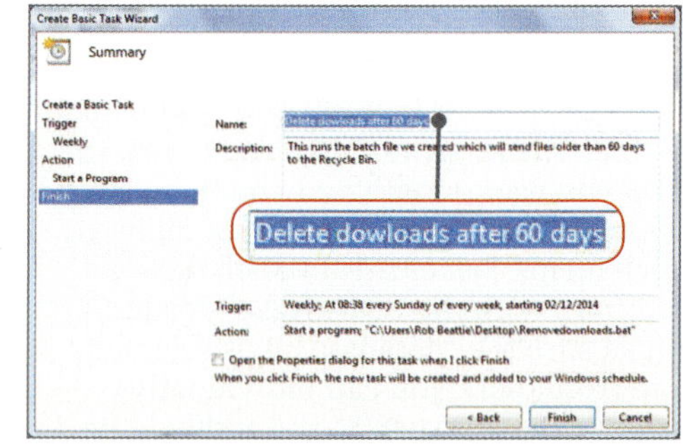

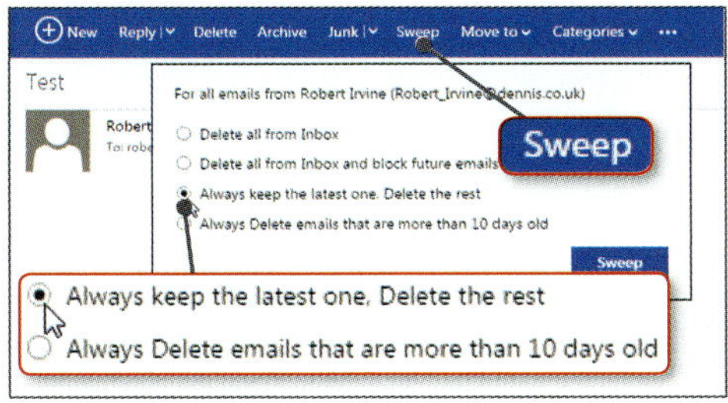

one and delete the rest (which is useful for newsletters); or delete all emails from that person or company.

There's no obvious way to do this in Gmail but you can clear out an over-stuffed inbox by searching for emails received before a specific date, then selecting them from the list of results and then archiving them yourself. For example, if you want to find emails received before July 2014, type: in:inbox before:2014/07/01 into the search box above your inbox, then click the 'select all' option in the top-right corner and choose Delete. Alternatively, you can choose to only delete read, unread, starred or unstarred messages.

Clear data from your browser

Internet Explorer and Firefox can both be set to clear your browsing history (and other private data) every time you close them. In IE, click the cog icon in the top-right corner and choose Internet Options. Make sure the General tab is selected and find the 'Browsing history' section. You can either put a tick next to 'Delete browsing history on exit' or click the Settings button next to it, click the History tab and choose the number of days to keep pages in the history.

In Firefox, open the Tools menu, choose Options and click the Privacy tab. In the History section, open the drop-down menu next to 'Firefox will', choose 'Use

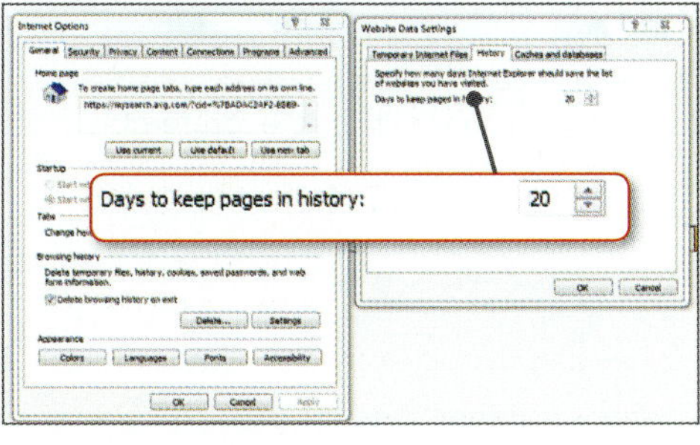

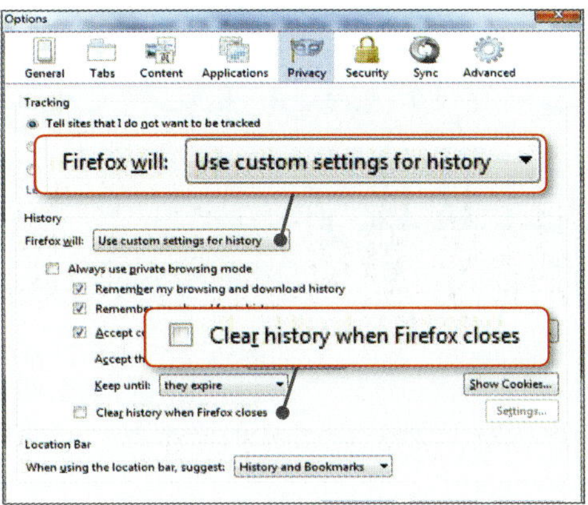

custom settings for history 'and select 'Clear history when Firefox closes'. To delete only your most recent browsing history and cookies, click the new Forget option on the toolbar.

We couldn't find an easy way of doing the same thing with Chrome – which is surprising considering that it's regarded as the most 'cutting-edge' browser – but you can always clear the history manually or use an add-on such as Click&Clean (www.hotcleaner.com) to do the job.

Delete duplicate files in a jiffy

It's easy to make a temporary copy of a file or folder and then forget to remove it later. To save the extra space, you can install Duplicate Cleaner Free (www.digitalvolcano.co.uk), run the program in Regular Mode and tell it to find duplicates with the same content and

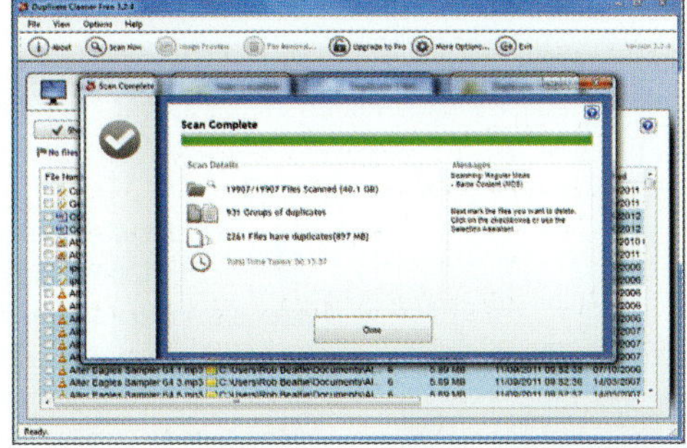

the same filename (you can get more creative later). Click the Scan Location tab and choose which drive or folders to scan, then click Scan Now and await the results. You can run Duplicate Cleaner by adding it to Windows Task Scheduler – see 'Delete your downloads after 60 days' on the facing page for how to set up a routine. And have a look at Web User's Top Tips (bit.ly/webuser359) for more about deleting duplicate files.

Remove empty folders (but carefully)

If you regularly come across empty folders on your PC, you can quickly get rid of the lot by using the free tool Fast Empty Folder Finder from bit.ly/empty361. This finds empty folders on your hard drive, shows you a preview of their contents (so you can be sure they really are empty) and gives you the option to delete them permanently (this is misspelt in the software as "perminately"!). Take care not to delete apparently empty system folders or you could cause serious problems – if you're unsure, leave the folder alone.

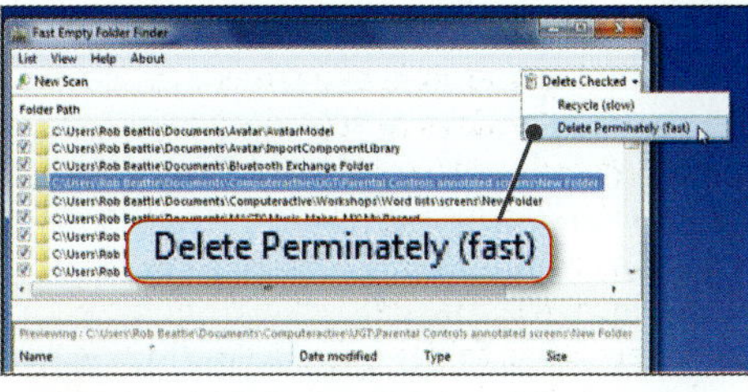

Delete old text messages automatically

Most text messages you receive will never be read again, so why not set your phone to delete them after a set time? On an iPhone, tap Settings, Messages, scroll down to Message History and tap Keep Messages. The default is Forever, but you can choose to keep messages for one year or 30 days.

If you've got an Android phone, you can set it to delete messages when you reach a certain number, rather than after a period of time. Open the Messaging app on your device, tap the menu icon and choose Settings. In the Storage section, make sure 'Delete old messages' is ticked, then tap 'Text message limit' and specify a number.

Create a fake virus to test your PC's security

You depend on your PC's antivirus to keep you safe, but how can you be sure that it's working properly? EICARgen is a fake virus that you can run to assess how powerful your antivirus is. It's an easy, free and safe way to check your antivirus is working properly. Here's how to do this in a few simple steps.

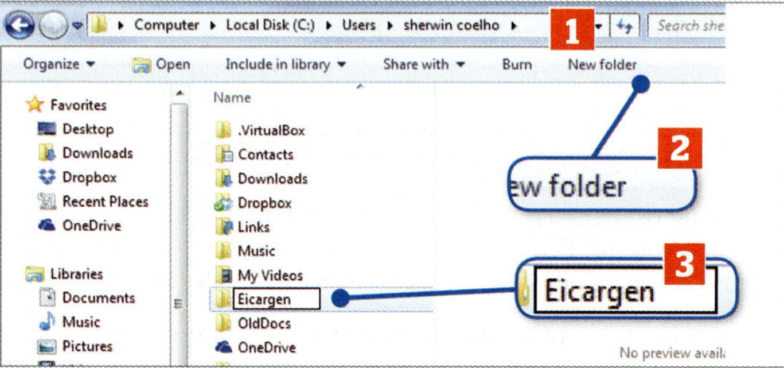

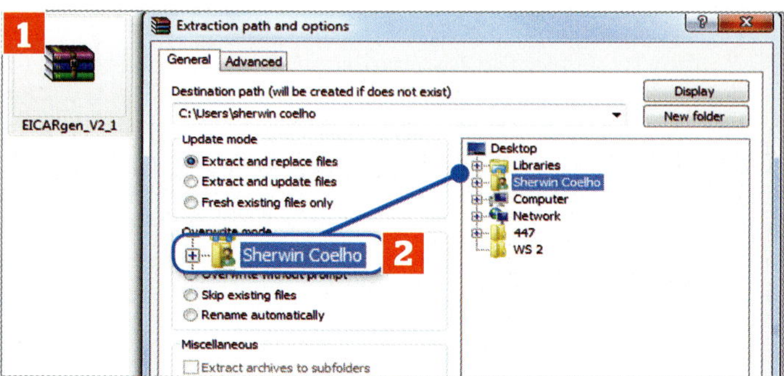

1 EICARgen is a zipped file, so you need a program that manages those (such as 7-Zip, PeaZip, WinZip or WinRAR). We're using the free WinRAR (www.snipca.com/15898), one of our favourite free programs. To download and install it, click the version (32bit or 64bit) that corresponds to your PC at the top of the web page. To find out your PC's version, right-click Computer on your Desktop or Start menu, Properties, then look under 'System type' in the System section. Next, create a new folder on your PC to save the extracted EICARgen file to. Open Computer, C Drive, Users and the folder with your Windows username **1**. Now click 'New folder' **2** and name it Eicargen **3**.

2 Now go to www.snipca.com/15896, scroll down and click the 'EICARgen_V2_1.zip' link (below the video) to download it. To extract the contents of this file to the Eicargen folder you created, navigate to the 'EICARgen_V2_1' zipped file (in your Downloads folder) **1**, right-click it, then click 'Extract files'. In the pane that opens click the '+' symbol next to your name **2**, select the Eicargen folder you created (in Step 1), then click OK. (This step may differ slightly if you're using a different file-compression program).

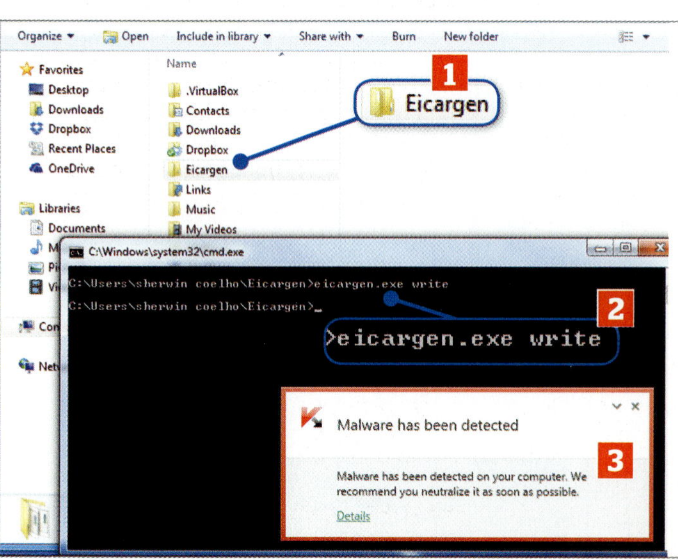

3 You now need to run the file from the Eicargen folder using Command Prompt. Navigate to the Eicargen folder, press and hold the Shift key, right-click the folder **1**, then click 'Open command window here'. Type `eicargen.exe write` **2** in Command Prompt, then press Enter. Our favourite antivirus program (Kaspersky Internet Security 2015) detected the file as malware **3**. If yours doesn't, update your antivirus and repeat this step. If you still don't see a security warning, then consider replacing your antivirus program with a better one, preferably Kaspersky.

Secret tips for OneDrive

Use Word and Excel for free

There's much more to Microsoft's cloud service OneDrive (https://onedrive.live.com) than storage space. Your OneDrive account integrates automatically with Office Online (https://office.live.com), a free, slimmed-down version of Office 365 (£7.99 a month, www.snipca.com/15604).

Once you've signed up for, then into, OneDrive, you won't have to open Office Online in a separate tab or window.
Just click '+Create' at the top left of the OneDrive window and choose a file ('Word document', 'Excel workbook' and so on). Any work you do saves to your OneDrive account, automatically and instantly. So if your internet suddenly dies on you, your work is safe.

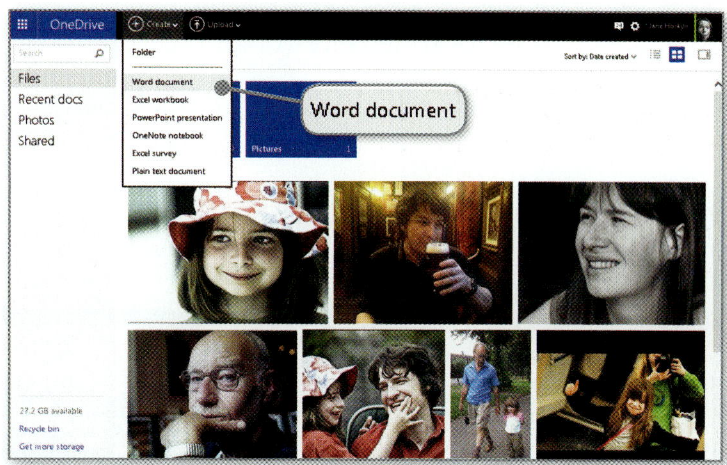

Click a file type in OneDrive to open a new Office Online document

Back up your photos and double your storage

OneDrive gives you 15GB free the moment you sign up, which is pretty generous (Dropbox only gives you 2GB free). But you can double that to 30GB by installing OneDrive on your tablet or phone (Android www.snipca.com/15600; iOS www.snipca.com/15601) and switching on Camera Backup.

Besides expanding your storage, Camera Backup automatically saves all your device's photos and videos to your OneDrive account. By default, it only does this via Wi-Fi, to avoid landing you with a huge mobile-data bill.

Be aware that if you've already enabled your Camera Backup bonus using one device, you won't get it again by enabling it on a different device. Also note that the recent stories about OneDrive offering 100GB to anyone switching from Dropbox had prohibitive strings attached: the offer was US-only and it has expired.

Save your photos and get more storage with OneDrive's Camera Backup

Edit your OneDrive documents offline

If your internet connection goes down a lot, install OneDrive on your PC (www.snipca.com/15606 for Windows 7 and 8; it's pre-installed in Windows 8.1). Now, any work you do in Office Online is not only saved to OneDrive online, but also to the OneDrive folder on your computer.
As long as you have Office installed, simply click the file and it'll open in your installed version of Word or Excel (see screenshot above). Any changes you then make are saved to your OneDrive account the next time you go online.

Prevent OneDrive clogging up your hard drive

OneDrive's PC version syncs all your OneDrive files to your PC by default. Frankly, that's daft. The whole point of cloud storage is to give you extra room for your files. To change this, right-click the OneDrive cloud icon in your system tray (you'll need to have the PC version installed and be signed in), click Settings, then 'Choose folders'. Instead of 'All files and folder on my OneDrive' (default), click 'Choose folders to sync' and untick any folders you don't want to sync.

Back up Gmail attachments automatically

IFTTT (https://ifttt.com) lets you automate rules for various tools. You can tell it to save all incoming Gmail attachments to a OneDrive folder (www.snipca.com/15609). First, you have to create a free IFTTT account, then click Activate in the link above (to connect IFTTT to OneDrive), then Yes and Done (to confirm). Finally, click Add Recipe.

There are are dozens more Recipes for OneDrive at www.snipca.com/15609.

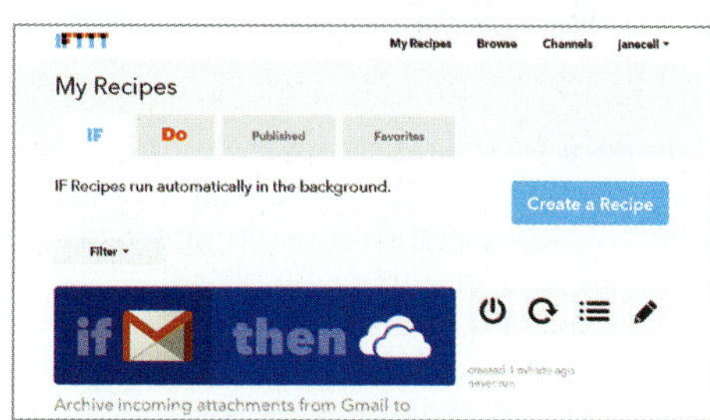

Automatically save files from Gmail and other services to OneDrive using IFTTT

Best free back-up software

Backing-up your documents, photos and videos is a vital task, yet most of us still can't be bothered to do it. We test five of the best free back-up tools to find out which one you should use

SyncBackFree | bit.ly/syncback366 |

FEATURES ★★★★★ **PERFORMANCE** ★★★★★ **EASE OF USE** ★★★☆☆

What we like

Most free back-up software creates and keeps copies of your files and folders in a specified location, but SyncBackFree is the only one we reviewed that syncs back-ups so any changes made to either folder are mirrored in the other.

Its range of tools puts it head and shoulders above other free back-up programs and it's one of the few we reviewed to offer scheduling tools in its free version, by linking directly into the Windows Scheduling tool. This means you can set up regular back-ups from within the program and still be sure that the back-up will run, as long as your computer is switched on and running Windows.

When you start SyncBack, an icon appears in the notification area. However, it doesn't remain in place when you reboot Windows. If you want SyncBack to launch with Windows, you have to go into the Preferences menu, choose Settings and tick the 'Start with Windows' box. We like that the software doesn't presume you're going to want to do this, yet makes the option easily accessible in case you do.

SyncBack looks a little overwhelming at first but it is mostly configured through a relatively simple step-by-step interface. When you're configuring a back-up, there is a lot of text displayed on screen that tells you exactly how your back-up will run, so you can tweak the settings if you want to. While this might be a bit overwhelming for beginners, anyone who wants more control over their back-ups than simply clicking and hoping should relish the chance to get into the nitty-gritty detail.

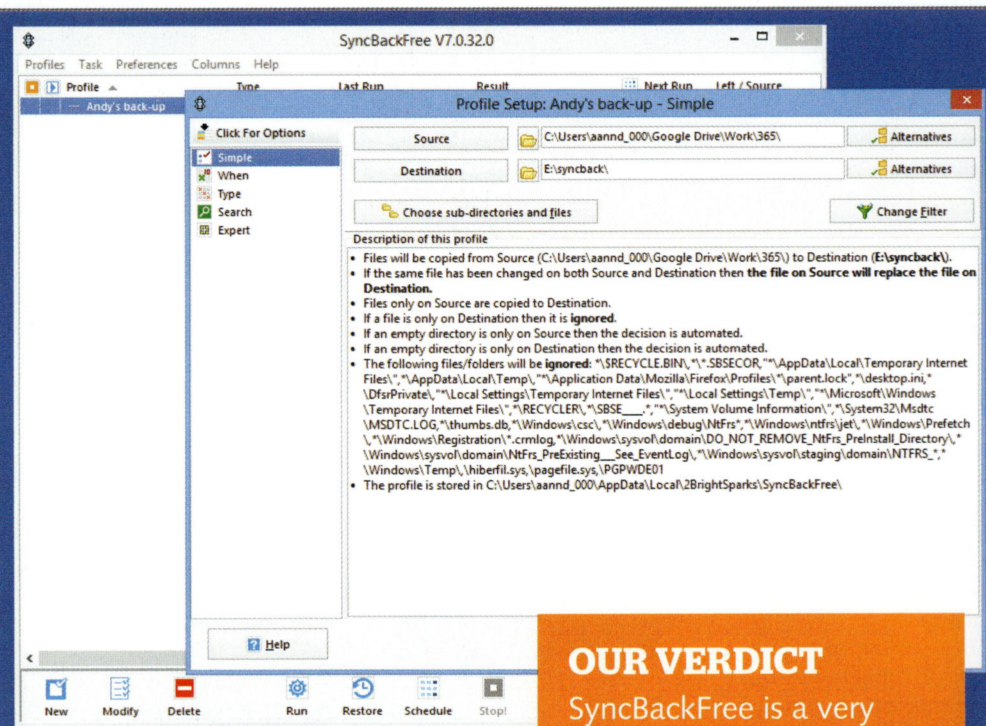

How it can be improved

SyncBackFree's main weakness is its interface. The program isn't difficult to use, because you are essentially guided through a wizard-style series of steps to create or update a back-up, or sync your files between two folders. However, being faced with a screen crammed full of text can be confusing. Stick with it, though, because it's worth the extra effort.

OUR VERDICT

SyncBackFree is a very capable program that gives you plenty of control over how it can be used. Its text-heavy interface may put off novices, but if you know what you need from your back-ups and you're prepared to spend time configuring the options, SyncBackFree has everything you need.

EaseUS Todo Backup Free 8.0

www.easeus.com | ★★★★☆

FEATURES ★★★☆☆ PERFORMANCE ★★★★☆ EASE OF USE ★★★★★

What we like

EaseUS Todo Backup's interface is much simpler and clearer than SyncBack's, which makes it a lot easier to use, but it doesn't have the same breadth of tools as SyncBackFree.

Todo Backup's different options can be easily accessed from the bar across the top.

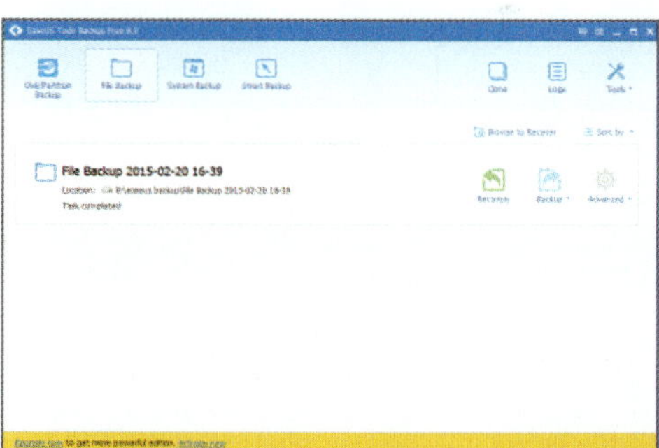

You can back-up entire drives or partitions; clone a drive if it needs replacing; make a system back-up in case your PC breaks down; and create standard back-ups of any files and folders of your choosing. Each process is broken down into simple steps, clearly presented. Even the option to restore a back-up only appears once you've created one, which keeps the interface uncluttered and tidy.

The software has a Smart Backup option, which performs a quick, regular scan of your selected folders and backs up any changes it finds. This is a great way to keep important folders regularly backed up.

How it can be improved

Todo Backup's sync tool is only available in the paid-for version, which means it's missing a vital tool that SyncBackFree manages to include.

OUR VERDICT

We love the way EaseUS Todo Backup Free is organised. Its interface is clear and easy to use, and includes lots of large icons that don't overcomplicate the process of getting the back-ups you want. It doesn't have as many options as SyncBack, though.

Iperius Backup Free

www.iperiusbackup.co.uk |

FEATURES ★★☆☆☆ PERFORMANCE ★★★★☆ EASE OF USE ★★★★☆

What we like

Creating a back-up with Iperius is easy – just choose your folders and files, and set filters for file extension or size to exclude anything you don't want. You can then perform either a full or incremental back-up, or use Iperius's handy best-of-both-worlds option, which saves a full back-up alongside versions of files that have changed. Once you've created a back-up, you can use the software to schedule it. Iperius launches with Windows by default, which is a bit presumptuous, but means you don't have to set it up yourself.

How it can be improved

The free version of Imperius only lets you back up to a local drive. There are online back-up tools linked to from the software but they all lead to screens nagging you to upgrade.

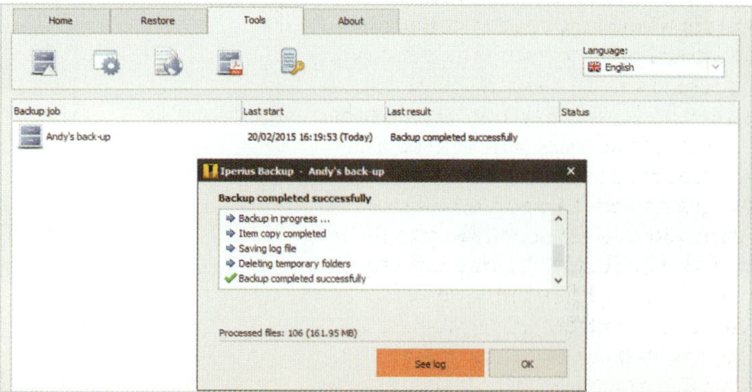

OUR VERDICT

Iperius Backup Free is a simple back-up tool with some interesting options. Its ability to run incremental back-ups alongside the standard ones is very handy. However, SyncBackFree offers a wider range of advanced features.

BEST OF THE REST

Paragon Backup & Recovery 14 Free

bit.ly/paragon366

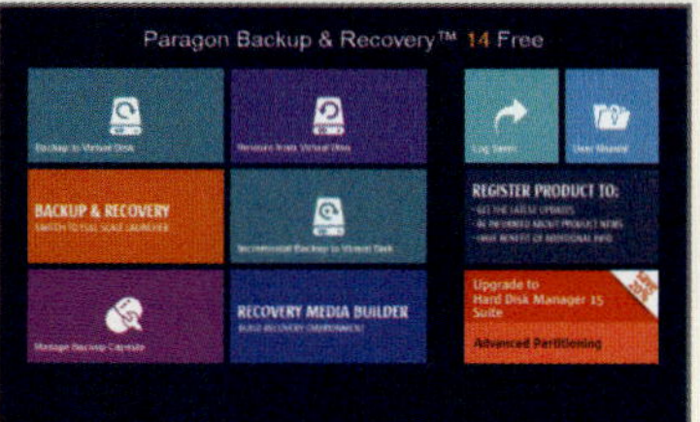

Paragon's Backup & Recovery software only works with entire drives, but it's a good option if you want to create a complete back-up. The lack of extras keeps things simple, but the program's more complex mode is barely worth it, because most of the options need the paid-for upgrade to activate them.

AOMEI Backupper Standard

www.aomeitech.com

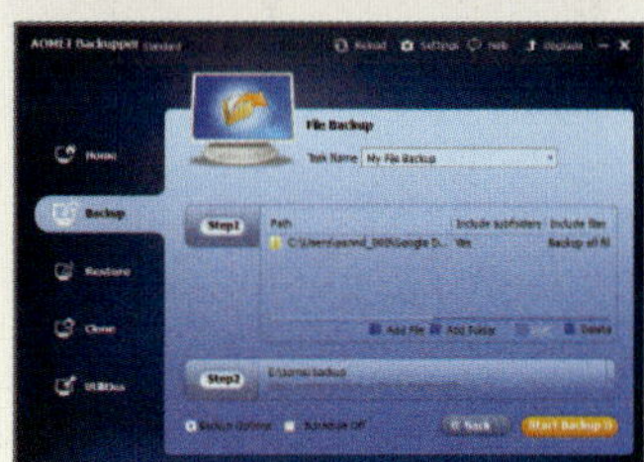

AOMEI Backupper Standard has an attractive interface that's easy to use. It offers a good range of options and tools that let you perform actions such as spanning discs and shutting down your PC when back-ups have finished. However, it saves back-ups in its own format so you can't explore them without installing the software.

Chapter 3

Great system utilities

We uncover all manner of system tools that will help your PC run more smoothly and add powerful new features

One of the best things about Windows is the availability of thousands of free utilities to help you get more out of your PC. Windows is a bit like a surly teenager – it's not great at cleaning up after itself. However, there are dozens of free utilities that can help keep your operating system tidy, and we walk you through how to use some of the best. We'll also reveal how to better organise your Desktops, find long lost serial numbers for software applications, and even show you how to install a guest operating system, so you can run two versions of Windows on the same PC!

CONTENT

Make your PC run like new

You don't have to put up with a slow PC or replace it with a new one. Here are 17 ways to get your computer working like new again, most of which won't cost you a bean

Wipe and restore your PC

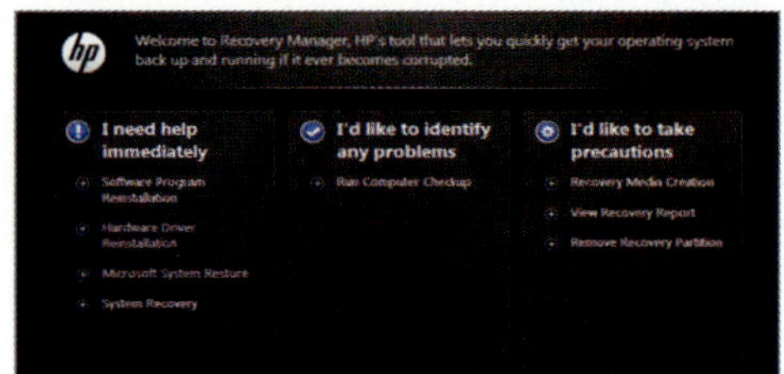

Most PC manufacturers include a recovery partition and software for using it – such as HP's Recovery Manager

1 Restore your PC to factory settings

Cost: free

We'll start with one of the most effective (free) ways to get your PC working like a spring chicken – and that's by restoring it to its original factory state.

These days, most PC manufacturers include something called a recovery partition – a hidden section of your hard drive that includes everything you need to restore your PC to its factory state. Bear in mind, of course, that the restoration process will wipe all current data from your PC. That means all your personal files, settings, installed programs, updates and customisations will be completely erased. Therefore it's vital you back up everything first.

If you're still happy to proceed, then the next steps depend on the make and model of your PC. Most Windows 8/8.1 computers, for example, have the option to restore from within the operating system (OS) itself.

In most other cases, accessing the recovery tools will involve tapping a particular key or key combination while Windows is booting, and then working your way through a few straightforward on-screen instructions. We can't offer specific advice for this, as different manufacturers use different procedures, so refer to your PC's manual.

Be aware that your computer may restart several times. Don't interrupt it until you see a message telling you the reset has completed, or until you're prompted to set up Windows. The entire process is likely to take up a significant amount of time, so you may need to clear your diary for the day.

2 Reinstall Windows

Cost: free

Reinstalling your current OS is similar to restoring your PC, except that it involves installing a clean copy of Windows from the CD or DVD it came on. This requires the disc itself, as well as the unique 25-character product key that came with it. If your PC didn't come with a Windows disc, then it's likely that the manufacturer provided a recovery partition instead (see previous tip).

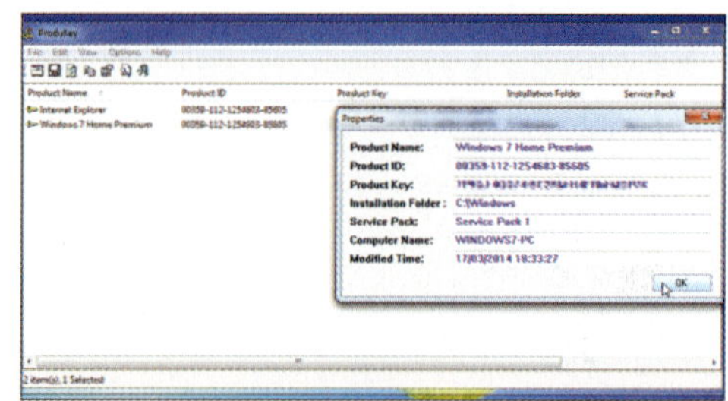

Check your Windows 7 product key using free tool ProduKey

If the Windows disc that originally came with your PC has been lost or damaged, then contact your PC's manufacturer to obtain a replacement.

If you bought a copy of Windows yourself, you can re-download it from Microsoft directly. The process is slightly different for Windows 8/8.1 (see below), but Windows 7 users should visit www.snipca.com/15396 and fill in the form, then download the disk image (ISO) file. You'll need the Windows product key for this. If you can't find the product key anywhere, download the free portable tool ProduKey (www.snipca.com/15400). Unzip and run the program, and it will tell you what your Windows product key is.

Once you've downloaded the Windows 7 ISO file, you'll need to create a bootable DVD (using a blank disc) or USB stick from the file. Use Microsoft's free Windows USB/DVD Download Tool (www.snipca.com/15431) to do this.

3 Upgrade to Windows 8.1

Cost: £73+

Windows 7 (or earlier) users may want to consider upgrading to a newer version of the OS instead of reinstalling the old one. Windows 8.1 is a massive improvement on the original Windows 8 release. It's also a lean, economical OS that's likely to make your PC feel faster and more responsive than ever.

A copy of the standard edition of Windows 8.1 currently costs around £73 from Dabs.com (www.snipca.com/15481), or £99.99 if you download it from the Microsoft Store (www.snipca.

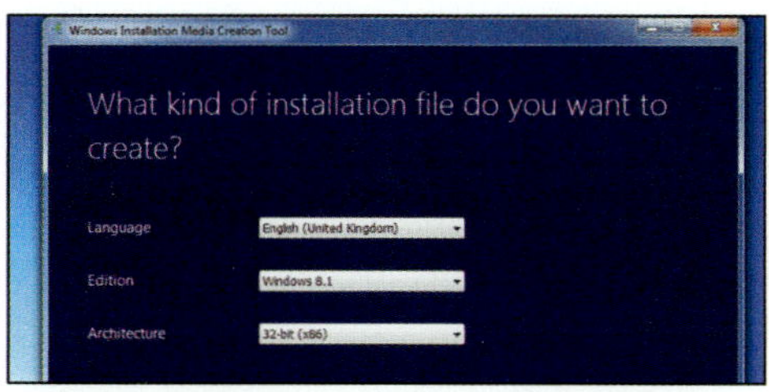

Create a Windows 8.1 ISO file using the free Windows Installation Media Creation Tool

com/15405). Be sure to buy the correct version; Windows 8.1 comes in 32bit and 64bit varieties. To check which you need, click Start, then right-click Computer and select Properties. Look under System Type to see whether 32bit or 64bit is listed.

The steps required for the upgrade process vary slightly, depending on whether you bought a physical Windows 8.1 disc or a downloadable copy. Alternatively, you might want to wait for the launch of Windows 10, which will be a free upgrade for users of Windows 7 and 8.

4 Restore your PC from within Windows 8.1

Cost: free

Windows 8.1 has built-in tools for restoring your PC to factory settings from within the OS itself. Press Win+C, click Settings, 'Change PC settings', 'Update and recovery', then Recovery.

The first option you then see ('Refresh your PC without affecting your files') will reinstall Windows leaving all your personal files intact – though we strongly recommend backing up everything beforehand. You'll need to reinstall programs after the process is complete. The second choice, 'Remove everything and reinstall Windows', wipes it clean and returns your PC to its original condition.

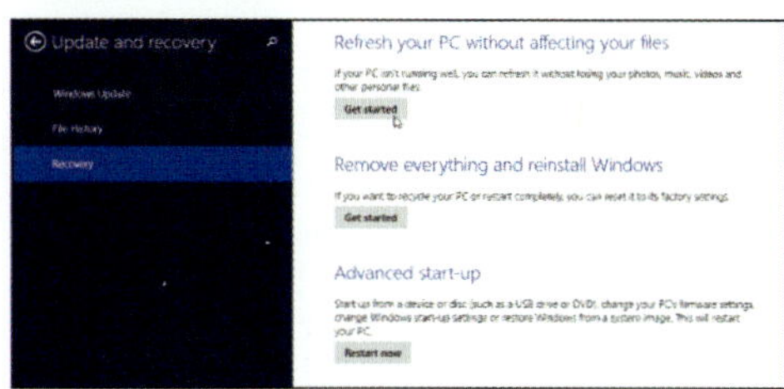

Reinstall Windows 8.1 without deleting your files using the built-in Recovery tool

In both cases, if you updated from Windows 8 to 8.1, you'll find that Windows 8 will be back once the process is complete. You'll need to update to 8.1 manually, using the steps outlined by Microsoft (www.snipca.com/15434).

5 Switch to a non-Windows operating system

Cost: free

If you're installing a system from scratch, who says you need to stick with Windows? Why not jump ship to another OS entirely?

Those looking for maximum speed should consider switching to a free, lightweight Linux installation, such as Lubuntu (http://lubuntu.net), an XP-like OS that's great for older PCs.

Try it first without affecting Windows by downloading the ISO from the link above, burning it to a DVD and booting from the disc.

If your main aim is to make your PC faster and more stable, don't be tempted to install Windows 10 until the operating system has been fully completed and launched, which is likely to be in autumn 2015.

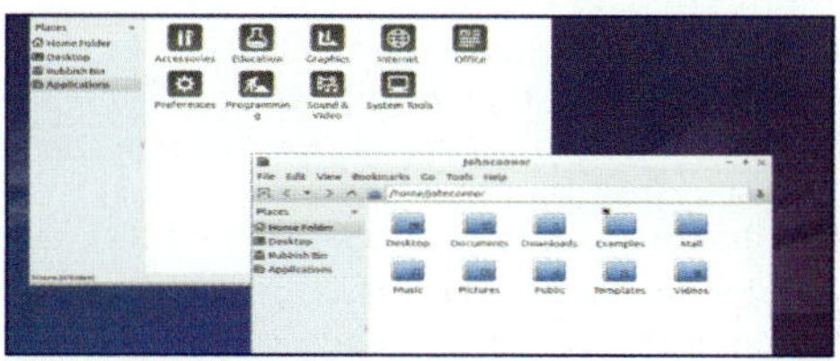
Lift the load on your PC's resources by running the free, light, XP-style OS Lubuntu

Remove outdated software and hidden junk

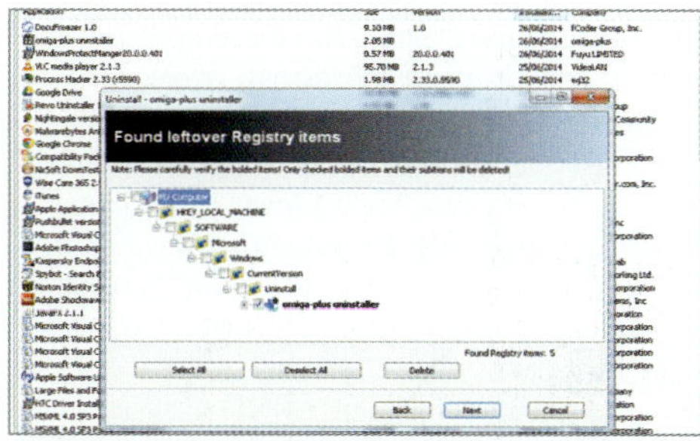

Get rid of unwanted programs and their Registry leftovers using Revo Uninstaller

6 Uninstall programs you don't use

Cost: free

Uninstalling unwanted software is a good way to keep your computer lean and mean. Open the Control Panel, click 'Uninstall a program' and scroll through the list. Be ruthless. You can always reinstall something if you miss it.

There are plenty of free third-party software uninstallers, too. If you only choose one it should be Revo Uninstaller (www.revouninstaller.com), which has an easy-to-use design and four levels of thoroughness: Safe and 'Built-in', which use Windows' uninstaller; Moderate, which removes any associated Registry entries along with the program; and Advanced, which is the ultimate solution for stubborn, troublesome programs that litter your system with all kinds of leftovers.

7 Remove bloatware and hidden junk

Cost: free

PC manufacturers sell their systems pre-loaded with unnecessary programs and tools (often called 'bloatware'), many of which can be uninstalled via the Control Panel. One side effect of restoring your PC from a recovery partition is that all the pre-installed software will also be restored. So after carrying out the restore procedures we described earlier, comb your PC for bloatware and remove anything you don't want. If you're unsure what to uninstall, use a free tool called SlimComputer (http://slimcomputer.com) to help you identify and remove resource-hungry programs, adware and more besides.

Not all the items that slow your computer are easy to find, but purging your PC of junk will have a beneficial effect. Our favourite tool for this task is CCleaner (www.piriform.com/ccleaner),

Remove hidden junk and uninstall software using SlimComputer

which analyses your hard drive and quickly relieves it of thousands of hidden temporary and unused files. You can find out how to get the most from CCleaner with our step-by-step guide on page 56.

8 Disable startup items

Cost: free

Programs or processes that are set to run automatically every time Windows starts are the biggest culprits when it comes to slow boot times. Disable anything you don't need. In Windows 7, click Start, type msconfig.exe and press Enter. Click the Startup tab and untick any items you don't want.

In Windows 8 and 8.1, right-click the taskbar and select Task Manager. Click 'More details' to expand the list if necessary (it's usually expanded by default), then click the 'Start-up' tab. Right-click an item you don't want to run at startup, then select Disable.

For help deciding which startup items you can safely disable, use the free online tool Should I Remove It? (www.shouldiremoveit.com). The 'What is it?' button next to each item takes you to an online database with information that can help you establish whether or not you need it. Alternatively, you could search for the item online. Windows 8/8.1's Task Manager even offers a handy 'Search online' option when you right-click a startup item.

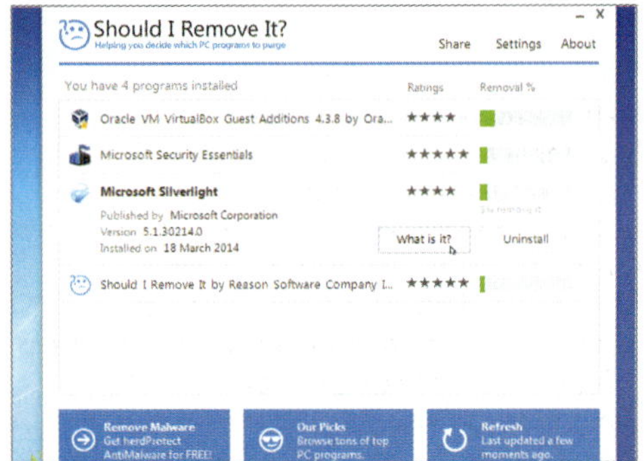

Find out what's safe to remove from your startup list using free online tool Should I Remove It?

9 Update programs you use regularly

Cost: free

When software is released, it usually still needs refining with subsequent updates and security patches. So keeping your programs and applications up to date can help improve your PC's performance.

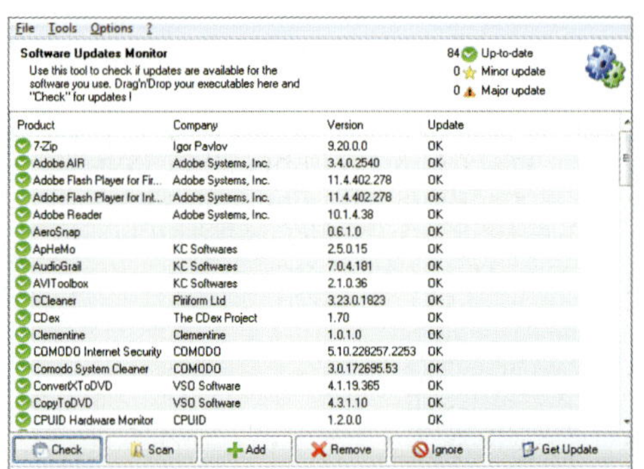

Update all your software at once with SUMo

We're assuming you've already set Windows to update automatically (if not, open the Control Panel and click 'System and Security', Windows Update, 'Change settings'). Keeping all your other software up to date can be time- consuming, but thanks to a free tool called SUMo (short for Software Updates Monitor, www.snipca.com/ 15437) you don't have to. The program automatically detects all the software on your PC, sends you a notification when updates are required and lets you get them with the click of a button.

We'd recommend downloading the tool's portable version, to avoid any junk in the installer. Under SUMo, click the small ZIP folder icon under the blue Download button. Save and extract the file ('sumo.zip'), then run the file 'SUMo.exe' to instantly run the program.

10 Use older programs or free online alternatives

Cost: free

Newer programs tend to make more demands on your system, while older ones are often less resource-hungry. One easy way to make your PC feel more responsive is to revert to an older version of a program. But there are drawbacks to this approach. Obviously, older programs may not have all the features found in the latest editions. Some, like Office 2003, may no longer be supported by the manufacturer (read Microsoft's confirmation at www.snipca.com/15438). Others may suffer compatibility problems with newer versions of Windows. There's also the risk that security flaws in older products won't be fixed, potentially leaving your PC exposed to attack.

Another alternative is to use up-to-date free programs, which are often less demanding than their paid-for equivalents – especially if they work entirely online, like Google Docs (www.snipca.com/15439). It not only uses less memory and no hard-drive space but also, if you use it instead of Microsoft 365, you'll save £80 a year.

11 Remove adware and spyware

Cost: free

Adware, spyware and similar miscreants can drag your PC's performance right down, and are often hard to identify and remove.

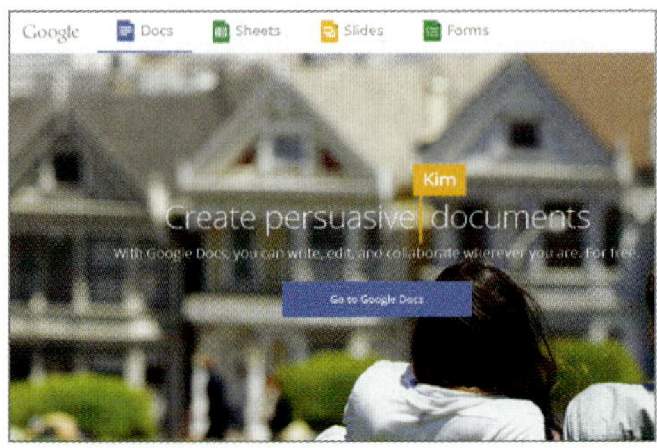

Save memory, space and money by switching to free online tools such as Google Docs

Your security software will hopefully catch anything that attempts to invade your computer but if you really want to breathe new life into your PC, you should definitely run a dedicated scanner to root out hidden malware. There are several great free scanners to choose from, including Malwarebytes Anti-Malware Free (www.malwarebytes.org), AdwCleaner (www.snipca.com/15441) and SuperAntiSpyware Free Edition (www.superantispyware.com). None of these should clash with your existing security software.

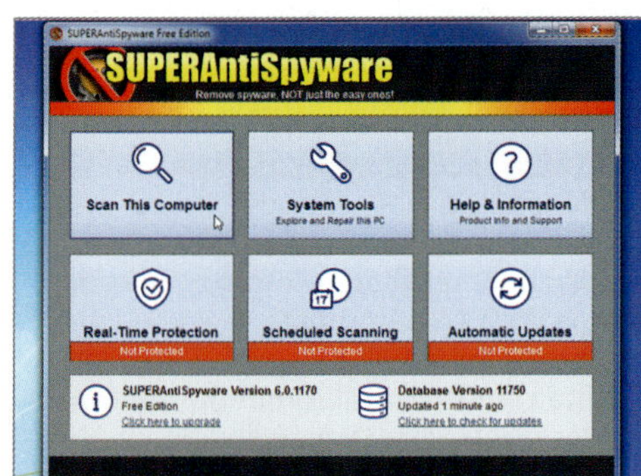

Find and remove adware and spyware using the free version of SuperAntiSpyware

Upgrade your PC's hardware and drivers

12 Get the latest drivers
Cost: free

As with other software, hardware drivers are usually updated multiple times following the initial release, providing performance boosts, compatibility fixes and more. Using older drivers could result in unnecessary speed drops, bottlenecks, crashes and other problems. Manually keeping all your drivers up to date would be a full-time job. Instead, install SlimDrivers Free (www.snipca.com/15419). It scans your system and informs you of any out-of-date drivers. And, unlike many of the other free driver scanners available, SlimDrivers Free also lets you download the latest updates with a click.

Discover which drivers are out of date by running SlimDrivers Free

13 Update your PC's firmware
Cost: free

The free FirmwareTablesView (www.snipca.com/15442), instantly lists all your PC's installed firmware – that is, the software embedded in your various components (hard drive, video card) and accessories (external drives, digital cameras) to make them work.

FirmwareTablesView can't find and apply firmware updates for you. In fact, there's no easy, automated solution to this problem, so you'll have to visit the manufacturers' product pages on a device-by-device basis. Updating ('flashing') firmware can be a tricky process and can even damage the device if carried out incorrectly, so only do it if a manufacturer specifically recommends it.

14 Remove old PC devices
Cost: free

Eventually, manufacturers stop supporting older devices. You may, for example, find there's no Windows 7 driver for that old flatbed scanner you bought in 2005. In some cases, you may be able to find a driver that makes your old gadget work with your newer OS, but this can often come at the expense of functionality or performance.

If you suspect any of your older devices or components might be hampering your PC, remove them via the Device Manager (in Windows 7: click Start, right-click Computer then select Manage. In Windows 8/8.1: go to Start, type device and select Device Manager in the results). Locate the device in question, then right-click it and select Uninstall. Then physically unplug the device and restart your PC to see if this makes any difference.

Use Windows' built-in Device Manager to uninstall old PC accessories

15 Add more memory
Cost: from £30

If you're happy to spend a bit of cash to reinvigorate your PC, then there are few better investments than adding memory. To give you an idea of cost, 4GB of RAM should set you back about £30 online.

To find out how much memory you have, what type your PC uses and how much more you can add, run Speccy (www.piriform.com/speccy). You should also run the free online hardware-analysis tool from Crucial (http://uk.crucial.com) and click the 'scan your system' button. This will automatically install and run a special free tool that will analyse your PC and tell you what you need to know about its memory and other specifications. You don't necessarily have to buy your memory from Crucial, so shop around.

16 Install an SSD
Cost: from £50

Upgrading your hard drive doesn't just give you more storage. Opt for an SSD (solid-state drive) instead of a traditional disk-based hard drive and you can give your PC a significant speed boost. These drives are a little pricier than standard hard drives (about £50 for 120GB, if you buy online), but they don't have any mechanical parts, which makes them able to read and write data much faster than traditional drives. The result is shorter boot times and snappier overall performance.

SSDs like this Samsung model are more robust than traditional hard drives

17 Give your PC a physical spring clean
Cost: a couple of pounds

One thing's for sure – your PC was a lot shinier when you first bought it. To really make it feel like new, give it a good clean.

Wipe the screen with a microfibre cloth or duster. Turn your keyboard upside down and shake out the crumbs, and give it a going over with an anti-bacterial wipe. Clean any dust that's collected on the underside of your mouse with a moist cotton bud.

Desktop PC owners should consider opening the case and, armed with a can of compressed air, blow away the dust that has collected inside. Make sure your PC is switched off and unplugged if you're going to do this and take care.

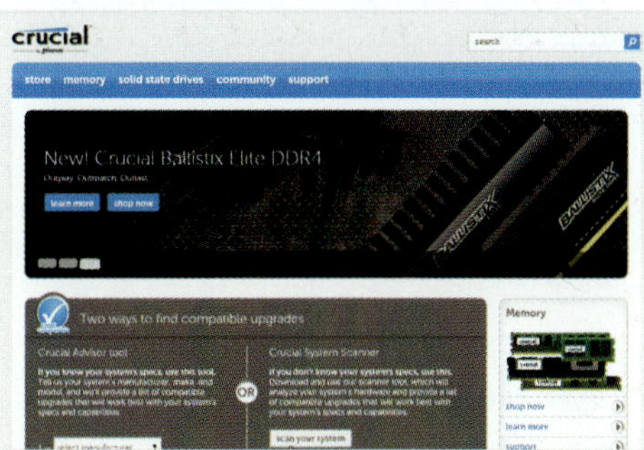

Click 'scan your system' on the Crucial website to discover your PC's hardware specifications

Recover your files when Windows crashes

Computer crashes can result in loss of data. Lazesoft Recovery Suite Home Edition is a free program that lets you create a bootable drive that you can use to boot into your crashed PC, fix the problems and recover any lost files. The program is packed with features, but has an easy-to-use interface with clear instructions for every task.

1 Go to www.snipca.com/15830 and click the green Download Now button. Click the downloaded setup file, Run, Yes, Next, select 'I accept the agreement' **1**, click Next (three times) **2**, then Install. Once it's installed, tick 'Launch application', then Finish. You'll see the main Lazesoft Recovery screen with five options.

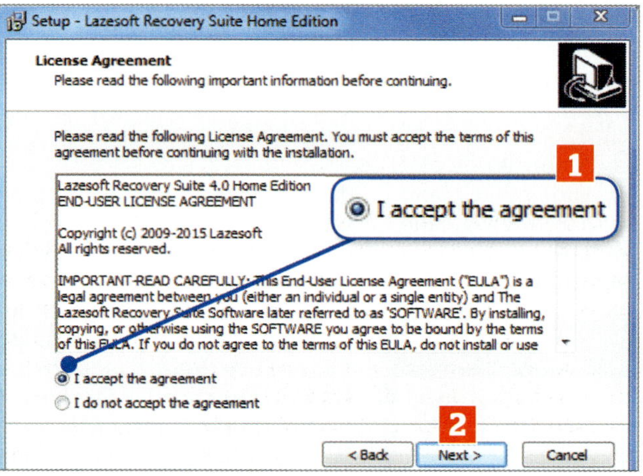

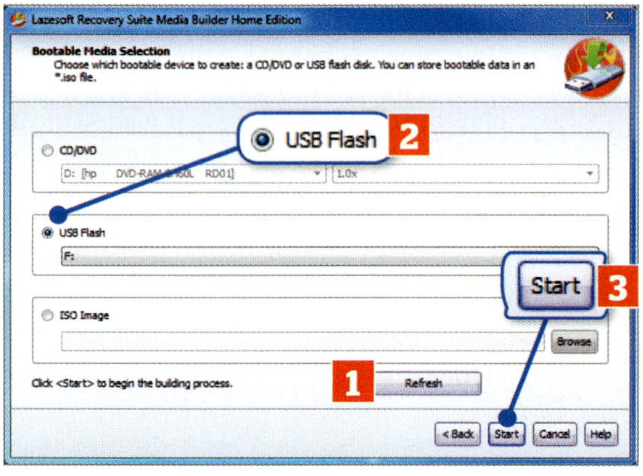

2 We'll first show you how to create a bootable disc. Insert a blank CD or USB stick into your PC. Click Burn CD/USB Disk in Lazesoft, then Next. Select whether you want to create a CD/DVD, 'USB flash' or ISO Image (that you can later save to an external drive). Click Refresh **1** if your CD/DVD or USB stick doesn't appear immediately. We selected USB Flash **2**. Now click Start **3**, then Yes. The creation process took about seven minutes on our Windows 7 PC. After it's finished, you'll see two links: 'How to boot from USB flash device' and 'How to boot from CD/DVD'. We explain this process in the next step.

3 The next time your PC crashes, insert your bootable CD/USB stick into it and restart your PC. As it boots, make a note of the brief notification telling you which key to press to access the Boot Menu in your BIOS (F2 on most PCs). Restart your PC and keep pressing that key as it boots. In your Boot Menu, select 'USB drive' as your First/Primary Boot Device, then click Lazesoft Live CD. Your PC will now boot in Safe Mode, displaying the Lazesoft Recovery Suite main window. Click Windows Recovery **1**, then OK. You'll now see a screen with four solutions to common crash problems. If you're unsure which option to choose, select One Click Fix Crash Solution, click the One Click Fix button, then Finish. Close that window, then click Reboot **2**.

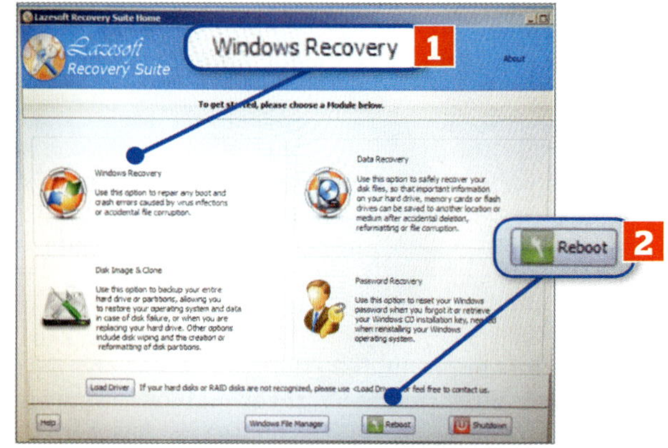

4 When your PC reboots, you should see the files you may have lost during the crash in their original locations. If you can't find them, it's possible they've been deleted from your PC. Fortunately, Lazesoft's powerful Data Recovery options can help you find and restore files or folders that have been deleted from your PC or external drives (such as USB sticks). It even lets you find and recover files that have been deleted using Shift+Del and those that have been emptied from the Recycle Bin. Open Lazesoft and click Data Recovery to see four scan options.

5 Each of the scan options works more or less the same way: select the drive you want to scan for deleted items, wait for the scan to complete, then tick the items you want to recover from a list. We'll show you how to use Fast Scan but if you can't find your files using this, then try one of the other (more thorough) options. Click Fast Scan, then select the relevant partition **1** – the drive letters **2** will correspond to your PC's drive letters. Click Start Search **3** to begin scanning, then OK when the scan has finished.

6 Next, click the dropdown menu beside the relevant drive letter **1** to see a list of folders that Lazesoft has recovered files from. Click any folder to see its deleted files in the main section. If you see 'Deleted and probably good' **2** in the File State column, it means those files can be recovered. Tick the files you want to recover, then click Save Files **3**. Now select the folder you want to save the recovered files to, then click Select Folder. After restoration, open the folder you chose and you'll see a folder named Recovered Data. Navigate through its sub-folders to access your recovered files.

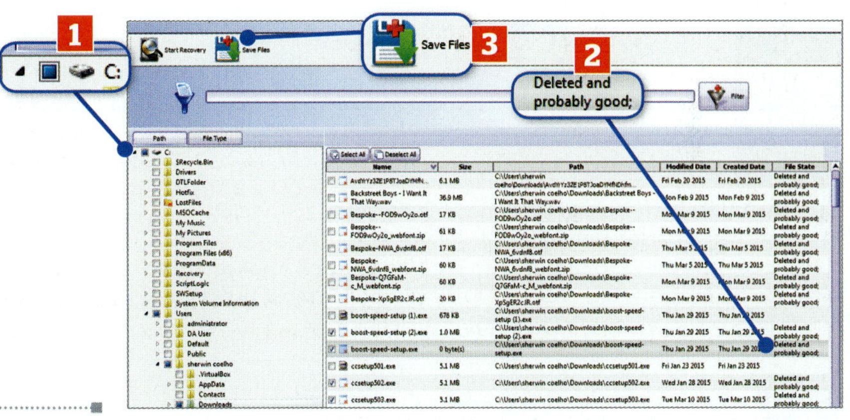

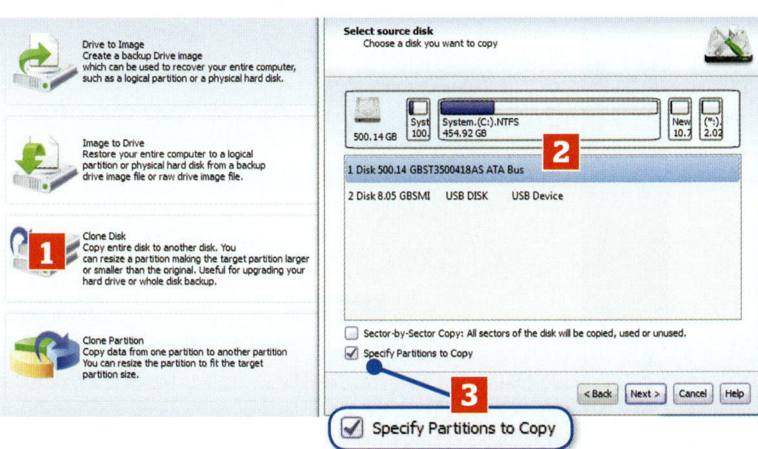

7 We'll now show you how to clone an entire partition to an external hard drive. This is handy if you need to quickly transfer or back up data. In the main Lazesoft screen, click 'Disk Image & Clone', Clone Disk **1**, select the drive you want to clone **2**, tick the second box **3**, then click Next. Now untick any partitions on that drive that you don't want to clone, click Next, select your connected hard drive, then Next again. Finally, select 'Fix partitions to entire disk', click Next, Start and OK. You'll need to restart your PC to see your cloned drive. Read tutorials on Lazesoft's other features at www.snipca.com/15839.

Clean and speed up your PC with CCleaner 5

EXPERT TIP

You can boost CCleaner's performance by installing CCEnhancer from SingularLabs (bit.ly/ccen361). This adds support for cleaning more than 1,000 additional programs. Run it to download the latest program definitions. When it's finished, run CCleaner as normal. The newest version of CCEnhancer adds full support for CCleaner 5, has a similar flattened interface and sorts out several bugs.

The more you use your PC, the more it fills up with junk. Temporary files, cached content, error reports, log files, most recently used (MRU) lists and an overflowing Recycle Bin can all eat into your hard drive's free space. All this junk makes your computer run much more slowly than it should. You can clean it up manually, but it's much quicker and easier to use software dedicated to the task.

CCleaner is a free favourite of ours that, according to its developer, has been downloaded over a billion times – and with good reason. It's thorough, but doesn't remove anything vital to the smooth running of your PC, and comes with a range of tools you can use to free up additional space and fix potential errors.

The software has recently been updated to version 5, which has a new, modern look, offers improved performance and is even better at cleaning up after Google's Chrome web browser, saving even more space.

CCleaner: www.piriform.com/ccleaner | 10 mins | Windows XP, Vista, 7, 8+

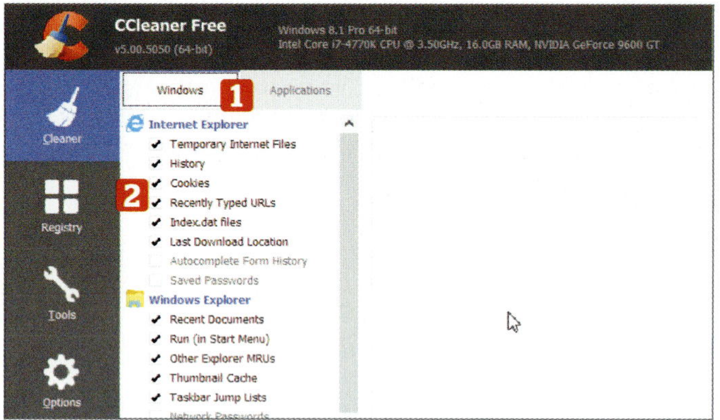

1 The biggest change to CCleaner 5 is the interface, which now has a flatter, Windows 8-inspired design. As before, you can choose the areas to target from the Windows or Applications tabs. **1** The pre-selected choices **2** will be fine for most users' needs and will give your PC a good, safe clean.

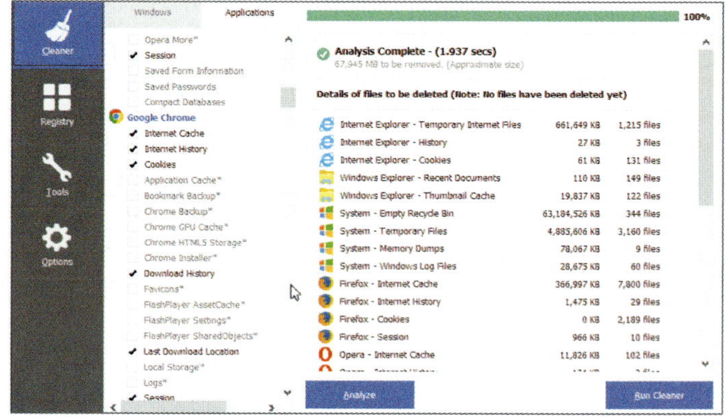

2 Click the Analyze button **1** to make CCleaner check to see what can be removed. If you have any browsers open, you'll be asked if you want CCleaner to close them. Browse the summary **2** and double-click any of the items to get more information about what will be cleaned.

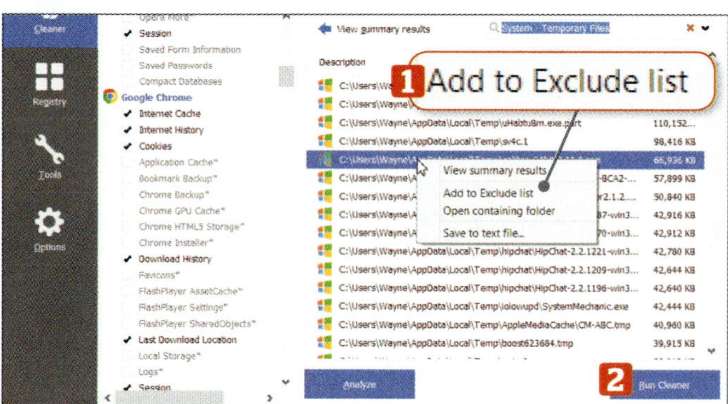

3 If there is an item you don't want to remove, right-click it and choose 'Add to Exclude list'. **1** When you're happy with everything, click the 'Run Cleaner' button. **2** The cleaning process is usually quick.

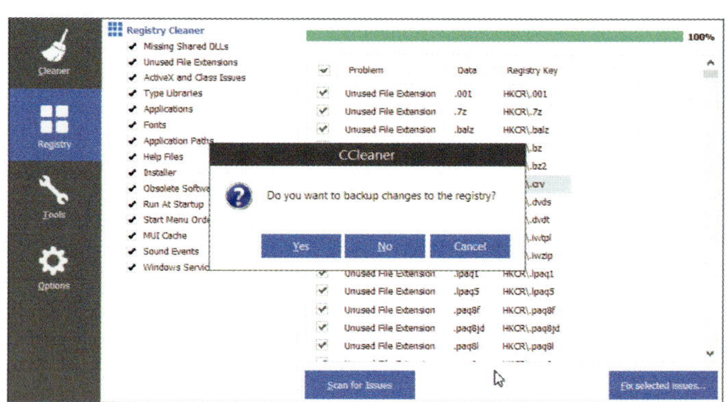

4 CCleaner has a Registry cleaner **1** that removes cruft. Choose the areas to include, **2** then click 'Scan for Issues'. **3** Deselect any items you don't want fixing, then click 'Fix selected issues'. **4** You should back up the Registry before cleaning.

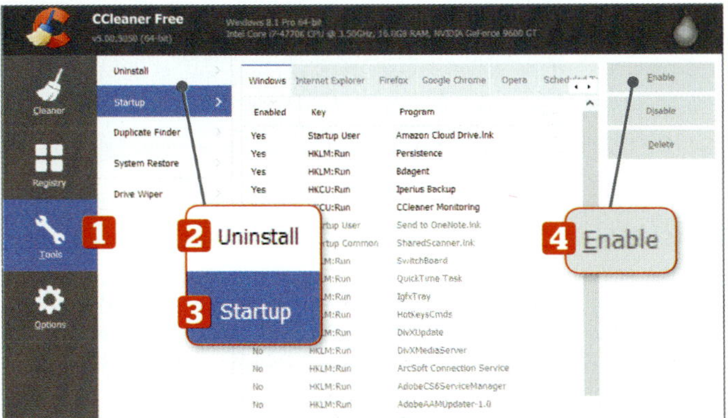

5 The Tools section 1 hosts advanced features. Uninstall 2 lets you remove or repair programs, and rename or delete their entries. Startup 3 lets you enable, disable and delete programs that start with Windows. Click Enable 4 to sort the list.

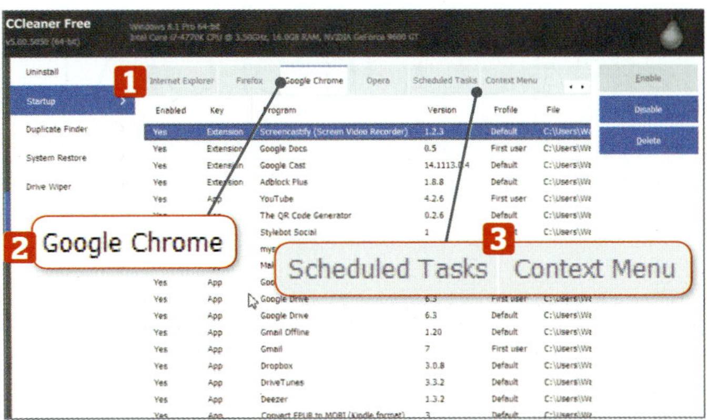

6 You can manage and remove browser extensions, plug-ins and helpers. 1 CCleaner 5 improves item detection in Chrome, and can disable or delete more elements. 2 You can tidy Scheduled Tasks and the right-click Context Menu 3, too.

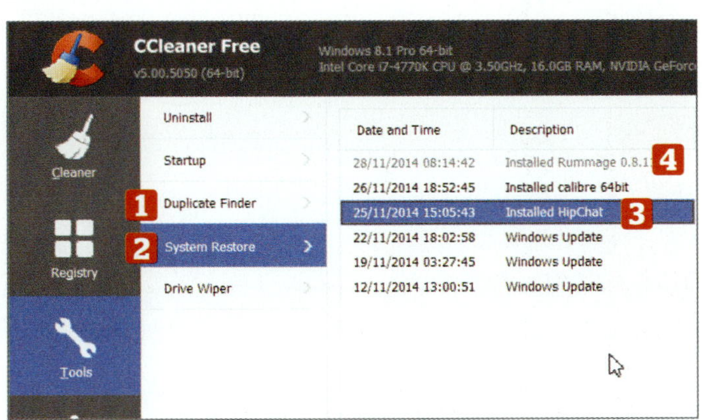

7 Duplicate Finder 1 tracks down duplicate files, such as identical photos in different folders. You can configure the search criteria in lots of ways. System Restore 2 lets you remove past restore points 3 to free up space. The most recent point is greyed out and can't be removed. 4

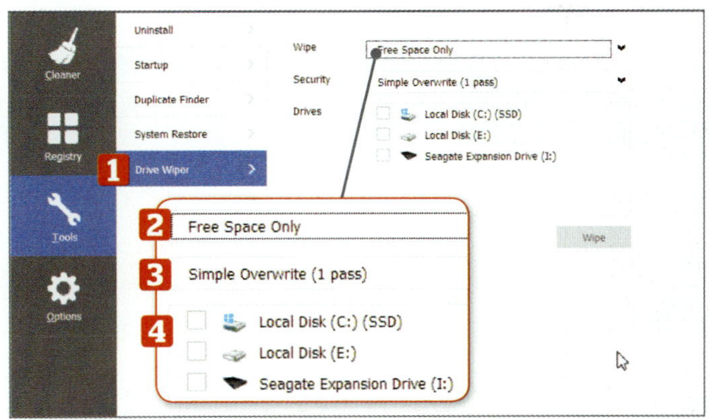

8 If you're planning on selling or passing on your PC, Drive Wiper 1 is a useful tool for securely erasing the hard drive. Select the type of wipe you want 2 (entire drive or just free space, which prevents recovery of deleted files) and the number of overwrites. 3 Then choose the drive. 4

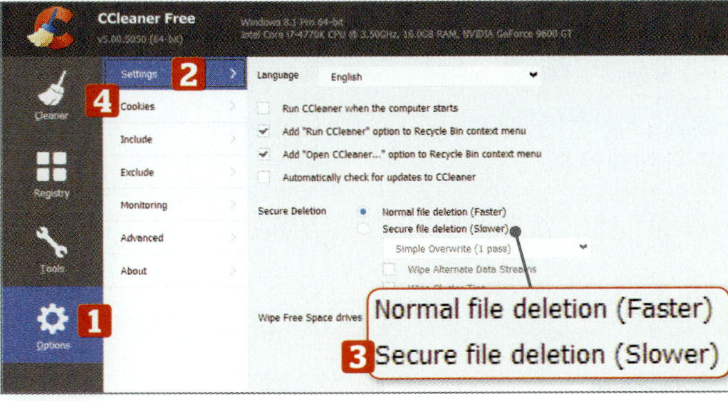

9 To configure CCleaner, click Options 1 and go to Settings. 2 You can set how files are removed and choose to delete them securely. 3 The Cookies section 4 lets you add any browser cookies to a 'keep' list, so they won't be removed.

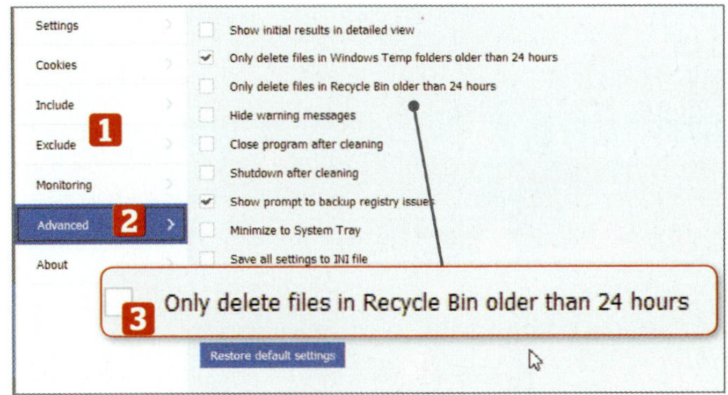

10 Include and Exclude 1 let you specify files and folders to remove or ignore; Advanced 2 gives you more options, such as only deleting Recycle Bin content that's at least a day old. 3 It's also where you can enable or disable warnings.

Take control of your hardware drivers

EXPERT TIP
In order to back up your drivers so that they can be restored without having to perform a more drastic system restore, you'll need to buy Driver Booster Pro, which costs $22.95 (around £15).
This also unlocks a range of other premium features, including tools to further enhance your hardware's performance.

Out-of-date drivers can slow your PC's performance and even stop your hardware from working properly. The free version of IObit Driver Booster 2 identifies old drivers and lets you update them with a single click so that your PC keeps running smoothly. The program can be set to perform scans on a daily, weekly, fortnightly or monthly basis. It detects newly installed devices, scanning them to make sure that you're using the most up-to-date drivers. It's also handy for browsing or exporting a comprehensive list of your installed drivers.

The program automatically creates a system-restore point when you update your drivers, which means you can return to the previous configuration if anything goes wrong. There's also a handy option that lets you set the program to ignore any out-of-date drivers that you don't want to update.

IObit Driver Booster: bit.ly/driver363 | 10 mins | XP, Vista, 7, 8+

1 Download and install IObit Driver Booster, taking care to untick the box that installs Advanced SystemCare Free, 1 unless you want it. When you run the program, it performs a scan before showing the number of outdated drivers on your PC.

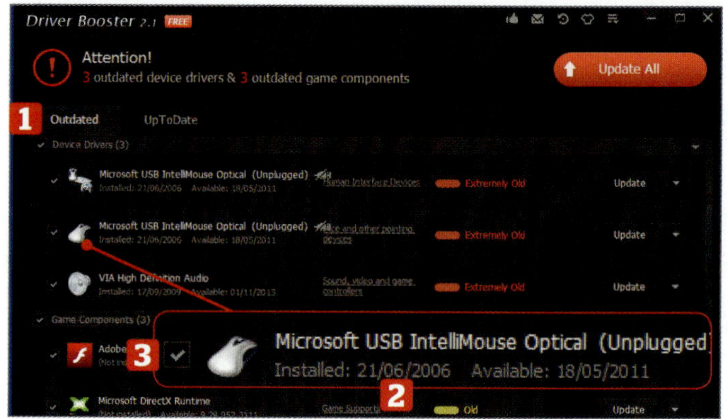

2 Check the names of the outdated drivers 1 and the dates that they were installed. 2 If a driver is required for a device you no longer use, you can untick the box next to it 3 to exclude it from the update.

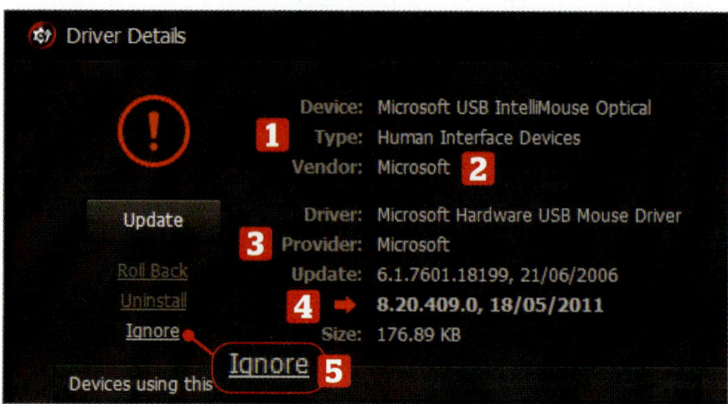

3 For more information about a driver, click the drop-down menu alongside it and select Details. Here you can see its Type, 1 Vendor 2 and Provider, 3 as well as the latest version available. 4 To hide it from future scans, click Ignore 5 and then Yes.

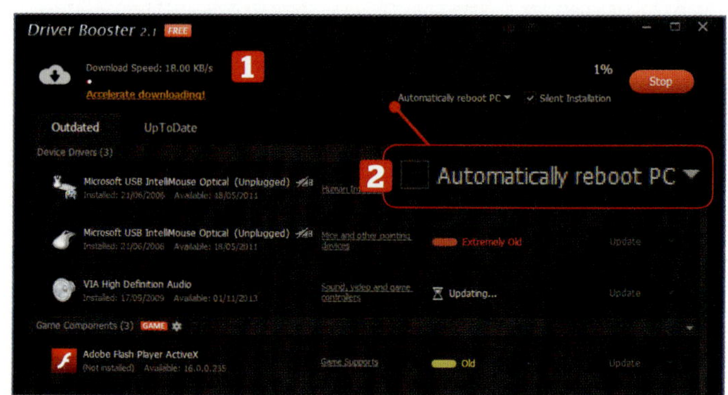

4 Unless you require Game Components, untick the relevant box to avoid installing them. Next, click Update Selected and OK. A progress bar will appear. 1 Tick 'Automatically reboot PC' 2 if you want your computer to restart once the drivers have been installed.

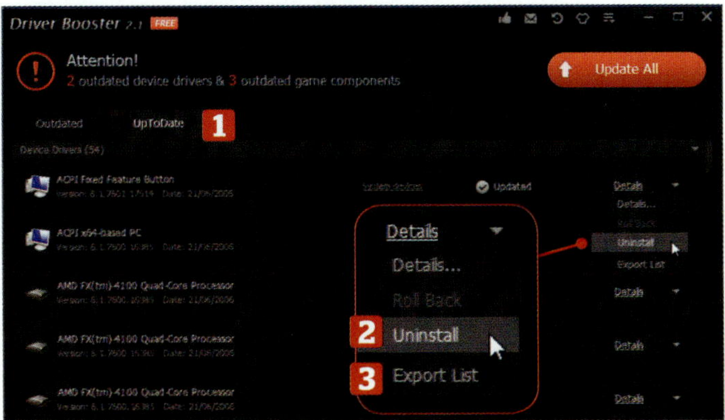

5 Select the UpToDate tab 1 to see a comprehensive list of all your up-to-date drivers. Click the drop-down menu next to a driver and select Uninstall 2 to remove it, or click Export List 3 to save the list of drivers as a text file.

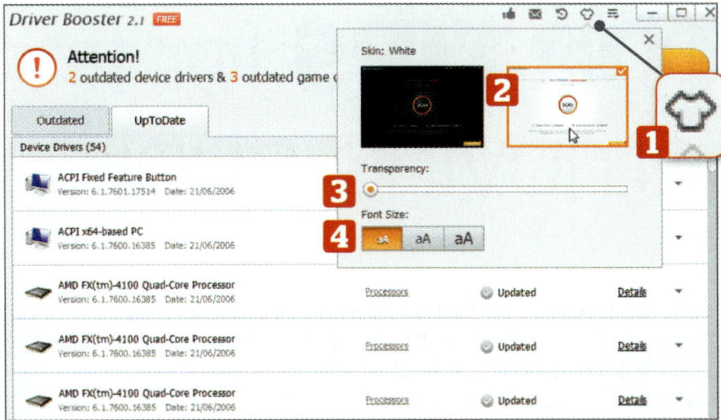

6 You can change the appearance of Driver Booster by selecting the T-shirt icon 1 in its toolbar. A pop-up appears, letting you choose an alternative white skin. 2 You can also adjust the program's transparency 3 and font size. 4

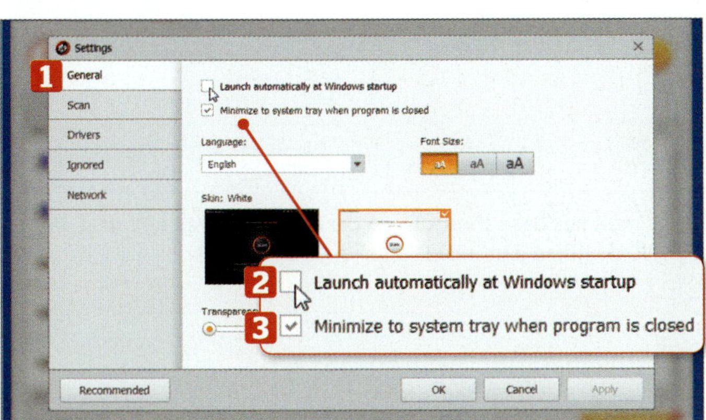

7 For more settings, click the three-line icon, then click Settings. On the General tab, 1 you can choose to launch the program on start-up. 2 By default, it is set to minimise to the taskbar's notification area when closed. 3

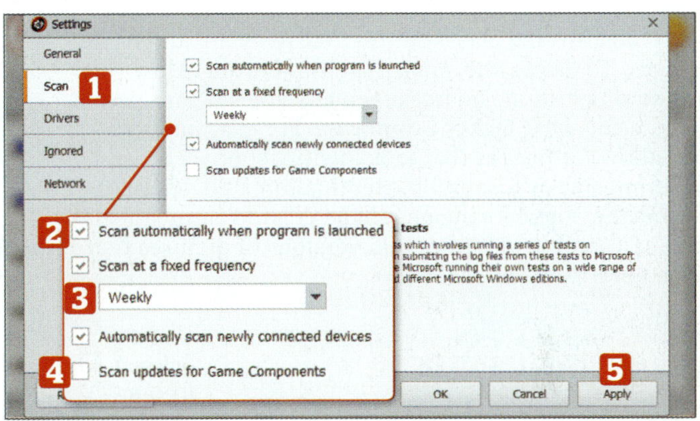

8 Click Scan 1 to see the settings related to scanning for new drivers. By default, the program scans when it's launched 2 and will carry out a weekly scan. 3 Turn off scans for game components by unticking the box. 4 Click Apply to save any changes. 5

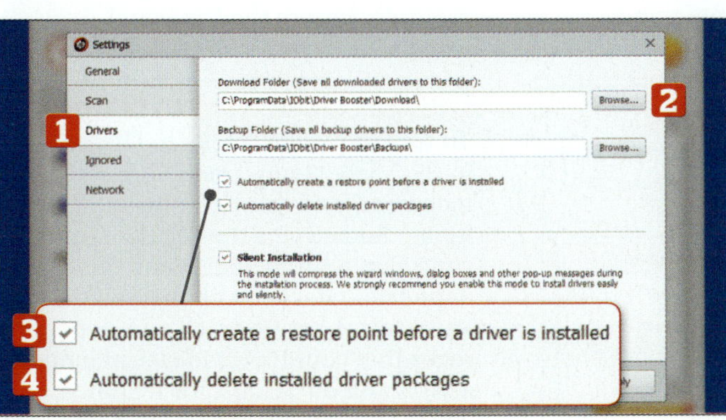

9 The Drivers tab 1 lets you choose where to save downloaded drivers. Click Browse 2 and select a new folder. By default, the program automatically creates a restore point before drivers are installed 3 and deletes the driver packages afterwards. 4

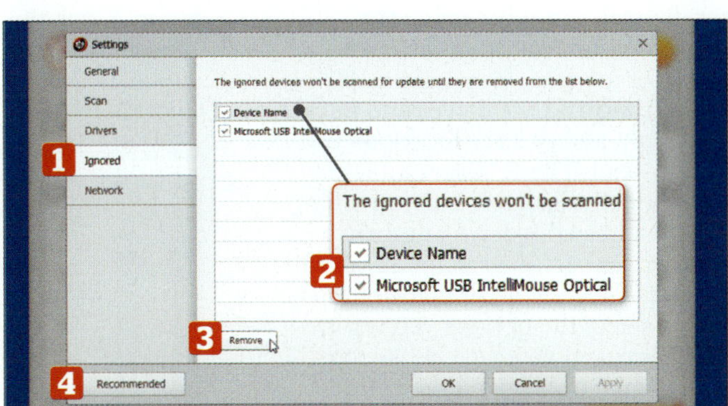

10 Click the Ignored tab 1 to see a list of drivers that you've set Driver Booster to ignore. You can remove items from the list by selecting them 2 and clicking Remove. 3 To restore the program's settings to the recommended configuration, click Recommended. 4

TOP TIPS for finding and removing duplicates

Find duplicate images that differ only slightly

Failing to erase photos from your camera, syncing with online storage and abandoning edits can all lead to duplicate images on your PC. Fortunately, the free tool SimilarImages (bit.ly/similar359) can track them down and delete them. Run it and click the plus button on the right to add folders to scan, such as C:\Users\YourName\Pictures. Click the scan (magnifying glass) button to display any duplicate images. To delete one, click the cross button below.

The slider on the home screen lets you set parameters that define what makes a duplicate. For example, you can allow for images that look identical but are a different size or resolution. 'Semi-automated deletion' means the duplicate image will be deleted automatically. You can set this to remove old versions of pictures that have been tweaked.

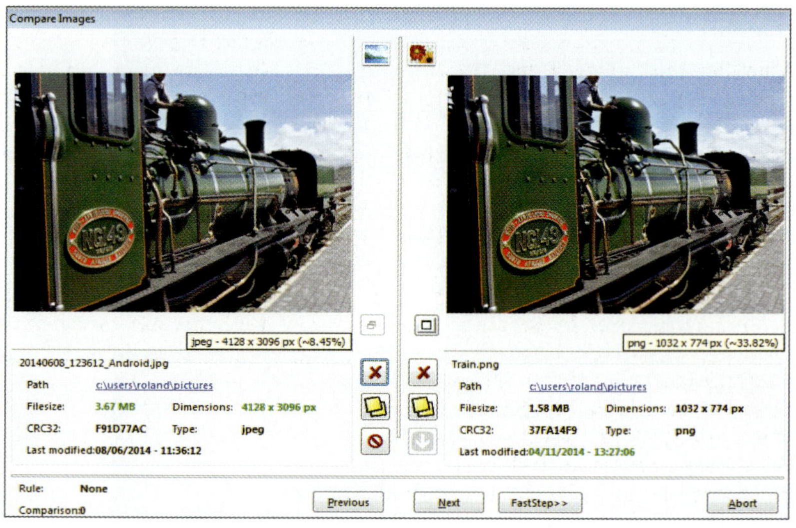

The photo on the right has been shrunk by 75 per cent and saved as a .png, but SimilarImages still identified it as a duplicate

Use a general-purpose duplicate finder

Some software for finding duplicates has been designed for specific types of files, such as photographs or music, but there are also general-purpose tools that let you track down all types of files. Auslogics Duplicate File Finder (bit.ly/dupff359), for example, leads you step-by-step through setting the parameters for scanning the hard drive.

Run it, expand the drives and folders on the left, and tick the locations you want to scan. The C:\Users folder is automatically selected, but you might want to add a USB drive or other location. You can search for all files or specific types, such as photos or music. Simply select the options you want. Click Next and you can choose to ignore small or large files, or clear both options to find all duplicates, regardless of size. The option to ignore file names means that duplicates are found even if they have different names. The final option is to send deleted duplicates to the Recycle Bin, Rescue Center or to permanently delete them. We recommend one of the first two because they let you restore deleted files, in case you change your mind.

Click Search. When the results are displayed, click the arrow next to Select and choose 'Select one in each group'. Click the arrow again and choose 'Invert selection' to mark all duplicate files except for one of each. Click Delete Selected Files, but remember that files sent to the Recycle Bin or Rescue Center are still on the drive. To free the space, you still need to open the Recycle Bin or Rescue Center and delete them, once you're sure you don't need them.

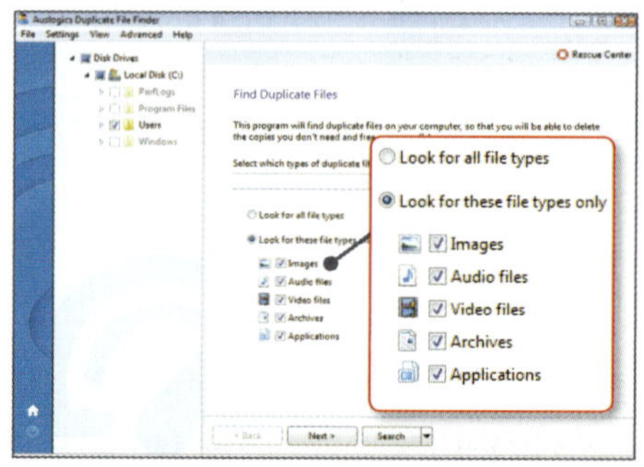

Auslogics Duplicate File Finder is easy to use and finds all types of duplicate files

• Be sure to select 'Custom install' during installation and deselect the bundled extras. When using the program, ignore the View and Advanced menus.

Delete duplicates in iTunes

To find duplicate tracks in iTunes, go to the View menu (press Ctrl+B for the menu bar) and select 'View duplicate items'. Sometimes the results iTunes comes up with are not identical duplicates, so check before you delete anything. A studio track and a concert recording could have identical names, artists and durations, for instance, but you might still want to keep both versions. Sometimes an extended version of a track has the same name and title as the original, but a different length. It's best to listen to a duplicate

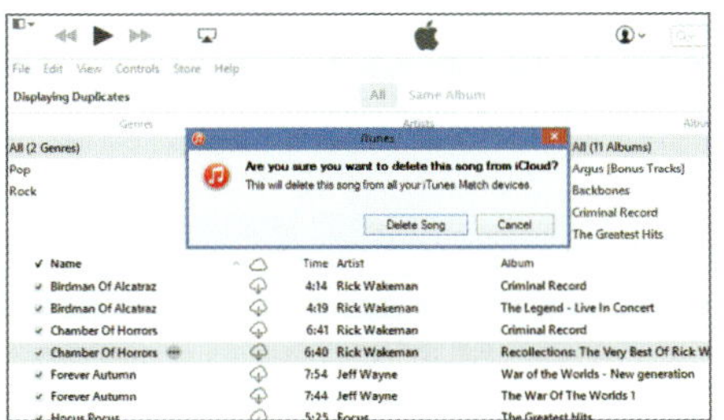

View duplicate tracks in iTunes, then right-click them and delete them

track to check. If you still want to delete it, right-click it and choose delete.

Finding other audio duplicates

Duplicate Cleaner Free (bit.ly/cleaner359) has special features for finding audio duplicates. Run the program and select the Search Criteria tab, then the Audio Mode sub-tab. There are options to find tracks with the same or similar artist, title, album, filename or file date. On the Scan Location tab, choose which folders to scan, such as the Music folder, and click Scan Now.

After scanning, click the magic-wand button to mark files. Select Mark, 'All but one file in each group' to leave just one track in each group of duplicates. A useful option is Mark, 'Select by audio tags in each group', which lets you choose to mark the longest track, or the highest bit rate or sample rate.

Clean your contacts

If you use Gmail on your PC and mobile devices, you may have duplicate contacts. Open Gmail on the PC, click Gmail on the left and select Contacts. Click the More button and select 'Find & merge duplicates' to display a list of your duplicate contacts. Click the Merge button at the bottom to combine them into single contacts.

Scrubly (www.scrubly.com) is a website that removes unwanted duplicate contacts from various sources, such as Gmail, Outlook and Google apps. It can import Facebook, Twitter and LinkedIn contacts, and it can help to resolve conflicts, such as different fields in duplicate contacts or the same phone number for home and work. It is free for up to 250 contacts.

TAKE IT TO THE NEXT LEVEL

More advanced tips for when you're feeling brave

Advanced de-duping

CloneSpy (clonespy.com) is an advanced tool for finding duplicates. It's a bit more complicated than some of the other tools we've mentioned, but it has powerful features. When it launches, it displays three empty lists on the left. The top two are called Pool 1 and Pool 2.

The simplest way to use CloneSpy is to select 'Pool 1 only' in the Mode section, then click Add Folder and select one or more folders on the hard drive. Select Duplicates in the 'Search for' section, then 'Ask user' in the

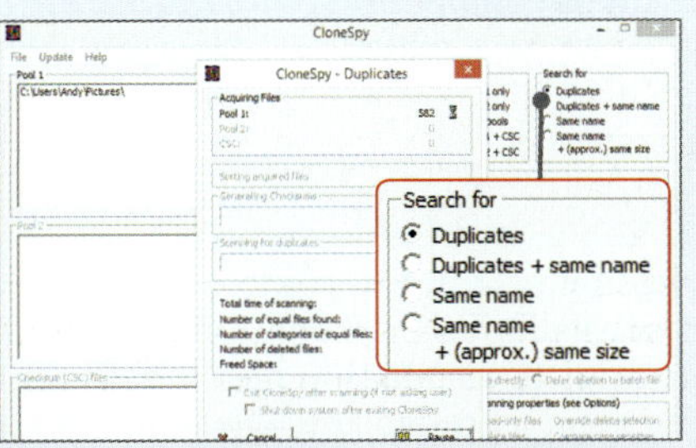

Use CloneSpy's Pool 1 to compare files in one or more folders

Action section. Click Start Scanning. When the scan has finished, a list of files is displayed, which can be selected and deleted. To make the process more efficient, use 'Preselect files' in the bottom-left corner of the results window, which provides options to select files by various criteria, including the oldest, newest, shortest- or longest-name duplicate.

Taking CloneSpy further

To further fine-tune the deletion of duplicates, select 'Both pools' in the Mode section to compare files between Pool 1 and Pool 2. You can then choose to automatically delete duplicates solely in Pool 1 or Pool 2 by going to the Action section.

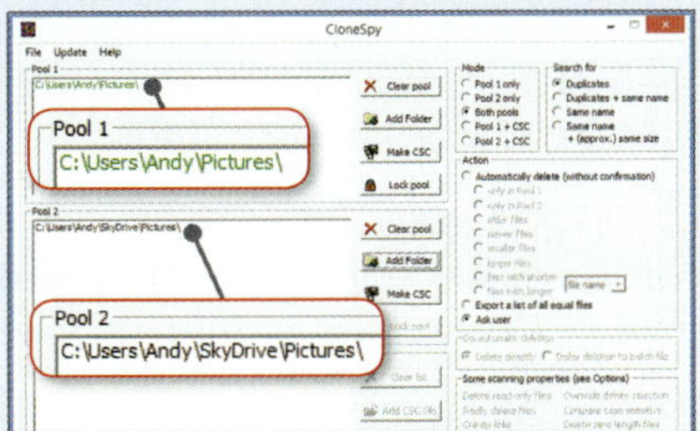

Using both pools lets you compare one drive or group of folders with another

Automatic mode lets you skip having to manually select and delete each duplicate by choosing which folder or hard drive to clean. So if you have a USB drive, for example, you could delete all copies of files on the PC's hard drive in Pool 1 and keep all files on the USB drive in Pool 2. Or you could delete the duplicates on the USB drive, keeping the copies on the PC's hard drive.

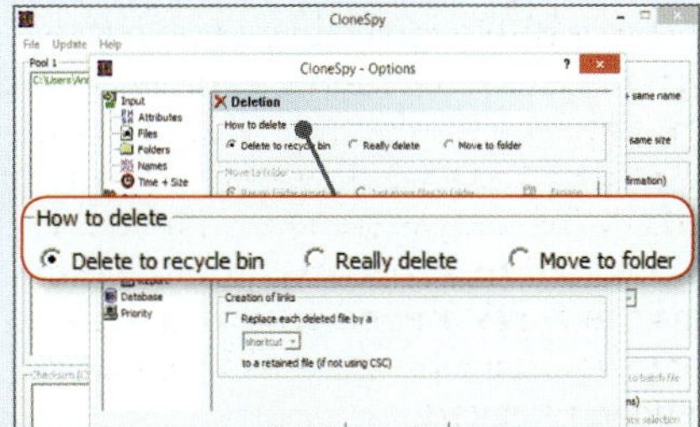

You can choose where to send your deleted duplicates

Configure CloneSpy

There are numerous options for customising CloneSpy. Selecting File, Options, Deletion and 'How to delete' lets you choose to completely delete files, send them to the Recycle Bin or move them to another folder. The latter two options will not free up any drive space, but you can recover your files and put them back if you change your mind.

The Time and Size options let you determine which files to scan. If the folders being scanned contain large files that are hundreds of megabytes in size, such as video clips, the scan could take a very long time. To exclude these large files, go to the 'Size of files' section, tick 'smaller than' and set it to 50MB. Conversely, if you only want to check large files you should make 50MB the minimum file size.

In the 'Time of files' section you can choose to ignore files that are newer or older than a certain date. Set the 'newer than' date to last week, for example, to only scan and delete duplicates of files created in the last seven days.

Install a guest OS with VirtualBox

Explore the VirtualBox wiki site

VirtualBox can be confusing at first, so make friends with its wiki site (www.virtualbox.org/wiki) before you get bogged down in buttons and menus.

The site guides you through every step of the way, from installing it (www.snipca.com/15749) to running multiple VMs from a remote server (www.snipca.com/15750). The Community section (www.snipca.com/ 15751) provides links to a forum, live Internet Relay Chat and (if you're really confident with VirtualBox) 'Test builds'.

Click the small Preferences link at the top-right of any page to set up keyboard shortcuts, create an account and store and restore browsing sessions – a useful feature in a site this size.

VirtualBox is open-source software and the site is community-run, but it's all overseen by Oracle (www.oracle.com/uk), which helps to ensure the information is up to date.

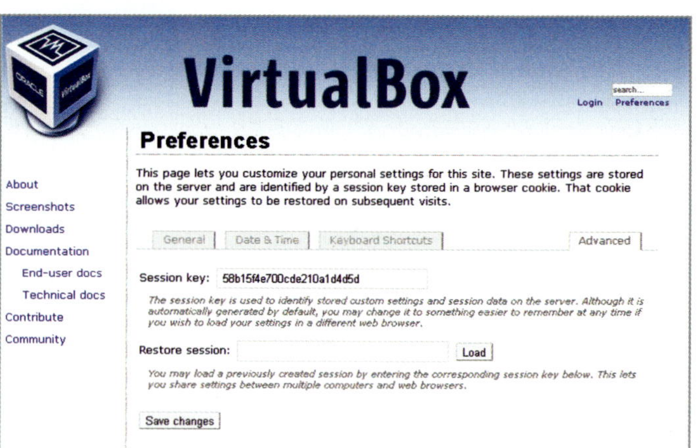

Store your sessions on the VirtualBox site in case you need to retrace your steps

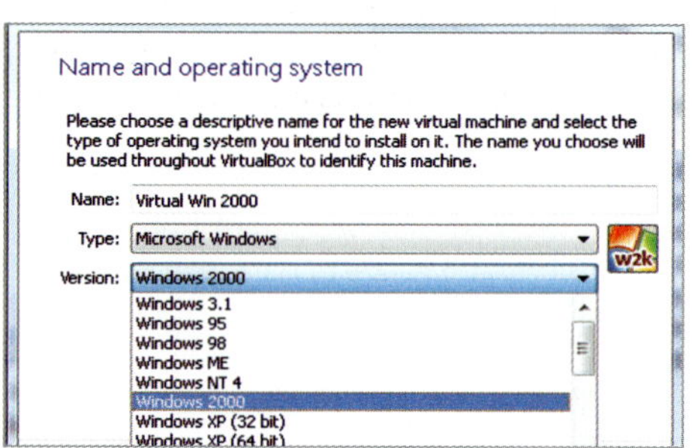

Choose a 'guest operating system' to run in a virtual machine (VM) using VirtualBox

Run a guest OS in your PC

VirtualBox (www.virtualbox.org) is our favourite tool for creating virtual machines (VMs) – such as the one we've been using to run the Windows 10 Technical Preview. By running the Preview in a VM rather than installing it directly on your PC, you can isolate it from your main operating system (OS). In VirtualBox parlance, that makes Windows 10 the 'guest operating system'.

To create a VM, run VirtualBox and click New. Use the dropdown menu to choose the guest OS you want to install (see screenshot below above), then allocate some of your PC's memory and hard drive space to it. You don't have to make any decisions here – provided you've got enough RAM and space to spare, you can simply use the default settings.

You won't be able to run a guest version of Windows unless you have its installation CD handy, or at least a legitimate installation file (usually an ISO file) and a licence key. The Windows 10 Technical Preview is free, of course, but you still need a licence key, which Microsoft puts on the download site.

Speed up your virtual machine with extra memory

Virtual systems need memory, just like your main OS does. When you create a VM, VirtualBox allocates a default amount of RAM to it, but you can allocate more by moving the memory slider to the right. You can change this later from the System section of the VM's Settings menu.

We'd recommend allocating at least 2GB (2000MB) of RAM to a VM running Windows 7, 8/8.1 or 10. Be aware that your PC's RAM is finite. If you allocate more of it to a VM, your main OS and other programs may slow down.

Roll back to a Snapshot

VirtualBox lets you store 'Snapshots' of VMs as you go along, so you can roll back if things go wrong – a bit like system restore points in Windows.

For example, if you want to use a VM to test a program you're not sure about, create a Snapshot of the VM before you install the program. To do this, select the VM in VirtualBox, right-click Current State and click Take Snapshot (see screenshot below). Then click Start to run the VM, and install the software you want to test. When you've finished using it, you can restore the Snapshot to remove all traces of the program.

Hack VirtualBox with extensions

VirtualBox also supports extensions, and you can download packages of them from the VirtualBox wiki site. Click Downloads in the left-hand menu, then 'All supported platforms' and save the file to your Desktop. You can then install the package from the Devices menu of a running VM (click 'Insert Guest Additions CD image...'). For this to work, you'll need to have allocated virtual-drive space to the VM when you created it, and you'll need to be running the latest version of VirtualBox.

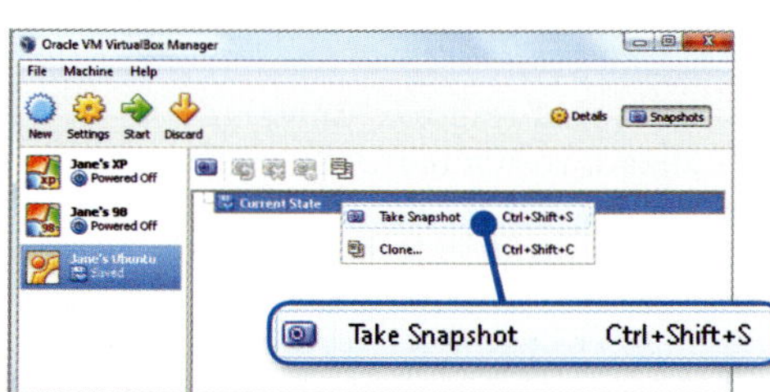

Take a Snapshot of your virtual machine so you can turn back the clock if necessary

The same Desktop, every time

Windows can be infuriatingly random in the way it opens programs; sometimes they're in the same place as when you closed them, other times not. WinDock lets you configure how you like your Desktop arranged. When you drag new windows to certain 'trigger' points, they'll resize and slot into pre-defined spaces, making it quick and simple to have your software arranged how you like it.

WinDock: bit.ly/windock359 | 5 mins | XP, Vista, 7, 8+

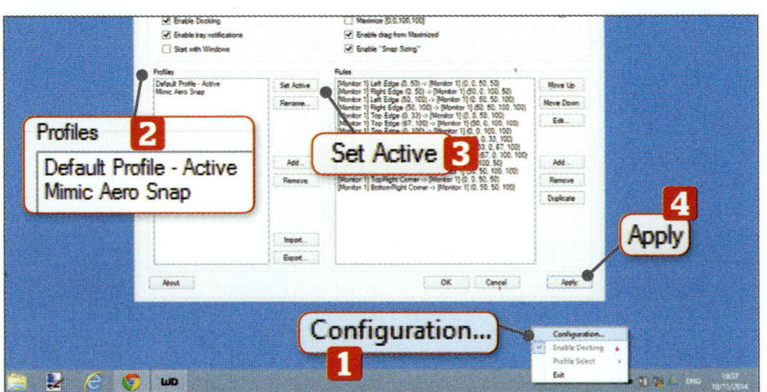

1 Right-click the WinDock icon and choose Configuration. 1 To switch between the two pre-configured profiles, select one, 2 click Set Active 3 then Apply. 4 Drag and drop the WinDock window to the edges of the screen to see it snap to different areas.

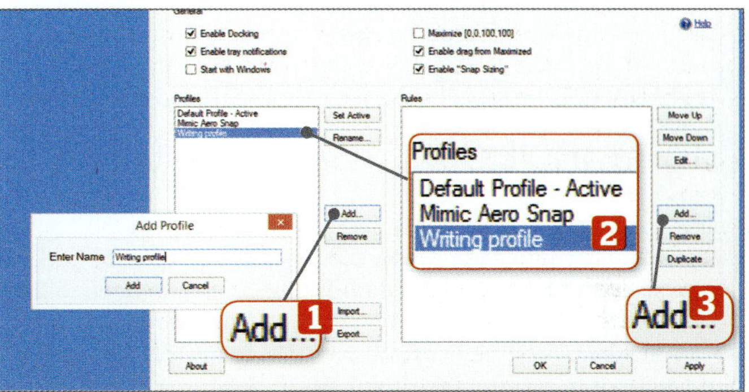

2 To create a profile of your own, click Add 1 and type a name into the Enter Name box of the Add Profile window. Once created, it will appear in the Profiles list. 2 To add a new rule, click the other Add button 3 to bring up the Add Rule window.

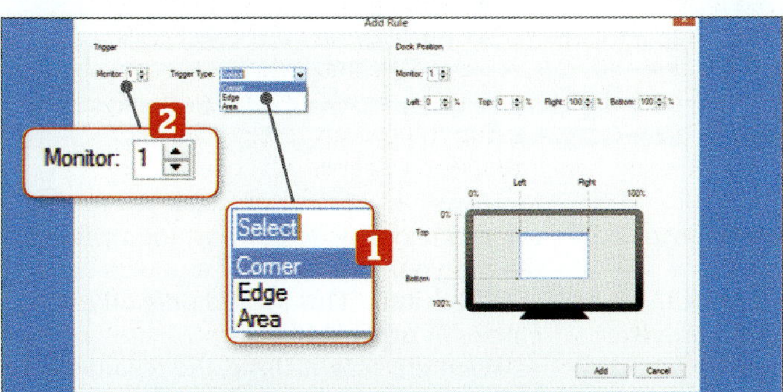

3 In the Trigger section, use the Trigger Type menu to select the first trigger position. 1 When you drag a window's title bar to that position, it will move the window to the Dock Position. Set up multi-monitor triggers 2 if you use more than one screen.

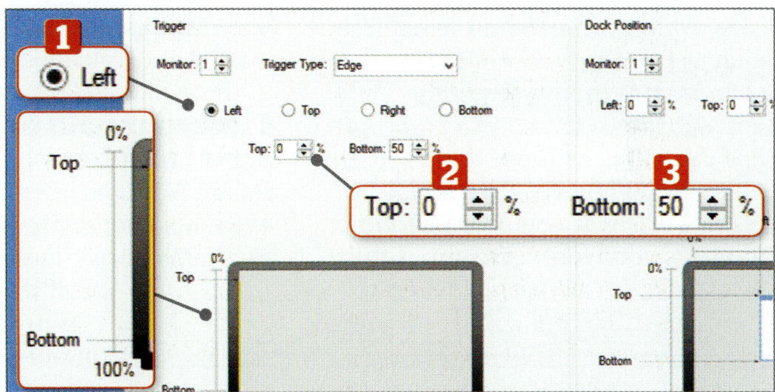

4 Set the position for your selected trigger. An Edge trigger, for example, lets you choose an edge, 1 then a section of that edge. Here, we've set the top to 0% 2 and the bottom to 50% 3 so that our trigger will be located in the top half of the left edge.

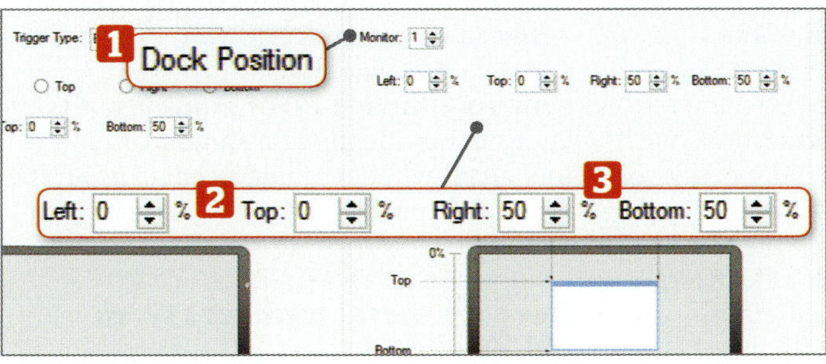

5 Choose where the window will sit in the Dock Position section. 1 Set the positions of the four corners as percentages of the screen. We've set this one to dock in the top-left quarter by setting Left and Top to 0% 2 and Right and Bottom to 50%. 3

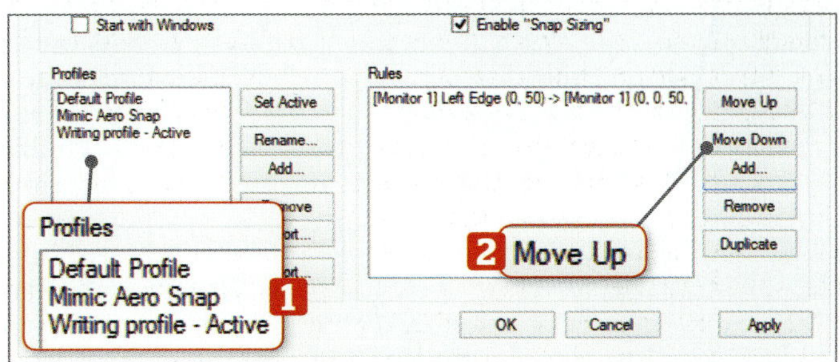

6 Click OK and make sure your profile is active. 1 Pick up your window by the title bar and drag it to the trigger position. It will dock into place. Add more rules in the same way. You can give rules priority by moving them up the list. 2

Find your lost serial numbers

Without your software serial numbers, you can't re-install the programs you paid for – including Windows. Use these free tools to find lost licences

Have you written down the serial numbers, licence codes and product keys for every program you've ever paid for, and filed them all in a safe place? No? We haven't, either.

Serial numbers are boring until you need them. They're certainly not as interesting as technical specifications such as your processor's speed and your hard drive's cache size, which you can find using free tools such as Speccy (www.piriform.com/speccy) and the Windows Upgrade Assistant website (www.snipca.com/14911).

But as fascinating as those 'tech specs' are, they're far less useful than serial numbers in a crisis. If you ever need to wipe your PC, you won't care about the speed of your processor – you'll want the licence details for all those programs you paid for, including your operating system (OS). Or the programs will be lost forever.

Here we reveal the best free tools, including a couple of notable newcomers, for digging up the serial numbers you (and we) never got round to writing down.

Generate a text file of any PC's paid software licences using LicenseCrawler

Find your paid programs' serial numbers

Belarc Advisor (www.snipca.com/14906) is even more adept at revealing your installed programs' serial numbers than it is at profiling your PC specs.

When we ran the Advisor on our PC, it quickly found several serial numbers we assumed we'd lost, including those for Kaspersky antivirus, Microsoft Office and Adobe Photoshop Elements. Belarc even listed its own serial number, despite the fact it's a free program.

Unlike the other tools we'll mention here, Belarc Advisor needs to be installed before you run it. Click the red, white and blue 'Click Here To Download... Belarc Advisor' box, run the installer, then click OK to dismiss the pop-up advertising Belarc's new Android security app (www.snipca.com/14907). There's no adware to opt out of. Click Yes to check for new security definitions, then click OK to scan your PC for serial numbers and specifications. This should only take a couple of minutes.

When the scan is done, the results open automatically in your web browser. Click Software Licenses on the left to skip straight to your serial numbers.

No information is sent to a server – it's stored in your browser for your eyes only, which is why you won't see 'http' or even 'https' in the address bar. You can save the page in your browser bookmarks or as a PDF for quick access later on, but ideally you should run the tool again whenever you need an accurate, up-to-date profile of your PC and its software.

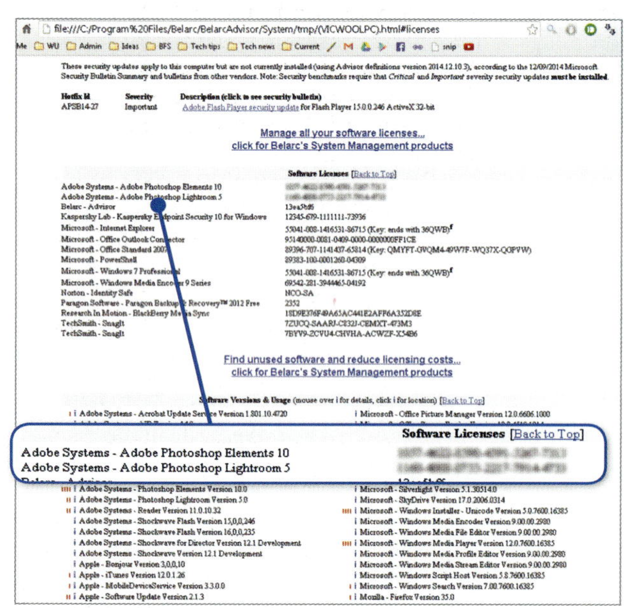

Discover your installed programs' serial numbers in minutes using Belarc Advisor

Recover serial numbers from old PCs

New program LicenseCrawler (free from www.snipca.com/14889) also scans your PC for serial numbers, but it's a portable program, so you can run it from a USB stick on any PC. This makes it ideal for

WHEN TO LOSE YOUR KEYS ON PURPOSE

As you can see, it's easy to recover serial numbers from a new or old PC. Bear that in mind next time you're thinking of selling an old laptop on eBay. Its next owner can use your licensing leftovers to re-install your bought software – which, in turn, prevents you installing it on your new PC.

```
C:\Windows\system32\cmd.exe
Microsoft Windows [Version 6.1.7601]
Copyright (c) 2009 Microsoft Corporation.  All rights reserved.

C:\Users\Jane Hoskyn>smlgr /dlv_
```

Type this command to get your Windows Activation ID

Don't just find your serial numbers in the Registry and delete them. Paid software has to be 'deactivated' before you can re-install it somewhere else. You can find specific deactivation guidelines on the software maker's website; you'll often need your serial number to complete the process.

The most important program to deactivate is your Windows OS. To do this, 'uninstall' your Windows product key via the command line. Open the Command Prompt as an administrator, type slmgr /dlv (see screenshot) and press Enter.

Make a note of the Activation ID. Actually, make a note of everything you see, and save it to an external hard drive.

Back in Command Prompt, type slmgr / upk, followed by another space, followed by your Activation ID, then press Enter to see a confirmation pop-up.

Besides depriving the PC's next owner of a freebie, uninstalling your product key means you can use it again, for example by installing your old OS in a partition or virtual PC on your new computer.

recovering licences from old computers (Windows 95 or later), including those that can't or won't connect to the internet, or from the PC of a friend who has no idea what a software licence is, let alone where to find one.

You have to download LicenseCrawler from one of the mirror sites listed on its download page; we chose FreewareFiles (www.snipca.com/14891). FreewareFiles is a useful site, but we'd strongly recommend using an advert-blocking extension such as Adblock Plus (https://adblockplus.org) to get rid of adverts disguised as Download buttons.

Sadly, the ads don't stop there. When we ran LicenseCrawler and clicked Start Search, we saw a series of pop-ups advertising other programs. It almost made us drop LicenseCrawler from this feature. But the pop-ups quickly vanished without leaving any adware behind, and once the program got down to work it was extremely efficient.

You can see which section of the Registry LicenseCrawler is scanning at any time, and all retrieved serial numbers are displayed in plain text in the program window. Click Stop Search once you've found the number you need, or let the scan complete. If you're planning to wipe and restore the PC, make sure you save your retrieved info on an external hard drive or USB for safekeeping.

A couple more tips: ignore the 'you must register' warnings – the program is free for unlimited personal use – and don't be put off by the captcha-style requirement to click a number when you run it. The developer is over-cautious, but not malicious.

Instantly see your Windows product key

Microsoft calls your OS serial number the 'Windows product key', with confusing consequences. If you search Google for 'Windows key' you'll get loads of results about your keyboard's Windows button.

New program WinKeyFinder (free from www.snipca.com/14897) calls them 'CD keys' instead, which either clears up or adds to the confusion (we haven't decided). What matters is that it's really easy to use – much quicker and simpler than the tools we've mentioned so far – and doesn't need installing.

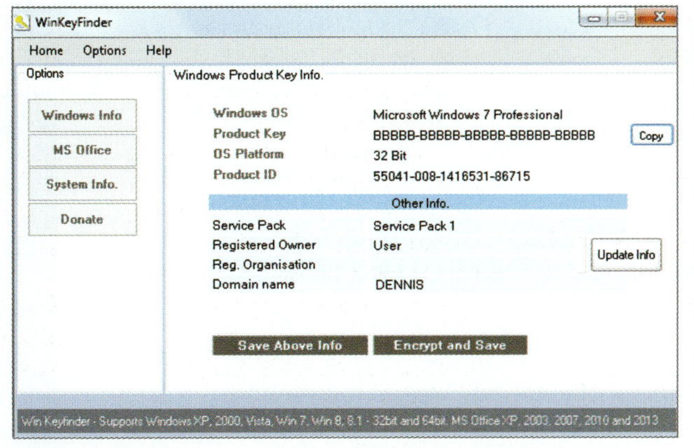

Get your Windows and Office product keys in seconds using WinKeyFinder

Run the program on any PC (Windows 98 and later) to instantly see its Windows and Office product keys. From the program window you can copy and print your keys with one click; encrypt them so no-one else can see them; and change the Windows registration details stored on your PC. Keep these details safe, ideally away from your PC, because you'll need them if you ever re-install your operating system.

The stable release of WinKeyFinder works on Windows 7 and earlier, and the latest beta on Windows 8/8.1. But, unusually for a new program, WinKeyFinder works best on Windows XP, where it lets you change your Windows and Office product keys with one click.

Why would you want to do that? You may have to. If you discover that your current version of XP or Office 2000 is pirated or illegal, you can use WinKeyFinder to change the dodgy key to a new, legal one without having to reinstall Windows. The process involves an automated Registry tweak, so create a system restore point first, just in case anything goes wrong during the process.

You can also change your product key in Windows 7 or Vista, but you will need to do it manually – the WinKeyFinder website has a tutorial to walk you through the process (www.snipca.com/14903).

Organise your programs on virtual Desktops

Windows 10 will let you organise your programs across several virtual Desktops. Linux and Mac users already have this option, but if you want it on your PC now, here are six free alternatives that run on any version of Windows, from XP to 8.1

Dexpot | dexpot.de | ★★★★★

FEATURES ★★★★★ **PERFORMANCE** ★★★★★ **EASE OF USE** ★★★★☆

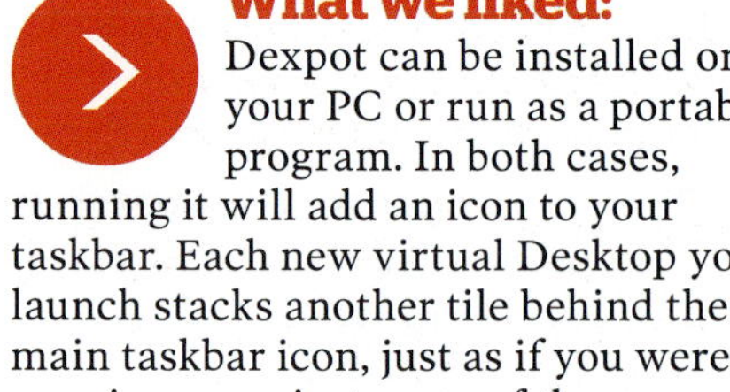

What we liked:

Dexpot can be installed on your PC or run as a portable program. In both cases, running it will add an icon to your taskbar. Each new virtual Desktop you launch stacks another tile behind the main taskbar icon, just as if you were opening more instances of the program. Hover over the taskbar icon and thumbnails of your Desktops appear, so you can see what's happening on each of them.

The software also installs an icon in the notification area. Right-clicking it provides access to a multitude of settings and tweaks that can be applied to one or all of the Desktops. You can have different screen resolutions and wallpapers, and do clever things such as turn off the taskbar and remove Desktop icons. You can also click the Start-Up tab to have certain tools available in specific Desktops when you launch them.

There are also sophisticated tools that let you add rules, so if a specific event occurs (such as the launching of a particular program) you can set Dexpot to perform a task (such as moving it to a particular Desktop).

Dexpot can run up to 20 different Desktops if your PC can handle them, though it defaults to a manageable four. Specific applications can be permanently pinned to one particular Desktop, so you always know where they are.

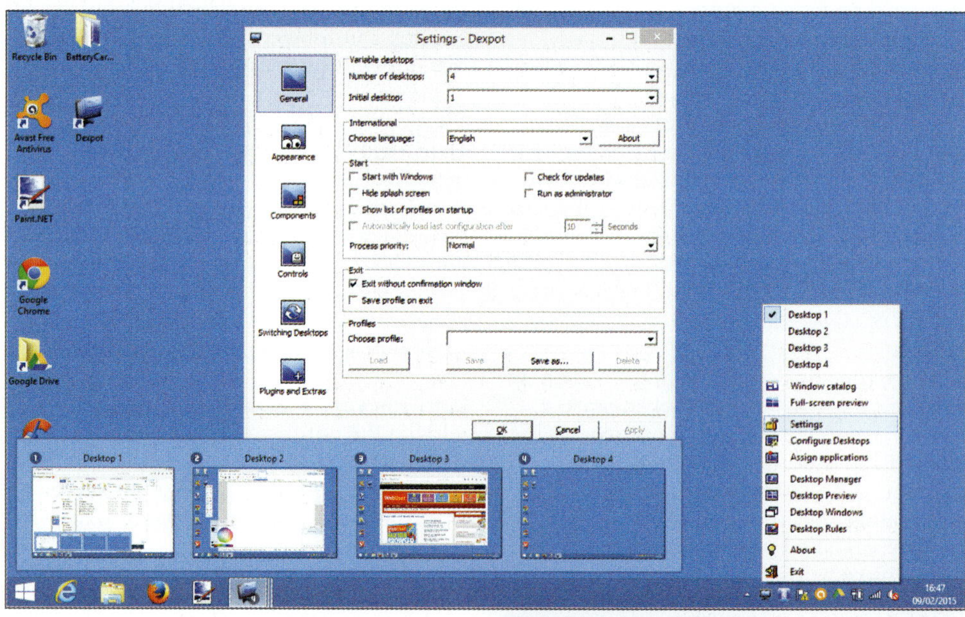

The range of Dexpot's tools sounds overwhelming, but most of the options are tucked away in menus so the basic program is kept easy to use.

How it can be improved:

The installable version bundles a PUP (Potentially Unwanted Program) with its installer. Dexpot is very upfront about it and it's easy to deselect to avoid, but it could still catch out the unwary.

OUR VERDICT

Dexpot is by far the most sophisticated program reviewed here. However, it manages to provide a huge range of tools without being over-complicated

Desktops | bit.ly/desktops365 | ★★★★☆

FEATURES ★★☆☆☆ **PERFORMANCE** ★★★★★ **EASE OF USE** ★★★★★

What we liked:

Sysinternals Desktops is almost the opposite of Dexpot, because it's tiny and has very limited features. The program is completely portable, so you can't install it, even if you want to. When you first launch Desktops, you can choose whether you want the software to start every time you launch Windows, and select a keyboard shortcut to switch between its four Desktops. You can also click the icon in the notification area to see a preview of all your Desktops and choose between them.

The Desktops are only created when you start using them, so the first time you switch to a new Desktop, the screen will go blank. However, once it's launched you can seamlessly flick between the Desktops you're using. There's also an option you can access from the icon in the notification area that shows you thumbnail previews of the Desktops, which you can click to select.

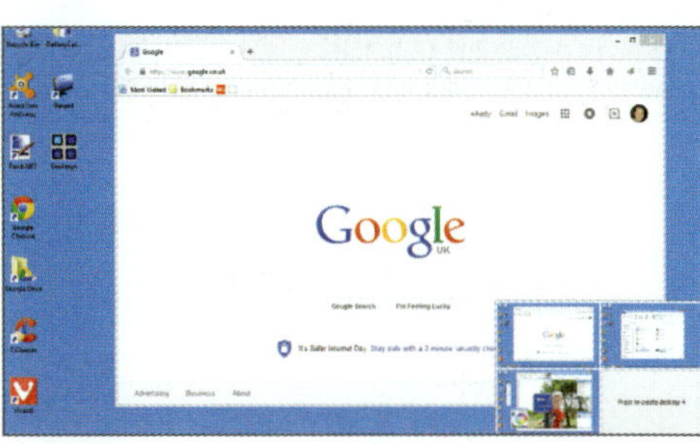

How it can be improved:

We found Desktops erratic in Windows 8.1: the Start button only worked in the first Desktop, though we could open it on the second. However, anything launched from it would open back on Desktop 1.

OUR VERDICT
Desktops is a bit limited and doesn't have anything like the number of tools that Dexpot has. However, it's very compact and if all you want to do is run programs in virtual Desktops, it's an excellent option.

Virtual Dimension | bit.ly/virtual365 | ★★★★☆

FEATURES ★★★☆☆ **PERFORMANCE** ★★★★☆ **EASE OF USE** ★★★★★

What we liked:

Virtual Dimension doesn't appear to have been updated since 2005 but it's still surprisingly capable. It isn't as slick as even the least sophisticated rivals we've reviewed here, but what it lacks in flashy tricks it makes up for in useful, useable tools.

Rather than displaying a full preview thumbnail of each Desktop, like Dexpot and Desktops do, it uses a small box containing program icons. Although this doesn't look as attractive, it's much clearer at showing which programs are open in each Desktop.

It also means that you can perform clever functions such as dragging individual program icons from one Desktop thumbnail to another, which makes moving them around simpler than in most of the other virtual-Desktop software. You can also right-click the program icons for special options.

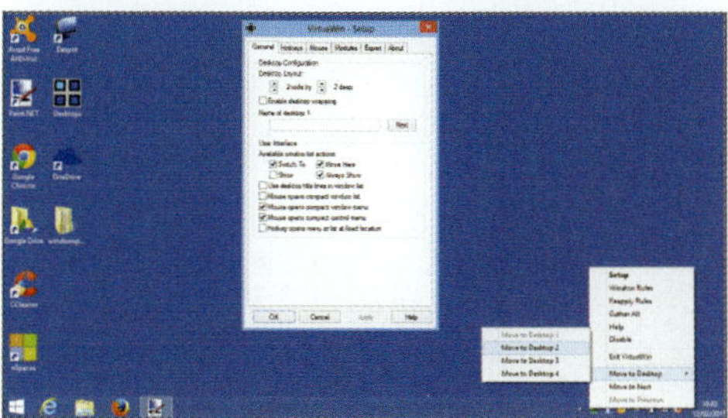

How it can be improved:

Virtual Dimension starts numbering Desktops at zero, rather than one, which we found confusing.

OUR VERDICT
This is an old program and it certainly looks it. However, it works surprisingly well, and some aspects of the old-fashioned interface, such as using program icons instead of full preview thumbnails, actually provide it with extra tools that are missing from the other, newer programs.

BEST OF THE REST

VirtuaWin

virtuawin.sourceforge.net

VirtuaWin offers up to nine Desktops and has a good selection of tools, with add-ons that provide access to even more. Navigation between Desktops is simple and effective: hold down Alt+Control and press the cursor keys to rotate through them. However, configuration is made complex because although the program uses a straight-forward Windows menu system, there's too much text and too many tick boxes.

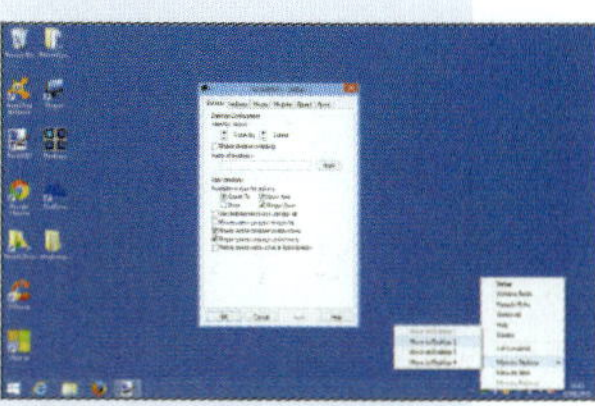

WindowsPager

windowspager.sourceforge.net

WindowsPager worked fine when we tested it in Windows 7, but it won't work with Windows 8 or above. Thumbnails for its four Desktops integrate into the taskbar, sitting to the left of the notification area. Rather cleverly, you can move programs from one Desktop to another by right-clicking the relevant title bar. It was only the lack of Windows 8 support that stopped this simple program getting an award.

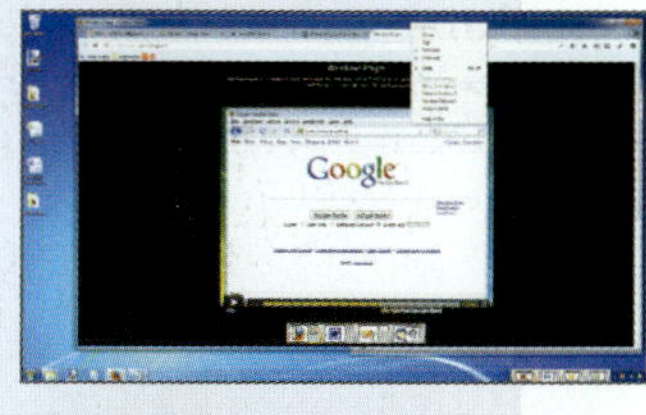

nSpaces

www.bytesignals.com/nspaces

Switching to a new nSpaces Desktop takes you to a blank screen with only the Start button still present – all your Desktop icons and pinned Taskbar programs are left behind. However, you can have a different wallpaper on each Desktop to easily tell them apart. We found that nSpaces worked in Windows 8, but not particularly well. It also relies on keyboard shortcuts to perform tasks, which you have to learn in order to use the program efficiently.

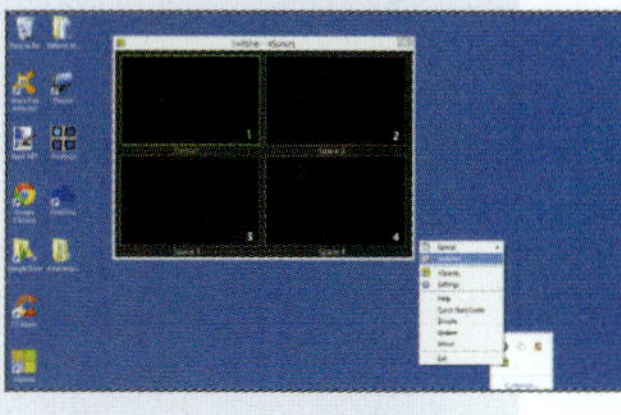

Chapter 4

Great software for the Office

We all need to get down to work at some point. In this chapter, we reveal the best free productivity tools and explain how to use them

When you think of business software, you think of expensive suites from companies such as Microsoft. However, there's plenty of great free office software out there, which will help you to word process documents, plug numbers into spreadsheets, make compelling presentations and much more. This chapter also covers some features that you don't find in traditional "office" packages, such as making free telephone calls, managing your personal finances and signing electronic documents. Enough talk – it's time to get down to work!

CONTENT

Best free office suites

Why pay for Microsoft Office when you can get a powerful, full-featured office suite for free? We review six of the best options

LibreOffice | www.libreoffice.org | ★★★★★

FEATURES ★★★★★ PERFORMANCE ★★★★☆ EASE OF USE ★★★★☆

What we liked:

LibreOffice gives you the feeling that you're using a proper, professional product that's comparable to Microsoft Office, but completely free. It has much of the same look and feel (especially if you prefer the pre-2007 version of Office, without the ribbon bar) and many of the same functions; useful as they are, none of the other office suites we've reviewed comes close. The standard download includes seven tools - Writer, Calc, Impress, Draw, Base, Math and Charts – while FreeOffice and WPS Office only offer word-processing, spreadsheet and presentation programs. Interoperability with Microsoft Office is generally good across all the modules, so you shouldn't experience any problems opening files.

LibreOffice makes extensive use of its Sidebar to compensate for the lack of a ribbon and here you'll find formatting options and other useful tools. Arranging the screen like this makes perfect sense and makes better use of space than FreeOffice's equivalent, which is mainly used for tips and to promote its paid-for version.

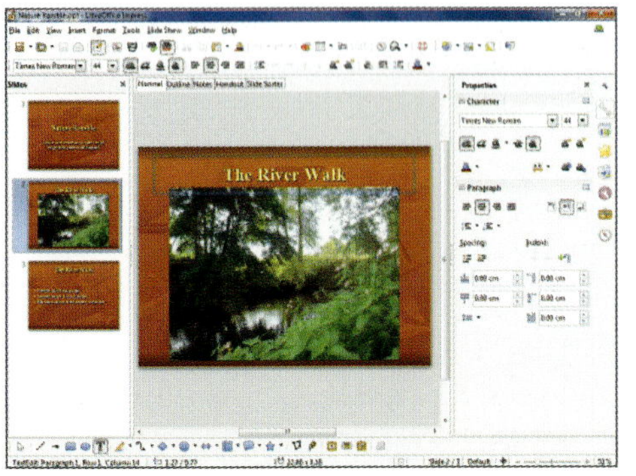

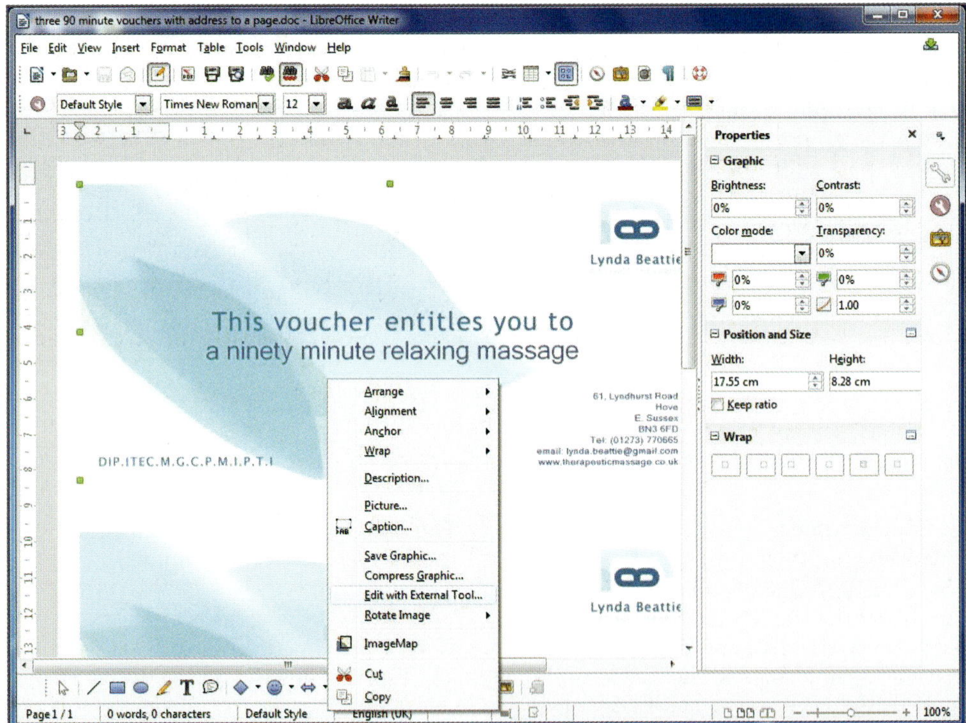

The interface is consistent across all programs in the suite; many of your favourite Microsoft Office keyboard shortcuts work just fine; and we also liked the Carlito and Caladea fonts, which are designed to mimic Office's default fonts, Calibri and Cambria.

How it can be improved:

The developers need to keep on top of Microsoft Office file formats and although copyright restrictions prevent LibreOffice from copying Office's ribbon, we'd prefer its interface to have a flatter, more modern look.

OUR VERDICT

Despite the occasional compatibility problems with complex documents, spreadsheets, presentations and databases, LibreOffice is a remarkable piece of work that stands toe-to-toe with Microsoft Office any day.

WPS Office Free | bit.ly/wpsoffice369 | ★★★★☆

FEATURES ★★★★☆ **PERFORMANCE** ★★★★☆ **EASE OF USE** ★★★★☆

What we liked:

WPS Office's Metro-style interface makes you feel like you're using software that's up to date and cared-for. It has a good level of Microsoft Office compatibility (although creators of complex documents who swap files back and forth may experience some problems) and it's fast.

We particularly liked the Skin Management feature, which lets you change the look and feel of WPS Office with a single mouse click, and the selection of templates. These include attractive and useful document layouts, as well as good starting points for presentations and spreadsheets. There's also a paragraph-formatting control that lets you adjust indentations and spacing by dragging the highlighted edges with your mouse pointer.

WPS Office's spreadsheet supports over one million rows and 16,000 columns, while its presentation tool offers more than 50 transition styles and handles PowerPoint presentations.

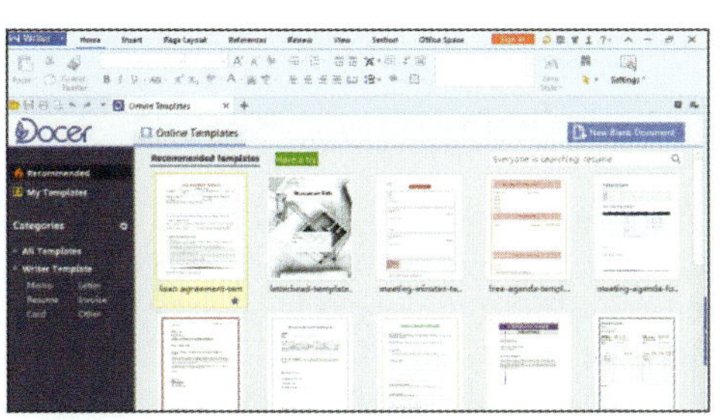

How it can be improved:

The latest version (www.wps.com) forces you to download the Premium Edition that reverts to the free version after 30 days, so we've reviewed an older version.

OUR VERDICT
Although it can't compete with LibreOffice in terms of features, WPS Office has a smart interface, good compatibility with Microsoft Office and useful templates.

SoftMaker FreeOffice | www.freeoffice.com | ★★★★☆

FEATURES ★★★★☆ **PERFORMANCE** ★★★★☆ **EASE OF USE** ★★★★☆

What we liked:

As with WPS Office, SoftMaker provides a word processor, spreadsheet and presentation tool, but while it lacks the same good looks and configurable interface, its familiar 'Office 2003'-style layout makes it very easy to find your way around.

Unlike LibreOffice, there's no unified 'dashboard', but no matter which program you're working in, the other two can be accessed directly from the toolbar. There are neat touches elsewhere as well, including a 'Save As PDF' icon on the toolbar and a continuous page view which is useful for browsing long documents. Compatibility with Office is generally good and, like the other suites reviewed here, FreeOffice will open password-protected documents and spreadsheets, has a decent mail-merge tool and offers a 'master styles' feature in the presentation program that's as easy to use as the one in PowerPoint.

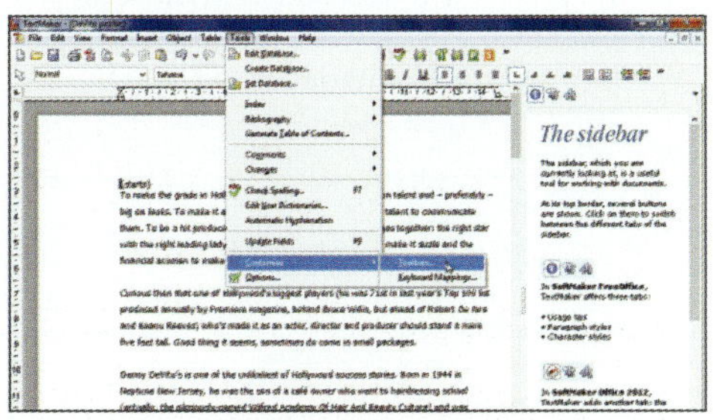

How it can be improved:

You have to sign up with a valid email address to get your licence code, which seems unnecessary for a free program. Conditional formatting created in Excel sometimes gets lost and the word processor needs a grammar checker.

OUR VERDICT
This is a solid Microsoft Office alternative for people who only need word processing, spreadsheet and presentation tools, but it lacks the visual pizzazz of WPS Office.

BEST OF THE REST

Apache OpenOffice

www.openoffice.org

We've only omitted OpenOffice from the top three because it's so similar to LibreOffice, with which it shares a tortuous history (they originate from the same suite). Although in many ways it's still the same product, LibreOffice is updated much more frequently these days and OpenOffice is beginning to fall behind. However, it remains a great free office suite.

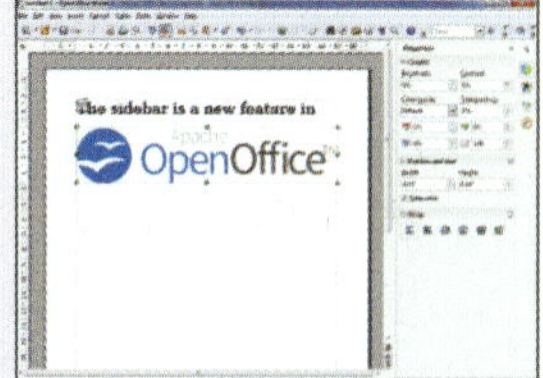

SSuite Excalibur

www.ssuitesoft.com

This suite offers a word processor and spreadsheet (with a few bolt-ons), but offers precious little compatibility with Microsoft Office. However, it reads and writes RTF and XLS files, as well as offering its own proprietary formats. It's worth looking at if all you need is a word processor and spreadsheet combo – wear your sunglasses, though, as the interface is rather garish.

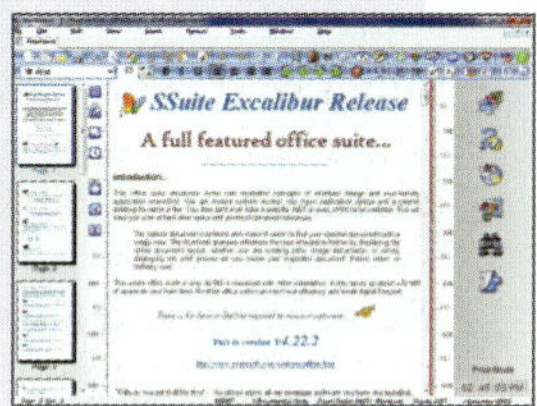

Calligra

www.calligra.org

Probably thanks to its origins in the Linux world, Calligra's the wackiest suite of the bunch. You get Braindump (mind-mapping), Flow (diagrams and flowcharts), Karbon (vector illustrations), Kexi (database), Krita (painting), Plan (project management), Stage (presentations), Sheets (spreadsheet) and Words (word processing) – everything you get with LibreOffice plus a couple of extras. Sadly, Office compatibility is uneven (especially with password-protected files) and performance is a bit sluggish. There's plenty of bang-for-no-bucks, though, and an unusual interface that makes good use of the sidebar.

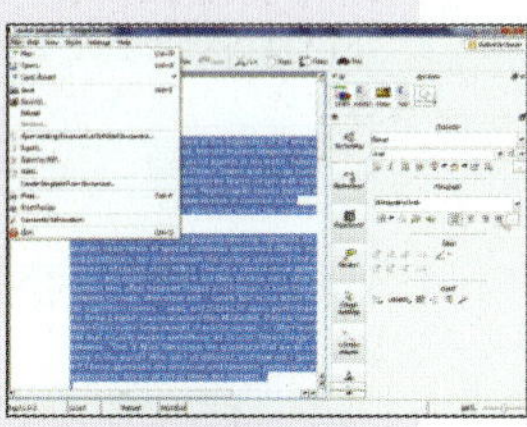

Use LibreOffice's new tools

As good as Microsoft Office is, its Home and Student edition is restricted to a single PC, while Office 365 requires that you sign-up to an annual subscription. LibreOffice (www.libreoffice.org) is an excellent free alternative that's evolved from the same code as the OpenOffice suite. It comprises six applications: Writer (word processor); Calc (spreadsheet); Impress (presentation and slideshow creator); Draw (vector drawing program for creating diagrams and flow charts); Base (database); and Math (editor for mathematical equations). It's now been redesigned with several useful new features that make working with documents and spreadsheets even easier.

TOOLBARS
The Standard and Formatting toolbars have been reorganised with frequently used features replacing less commonly accessed commands

IMPROVED STATUS BAR
The status bar is now much easier to read. … is where you'll find w… counts, document positions and other d…

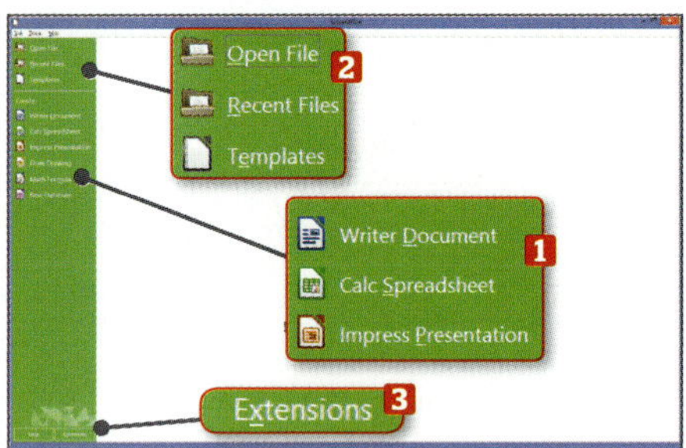

1 You can launch any of LibreOffice's modules through the Start menu, or open LibreOffice's own program menu and choose from the sidebar. **1** You can also open a file, browse recently saved files and explore templates. **2** Extensions **3** lets you add extra tools to the software.

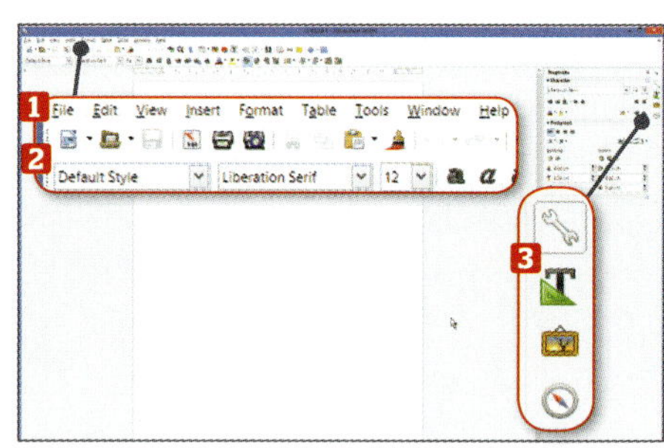

2 Writer, the word processor, is the main component of LibreOffice. If you've used it before, you'll see the interface has been given a makeover. There's a menu at the top, **1** with toolbars and buttons below. **2** On the right is a sidebar for its properties, styles and gallery. **3**

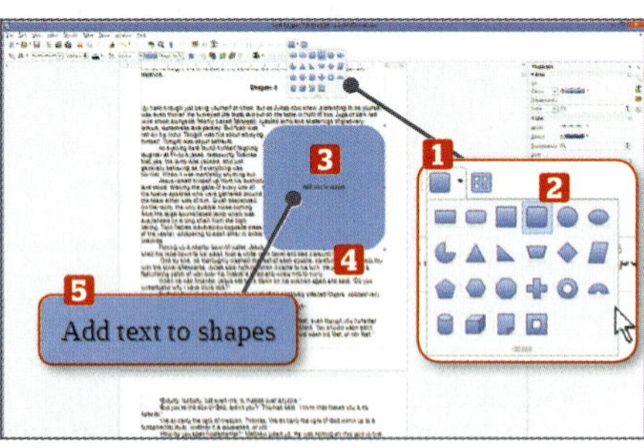

3 While it's been possible to add coloured shapes to documents for a while, LibreOffice now lets you add text to the shapes. Click the Basic Shapes button, **1** choose a shape **2** and draw it on to your document. **3** Make the corners rounded, if you like. **4** Double-click the shape to add your text. **5**

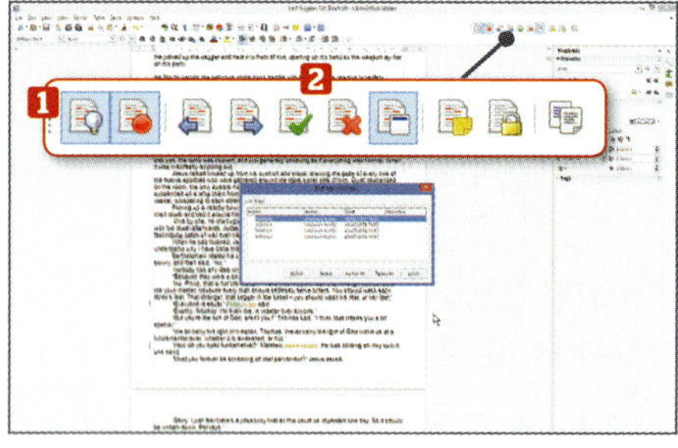

4 The Track Changes tool has new buttons and icons, **1** which you can select from View, Toolbars, Changes. The commands to accept and reject changes **2** jump to the next change automatically, so it's easy to work through a document with lots of alterations. This is especially useful if you collaborate on documents.

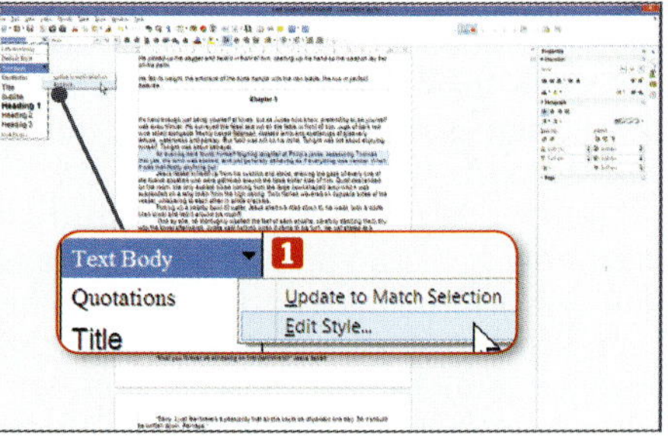

5 Document styling has been streamlined in the new release, so if you're pleased with a change you've made to a paragraph style, title or heading, you can quickly apply the same change to any other part of the document. Click the down arrow next to a style **1** to edit or update it to match the text you've highlighted on the page.

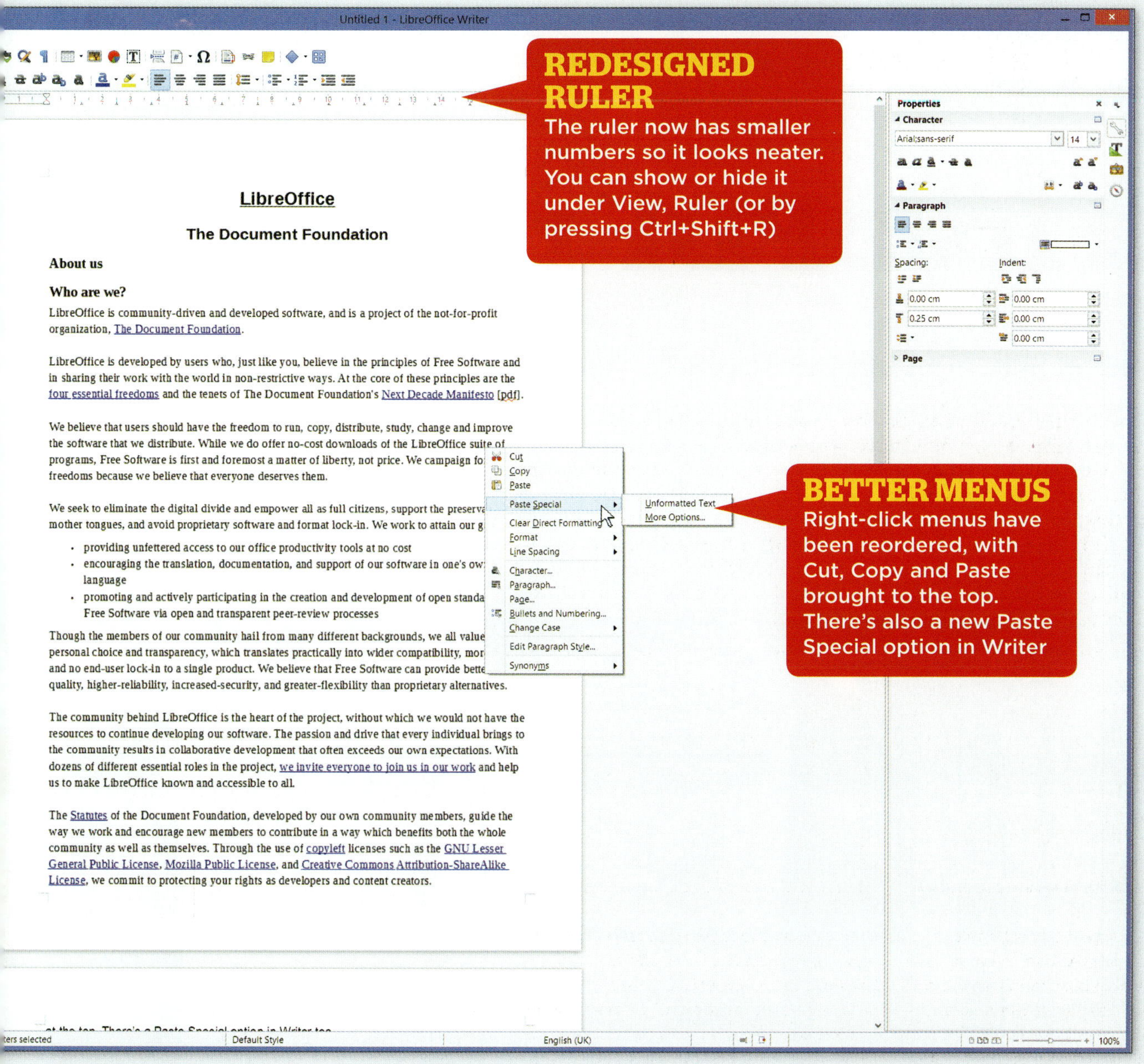

REDESIGNED RULER

The ruler now has smaller numbers so it looks neater. You can show or hide it under View, Ruler (or by pressing Ctrl+Shift+R)

BETTER MENUS

Right-click menus have been reordered, with Cut, Copy and Paste brought to the top. There's also a new Paste Special option in Writer

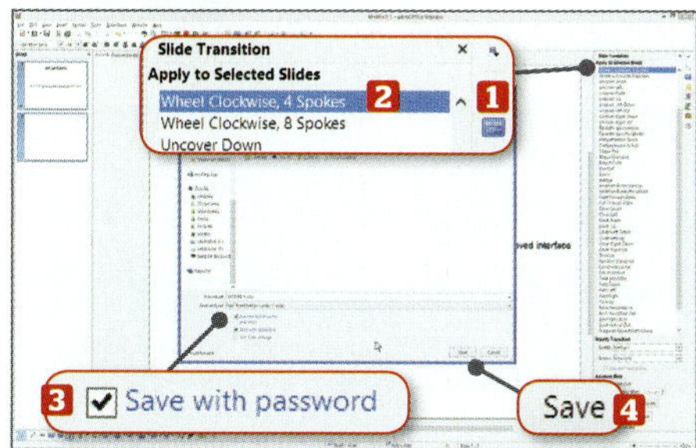

6 Impress now supports OpenGL (hardware-accelerated) transitions. Click the Slide Transitions button in the sidebar **1** to choose a type. **2** Slideshows can be password protected to prevent tampering. Go to File, Save As and tick 'Save with password'. **3** Click Save **4** and enter the password twice.

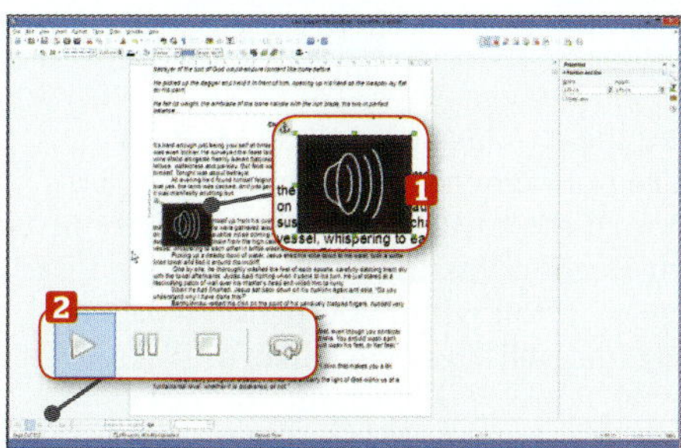

7 LibreOffice lets you add audio and video files to your documents and play them using the built-in media player. Go to Insert, Media, 'Audio or Video' and browse for a file. Click the media icon **1** and a player will appear below. **2** Version 4.4 supports a wide range of additional media types.

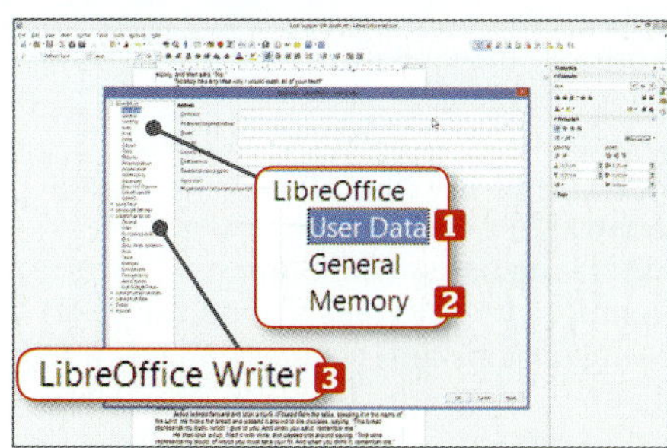

8 You can customise LibreOffice through the Options menu. Go to Tools, Options. Enter your information under User Data. **1** Use Memory **2** to manage the number of 'undo' steps and set LibreOffice to load at Windows start up. You can configure the word processor under LibreOffice Writer. **3**

Best free PDF readers

Adobe Reader is still most people's default PDF reader, but are there better alternatives available? We test five free competitors

Foxit Reader | bit.ly/foxit360 | ★★★★★

FEATURES ★★★★☆ **PERFORMANCE** ★★★★★ **EASE OF USE** ★★★★★

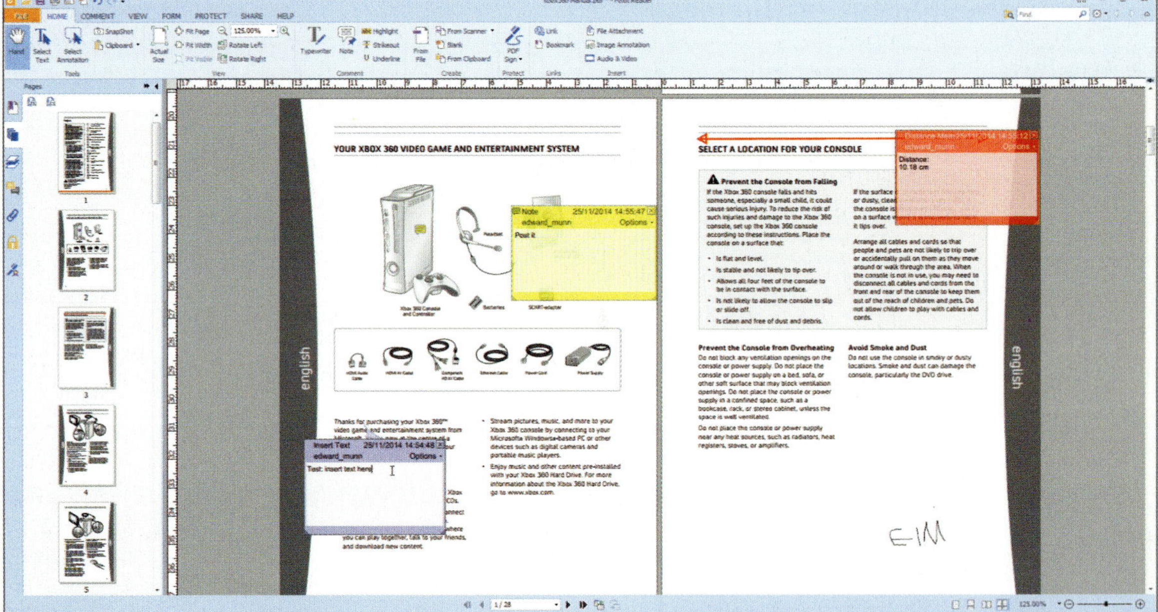

What we liked:

Foxit Reader has the best range of features of all the free PDF readers we tested. Its annotation tools are excellent, letting you attach notes or files to any section of a PDF or use the mark-up tools to indicate where text should be inserted, deleted or replaced. And when you've finished working on your PDF, you can use its helpful Summarise Comments option to create a PDF summary of all your annotations.

It doesn't have OCR (optical character recognition), which is PDF XChange Editor's (opposite page) best feature, but you can sign a form in your own handwriting using PDF Sign.

Foxit Reader provides a good range of viewing options and we particularly liked its Loupe and Magnifier tools, which let you enlarge a specific section of the layout without having to zoom in on the entire page. The Continuous Facing viewing mode, which displays the document as spreads rather than single pages, is particularly handy if you want to replicate a magazine layout or use the full width of a widescreen monitor.

The software's user interface is easy to use and you can customise the ribbon toolbar to suit your requirements, even reverting to Classic Toolbar Mode if you're not keen on the ribbon style.

One of the things we most liked about Foxit Reader was that it appears as a PDF Printer option when you print in other programs, which is very useful if you want to convert documents to PDFs quickly and easily. If you're working with drawings or plans, the program's Measure tools and Rulers will also come in handy.

How it can be improved:

The addition of OCR and security tools (such as document encryption) would make Foxit a more complete PDF reader. Users of eBook readers might also appreciate ePub and Mobi file compatibility, too.

OUR VERDICT

Foxit Reader's wide range of features and easy-to-use interface make it the perfect tool for reading and annotating PDFs. However, it lacks some of the more advanced tools offered by PDF XChange Editor.

PDF XChange Editor | bit.ly/xchange360 | ★★★★☆

FEATURES ★★★★☆ **PERFORMANCE** ★★★★★ **EASE OF USE** ★★★★☆

What we liked:

PDF XChange Editor's standout feature is undoubtedly its optical character recognition (OCR). This handy built-in tool lets you turn image-based PDFs into files with selectable text, which is useful if you need to annotate, search or copy text from a scanned document.

This was the only PDF editor we tested, and it includes editing features that aren't available in the other programs in this test, such as the Edit Content tool, which lets you change a file's text. You can try PDF XChange Editors' more advanced editing tools, but your documents will be marked with a DEMO stamp unless you buy the Pro version for $43.50 (around £28).

Like Foxit Reader, the annotation tools are easy to use, if a little less advanced. We were pleased to find that the Summarize Comments function was available when we tested it, despite being listed as a Pro-only feature on the program's website. PDF XChange Editor's security options will also appeal to those who want to password protect their documents.

How it can be improved:

PDF XChange Editor's interface is cluttered with features that are only available when you upgrade to the Pro version of the software. Unlike Foxit Reader, you can't use the program as a PDF printer and the option to add a signature to a document is only available when you buy a licence.

OUR VERDICT

PDF XChange Editor has plenty of standout features, including optical character recognition, but its interface is cluttered with locked Pro tools and it lacks some of the more basic functions that make Foxit Reader a better program for everyday use.

Adobe Reader | get.adobe.com/uk/reader | ★★★★☆

FEATURES ★★★☆☆ **PERFORMANCE** ★★★★☆ **EASE OF USE** ★★★★★

What we liked:

Adobe Reader's annotation tools are as good as those of Foxit Reader. Whether you simply want to add sticky notes to your PDF or you need to mark up detailed text corrections, this program is perfect for the job. You can even attach a file or audio recording to your PDF.

It doesn't have as many features as some of its rivals, but this means it has one of the simplest interfaces of all the software we tested. The toolbar contains only the most important features, while others can be selected from three sidebar tabs. Like Foxit Reader, Adobe Reader lets you add a signature to forms and there's even an option to collect someone else's signature using the Adobe EchoSign service.

How it can be improved:

Adobe Reader lacks some of the tools of our two top scorers and, like PDF Xchange Editor, some tools can only be unlocked if you pay. We also didn't like the installation file being packaged with McAfee Security Scan Plus, which could clash with other security software.

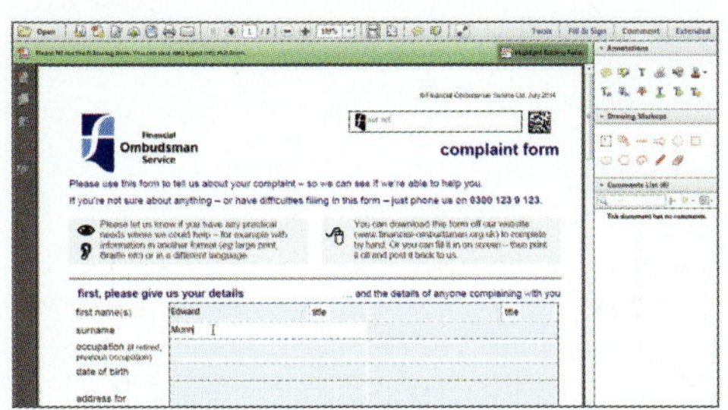

OUR VERDICT

Adobe Reader is good, reliable software for viewing and annotating PDFs. However, its features come up short when compared to Foxit Reader and XChange PDF Editor.

BEST OF THE REST

Nitro Reader 3

www.gonitro.com/pdf-reader

Nitro Reader is a simple, easy-to-use PDF reader that offers tabbed viewing and basic annotation tools. Like Foxit Reader, you can use it to convert files to PDFs and to sign your documents. There's even a handy Getting Started dialogue when you launch the program to help you grasp its important features. Unfortunately, its annotation tools are basic.

Google Chrome

www.google.co.uk/chrome

Chrome has its own built-in PDF reader that is enabled by default. It's very useful if you want to read documents without installing any other software. You can save, search and print PDFs using the browser, and it will also let you fill in forms. However, there are no options to annotate PDFs or convert files.

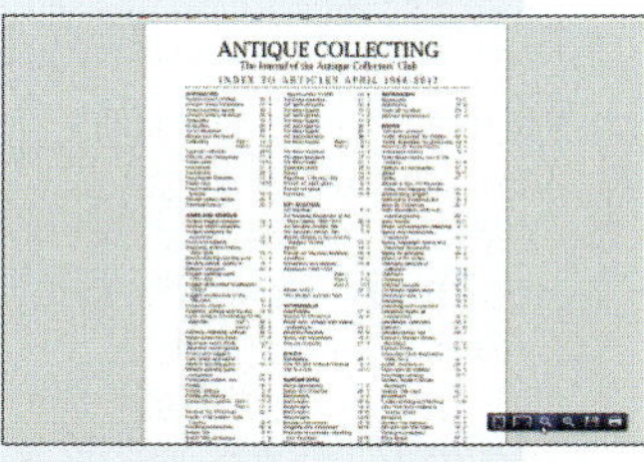

Sumatra PDF

bit.ly/sumatrapdf360

Sumatra's unique selling point is that it lets you view ePub and Kindle files as well as PDFs. Indeed, its good range of viewing options and handy search function make it perfect for reading digital books on your PC. The developer also provides a portable version of the program, which is useful if you want to read PDFs on a PC without installing any software. However, Sumatra is very short on other features and it was the only program we tested that doesn't let you fill in forms.

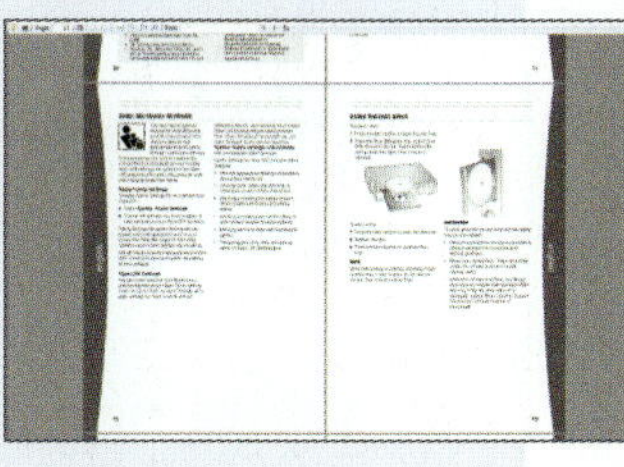

Manage your finances for free

There's plenty of software out there to help you keep your finances in good order. We round-up the pick of the free packages

Nobody enjoys the annual post-Christmas comedown of filling in your tax return. Tackling the taxman's unreliable website is bad enough, and worse still if your financial records are nothing more than mere scraps of paper. It all snaps into sharp relief, when having paid your tax bill, you head online to find out exactly how much money is left in your bank account.

At which point, you can either cross your fingers and hope you've got enough to get by, or take control of your budget using personal-finance software. Quicken (www.quicken.com) and Microsoft Money (MSM) used to be the programs of choice for balancing household books, but neither program is now supported in the UK. Microsoft offers a workaround if you still want to use MSM (see box opposite), but there are better, newer options.

A quick Google search for personal-finance software will throw up some great paid-for programs, such as AceMoney (www.snipca.com/15636, $39.99/£27) and You Need A Budget (www.youneedabudget.com, $60/£40). But if you're really cash-savvy, you'll use free software that's just as good.

Be your own accountant

Open-source program GnuCash (www.snipca.com/15625) is the closest thing to Quicken and MSM, and it's completely free. It's the best choice for those with lots of accounts to juggle: bank accounts, savings, pensions, insurance and so on. In fact, it's so powerful than many small businesses rely on it.

You can see multiple accounts in one window, generate a detailed balance sheet, see your cashflow represented in chart form, and export a valuation of your stocks, shares and other investments.

Like MSM, GnuCash supports OFX (Open Financial Exchange) files, which many banks use to store your bank-account data. You can download the files securely via your bank's website and import them into GnuCash, which saves you having to type in all your transaction history manually. Check with your bank whether you can download your data this way. Barclays, for example, does support OFX files, but it calls them 'Microsoft Money files': www.snipca.com/15627). GnuCash has a whole wiki site dedicated to explaining OFX (www.snipca.com/15626). You can also import your old Quicken files (QIF) into GnuCash.

We had a spot of bother installing GnuCash at first, but we got round it by choosing 'Full installation' (default) during setup. Normally, we'd recommend carrying out a 'Custom installation', but this stopped the program installing properly. 'Full installation' went ahead without a hitch, and there were no unwanted extras to opt out of. If you prefer to avoid installing it altogether, there is a portable version of GnuCash (www.snipca.com/15629).

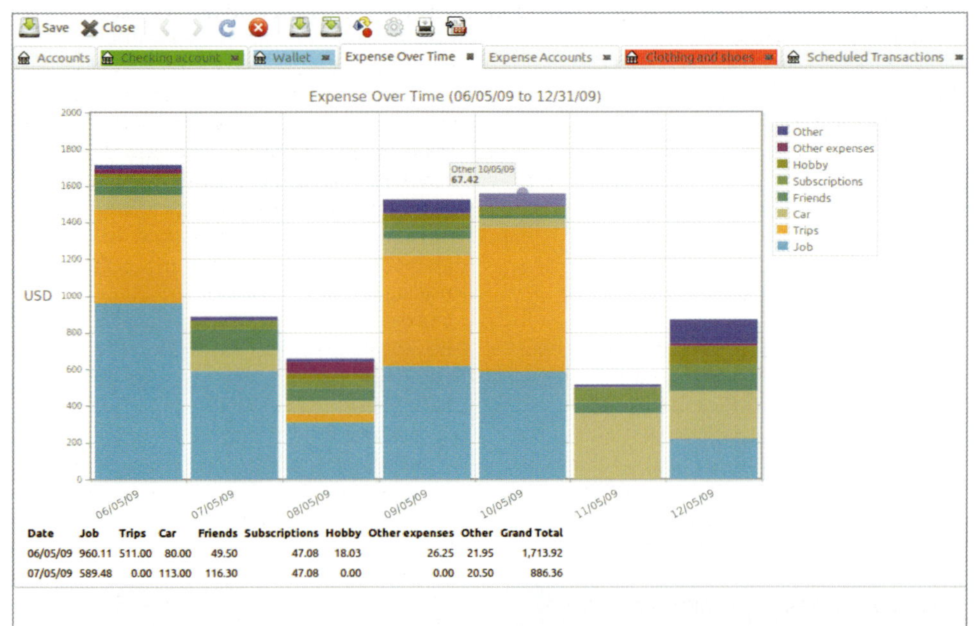

Track your accounts and expenses in detail with GnuCash

Plan your monthly spending

GnuCash may be a powerful tool but it's also rather complex – too complex if all you want is to keep an eye on your

RENEW YOUR OLD MICROSOFT MONEY

Microsoft Money (MSM) is to personal-finance software what Windows XP is to operating systems: long-established and well-loved, but no longer supported by Microsoft. There's been no new version since Money 2006 (despite a campaign by our sister title PC Pro magazine: www.snipca.com/15652), and Microsoft withdrew support in 2009. So if you have an old version of MSM on your PC, you can't run it safely. Given that it was a paid-for program, you'd be justified in thinking that Money was a waste of money.

But there may be life in your old MSM data yet. In 2010, Microsoft released the free program Money Plus Deluxe Sunset (www.snipca.com/15658), which lets you open, convert and manage most old MSM files, as well as QIF (Quicken) files.

Initially, MSM Sunset only worked in the US, but we gave it a try and it seems to work fine here. Download and run the installer, accept the licence agreement (which is free) and sign up using your Microsoft account or with a new password.

MSM Sunset can be used as a standalone program too, but we wouldn't recommend it. There's no support and its future is uncertain. If you want to start managing your cash from scratch, use GnuCash or BudgetSimple instead.

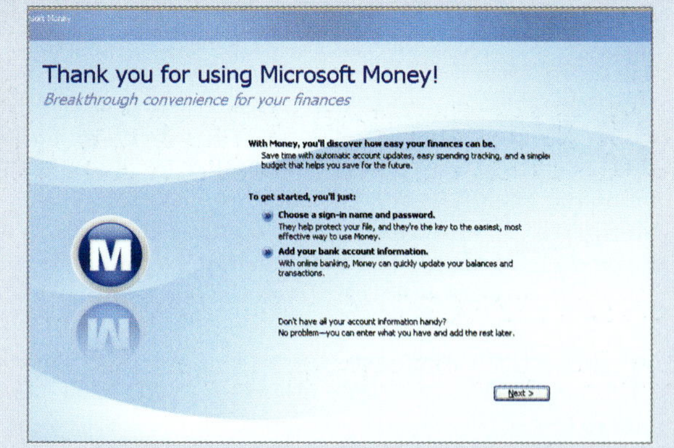

Microsoft Money Deluxe Sunset lets you access your old Microsoft Money data

monthly outgoings. For basic cash control, we recommend BudgetSimple (https//www.budgetsimple.com), which lives up to its name with a wonderfully fast and easy free web-based tool that doesn't require any downloads at all.

Start by creating a free account. Click Register at the top right, choose a password, then click through the welcome screens until you reach a comparison table of the tool's free and paid-for versions. Click Get Started under 'Basic free'. (Even if you wanted to use the paid-for Plus Account, you can't – it's US-only.)

You're then walked through a setup process. This simply involves typing in your sources of income and expenditure, broken down into bills, groceries, savings, phone contract and so on. You can edit these categories to suit your needs. Anything you type into BudgetSimple is encrypted (hence the 's' in the 'https' URL prefix), so no one, including people who work at the website, can read anything you type or see.

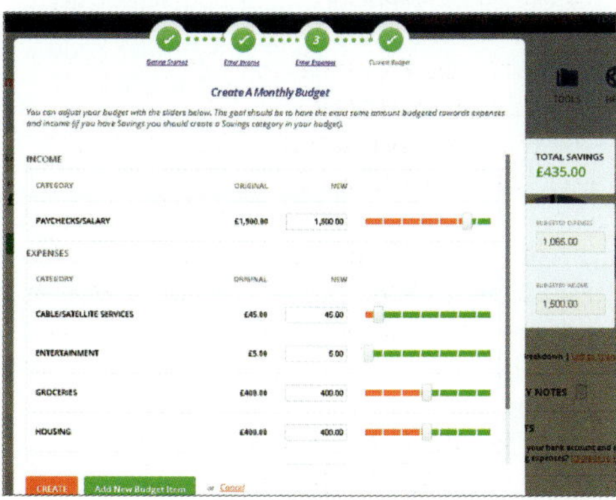

Balance your books at a glance using BudgetSimple's free online planner

Once you've entered your figures (which you can amend later), the tool works out how much you've got left to spend (or how much you're over-spending) and displays it as a bar chart and pie chart, so you can instantly see your balance.

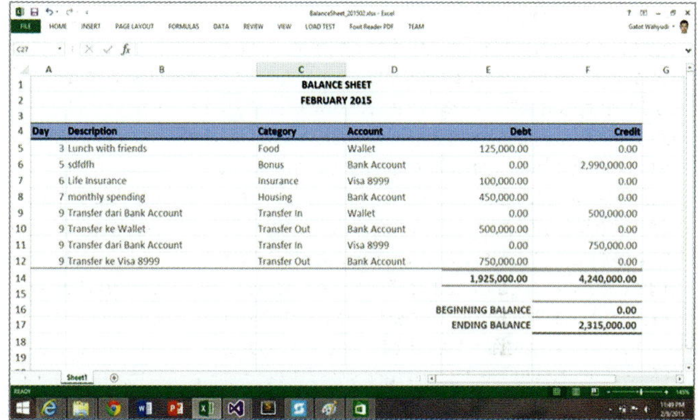

BALANCE SHEET
FEBRUARY 2015

Day	Description	Category	Account	Debt	Credit
3	Lunch with friends	Food	Wallet	125,000.00	0.00
5	sdfdfh	Bonus	Bank Account	0.00	2,990,000.00
6	Life Insurance	Insurance	Visa 8999	100,000.00	0.00
7	monthly spending	Housing	Bank Account	450,000.00	0.00
9	Transfer dari Bank Account	Transfer In	Wallet	0.00	500,000.00
9	Transfer ke Wallet	Transfer Out	Bank Account	500,000.00	0.00
9	Transfer dari Bank Account	Transfer In	Visa 8999	0.00	750,000.00
9	Transfer ke Visa 8999	Transfer Out	Bank Account	750,000.00	0.00
				1,925,000.00	4,240,000.00
				BEGINNING BALANCE	0.00
				ENDING BALANCE	2,315,000.00

Export your balance sheet to Excel using Windows 8.1 app Selffina

We love the fact that, even though BudgetSimple is US-based, it displays your accounts in pounds rather than dollars if you're a UK user.

The site also has tools for helping you save money for specific projects (for instance, a long holiday or home improvements) or managing a debt (for example, a credit card or mortgage).

Back up your budget online

Free new Windows 8.1 app Selffina (www.snipca.com/15618) lies somewhere between GnuCash and BudgetSimple in terms of its complexity. You can keep it simple by just using it to plan your spending, or set it up to track various accounts, credit cards, transfers and investments.

Either way, all your data is password-protected and can be exported to Excel as a backup. You can also link your account securely with OneDrive, so all your plans and transactions are backed up securely in your cloud storage (for tips on getting the best out of OneDrive, see page 45). Selffina also works on Windows Phone but not, as yet, on Android or iOS.

If you want to manage your cash on your tablet or phone, your best bet is to use a secure web-based tool like BudgetSimple. There are plenty of free mobile money-management apps, but their functions are very limited unless you link them to their paid-for Windows counterparts. If you do decide to spend money on a program that syncs between your PC, tablet and phone, You Need A Budget is the best option (Android www.snipca.com/15650; iOS www.snipca.com/15651), and it has a very helpful website (www.youneedabudget.com/support).

Make free video calls in Firefox

When it comes to video-calling, there are plenty of options. While Skype is popular, we know from your emails to Problems Solved that it's not perfect. If you want an alternative, the Firefox browser comes with a new feature called Firefox Hello, which lets you make free video calls directly from your browser. You don't need to install anything, you can start chatting without an account, and it even lets you make video calls to mobile devices. The person you're calling can receive the call in Firefox, Chrome or Opera browsers (Internet Explorer and Safari are not supported).

1 To use Firefox Hello, you need to be running Firefox 35 or later. To install this, go to www.snipca.com/15112, click the green Free Download button and follow the instructions. If you already have Firefox, update it by clicking the menu button at the top right **1**, the Help menu **2**, then About Firefox. You'll see a pop-up window that will update Firefox, then restart it if necessary.

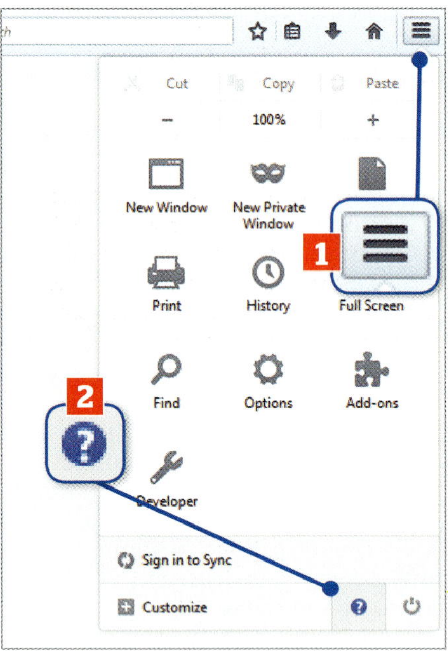

2 Next, you need to add Hello to your browser. We'll add it to the extensions toolbar (at the top right beside your search bar). Click the menu button (three lines), then Customize at the bottom. You'll see an 'Additional Tools and Features' page **1** with several options, including Hello (a smiley face icon). Click and drag that icon to the Firefox extensions toolbar **2**, then click Exit Customize **3**.

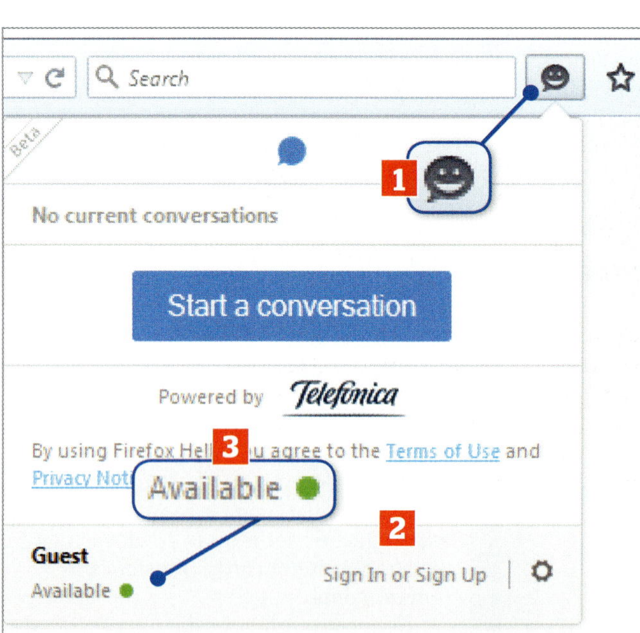

3 To start using Hello, click its icon **1**, then Get Started. You can begin video calling immediately by clicking the blue 'Start a conversation' button. If you prefer to log into your Firefox account first, click Sign In or Sign Up **2** and follow the instructions. Your email address will now appear at the bottom, above your status. You can change your status by clicking Available **3** and selecting Do Not Disturb.

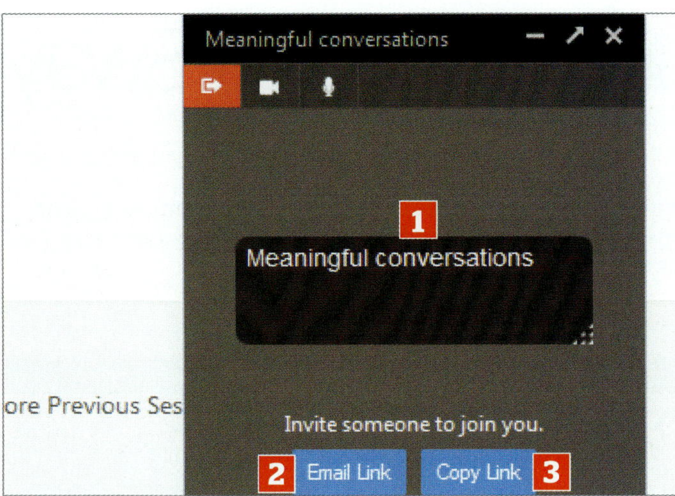

4 Next, grant Firefox permission to access your webcam and microphone. A small video-call window will then appear at the bottom right of Firefox. Type a description of your call in the 'Name this conversation' box 1 if you want. Next, click Email Link 2 to open a pre-written email containing the link to your video call and send this to whoever you want. Click Copy Link 3 to copy the video-call link to your clipboard from where you can paste and send it to anyone – using another email account, for example, or by posting it on Facebook.

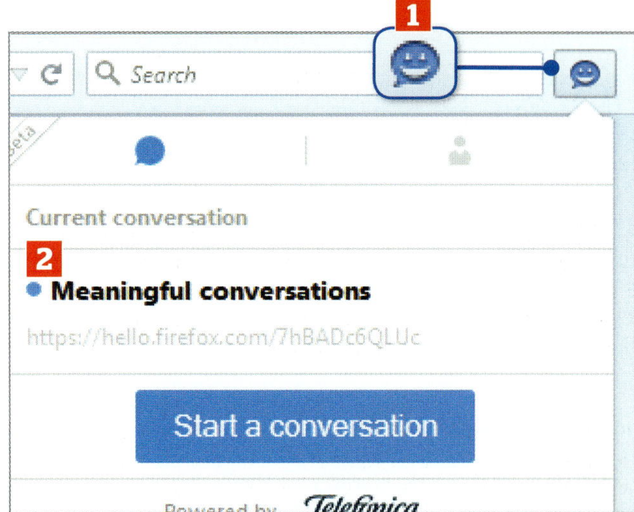

5 Once you've sent the link, wait until the recipient clicks it. It will work as long as they use Firefox, Chrome or Opera (on mobile or PC). While waiting, you can either click the Hello icon and launch more calls or browse the web. When your contact clicks the link, they'll be taken to your video-call window, where they need to click 'Join the conversation'. If you closed your video-call window, the Hello icon will turn blue 1 to let you know someone's calling. Click the icon, then the conversation with the blue circle next to it 2.

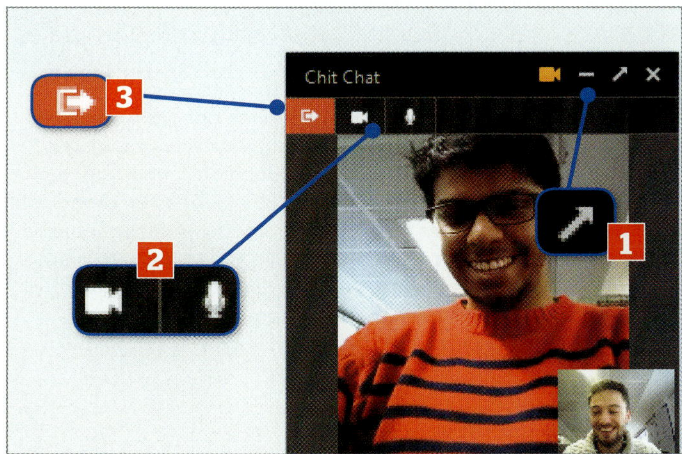

6 You can now begin chatting with your contact (this will be a voice-only call if neither of you has a webcam). You'll need to control your speaker and microphone volume via your PC because there are no settings to do this within Hello. To make your video-call window full screen, click the diagonal arrow 1. To stop your camera or mute your microphone, click the relevant icons 2. Click the red icon 3 to terminate your call.

7 Every call link is saved as a 'conversation' in Hello. Just click it to start another call with your friend. If you want to delete a link, move your cursor over it, then click the red trashcan icon 1. Click the blue icon 2 to copy a link (which you can email to more people). The contact icon 3 lets you import contacts from your Gmail account or add new contacts using their names and email addresses.

Make presentations using Microsoft Sway

Sway is the new free, online tool from Microsoft that lets you create scrolling presentations (called 'sways'). While PowerPoint offers a wide range of options, Sway's focus is on simplicity. You can add text, images, captions and files from your PC and arrange them as you like. Initially launched as an invite-only service, Sway can now be used by anyone with a Microsoft account. It's also available on iOS (www.snipca.com/15040), with an Android app coming soon.

1 Go to www.sway.com, click the green 'Get started!' button and log in with your Microsoft account. Next, click Create New at the top right to begin creating your first presentation (sway). Click 'Title your Sway' and name it **1**. You can bold up words in your title by highlighting them and clicking Emphasize **2**. A preview of your title will appear below. Click anywhere on the right-hand side of your page **3** to see how this will appear in your presentation. To switch back to your editing view, click the Storyline arrow at the top-left.

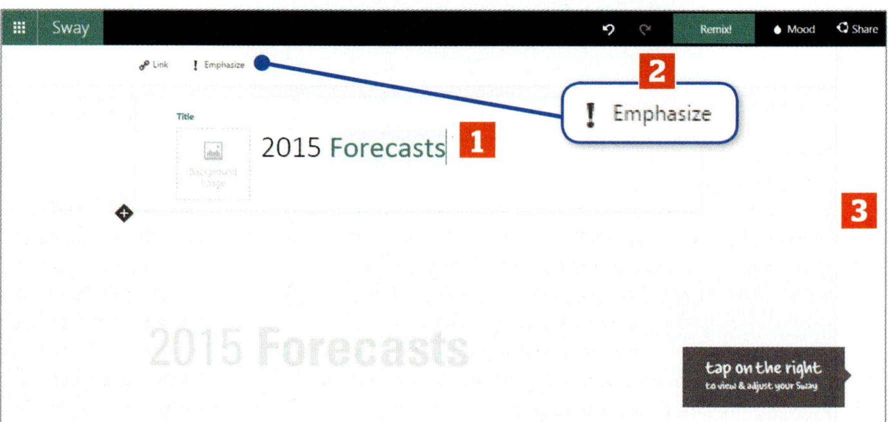

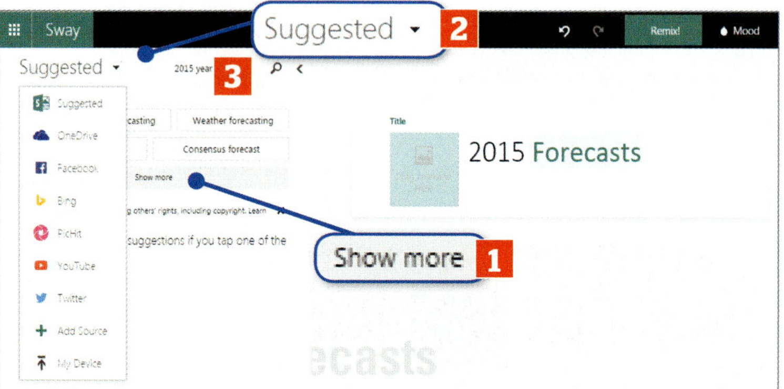

2 To add a background image to your title, click the Background Image box. A panel with options will slide in from the left with suggestions, by Bing, with relevant images you can click. If none of the suggestions match what you're looking for, click 'Show more' **1**. Click the Suggested dropdown menu **2** to use images from your PC, OneDrive or social-media accounts. External accounts will require you to log in to grant Sway access. Alternatively, search for the images you want by typing in the Bing search box **3** and pressing Enter.

3 Click the image you want and then click Add **1**. Alternatively, drag an image from the left-hand panel to the 'Drag an Image Here' box **2**. Click the small arrow icon **3** at the top to hide the left-hand panel and continue creating your presentation. If you want to replace your background image, click it, click the Delete icon that appears and repeat Step 2. When you're ready to proceed, click the small '+' symbol at the bottom left of your title and select which element you want to insert (Heading, Text, Media and so on).

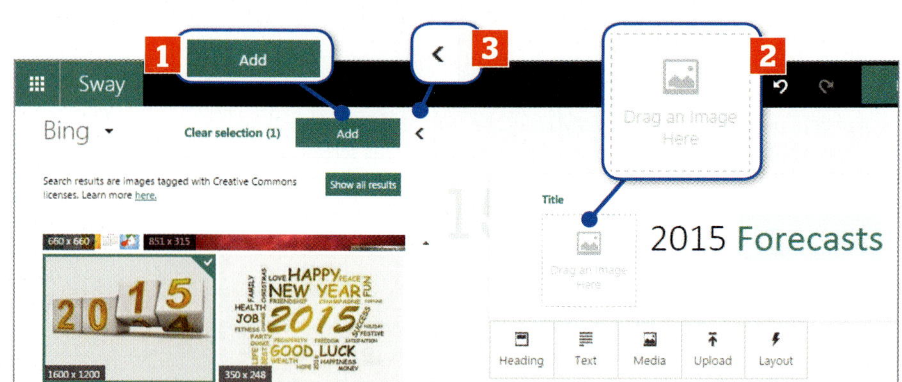

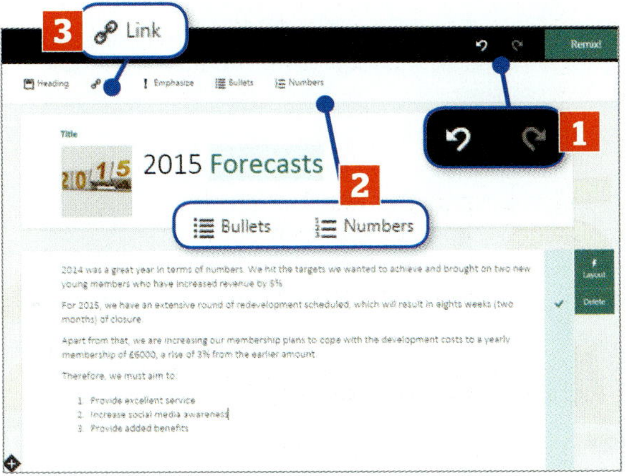

4 To add text, type or paste it in the field below and bold up the words you want (see Step 1). Features include undo and redo **1**, as well as options to create a list of bullet points **2**. To create links to web pages, highlight the relevant text and click Link **3**. Next, in the Web Link field paste the URL (web address) of the page you want to link to. You can change your layout by clicking Layout on the right and selecting an option from the left panel. The range of layouts is currently limited, but Microsoft says more will be added.

5 Click Heading at the top, type your heading and add an image (optional, see Step 2). Next, click the small '+' symbol at the bottom left. Click Upload to add files (such as Word documents or PDFs) from your PC. If your file is large, Sway will automatically break it down into headings, images and text sections. Caption your images by typing in the field provided. To reposition a section, click and drag its '=' symbol **1** up or down. To delete a section, click the panel on its right-hand side and tick it **2**. Do this for every section you don't want, then click Delete **3**.

6 You can also drag and drop sections on top f each other to group them into one section **1**, which is especially useful for images. To edit any image in the group, click the Group dropdown menu **2**. Click Add Content **3** to add more images. You can preview your sway by clicking on the right.

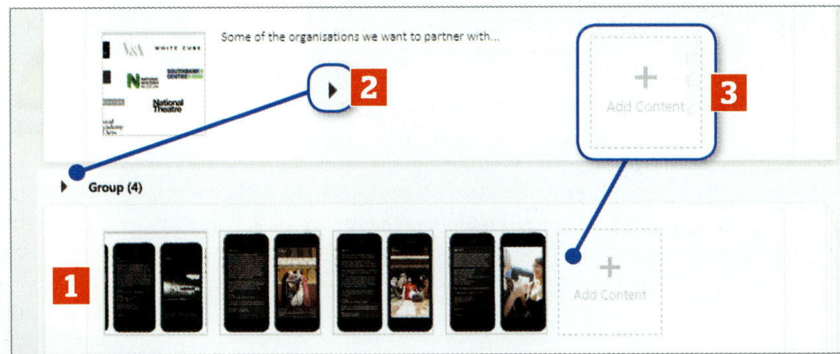

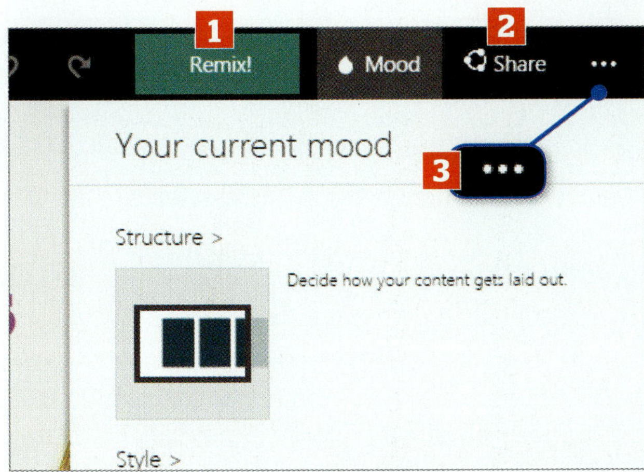

7 To personalise your presentation, click the Remix button **1**, which adds a theme to your sway. Keep clicking Remix until you're happy with the theme. The Mood option lets you modify your presentation's structure, style and colour. Structure lets you choose how you want to scroll through your sway (vertically or horizontally), while Style lets you choose from a variety of background layouts and fonts. Click Colour to modify your colour scheme. Click the Share icon **2** to create a link that you can email or embed in a website. Click the three dots **3** to create a new sway or leave feedback for Microsoft, so they can improve the service.

Chapter 5

Music and video treats

The web is stuffed full of audio and video delights that you can download, store and convert into different formats using your PC

Somewhere in the order of 300 hours of video is uploaded to YouTube every minute. In amongst all the videos of cats and people falling off logs are some TV and film classics that you can download and keep on your PC – but only if you know how! YouTube, nor any of the other video sites, really want you to find out how it's done. In this chapter, we'll explain how to record and keep audio and video classics off the web, as well as how to convert your home videos into the right formats, and provide tips on how to get the most from Windows Media Player using little-known features.

CONTENT

Record classic TV & film from the web

Discover where to find your old favourites online and how to save them for watching at your leisure

Setting up your video recorders

Record online video for free

Screen-recording is the direct digital descendant of VHS. You simply record what's playing or broadcasting on your PC's screen, then save it as a video file to watch when you want.

The very best tool for the job, Camtasia (www.snipca.com/15918), costs more than your first video recorder (£236.45 inc VAT, to be precise). You can buy a new iPad Mini 2 for less (www.snipca.com/15926). Fortunately, Camtasia has a more affordable little sister, Snagit (www.snipca.com/15919, £39.50; free 15-day trial). If you become very keen on screen-recording and want excellent results, Snagit won't disappoint.

There are free alternatives, but most force you to compromise on recording time. Jing (www.snipca.com/15921) records great-quality video, but only up to five minutes in length. Screenr (www.screenr.com) also lets you record up to five minutes and works entirely in your browser, without the need to download anything.

To record without time restrictions, use the free program Any Video Recorder (AVR, www.any-video-recorder.com). You can use it to record anything that moves, as long as it's on your PC's screen: YouTube videos, iPlayer broadcasts, Netflix shows and any TV or film gems you find.

AVR lets you select an area of your screen to record (useful if you want to carry on working in a different window), then automatically saves the recording to your hard drive as a good-quality MP4 video file.

Frame a video on your screen then click Rec to capture it using Any Video Recorder

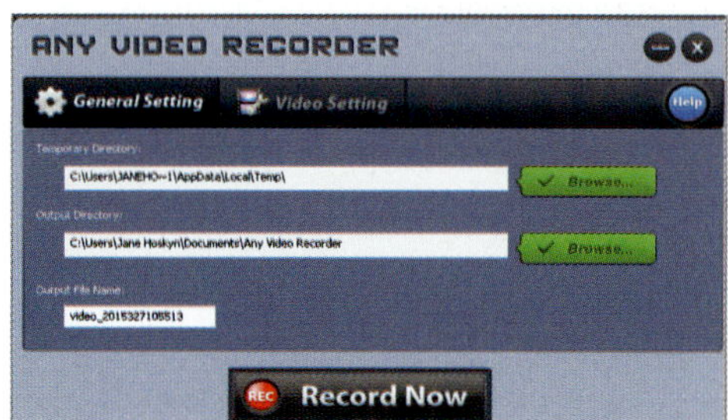

Any Video Recorder is the easiest tool for recording video as it plays on your Desktop

AVR's website has a strong hint of "too good to be true" and we braced ourselves for a truckload of adware in the installer, but there were no extras to opt out of at all. The installer correctly predicted that we'd see a Windows Security warning and assured us it was safe, so we clicked 'Install this driver software anyway' and didn't encounter any problems.

When the program opens, give it a test run by clicking the Record Now button. Your Desktop may disappear for a moment, which is a bit scary, but it will come back. Click Manual in the little blue window that appears. There's an automatic option that tries to detect any video playing on your screen, but it doesn't seem to work – at least not reliably.

After a couple of moments a red square will appear on your screen. Drag it to fit round the video you want to record, input a time limit if you want, then click the Rec button. You can also start and stop recording by pressing Ctrl+F7. When you press Stop, AVR processes and saves the MP4 to your chosen folder, which opens automatically in Windows (File) Explorer. Click it to play it in your default video player, or copy it to your tablet or laptop to watch while out and about.

If you want to crop or trim your recording, we recommend the excellent free online video editor WeVideo (https://www.wevideo.com). You can also convert your MP4s and other video files to alternative formats using WeVideo.

Download YouTube videos safely using VLC

The best place to find classic clips and shows is YouTube, the web's biggest video site. But YouTube is designed for watching videos online, not for saving them to watch offline, and its owner Google cracks down hard on attempts to get around this. That's why most of the "YouTube downloader" extensions you'll find online don't work, and many are unsafe.

Fortunately, there's no need to use them. You can either record YouTube videos as they play using Any Video Recorder, or you can download them using a hidden tool in our favourite media player, VLC (www.snipca.com/15928).

Downloading is more hit and miss than screen-recording, and in our experience it doesn't work with all online videos. But it

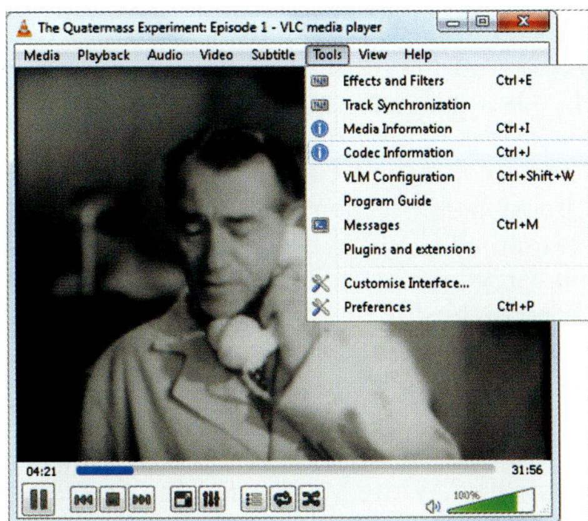

Use a hidden feature in VLC to safely download YouTube videos

does work with most YouTube videos, and it frees you from the need to play a video while you capture it.

First, go to YouTube and find a video you want to save, then copy its URL to your clipboard. Open VLC and click Media, then Open Network Stream. Paste the URL into the box and click Play. Your YouTube video will start playing in VLC.

Click Tools, then Codec Information (see screenshot left) and, in the box that opens, right-click the long line of text in the Location box at the bottom and choose Select All. Press Ctrl+C to copy the text, then paste it into your browser's address bar. When you press Enter, the video will open in YouTube's server. Right-click the video as it plays and select 'Save Video as' (see screenshot below), then choose a location on your hard drive to download the file to.

Type a name (say, quatermass) into the 'File name' box, followed by .mp4 (so in our example, the whole thing would read 'quatermass.mp4'). Press Save, and the file will download. Click to play it in your video player.

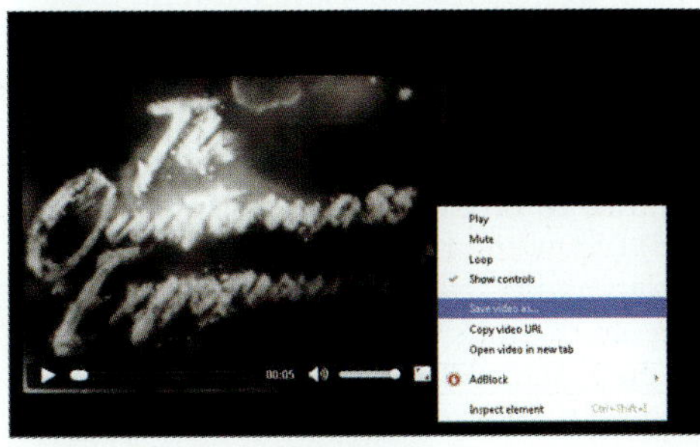

Open a video in YouTube's own server, then right-click to download it

Get YouTube classics on Laserdisc*

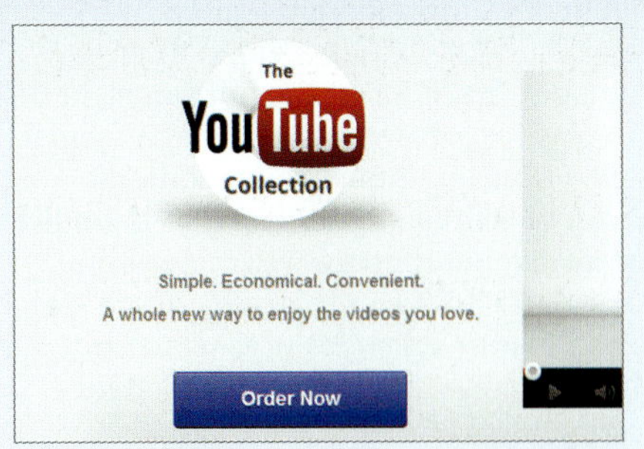

*Sadly not. This was one of YouTube's better April Fool's Day jokes. On 1 April 2012, the site's visitors were greeted with a little DVD icon next to the YouTube logo, and if they clicked the icon, up popped a promotional video for a new (and entirely fictitious) service called The YouTube Collection. Lucky users of this service could order any YouTube video for home delivery on DVD, VHS, Betamax and even Laserdisc, then enjoy "the complete YouTube experience completely offline".

Find the web's best classic TV shows and films

Find classic shows in seconds on YouTube

Now we've dealt with the technical stuff, we can move on to the fun part: watching telly. YouTube is still the first place we turn to – it's great for finding clips and entire episodes of a programme when you can't quite remember the full name. For example, type 'dixon dock' into the search box, and YouTube instantly offers a wealth of content from vintage police drama Dixon of Dock Green, including the first and second episodes in full. Narrow your search by clicking the Filters button at the top-left and clicking filters such as 'Subtitles/CC' (only see videos with closed-caption subtitles), 'Long (> 20 minutes)' (videos longer than 20 minutes; ideal for finding full episodes), and Programme (videos whose uploader has marked them as TV programmes).

To find whole series or groups of clips, use the Playlist filter. Type your search term, click Filters, then Playlist. For example, our 'dixon dock' search found playlists containing several Dixon of Dock Green episodes and much more.

In most cases, you won't have to record or download a YouTube video to watch it again later. There's every chance it'll still be there in a week, a month or a year. However, YouTube videos can get taken off the site, either by YouTube or by the person who uploaded them. So if you record your favourites and save them to your hard drive, you'll know you can watch them whenever you want – and without the need for an internet connection.

Watch the first episode of Steptoe and Son on The Internet Archive, and download it for free

What to record: 176 Monty Python sketches in one playlist (www.snipca.com/15922). For more comedy gold, search for 'Hancock's Half Hour' to find plenty of TV and radio episodes from East Cheam's finest. Britain's greatest ever comedy duos – Morecambe and Wise and The Two Ronnies – also crop up a lot on YouTube, with Christmas specials in full and classic sketches ('Four candles', André Previn etc).

Download vintage TV from The Internet Archive

The Internet Archive (https://archive.org) is an incredible resource of TV shows, films, audio clips and even computer games that are old enough to be out of copyright. Because of their licence-free status, you don't have to use third-party tools to record them – you can simply download them straight from the Internet Archive website, all for free.

The site is US-based, so its Television section (www.snipca.com/15946) has a distinctly American flavour, with transatlantic treats including The Three Stooges and You Bet Your Life, the legendary quiz show presented by Groucho Marx. Click a video to view it, and click 'MPEG4' at the bottom right of the player to download it in MP4 format.

To focus on home-grown content, click the British tag in the right-hand list (or go straight here: www.snipca.com/15947) and browse the results. Here we found classic episodes of Coronation Street (www.snipca.com/15939), The Avengers (www.snipca.com/15949) and Armchair Theatre (www.snipca.com/15948), all with free download links below the player.

What to download: The first episode of perhaps the best sitcom of all time, Steptoe and Son (www.snipca.com/15938). There are also episodes from the chilling 1950s sci-fi classic Quatermass and the Pit.

Collect classic Doctor Who episodes

The BBC keeps a tight rein on its content. The corporation's golden goose, Doctor Who, is particularly well guarded, and you won't find any classic episodes on the iPlayer.

YouTube has plenty of Doctor Who clips (such as Jon Pertwee's regeneration into Tom Baker: www.snipca.com/ 15950), but full episodes tend to get quickly removed following copyright requests. The Internet Archive has free downloadable Doctor Who audio clips, comics and ebooks (www.snipca.com/15955), but no episodes.

What's a Who fan to do? Go to Hell's Library (www.snipca.com/15936). Here, you'll find a link to nearly every episode of the 'classic' (20th century) Doctor Who, most of them uploaded by fans – and plenty of non-Doctor Who content, too. Most links open automatically in Google Docs (https://docs.google.com), where you can play the video in your browser or click the Download arrow at the top of the window to save the file. The Hell's Library FAQ (www.snipca.com/15952) recommends saving files as MP4 and playing them in VLC for offline viewing.

You can see all the original Doctor Who on Hulu, but you'll need a subscription and a proxy IP

The Doctor Who 'reboot' (21st century series) is all currently available on Netflix (www.snipca.com/15953, £5.99 a month) but the classic series is not. We found classic episodes on Amazon Instant Video (www.snipca.com/16004), but again they're not free. Most cost £1.89, with a series costing £5.99.

The best-quality source of classic Doctor Who episodes is US streaming site Hulu (www.snipca.com/15932). However, to use it, you'll have to pay a subscription ($7.99 a month, around £5.40) and pretend you have a US IP address by using the free Chrome extension Hola (www.snipca.com/15933). You won't be able to record episodes from Netlfix, Amazon or Hulu, though.

Some Like It Not: be aware that full-length films on YouTube are not always genuine

What to record: Watch and download the first Doctor Who episode, 'An Unearthly Child', from Hell's Library (www.snipca.com/15936). For just over a fiver, you can watch the whole classic 1973 series 'The Time Warrior', with Jon Pertwee, on Amazon (www.snipca.com/15954). And for a special treat, here are 707 Doctor Who episodes playing at the same time (www.snipca.com/15935).

Save classic films and find lost treasures

The best place to watch full-length films for free is Black And White Movies (www.bnwmovies.com). Click a thumbnail to choose a genre, then click a film's thumbnail to watch it using the built-in player, which has a full-screen mode. Films rated highest by users are listed at the top, with the brilliant courtroom drama 12 Angry Men (www.snipca.com/15968) leading the pack.

You can download films for free using Black And White Movies, but the process is trickier than with The Internet Archive. Click the little red download button a few lines below the player, then right-click one of the links (go for the one ending '.mp4' if available), click Save As and save the video file to your computer. Alternatively, use a screen recorder.

For more recent blockbusters like The Godfather you'll need a more conventional source such as TCM (www.tcm.com/watchtcm). The channel's website makes films available to view online for around a month after they've been shown on TV.

Download classics like 12 Angry Men for free from Black And White Movies

An inescapable problem with recording and downloading films is they devour gigabyte upon gigabyte of hard-drive space. We'd recommend investing in an external hard drive and saving your recordings to that to avoid clogging up your PC.

What to watch: If you're in a serious mood, watch the stunning silent classic Battleship Potemkin (www.snipca.com/15964). If you're not, join Charlie Chaplin for Twenty Minutes of Love (www.snipca.com/15965).

Record all radio from the web

You don't need to tune in 'live' to enjoy internet radio. We reveal how to record audio streams so you can enjoy them offline at your leisure

Not all radio shows are made available through on-demand services, or if they are, they are frequently only offered for a limited time. This means that if you miss something when it's first broadcast, you might never get the chance to hear it again.

Fortunately, there are plenty of free and easy ways to capture streaming audio on your PC and mobile devices, so you can keep the content to play forever, even when you lose your internet connection.

In this feature, we explain how to record web-radio streams, save radio broadcasts on Android and record BBC radio shows But first, we look at the legalities of recording streaming media.

Recording from the web FAQ

Is it legal to record streaming audio and video?

The short answer is yes. There's nothing in UK law to stop you doing this for personal use, although the site you're streaming from may prohibit capturing its content under its terms and conditions. For example, the music-sharing service SoundCloud (soundcloud.com, pictured right) lets you download tracks so long as the artist allows it and you do so using one of the site's own tools (rather than one from a third party).

SoundCloud also expressly states: "You must not copy, rip or capture, or attempt to copy, rip or capture, any audio content from the platform or any part of the platform, other than by means of download in circumstances where the relevant uploader has elected to permit downloads of the relevant item of content".

SoundCloud makes it clear that if you breach these terms, it is within its rights to terminate your account and could also take court action against you, should it choose to. In reality, it's unlikely to do this, unless you're a serial offender, but it's worth being aware of the warning if you're thinking of ripping music from the site.

If you're recording live television programmes or radio shows from the web, you must have a TV licence. The law is very clear on this. You don't need a licence to watch catch-up TV, but you do for watching or recording live broadcasts. This relates to all UK broadcasters, not just the BBC.

Are you allowed to share your recordings?

No, not really. UK copyright law has a time-shifting exception that lets you make a copy of a broadcast provided you do so in your own home; you copy from the original broadcast (meaning you shouldn't copy

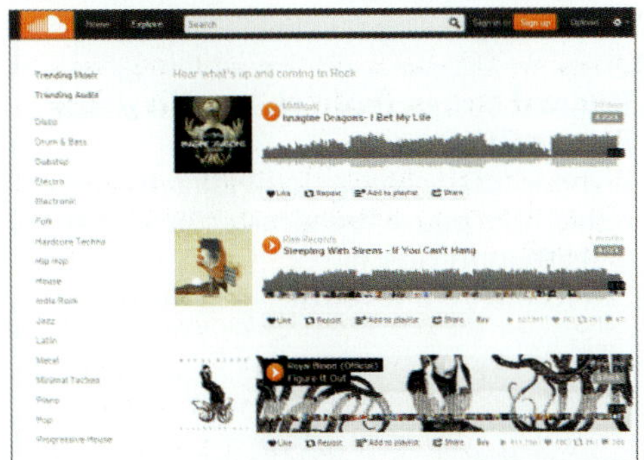

from someone else's copy, for example); and your reason for doing so is to view or listen to the broadcast at a more convenient time. The time-shifting exception does not allow you to share the copy with other people, or to upload it for them to then download.

It's obviously completely illegal to sell copies of recordings you make of other people's work. The law may not actually apply to all streaming audio and video (as opposed to broadcasts) because it depends on the media source, but it's probably best to err on the side of caution and avoid sharing anything you record. That said, you aren't likely to get into trouble for passing recordings on to friends and family, so long as the recipients don't do anything dodgy with them or try to profit from the recordings financially.

What is the difference between recording and downloading?

Under 'fair use' rules, if you record a song from the radio (including web radio), you are legally allowed to record that track for personal use.

This is because the broadcaster has already paid for the rights to play that song, so the artist, songwriter and record label have also been paid, which means everyone is happy.

If you download a song from a legal music service, such as iTunes, people also get paid. However, if you download the song from a website for free, without the copyright holder's permission, then no-one receives any payment, and the process is both morally wrong and illegal.

The lines can sometimes be blurred when it comes to recording and downloading something from a website, because the program you use to 'download' the content might in fact be recording a stream.

MINI WORKSHOP
Record web radio using VLC

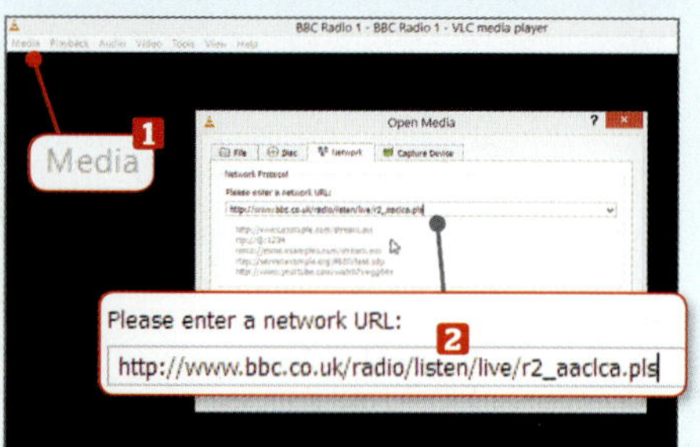

1 To listen to and record web radio through VLC Media Player, you'll need the URL of the radio station. There's a good list of stream addresses at www.listenlive.eu/uk.html. Copy the address of a station and, in VLC, click Media, **1** then go to Open Network Stream. Paste the URL into the address box. **2**

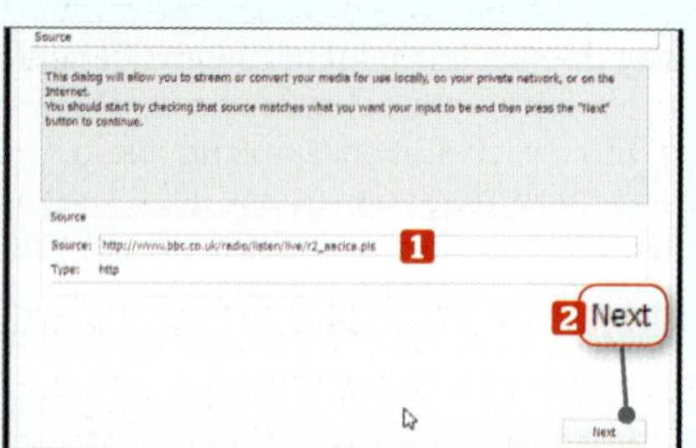

2 Click Play to start listening to your choice of radio station, which should begin streaming immediately. Go to Open Network Stream, click the down arrow next to the Play button and select Stream. The Stream Output box will open, showing your source. **1** Click the Next button. **2**

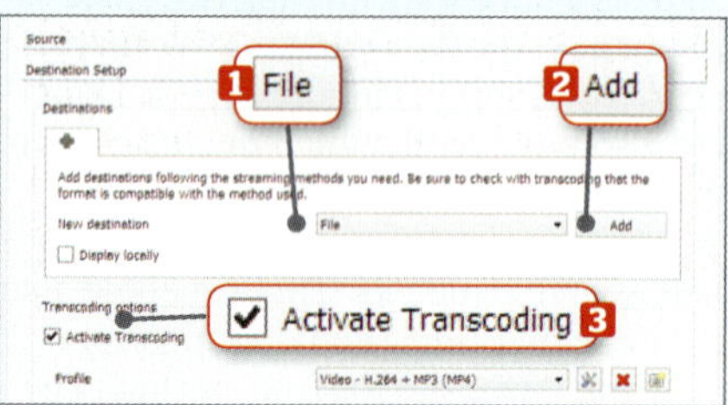

3 Under Destination Setup, make sure the New Destination is set as File **1** and then click Add. **2** Enter a name for the recording. You can specify a different save location. Untick Activate Transcoding **3** and click Next. Finally, click Stream. The counter will show the recording is in progress. Click Stop when it's done.

Record any audio from the web

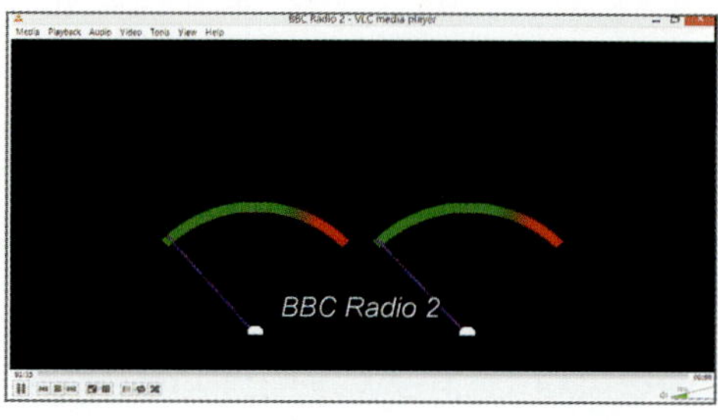

Record web radio streams using VLC

The brilliant free program VLC Media Player (www.videolan.org) doesn't only play audio and video files stored on your hard drive; it can also play and record streaming content from the web. Provided you know the URL for the audio or video source, the software can stream it directly to your Desktop. For example, if you know the web address for a web radio station (it will probably end in '.m3u', or '.pls'), you can tune in through VLC without needing to visit the website. Best of all, you can easily download the stream in MP3 format to listen to offline at a time that's convenient to you.

See our Mini Workshop on the left for full instructions on how to do this.

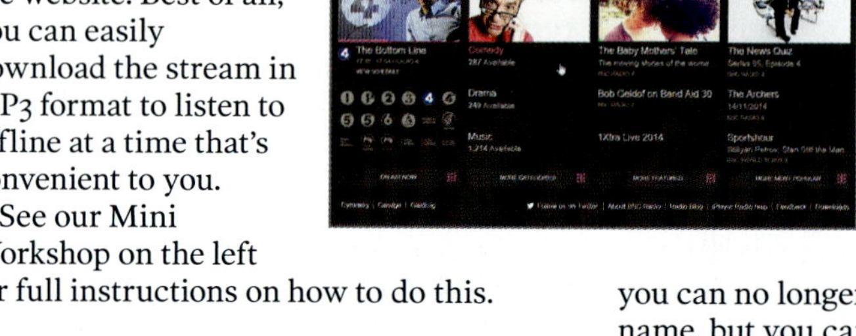

Record songs from the radio using StreamWriter

If you want to capture individual tracks rather than entire broadcasts, the superb tool StreamWriter (streamwriter.org/en) can record your favourite songs as they play on the web. You can either search for a track by name or browse a list of popular choices, and add your favourite tracks to a queue. The program will then monitor all the radio stations in its database and automatically record the songs you've selected when they are found playing anywhere. It also lets you record selected radio stations and programmes.

To listen to a recording in StreamWriter, simply click the Saved Songs tab, right-click a track and select Play. Sometimes the program will fail to record the full song to begin with, but if you leave it alone, it will eventually grab the entire track. You can limit the amount of bandwidth allocated to recordings to prevent StreamWriter from hogging your internet connection.

Record BBC radio shows

We've often recommended the excellent get_iplayer (squarepenguin.co.uk) for recording iPlayer television programmes, but the software can also record BBC radio, including live broadcasts and past shows, and export the audio in MP3 format. The BBC recently made changes to its feeds, so you can no longer search for a show by name, but you can search for a programme on iPlayer Radio (www.bbc.co.uk/radio) and use the details found there. You'll find full instructions on how to record BBC radio with get_iplayer at bit.ly/getiplayerguide359.

Alternatively, if it all seems too

streamWriter

File Community Stream Player Update Help

Streams | Title search | Lists | Saved songs

Search: Most played

Name	Last played	Played last day/week
Taylor Swift - Shake It Off	2 minutes ago	573 / 3236
Meghan Trainor - All About That Bass	7 seconds ago	509 / 2858
Sheppard - Geronimo	1 minute ago	368 / 2063
The Script - Superheroes	5 minutes ago	377 / 2013
Maroon 5 - Animals	7 seconds ago	336 / 1912
Marlon Roudette - When The Beat Drops Out	6 minutes ago	338 / 1857
Sam Smith - Stay With Me	4 minutes ago	334 / 1843
Ella Henderson - Ghost	8 minutes ago	295 / 1825
George Ezra - Budapest	3 minutes ago	315 / 1807
Coldplay - A Sky Full Of Stars	6 minutes ago	350 / 1791
Sia - Chandelier	20 seconds ago	344 / 1713
Calvin Harris Feat. John Newman - Blame	22 seconds ago	319 / 1711
Magic! - Rude	3 minutes ago	301 / 1706
Pharrell Williams - Happy	37 seconds ago	354 / 1576
Avicii - The Days	3 minutes ago	237 / 1464

complicated (honestly, it isn't), you can use BBC Radio Recorder (bit.ly/bbcradiorecorder359) instead. This tool, which you'll notice is actually called i-Sound Recorder when you download it, is much easier to use, and works very well, but the free version only lets you capture up to 100 seconds of radio. For unlimited recording, you'll need to buy the full edition for $29.95 (£19.15).

Use Audacity to record audio as it plays

Audacity (audacity.sourceforge.net) is an excellent, free multi-track audio editor that you can use to record streaming content to your PC. To do this, you'll need a 3.5mm (male-to-male) audio cable and (optionally) a pair of headphones and a microphone splitter. Plug one end of the audio cable into your soundcard's audio out (usually coloured green). Plug the other end into the microphone splitter, and the end of that into the line-in port (which is probably blue). Finally, plug your headphone jack into the spare port on the microphone splitter.

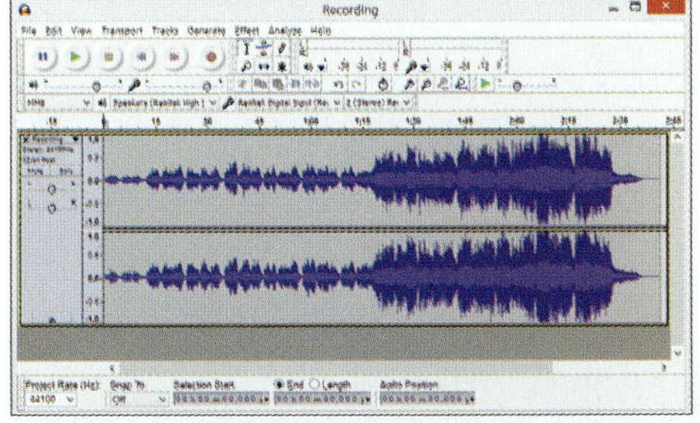

A simpler method (and the one to use if you don't have a microphone splitter) is to connect the audio cable to the audio out and line in. However, you won't be able to hear the streaming audio to prompt you to start recording.

Once you've set up your cable connections, open Audacity and set the recording input to 'line-in' (the wording of this will vary depending on your set-up). Start your stream playing, then hit Audacity's Record button. You'll know that the broadcast recording if you see a moving waveform.

You can pause and stop the recording at any time. To play it back, click Stop, then skip to the beginning of the track and hit Play. The file can be saved in WAV format, or as an MP3 if you install the LAME encoder from lame1.buanzo.com.ar.

Record radio broadcasts on your Android device

The free app Simple Radio Recorder (bit.ly/simpleradio359) gives you access to thousands of online radio stations on your Android phone or tablet. To find something to listen to, just click the magnifying glass and search by name. To record a show or song, go full screen and tap the Save button at the bottom. Agree to the terms, then give the recording a name. You'll be able to listen to your saved recordings under the MP3 tab. The app can automatically fetch cover art and save recordings to your device's SD card.

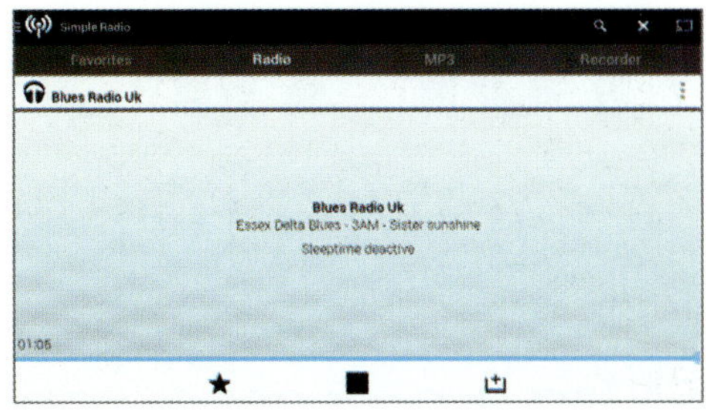

Record tracks from SoundCloud

As we mentioned in the legal Q&A, you're not allowed to use third-party programs to record music hosted on SoundCloud. However, if you want to take your chances anyway and promise to only keep songs for personal use, we can reveal that one of the best tools for the job is Apowersoft Free Online Audio Recorder (bit.ly/apowersoft359). This can record any audio stream, not only SoundCloud. Just start playing the track you want to capture and hit Record. It's very reliable and does a great job of recording streaming audio. See our Mini Workshop below to find out how to use it.

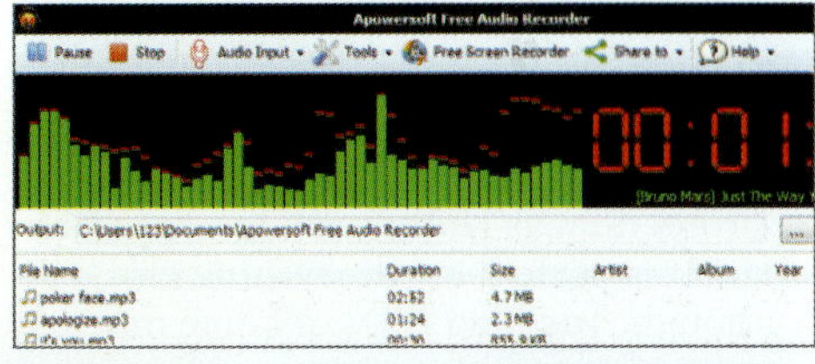

MINI WORKSHOP | Use Apowersoft's free software to record streaming audio

1 Download the program from bit.ly/apowersoft359. There's a Desktop version, **1** but you probably won't need it. Click the Start Recording button **2** to initialise the Java applet. Java is known to be a little insecure so you may have to give your permission to let it run in your browser.

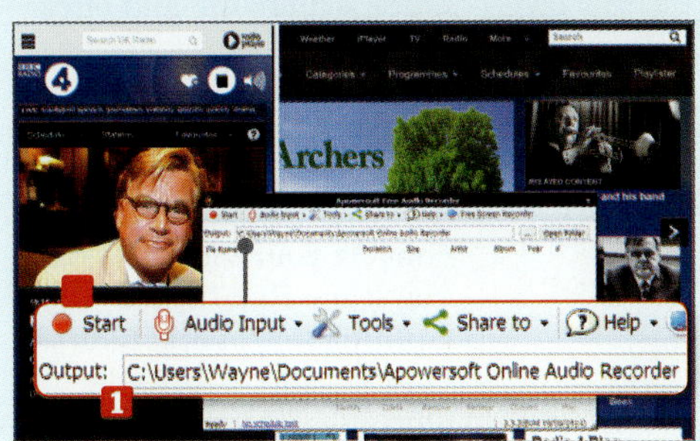

2 Once you've agreed to allow Java, Free Audio Recorder will load and open in a new window. It looks and behaves just like a regular program and is independent of your browser. Set an Output location, **1** then open a website with some streaming audio. Click the Start button **2** to begin capturing the sound.

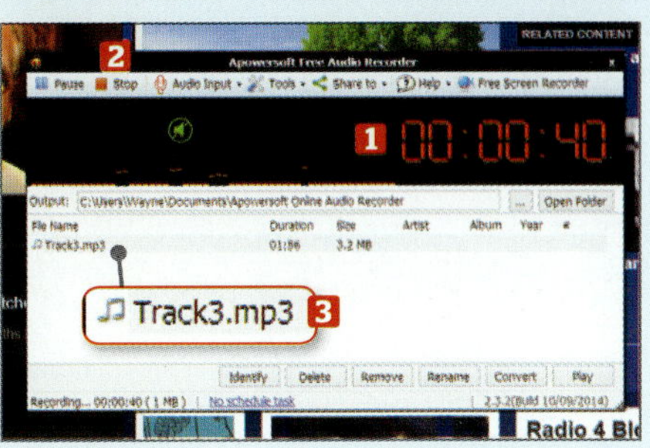

3 A graphic will show that the audio is recording, and you'll be able to see how much has been captured. **1** You can listen to the audio as it records. Don't do anything with your PC that uses sound as that will be recorded, too. Click Stop **2** when done and double-click a recording **3** to listen to it.

TOP TIPS for handbrake video converter

Use a preset to convert all your videos faster

HandBrake (handbrake.fr) makes it easy to convert videos from one format and size to another. Its presets configure all the settings automatically, simplifying the task to just a few clicks of the mouse.

Start HandBrake and click the Source button. Select File, then find and select the video file you want to convert. Click the Browse button to the right of Destination and select the folder and filename for the converted video. A logical place to store your clips is the Videos folder.

Select a preset on the right, such as iPad, iPhone or Universal (for a video that will play on any device), then click Start. It takes anything from a few minutes to a few hours for the process to complete, depending on the length of the video.

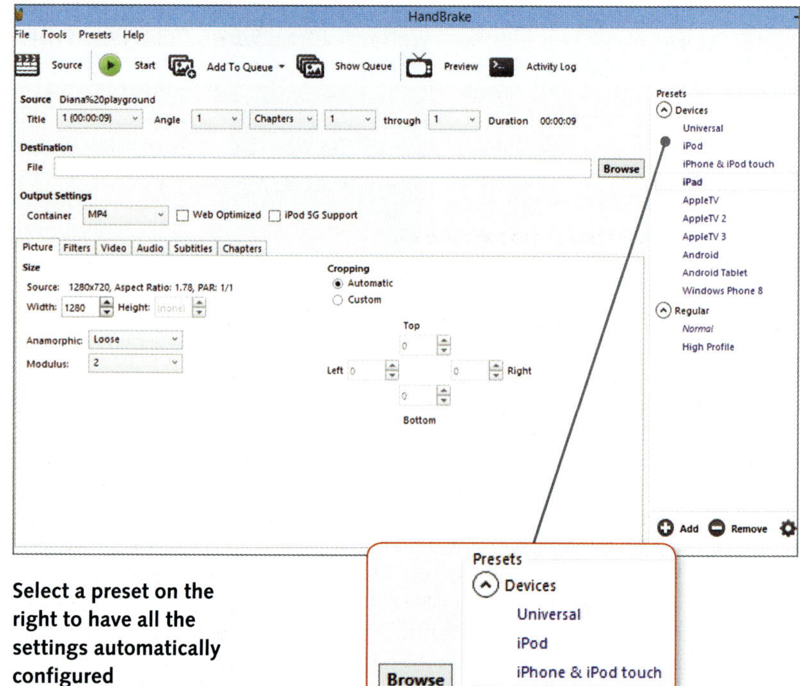

Select a preset on the right to have all the settings automatically configured

Rip DVDs and Blu-ray

HandBrake can copy and convert DVDs to other formats, but it doesn't work on discs that have copy protection, as Hollywood movies often do. It is perfect for everything else, though, and old DVDs of home movies capturing family events, weddings, birthdays and so on can easily be converted to view on your phone or tablet, or shared online at YouTube, Facebook and other sites.

Insert the disc in the drive and if it starts playing, click the player's Stop button and quit. Run HandBrake and click the Source button in the toolbar. Select the DVD to scan it. When this is done, click the Browse button to the right of Destination. Select a folder to save the movie to, such as Videos, then enter a filename and click Start.

If you have the time, you should optimise the video very slowly to get the best results

Compression vs speed

Are you in a hurry to convert your videos or can you leave HandBrake running for several hours? On the Video tab, under Optimise Video, you'll find a slider that lets you choose how long HandBrake spends compressing the video. If you drag the slider across to Very Slow, it will obviously take a long time to convert the video, but the resulting file will be much smaller. Drag the slider to Ultra Fast and the video conversion is up to 10 times faster, but the file size will be much bigger.

Batch conversion

The speed at which videos are converted can vary, but the main factors are processing power and video length. If you have a low-powered PC or lots of long videos to convert, you could be waiting hours for each one to complete. Set up a batch conversion and you can let it run overnight or when you are doing something else.

Click Source and select a video to convert. Choose a preset or manually select the conversion settings. Instead of clicking Start, click Add To Queue. After adding all the files you want to convert, click Start and leave HandBrake to carry out the task.

Picture size vs quality

The Picture tab shows the picture size of the source video and, below it, the

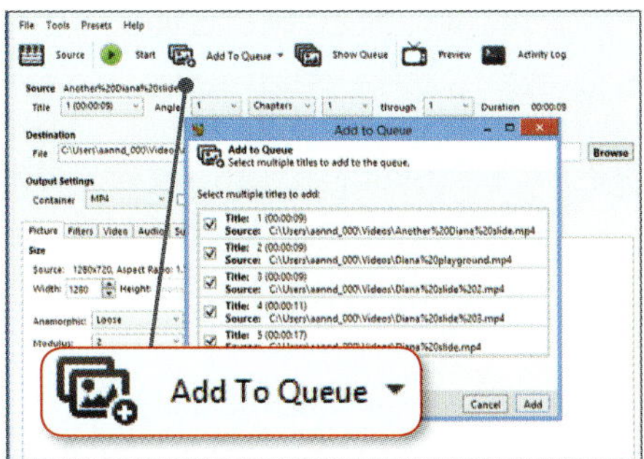

You can queue up several videos at a time for Handbrake to convert

size of the video it will be converted to. They don't have to be the same and the video picture size can be made larger or smaller. A video can always be viewed full screen no matter what size of screen you play it on. The video will be automatically scaled up if the picture is too small or scaled down if it is too big.

You can manually set the picture's dimensions on the Picture tab. There is no benefit to making it larger than the screen it will be viewed on; in fact, this is best avoided because it makes the file much larger. However, there are some benefits to making it smaller. If the video is HD quality (1,920 x 1,080 pixels) but you want to convert it to watch on a tablet, laptop or TV with a small non-HD screen, you can reduce the resolution. This will make the converted file size smaller. It's a good idea to do this if you need to save space on your PC's hard drive or device's storage.

Selecting standard DVD quality (720 x 576 pixels) as the output picture size will reduce the size of an HD-resolution video file. The playback quality will be no worse than a normal DVD. The space savings are considerable with a long movie, and the resulting file can end up being a fifth of the size.

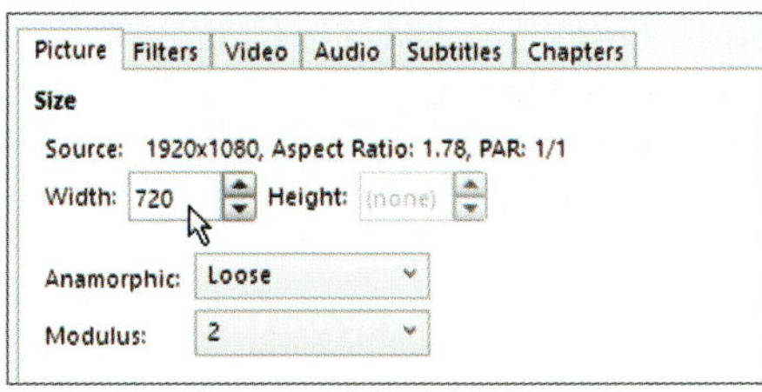

Match the picture width to your device's screen. The height is set automatically

TAKE IT TO THE NEXT LEVEL

More advanced tips for when you're feeling brave

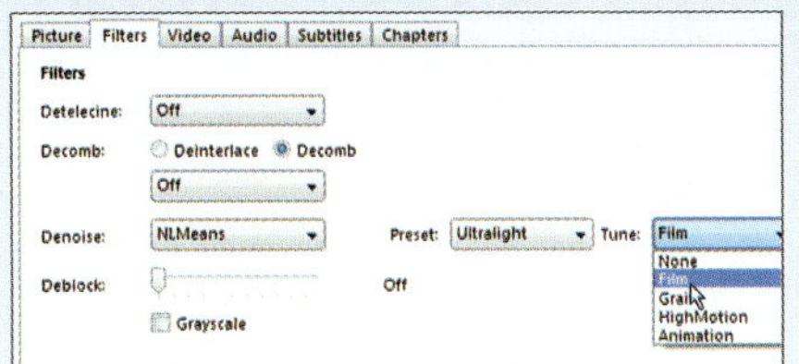

Use the Denoise and Deblock controls to repair poor quality videos

Clean up poor-quality videos

Old videos and low-light footage can often be marred by noise, grain and other imperfections, and instead of smooth areas of colour, the picture often displays dots and blocks.

Poor-quality videos can be cleaned up using HandBrake's Denoise and Deblock features. Select the Filters tab and, next to Denoise, select NLMeans. Denoising reduces the image quality slightly, so select Ultralight or Light in the Preset menu. Deblocking is set using a simple slider, but don't overdo it. Use the preview function to check the effects of these filters on the video quality before you convert it.

Work with ISO images

The best way to convert DVDs is to transfer them first to your computer's hard drive. This will make the conversion four times faster than if you do it directly from the DVD. You can also run HandBrake several times to convert the movie to different formats. A CD/DVD burner that creates ISO files will do the job, such as ISO Workshop (bit.ly/iso369) or Burnaware Free (www.burnaware.com).

Insert a DVD into the drive and, if it starts playing automatically, quit the player. Run ISO Workshop and click the Backup Disc icon on the homescreen. Click the Browse button under 'Save to image file' and select the filename and folder for the ISO file. In HandBrake, click the Source button and select File. Go to the folder with the ISO image and select it. You can then proceed as normal.

Preview videos

When converting a movie from one format to another, the size, frame rate, encoding parameters and more can be changed. If you want to take the guesswork out of how the finished movie will look, try previewing the result before you start.

HandBrake's Preview tool uses the popular free media player, VLC. If you don't already have it installed, get it from videolan.org.

To make sure HandBrake is configured to use it, go to Tools, Options and find VLC Player in the General section. If it's not there, click the Browse button and select VLC.exe to find the correct path. It is usually in C:\Program Files or C:\Program Files (x86).

Once VLC is installed and HandBrake is configured, click the Preview button in the toolbar. There is an option to set the duration, which refers to the number of seconds of video you want to convert. The default of 30 is fine. Longer previews are available but they take more time to create. Previews are stored in the destination folder; if you don't want to install VLC, just open the folder and play the preview clip in Media Player.

Quality vs file size

The quality slider on the Video tab has two purposes: one is to improve the quality of the converted video and the other is to reduce the file size. You can't do both so you'll have to choose between reducing the file size or increasing the quality.

Drag the slider down to 10 to increase the file size and quality, or drag it to 30 for a smaller file size and lower quality. This is useful if you want to create videos for uploading to the web. Check the quality using the preview facility to make sure it is good enough for your needs.

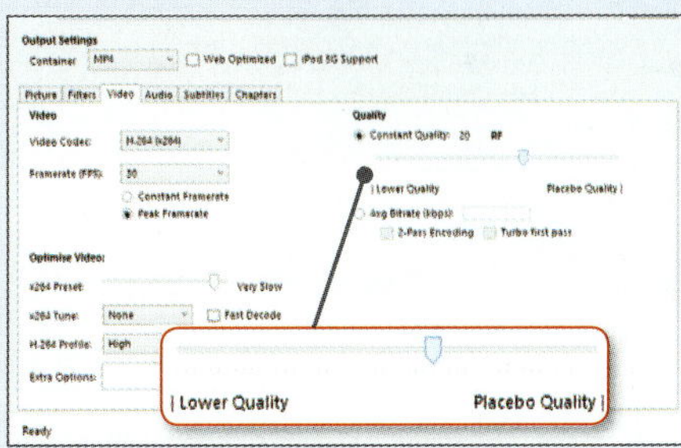

The Quality slider balances the size and playback quality of the final file

Download audio and video from any website

EXPERT TIP

We used FFmpeg to merge the audio and video files in this Workshop. It's a powerful audio- and video-conversion tool than can be used for a range of video-related tasks, such as grabbing content from a live video/audio source. It's entirely command-line based and takes time and patience to get to grips with, but it's worth persevering. Full documentation can be found at bit.ly/ffman366.

EagleGet is a brilliant tool that lets you download ad-free video and audio directly from the web. Compatible with most browsers, it also doubles as a general purpose download manager.

In this Workshop, we show you how to add EagleGet to Chrome, so you can rip files from any video site. The process of adding EagleGet to Firefox is similar, but if you get stuck you can find step-by-step instructions at bit.ly/eagleget366.

When using the EagleGet browser extension, the highest resolution versions of YouTube's videos are sometimes listed as 'hidden formats', which require you to download the video and audio files separately. To get around this, we'll show you how to combine these two files into one fully functional video using the command-line tool FFmpeg (www.ffmpeg.org). To install FFmpeg, you'll need an extraction tool such as 7-Zip (www.7-zip.org) and to be logged into a user account with admin rights.

EagleGet: www.eagleget.com | 20 mins | Chrome, Firefox, Internet Explorer

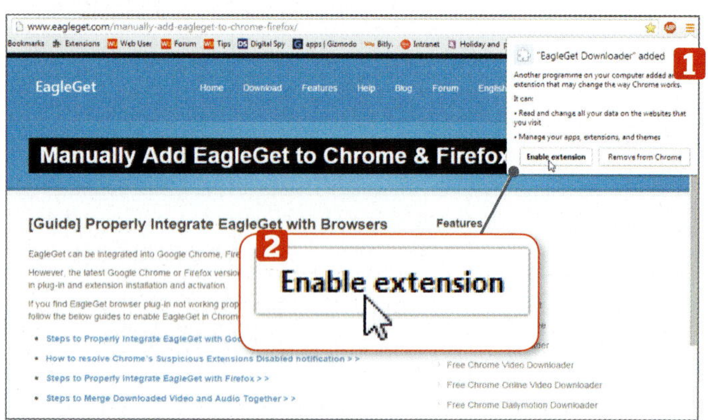

1 Download, install and run EagleGet. When Chrome launches, a pop-up appears saying that EagleGet Downloader has been added. **1** Read the information about what the extension can do, then click 'Enable extension' **2** to approve it.

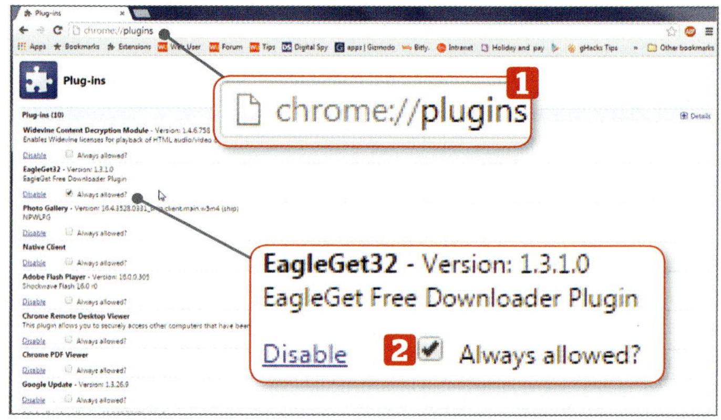

2 Type chrome://plugins into the address bar. **1** Find the EagleGet plug-in and make sure that it's enabled, and check that the 'Always allowed?' box is ticked. **2** Close your browser and restart your PC to complete the installation.

3 Visit YouTube and open a video you want to save. A Download button **1** appears above it. Click it to see a list of different files you can download. Each file's resolution is shown at the end of the title **2** with the file type in square brackets. **3**

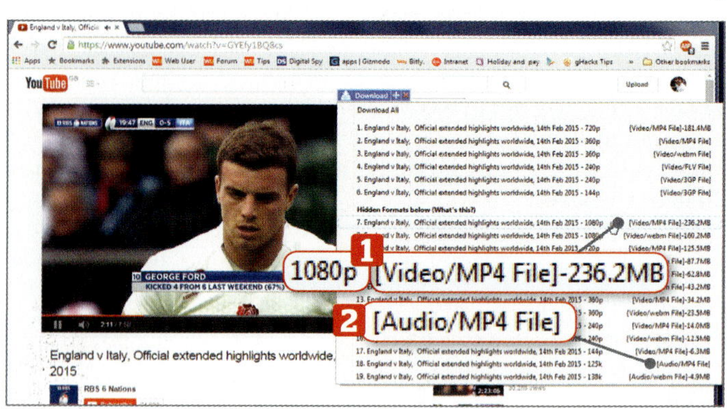

4 If you select an MP4 file from the top half of the list, the file will contain both video and sound. If, however, you select a 'hidden format' file, such as the 1080p MP4, **1** you'll need to separately download the audio file, **2** then merge the two.

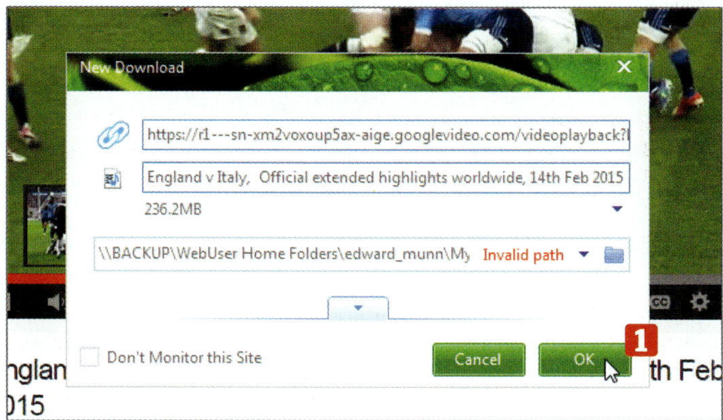

5 Click the file you want to save and a pop-up window appears. Choose a name for the file and the location you want to save it to, then click OK. **1** If you're downloading a 'hidden' format, repeat this step for the audio file.

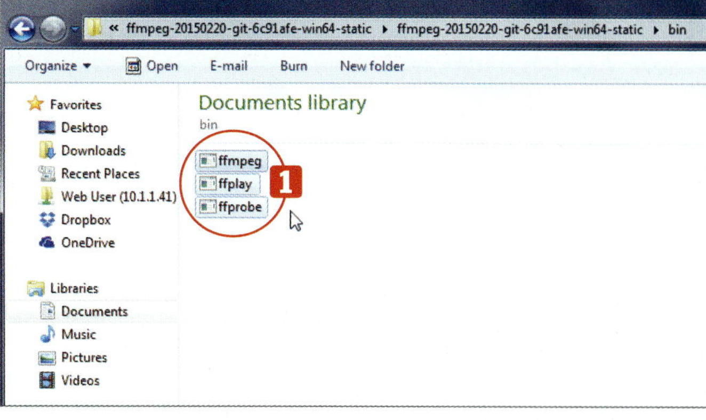

6 To merge the video and audio files, you first need to install FFmpeg (bit.ly/ffmpeg366). After downloading the correct version for your PC, extract the files using 7-Zip, locate the 'bin' folder and copy all its contents **1** to C:/Windows/System32.

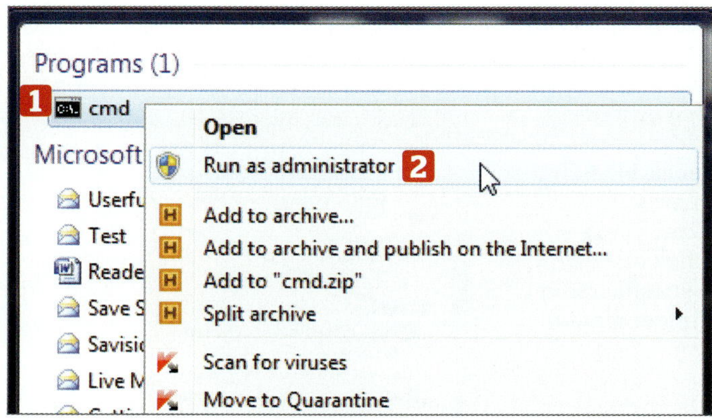

7 Next, type CMD into the Start Menu, right-click the program **1** and select 'Run as administrator'. **2** Your audio and video files must be saved to the same folder before you merge them and it's best if they have short, simple names.

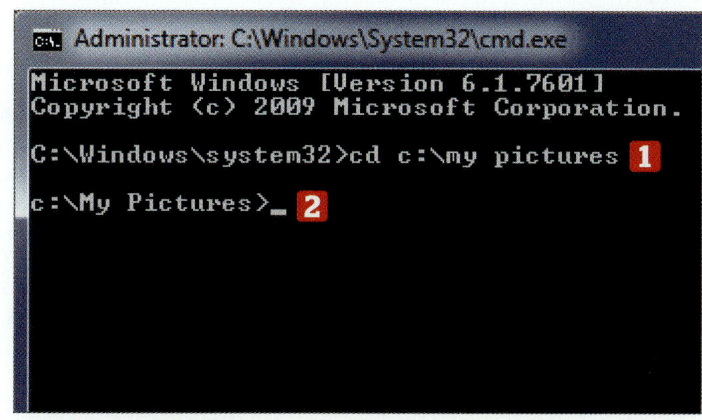

8 To tell Command Prompt where your files are saved, use the 'change drive' command `cd` followed by the file path of the folder the files are saved to, including the drive letter, for example `cd c:\my pictures`. **1** Press Enter and Command Prompt shows the new drive location. **2**

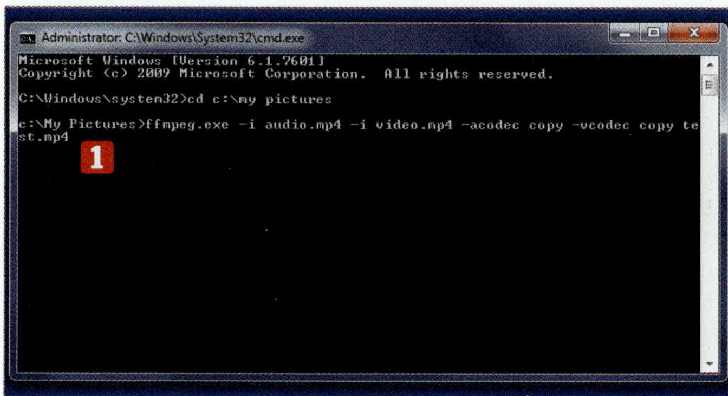

9 Next, type `ffmpeg.exe -i audio.mp4 -i video.mp4 -acodec copy -vcodec copy test.mp4` **1** where 'audio.mp4' is the name of the audio file, 'video.mp4' is the the video and 'test.mp4' is what you want to call the merged file. Press Return.

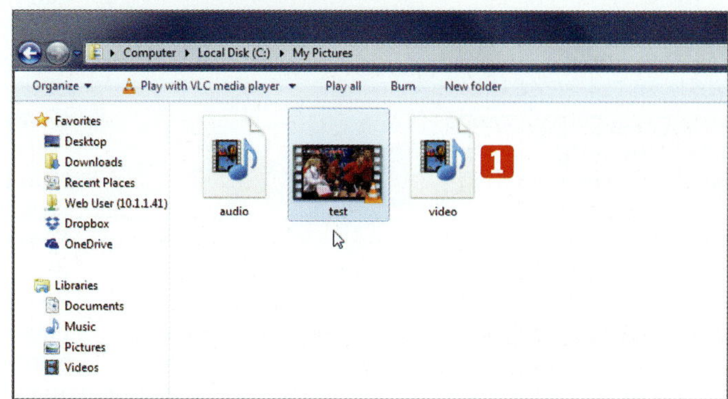

10 FFmpeg merges your files. If the process has been successful, no error messages will appear in the Command Prompt. Your merged file can be found in the same directory as the original video and audio clips. **1**

TOP TIPS for Windows Media Player

See the lyrics of the song you're playing

A little-known fact about Windows Media Player is that it supports third-party plug-ins that add new features. For example, you can download the Lyrics Plugin at www.lyricsplugin.com to display the lyrics of any track you play. Click the Download Now button under 'Lyrics Plugin for Windows Media Player', then double-click the downloaded file and follow the instructions to install it. Now open WMP, right-click the blue space at the top, click Tools, then 'Plug-ins' (see screenshot). You should see the Lyrics Plugin with a tick next to it. Next, start playing a track, then switch to the Now Playing view (by pressing Ctrl+3) to see the lyrics to that song.

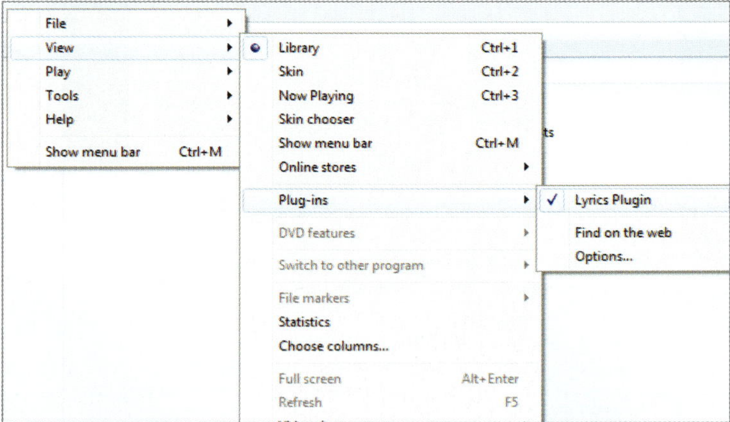

Download the Lyrics Plugin to sing along to your favourite songs

Use keyboard shortcuts to control your media

Using keyboard shortcuts is the quickest and easiest way to control your PC. Windows Media Player (WMP) has a whole range of keyboard shortcuts for perusing and playing your music and DVD collection. For example, press Ctrl+F to skip to the next track or DVD chapter or Ctrl+B to return to the previous one (an easy way to remember: 'F' for Forward and 'B' for Back).

If you don't have a media keyboard containing dedicated buttons for Play, Mute and so on, you can use the Function keys to carry out these tasks. The F7 key mutes/unmutes WMP's sound; F8 and F9 reduce and increase the volume respectively; and Ctrl+S stops a track playing. To see a full list of WMP keyboard shortcuts, go to www.snipca.com/15073.

Listen to internet radio stations

If you want a change from your personal music collection, you can tune in to any of the thousands of internet radio stations that are available via WMP. Right-click the light-blue section at the top (beside Play, Burn and Sync at the top right), then move your cursor to View, 'Online stores', and click Media Guide. You'll see a list of genres (including Jazz, Oldies, Country and Classic Rock) at the top. Click one of these to see a list of genre-specific radio stations, then click Listen under a radio station's thumbnail to play it.

Click the View menu, 'Online stores' then Media Guide to listen to online radio stations

Play all media formats on Windows Media Player

Windows Media Player supports a large number of audio and video formats by default, but there are still many formats, such as DivX and FLAC, that aren't supported. Thankfully, you can install the free K-Lite Codec Mega Pack, which adds support for hundreds of popular formats to WMP. Go to www.snipca.com/15078 and click the blue Direct Download Link (just above Publisher's Description). Once it's downloaded, open the installer, and keep clicking Next through all the menus until you reach the page prompting you to install additional software. Untick all the boxes, then tick 'No Thanks' to confirm you don't want these extras. Continue clicking Next to install the codec pack.

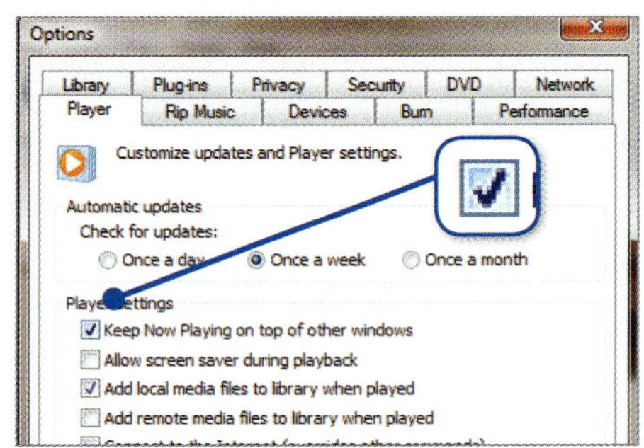

Tick the 'Keep Now Playing' box to keep an eye on your music when using other programs

Control your music when using other programs

If you want to have instant access to your music player when you're doing other things on your PC, you can choose to keep Windows Media Player's Now Playing window on top of your other open windows. Click Organize at the top left, then Options. In the window that opens, click the Player tab, tick the box next to 'Keep Now Playing on top of other windows', then click Apply and OK. Start playing a track, then press Ctrl+3 to activate Now Playing mode which brings up a small window displaying the track you're currently playing. You can resize this window by dragging its corners and access the music player controls by moving your cursor over it.

Chapter 6

Pursue your hobbies

Hobbyists will find plenty to do on their PC, whether it's creating a family tree, amazing digital photos or retro gaming

Getting into computing isn't just a hobby in itself, it can also help you get more from your existing pastimes. PCs are the perfect tool to help you compile a family tree, for example, turn your life story into an audiobook for future generations to enjoy.

Then there are the hobbies that are formed of computing itself: retro gaming or simulators that let you fly planes, drive trains or even take a tour of the planet. We've got all these covered. You can also stitch together your holiday snaps to make stunning panoramas, or stay home and forecast what the British weather will be like.

CONTENT

Best free family tree software

There are lots of free programs you can use to record information about your family tree as you research it. We test six of the best

MyHeritage Family Tree Builder 7 | bit.ly/family364 | ★★★★★

FEATURES ★★★★☆ **PERFORMANCE** ★★★★★ **EASE OF USE** ★★★★★

What we liked:

The main screen of Family Tree Builder looks like a table on to which you spread out a collection of index cards containing your family's personal details. The attractive and practical design of the interface makes it perfectly suited to the task at hand: you enter your data using a simple form, which has spaces to type details. It also has drop-down options, such as for dates, which you click to select.

This card-based system feels instantly familiar, even more so than a standard family tree view, which makes the program very straightforward to use. You click a name to bring that person's card to the foreground, then you can rearrange ancestors and descendents around it. You can also adjust a slider to show several generations at a time, and sort and view the data in different ways.

The card display is handy for editing your tree, but it isn't the best way of presenting it. For that, Family Tree Builder has a vast range of different printing options, from attractive charts to full reports, including PDF documents crammed with all your research. You can even add your relatives to a Google Map, which shows where major events such as births and deaths occurred.

The software includes an automatic back-up to the MyHeritage website. Files are uploaded and encrypted, and while you can publish your tree to the web if you wish, it doesn't happen by default, so you don't need to worry about privacy.

How it can be improved:

Family Tree Builder is linked to MyHeritage, so you end up being tied to that site if you want to publish your family tree online, though you can export it using the open GEDCOM standard. Frustratingly, some of the tools – such as merging and all-in-one charts – are only available if you upgrade to a paid-for account. Yet, none of these paid-for features are critical.

OUR VERDICT

MyHeritage has produced an excellent tool with a well-designed interface that looks friendly and is a pleasure to use. Some features have to be paid for, but you can easily build your family tree without them.

RootsMagic Essentials 7 | www.rootsmagic.co.uk | ★★★★☆

FEATURES ★★★☆☆ PERFORMANCE ★★★★☆ EASE OF USE ★★★★☆

What we liked:

Essentials is a cut-down version of the full RootsMagic software. All that's missing is the ability to automatically back up and print your finished family tree, so you're still provided with the tools you need to create it.

RootsMagic starts with a blank tree. You begin by entering a name and working back in time by adding parents, grandparents and so on.

The interface is very easy to use. The default 'add person' form lets you fill in a person's details, such as their name, and dates for their birth and death. You can also add other elements including occupation and nationality, and drop in religious events such as a christening or bar mitzvah.

This form takes you to what looks like an information card, where you can add more facts about a person as you discover them. If you add a marriage date, you're prompted to add a spouse, which can be a new person or someone whose details

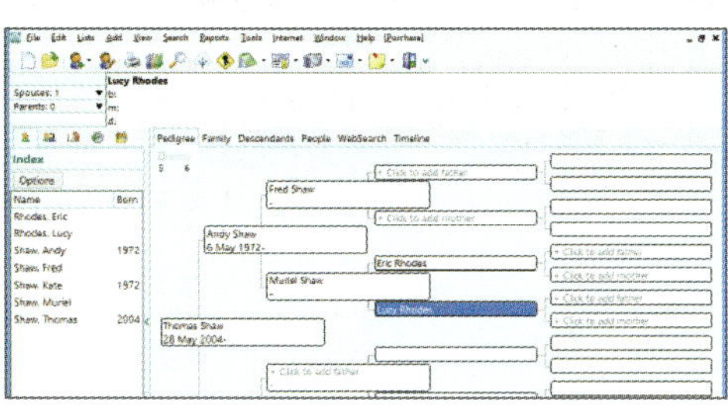

you've already added. The interface is very logical, and takes no time at all to get used to.

How it can be improved:

The biggest restriction to the free version is its limited formatting and printing options. If you try to use them, you get nagged to upgrade.

OUR VERDICT

The free cut-down version doesn't let you print and back up your tree. To get these options, you'll have to pay £20 for the Basic version, but it's a good price for a powerful tool.

Legacy Family Tree | www.legacyfamilytree.com | ★★★★☆

FEATURES ★★★★☆ PERFORMANCE ★★★★☆ EASE OF USE ★★★☆☆

What we liked:

Legacy Family Tree provides a wizard to introduce and guide you through the software. The program's data-entry forms aren't as dynamic as those in Family Tree Builder; to enter dates, you have to type them yourself, rather than choose a date from a calendar.

You enter all the facts about a person in this way, which makes the program uniform and straightforward, but decidedly dry: it's more like a database tool than a specially designed family history recorder.

Once you've added some information,

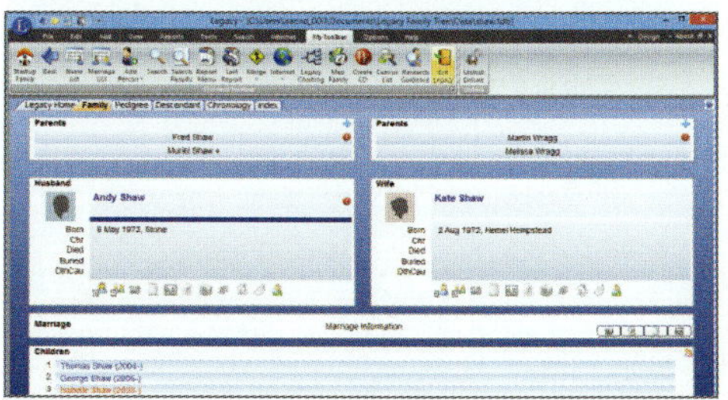

you can view the tree in a variety of ways including a card-like layout with ancestors above and descendents below, and a 'pedigree' view which shows ancestors branching off to the right. There are a number of views that aren't accessible in the free version, but you are given plenty of options for printing your information.

How it can be improved:

The software's wizard makes you go through a set-up section at the beginning, which forces you to customise details such as the colour scheme of the software when you'd probably rather get started right away on your family tree.

OUR VERDICT

The wizard is helpful in setting up the software, although it includes some unnecessary steps. The program works well, but some buttons are only there to nag you to upgrade to the paid-for version.

BEST OF THE REST

ScionPC

bit.ly/scion364

Our three leading programs all need to be installed, but ScionPC is portable, so you could keep both the program and data on a USB stick and run it from any PC. As a result it's small, not very intuitive and is best used as a simple family database. It doesn't have as many reporting options, so you might end up wanting to export the data, but that's easily done using the GEDCOM standard.

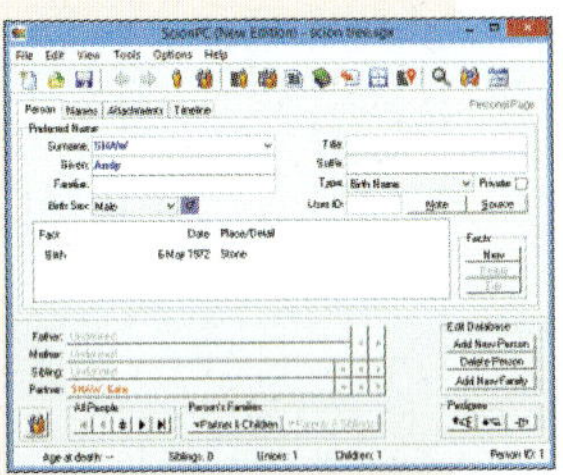

XY Family Tree

xyfamilytree.com

XY Family Tree is a small 4.3MB download. It's a no-nonsense program and more refined than ScionPC, but it's significantly harder to get started with than our three top picks. The interface largely revolves around individual records, though you can break out into a separate window if you want to view an entire family tree.

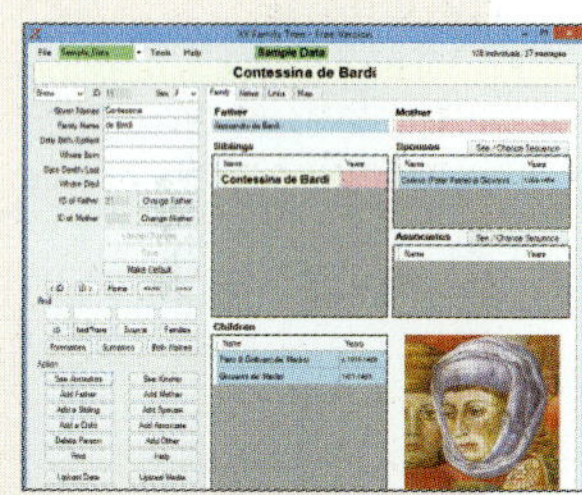

Gramps

www.gramps-project.org

Gramps is a well-respected open-source program, so you don't get nagged to upgrade to a paid-for version. However, the design of its interface is plainer and isn't as much fun to use as our top picks. We found it wouldn't install on a PC protected by Avast anti-virus, which we suspect to be a false positive, since other anti-virus software let it through, but you may want to proceed with caution until its developers can resolve the problem.

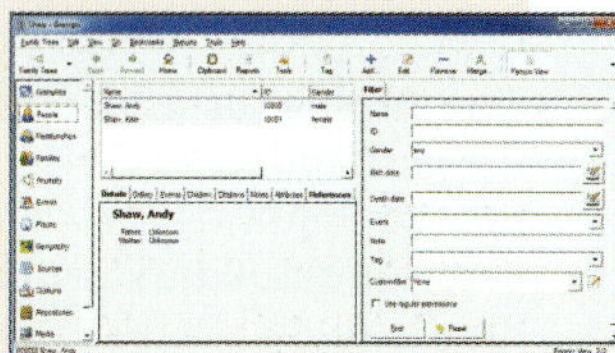

Run old computers on your modern PC

Hands up if you had a ZX Spectrum, Commodore 64 or another classic home computer in the Eighties? We take a walk down Memory Lane by finding the best way to emulate them on a modern Windows PC

BBC Micro

The machine that began the Eighties home-computer revolution in schools may be long gone, but you can relive its glory days at BeebEm (www.mkw.me.uk/beebem), a free emulator for Windows.

Install the software, fire it up and choose Run Disc from the File menu. Choose Games from the list of files and you'll be able to dive straight into several titles including Chuckie Egg, Cylon Attack and Snapper. Enthusiasts will find plenty of settings to fiddle with, such as turning the display green or amber to mimic an ancient computer monitor.

You should also head over to the BBC Games Archive (www.beebgames.com) where there are stacks of classic games you can download and play for free. You'll find full instructions on how to play the games in the Help menu.

For a quick play online with no commitment, go to bit.ly/micro364 and, when the emulator loads, hold down the Shift key and press F12 to load the classic space-based trading game Elite. For more games, open the Discs menu, choose STH Archive, select your game and, when the main screen appears, press Shift+F12 to start.

Commodore Amiga

The Amiga series of computers followed the Commodore 64 and were popular in the late Eighties. There are several paid-for emulators available (the FS-UAE Emulator at fs-uae.net is the best), but getting them up and running is so complicated that only diehard fans should attempt it. Instead, you can get some instant old-time Amiga action by going to bit.ly/amiga364 and following the instructions. The main Workbench screen (the Amiga Desktop) takes an age to load, but this is deliberate and the status messages are genuinely entertaining.

Once it has loaded, double-click the First Demos icon, then the ReadMe icon. Follow the instructions to enjoy some of the demos that came with the original Amiga back in 1985.

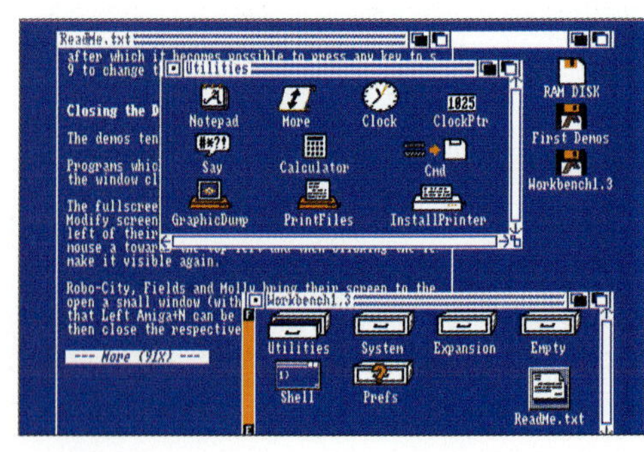

Commodore 64

If you owned Commodore's follow-up to the PET (read about it on Wikipedia: bit.ly/pet364), then you're not alone – it's still listed by the Guinness Book of Records as the best-selling computer of all time. For a revel in notalgia, head to www.c64forever.com and download the Free Express Edition of C64 Forever. The file is large, at 125MB, but it includes a whole stack of ready-to-play games, plenty of demos and emulators for 14 different Commodore machines.

The C64 emulator is a faithful recreation of the original, right down to the "now loading from disk, please wait approximately 1.5mins" message when you load a game. There's a paid-for version for $14.95 (around £10), which removes adverts and adds lots of advanced tools, but the free version is enough to keep any Commodore fan entertained.

If you don't want to download any software, you could try some of the online C64 emulators, although we didn't find them particularly good. If you still

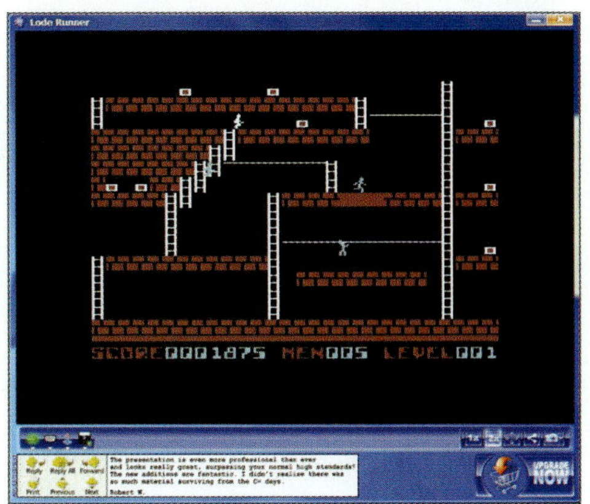

want to have a go, there's a Flash-based emulator at codeazur.com.br/stuff/fc64_final, complete with eight games (including Elite). Alternatively, try the JavaScript-based emulator at www.kingsquare.nl/jsc64, which has six games. There's also a decent online emulator for Survivor (www.schillmania.com/survivor), a 1982 game that, at the time, was one of the best shoot-em-ups available.

If you fancy playing C64 games on a mobile device, install the free Android app Frodo C64 (bit.ly/frodo364). We couldn't find an iOS equivalent, though a C64 emulator did exist briefly about five years ago (you can see it in action on YouTube at bit.ly/iphone364).

If your interest extends beyond merely playing the games, visit C64.com (www.c64.com). It's an online encyclopedia of C64 games, demos, interviews, articles, video clips and stills from famous games. Finally, don't forget the all-important Commodore 64 User Manual: www.lemon64.com/manual.

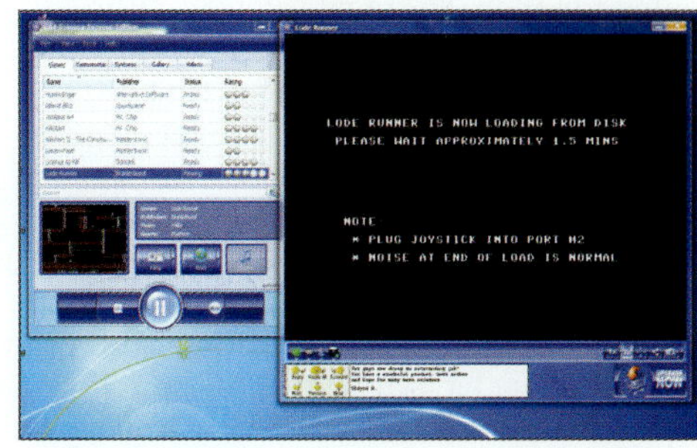

ZX Spectrum

One of the first stops for any Speccy fan should be ZXSpectrum4.net (www.zxspectrum4.net) – and not just for the wry tagline: "Why break new ground when you can dig up the past?" This emulator replicates every iteration of Sir Clive Sinclair's classic home computer, from the 16K model up to the +3, launched in 1987, with its 'revolutionary' built-in 3in Amstrad floppy drive.

This brilliant emulator requires no installation: just download and unzip it to begin. The free version comes with three games (including Manic Miner) and has

joystick support. A $10 (around £6.60) donation will unlock all the emulator's features and give you access to the site's extensive library of games.

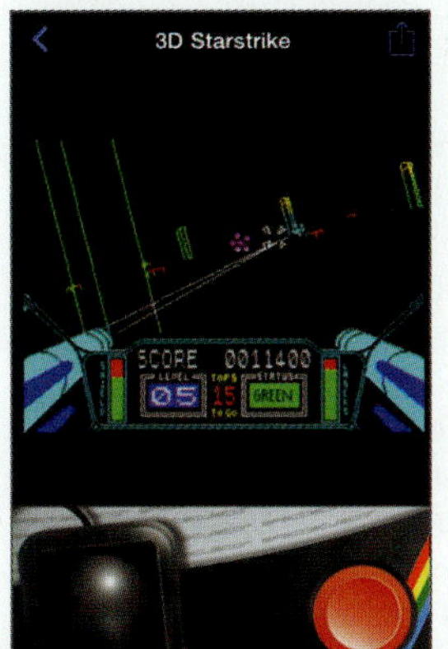

Fans of mobile gaming should check out Spectaculator (www.spectaculator.com) where you'll find not only a great emulator for Windows, but also iOS and Android devices. Spectaculator even includes a 'Load from Audio Source' feature that lets you load programs from the original cassette tapes, if you have them. If you've long since thrown them out, go instead to World of Spectrum (www.worldofspectrum.org/archive.

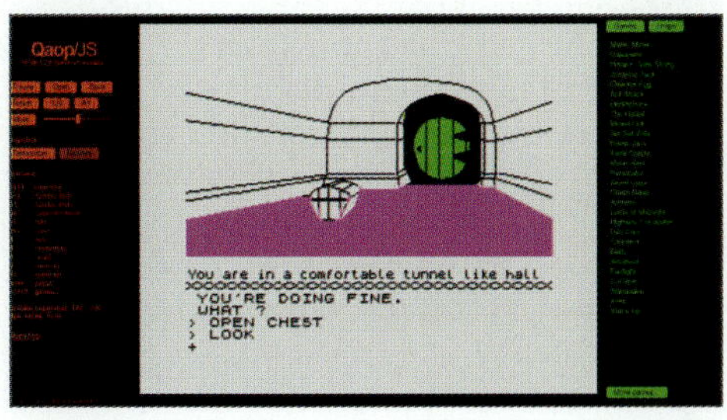

html) where you can choose from nearly 25,000 games. Spectaculator 8.0 is free for 30 days, after which it costs £10; the iOS version is priced £2.99, while the Android app is free with in-app purchases.

Alternatively, if you don't want to download anything but would like a quick fix of classic Spectrum games such as The Hobbit, Galaxians and Horace Goes Skiing, then scoot over to torinak.com/qaop where you'll find nearly 300 titles to play in your browser for free, handily organised by year. Usefully, you can save the current game as a snapshot and come back to it later.

Best free simulators

Simulator programs let you fly planes, drive trains and even get a goat's-eye view of the world from your PC or armchair. Here are our favourites

In 1903, Wilbur Wright (with a little help from brother Orville) built the world's first successful airplane. Nearly a century later, a man named Will Wright helped pioneer flight simulators. Who doesn't enjoy a coincidence like that?

Wright (Will, not Wilbur) wasn't responsible for the first-ever flight simulator, but he did invent the simulator genre with his 1989 game SimCity. It spawned numerous spin-offs, including SimCopter and SimFarm, and inspired a whole industry of programs, apps and websites that let you fly planes, tour real-world cities and explore deep space in amazing detail from the safety and comfort of your PC.

SimCity is still hugely popular, and a 'Special Edition' of SimCity 2000 for PC (www.snipca.com/15202) was free for a while. The game has now reverted to its usual price of £4.99 – still fantastic value, given how much you can spend on simulators (here's a PlayStation Ferrari wheel for a cool 500 quid: www.snipca.com/15203). We'd rather save our cash and fly, drive and orbit the world without paying a penny.

Fly a plane

Open-source program FlightGear (www.flightgear.org) has been around for nearly two decades now, but it's constantly being improved and is still leagues ahead of its free flight-simulator rivals.

The latest version 3.2 (www.snipca.com/15232) lets you man the cockpit of more than 400 passenger jets, helicopters, war planes, airships and even the Wright Brothers' Flyer. You've got even more choice where you fly, with 20,000 real-life airports rendered in amazing detail, and thousands of miles of real-world scenery in between (we say scenery; they say "seamless, continuous oblate ellipsoid world").

Choose your plane and explore the world in detail with FlightGear

YSFlight lets you join a squadron of high-speed jets – without slowing down your PC

It's a vast labour of love and obsession, put together by an army of volunteers who've also created the the fans' go-to site FlightGear Wiki (www.snipca.com/15208) and a detailed, free online manual (www.snipca.com/15209).

There is a catch. The program is huge, so it's a real pain to install. First you have to choose a download mirror (the options appear when you click 'Download Now!' on the homepage), then wait for the 1.2GB installer to download, and only then can you start setting up the program.

If you and your PC don't want the hassle, we'd recommend YSFlight as a memory-light alternative (http://ysfhq.com). This free, small (8.8MB) program works on all versions of Windows since 2000. While it won't win any CGI awards, it doesn't skimp on options. There are scores of aircraft to fly or just watch, missions to accomplish and free ("always free") extension packs for adding new routes, missions and vehicles. The vehicles range from Ferraris to Star Wars trucks (check the forum for the latest: www.snipca.com/15233). YSFlight even lets you customise the weather. If only you could do that in real life!

Drive a train

Finding train simulators online is like looking for hay in a haystack. There are so many, for every budget, platform and disposition, that it's hard to weed out the good stuff.

Steaming ahead of the pack is Open Rails (http://openrails.org), which is unbeatable and completely free. This open-source project is similar in style and scale to FlightRadar, with a mind-boggling choice of trains and tracks, as well as its own wiki site (www.snipca.com/15241), featuring a manual and forum.

Open Rails grew from the ashes of the classic Microsoft Train Simulator (MSTS), and most MSTS files (routes, extensions and so on) are supported by Open Rails. You can download many of these files free from the File Library section of Train Sim (www.trainsim.com), a kind of Internet Archive for train simulator fans. If you have an old copy of MSTS kicking around, visit Train Sim's 'How To...' section (www.snipca.com/15240) for advice on making it

AROUND THE WORLD IN 8 FREE SIMULATORS

Sorry, we haven't got room for 80, but this lot should keep you busy...

1 CLIMB MOUNT EVEREST and explore the Himalayan landscape with free app Mount Everest 3D (Android www.snipca.com/13215, iOS www.snipca.com/13217).

2 TOUR ROME at the wheel of the Giagi Driving Simulator (www.snipca.com/15246, click Tour), which requires the Google Earth plug-in (www.snipca.com/15247).

3 EXPLORE THE OCEAN FLOOR as a deep-sea diver (or a squid!) with the online Savage Seas simulator (www.snipca.com/15253).

4 GET INSIDE ENGLAND'S GOLD VAULT using the free Bank of England Virtual Tour app (Android www.snipca.com/13225, iOS www.snipca.com/13287).

5 DRIVE DOWN LAS VEGAS STRIP with the Google Maps-based version of 2D Driving Simulator (www.snipca.com/15245).

6 FLY A BETTY BOMBER OVER JAPAN with World War II simulator WarBirds (www.snipca.com/15256). Register to download free.

7 HEAD FOR THE BEACH in wonderful 8bit-style graphics, courtesy of free online game Holiday Sim (www.snipca.com/15263).

8 BE A GOAT and butt walls, cars, people and anything in your realistic 3D path, using free app Crazy Goat (Android www.snipca.com/15265, iOS www.snipca.com/15266). It's inspired by the brilliant, but paid-for, Goat Simulator (www.goat-simulator.com, £3.99 for Android and iOS, £6.99 for PC).

work in Windows 7 and 8.

We also like the free Train Sim app (Android www.snipca.com/15243, iOS www.snipca.com/15244). It's not related to the Train Sim website. Man the controls of numerous trains and speed through a wide range of 3D environments, including a city's underground network. There are no in-app purchases to worry about, so a child can use it without running up a bill.

Explore deep space

Join the space race with Rodina (www.snipca.com/15211), a vast computer-generated universe you explore from a virtual space station. Click the Direct Download link to get the installer. Rodina fans will also like Limit Theory (http://ltheory.com), a virtual universe that's currently only available as a free prototype (www.snipca.com/15235). We'll let you know when it gets a stable release.

If you'd prefer a more educational and less game-like journey through space, try the Solar Walk app (Android www.snipca.com/15214, iOS www.snipca.com/15215). The free version lets you explore Saturn and its moons in amazing detail, using your fingertips to zoom in and out. You can also see their positions on any given date and explore their geography and history. Other planets, missions and spacecraft are available as in-app purchases.

Explore a vast virtual universe from your own space station with Rodina

The biggest solar system exploration app had only just been released at the time of going to press. Space Simulator (www.space-simulator.com) will eventually be available for Android, iOS, and PC, but at the time of publication, only the iPad version of the software was available (http://apple.co/1FKtVmo).

If you're waiting for an Android or PC version to appear, you can kill time by taking control of the Apollo 11 Moon Lander (www.snipca.com/15248), a beautiful, free simulator that works entirely online (requires the Google Earth plug-in, www.snipca.com/15247). Finally, and purely for laughs, try your luck with Comet Landing Simulator (www.snipca.com/15216), inspired by last November's bouncing space probe Pilae (www.snipca.com/15239). Let's just say it's not the most authentic simulator we've come across...

Steam through the countryside on your PC using free simulator Open Rails

Use Google's £260 Earth Pro for free

Google recently made its £260 program Earth Pro available for free, giving Google Earth users a vast array of new features to play with. Here, we'll show you how to install the Pro version and explain how you can then record your own 3D flyover virtual tour of any place in the world. You can then add your own commentary and convert your recorded tour into a high-definition version.

You can also use Pro to quickly measure distances between two locations, calculate the distance of any route, and print high-resolution images of famous landmarks, none of which you can do in the free version.

Despite Windows 8 being omitted from the system requirements on Earth Pro's homepage, we can confirm it works with Micorosoft's latest operating system.

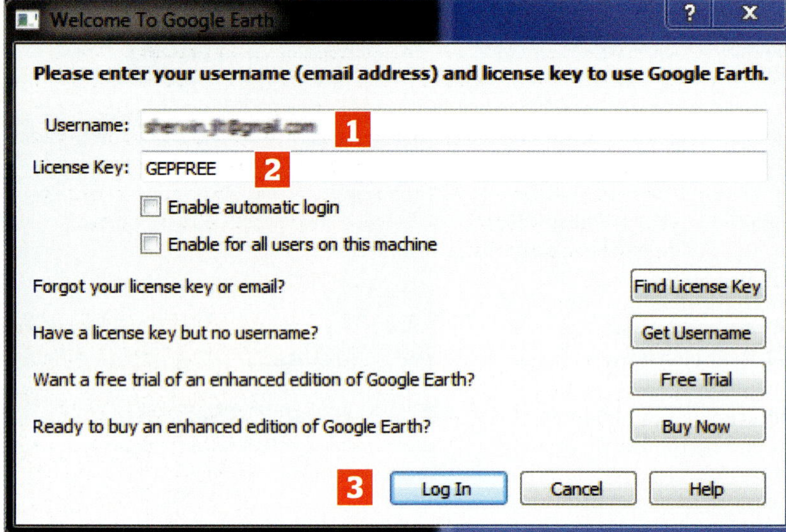

1 Go to www.snipca.com/15715 and click the blue 'Agree and Download' button at the bottom. Click the setup file that downloads to your PC, Yes, then wait for Google Earth Pro to download and install. On the login window, enter your Google email address in the Username field **1** , type GEPFREE **2** in the License Key field, and then click Log In **3**. Next, close the Start-Up Tips window, click 'Sign in' at the top right and log into your Google account using the same email address.

2 You'll now see the Google Earth globe. Click and drag it to rotate. Move the scroll wheel on your mouse up and down or use the slider **1** to zoom in and out. The two options at the top right **2** let you navigate the globe by tilting it on its axis and moving up, down, left and right. To switch on/off the globe's various layers (country borders, weather, photos from users, and so on), tick/untick those options in the Layers menu **3**.

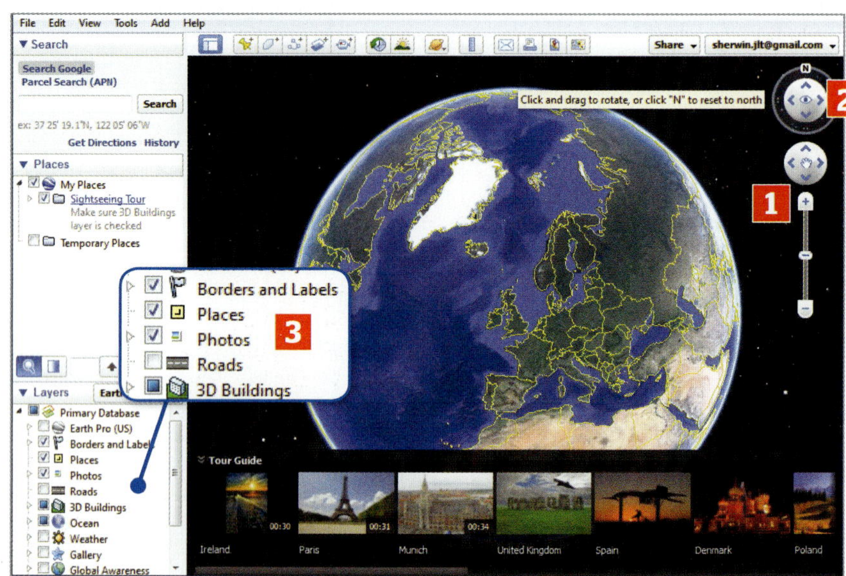

3 The Tour Guide thumbnails at the bottom contain short clips of 3D flyovers created by other users, which let you 'explore' a city. Type a city's name in the search field 1, then press Enter. If you cannot see the thumbnails, click the Expand icon beside Tour Guide 2. Click a thumbnail and use the playback controls 3 to view that tour and close it.

4 While the standard Google Earth lets you record your own city guide, Pro lets you do this in HD. To record your tour, find your chosen city/location on the globe. Use the onscreen controls to navigate from one point to the next (you'll find the transitions are smoother than if you use your mouse). Click the 'Record a tour' icon 1, then click the red Record icon 2 at the bottom left to begin recording. Click the mic icon 3 to record a voiceover for the tour. After you've finished, click the record icon again to stop recording and play back your tour. To re-record your tour, click the close icon and repeat this step.

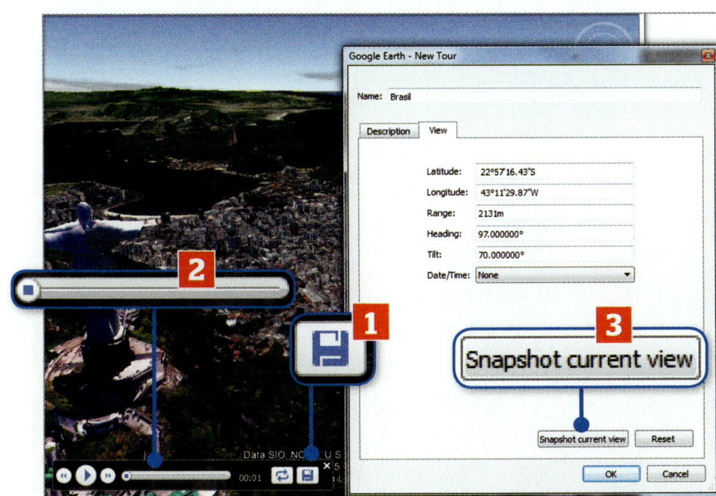

5 When you're happy with your tour, click the small floppy disc icon 1, name it, type a description in the Description field, then click the View tab. Here you can save the exact location of your recording as a 'snapshot'. Using the playback slider 2 navigate to a point in your video that best represents it, then click the 'Snapshot current view' button 3. This automatically fills out all the fields in the View tab based on the location of your snapshot. To add the date and time, click the Date/Time dropdown menu, click 'Time stamp', then click the month, date and time options and set them by moving the arrows.

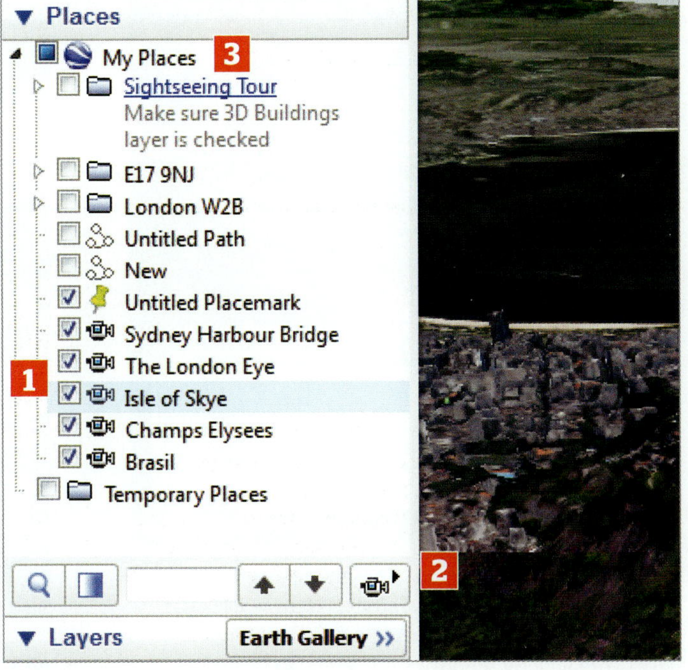

6 Recorded tours appear with a small videocam icon in the My Places section on the left 1. Double-click any tour to begin playing it, or click the tour, then click the video icon 2. Right-click any tour to see options to delete, rename or email it. Double-click any option other than a tour in the My Places section 3 to exit the tour mode.

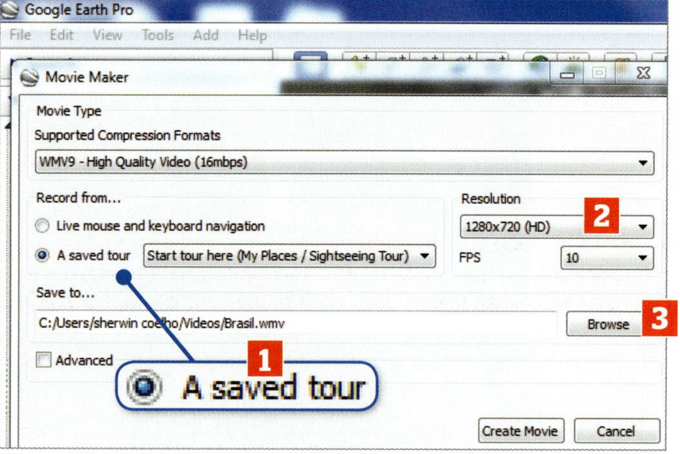

7 To convert your tour into HD, first click the Tools options at the top left, then Movie Maker. Select 'A saved tour' **1** and use the dropdown menu beside it to choose the tour you want to convert. Click the Resolution dropdown menu and select the resolution you – 1280x720 (HD) **2** is ideal. Click the Browse button **3**, navigate to the folder you want to save your HD tour to, name the file, then click Save. Next, click Create Movie. You'll now see a progress bar and once the creation process is finished, click Yes to watch the movie in your default video player.

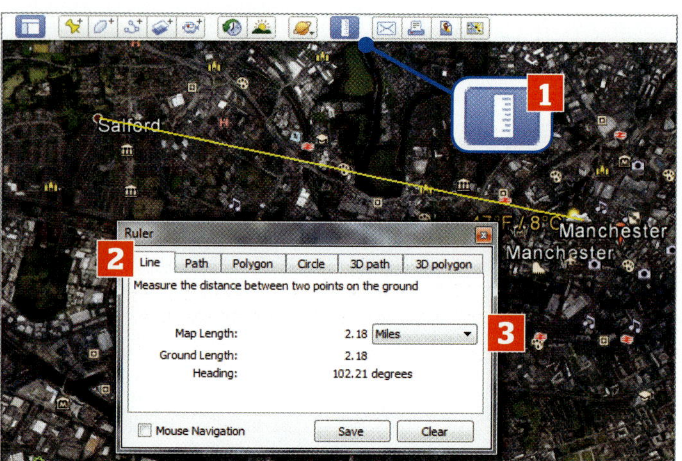

8 Google Earth Pro lets you measure the exact distance (as the crow flies) between two points on a map, then save this for future reference. Pro calculates the distance in any unit of measurement (anything from centimetres to nautical miles). Click the Ruler icon at the top **1**, then click the Line tab **2**. Click your first point of reference, then move your cursor to the second point and click it (to connect them with a yellow line). Click the Map Length dropdown menu **3** to choose the unit of measurement. Click Save and name it to store this measurement in the My Places section.

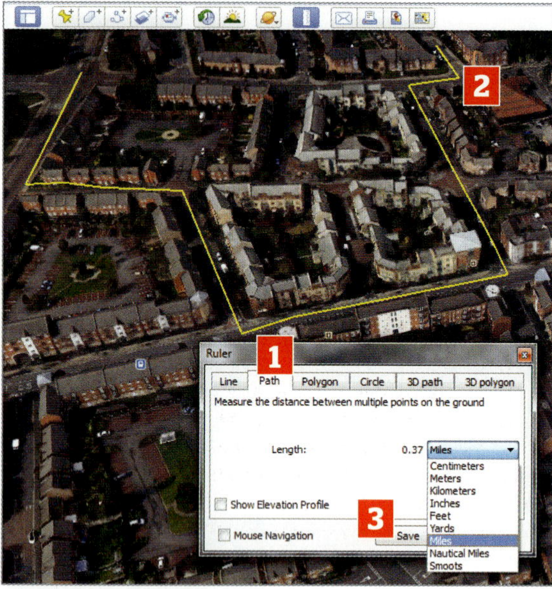

9 To calculate the distance of a route (via roads, for example), click the Path tab **1**. Now click the starting point, then click a second point on your route (when you change direction, for example) **2**. Continue clicking to plot points on your route until you reach your final destination. Press Delete on your keyboard if you need to undo the last point you clicked. Again, you can use the Length dropdown menu to change the unit of measurement, then click Save **3** to save this path to My Places.

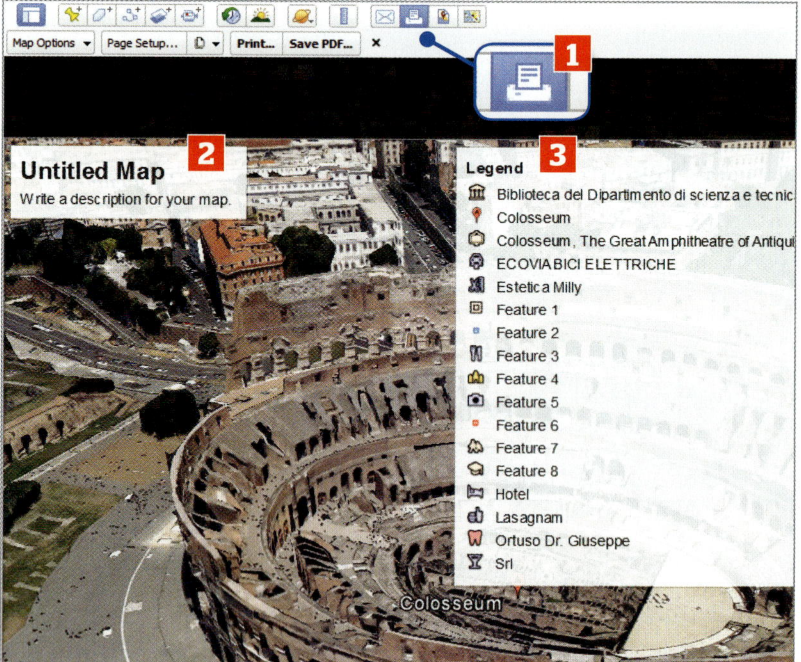

10 Another unique feature in Google Earth Pro is the option to print high-resolution images of any location on the map. Navigate to the place you want to print, then click the Print icon **1** at the top. You'll see two panes on the left and right. Click the left-hand pane **2** to name and describe your printout. Click the Legend pane on the right **3** and untick all the boxes to remove map markers (hotels, photos and so on). Next, click the Print button at the top, select your printer, then click Print.

Make amazing panoramas from your photos

Image Composite Editor (ICE) is a free Microsoft program (released in 2008) that creates stunning panoramas of your photos by merging them. It has now been updated with a new interface and includes new tools that let you fill in any missing gaps in your panorama and upload it to Photosynth – a Microsoft website that lets you zoom in and out of your photos.

1 For convenience, you should first create a folder on your Desktop and save the photos you're planning to use in your panorama there (in this Workshop, we'll merge five images). Before downloading ICE, you'll need to determine your version of Windows (64bit or 32bit). To do that, right-click Computer on your Desktop or Start menu, then click Properties and look under 'System type' **1**. Now go to www.snipca.com/16028 and click the Download ICE 2.0 option that corresponds to your PC. Next, click the Download button, then the setup file that downloads, and finally Run.

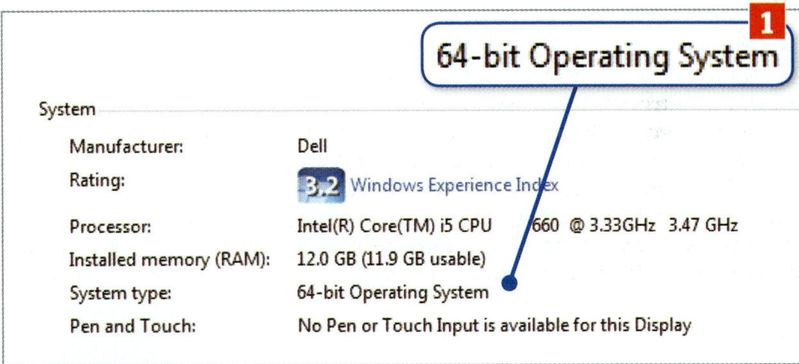

2 To work, ICE needs a feature called 'Microsoft Visual C++ 2013 Runtime Libraries'. If you don't have this, you'll be prompted to install it from the Microsoft website. Click Yes to go to the site, click the red Download button, tick the file that corresponds to your version of Windows, then click Next. Now click the downloaded file, Run, tick the terms and conditions box, then Install. When that's finished click Close. Now reopen your ICE setup file (in your Downloads folder), click Run, Next, tick I Agree **1**, click Next again **2**, select Everyone, then click Next (twice) to install it. When it's installed, click Close to open the program.

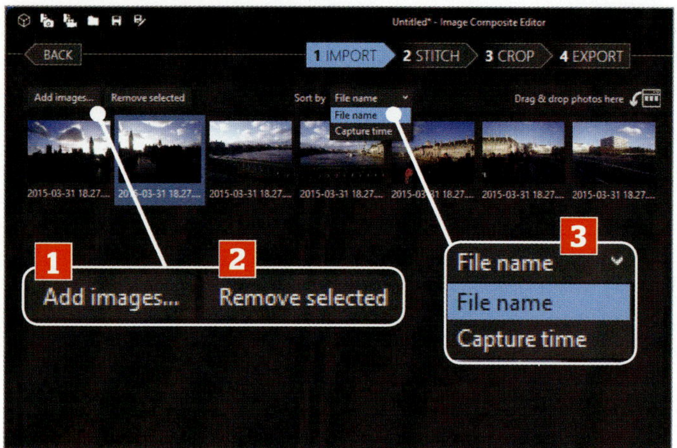

3 Click New Panorama From Images at the top left. Navigate to the folder you created on your Desktop, press Ctrl+A to select the photos, then click Open. You can add more by clicking 'Add images' **1** or by dragging and dropping them into the ICE window. To remove a photo, click it, then click 'Remove selected' **2**. You can organise your photos by name or by the time they were taken using the 'Sort by' dropdown menu **3**.

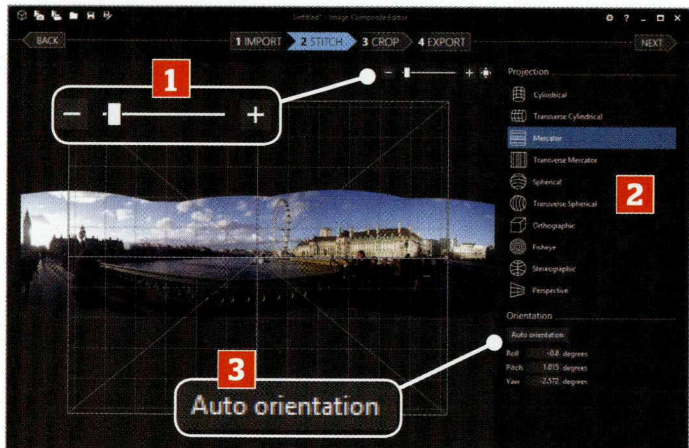

4 Make sure your photos are positioned in the order you want them merged (from left to right), then click Stitch at the top. ICE will merge them to create a single panoramic view. You can zoom in and out using the zoom slider **1** or by clicking the image and scrolling your mouse wheel. Click the different Projection styles **2** to try the visual effects and find the one that best suits your panorama. If your panorama isn't straight, click 'Auto orientation' **3**.

5 After selecting your Projection style (we selected Mercator – see screenshot), click Crop at the top (to change the Projection style, click Stitch to go back, select another Projection style, then click Crop). Next, click 'Auto crop' **1** to place a white (extendable) frame around your image. If there are empty black spaces **2** within your frame, click 'Auto complete' **3** to fill them spaces (this works best when filling flat expanses such as land or sky). The process can take a few minutes.

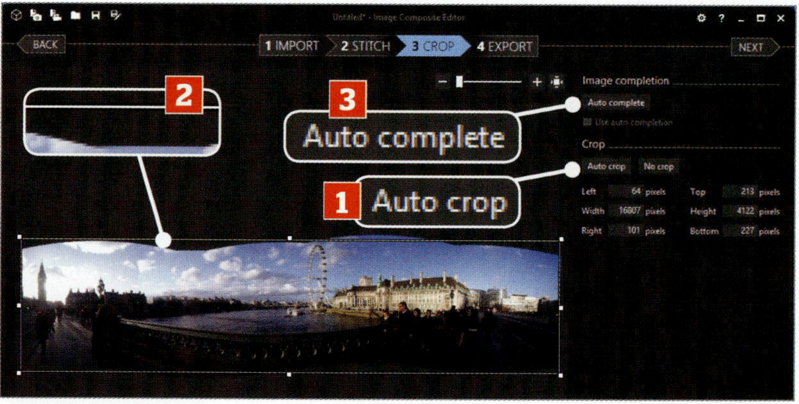

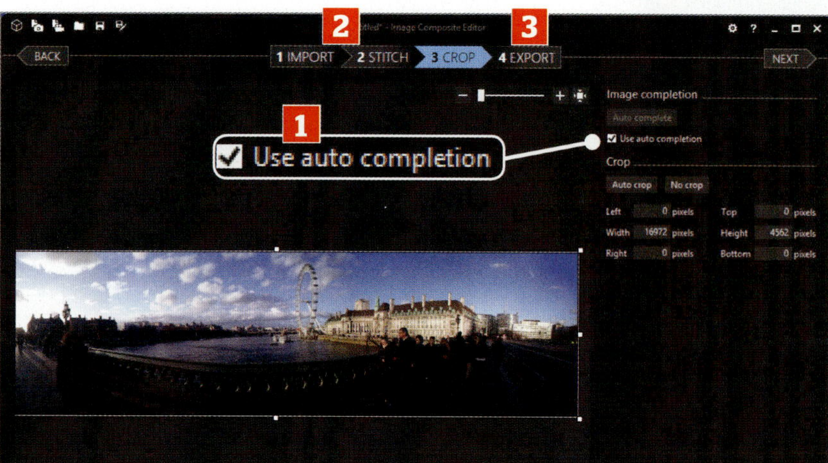

6 When that's finished, you should see a fully realised rectangular panoramic image. To compare this image to the pre-Auto complete version, untick 'Use auto completion' **1**. You can return to earlier stages of the process (such as Import or Stitch **2**) to make any changes. If you want to set the width and height (in pixels) of your panorama, type those values in the box on the right and click 'Auto crop'. When you're happy with your panorama, click Export **3**.

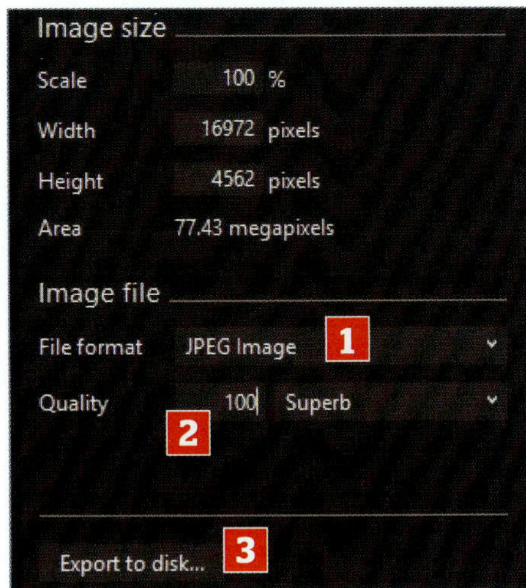

7 To save your panorama, click the Image dropdown menu, and select JPEG Image **1** from the 'File format' dropdown menu (this is the best format for saving panoramas). Next, click the Quality dropdown menu and select Superb (it's set to High by default). Now type 100 in the field beside Quality **2**. The resulting file will be larger but you'll see more detail. Finally, click 'Export to disk' **3**, name the file, save it wherever you want on your PC, then click Save.

8 The Deep Zoom dropdown menu **1** lets you create a high-resolution image that you can upload online, but it only works with certain Projection styles and on websites that support interactive (pan and zoom) elements. A better option is to upload your image to Microsoft's free Photosynth site, where others can view it using pan and zoom options. To do so, click Photosynth's dropdown menu **2**, then click 'Sign in' and log in using your Microsoft (Outlook or Hotmail) account **3**.

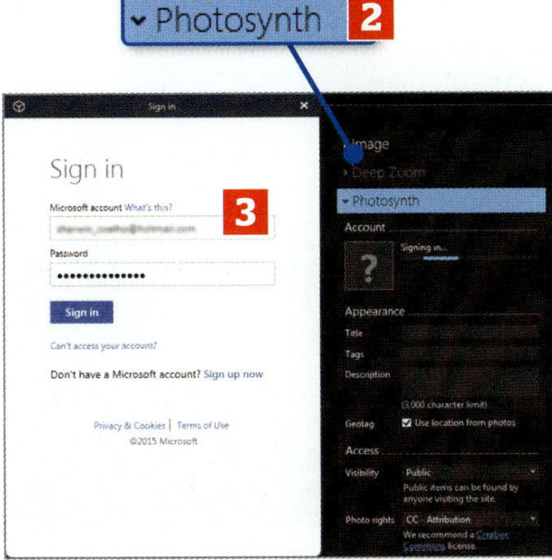

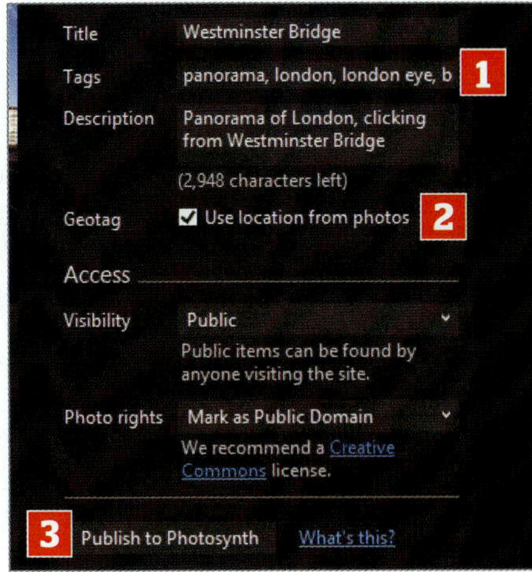

9 Now, create a Photosynth ID, then click 'Create account'. Next, give your panorama a title, tags (such as 'London') and a description **1**. Tick 'Use location from photos' **2** (to pin your image's location on a map – see Step 10). Now select Public from the Visibility dropdown menu to let anyone see your image, then click the 'Photo rights' dropdown menu and select whether you want to copyright your image or make it freely available for others to use. Finally, click 'Publish to Photosynth' **3**.

10 If you don't have Microsoft Silverlight installed, you'll be prompted to install it because panoramic photos on Photosynth can't be viewed without it. Click Install Microsoft Silverlight, then the downloaded setup file, followed by 'Install now' and Close. You'll now see an interactive (pan and zoom) version of your image on Photosynth. Use the controls **1** to zoom in and out of and pan across your image. You can edit your Title and Description **2** if you want. Clicking the Location tab **3** will display the precise location of your pictures in Bing Maps. If the pinned location is in the wrong place, click and drag it to the correct location, then click Save at the bottom.

Forecast the weather with your PC

Your computer can do far more than just check for rain. We discover the best free PC tools for predicting weather and even contributing to climate science

Britain is a weather-obsessed country. Don't take our word for it – survey company Brandwatch found that a fifth of all the internet's weather-based comments are made by British people (www.snipca.com/14949). When it comes to weather, we lead the world.

So why not get more actively involved in tracking and understanding our weather and climate? Using your PC, you can monitor global wind patterns in real time or trawl through historical records to see how the world's climate has changed in your lifetime. You can even play an important role in predicting meteorological patterns and contribute to international weather databases and climate studies.

Here, we reveal the best free tools for turning your PC into an interactive weather station.

See the rain that's heading your way

Rather than relying on TV weather forecasts or trying to gauge which one of the hundreds of weather websites is the most accurate, you can now monitor and predict the weather yourself.

Go to the website Sat24 (www.snipca.com/14927) to see a time-lapse view of the current weather above the UK (see screenshot above). You can view a range of weather conditions such as cloud banks, rain and lightning over the previous two-hour period.

The default map shows the weather across all of Europe, but click the dropdown menu where it says Europe on the left-hand side and select 'UK & Ireland' to see a more localised picture of the weather. At the bottom-right of the map, click 'Set up my location' to add up to three specific areas where you want to monitor the weather.

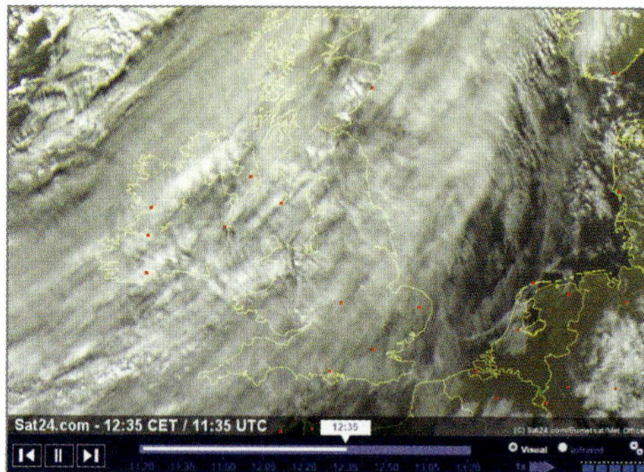

Track various weather conditions using Sat24's satellite-powered map

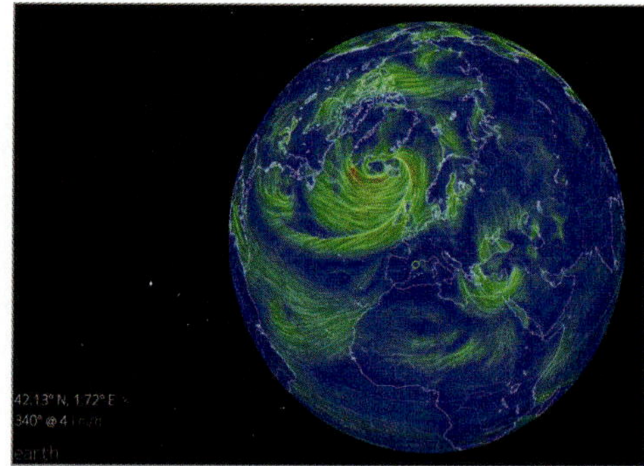
See the world's wind patterns moving in real time using online tool Earth

The free online tool Earth (www.snipca.com/14915) is more of a novelty than a weather-forecasting tool – but we love it. This interactive graphic globe (see screenshot above) displays wind currents around the world, so you can see what's heading your way. Watching the winds flow from one current to the next is mesmerising and gives you an overview on how these currents are all connected. To check out different parts of the world, click and drag the globe.

Be part of a forecasting supercomputer

The Climate Prediction project (www.climateprediction.net) harnesses the power of people's home PCs to predict the weather of the future.

The project, run by Oxford University, relies on the processing power of thousands of volunteers' computers to carry out complex calculations that help predict changes in the global climate.

To get involved, you first need to download and install the free open- source program BOINC (Berkeley Open Infrastructure for Network Computing) from www.snipca.com/14936. This tool lets you contribute to science projects like SETI (the Search for Extra-Terrestrial Intelligence, www.snipca.com/14937) and the medical initiative Rosetta (www.snipca.com/14938) as well as the Climate Prediction project. After installing BOINC on your computer, you can connect it to as many of these projects as you like, committing a small portion of your PC's processing power to each one. You can find instructions on setting up and using BOINC at www.snipca.com/14917.

BOINC runs quietly in the background, and you shouldn't notice any impact on your PC. Its creators recommend installing it in a partition or in a virtual PC such as VirtualBox (see our guide to VirtualBox on p62), but you don't have to.

TURN YOUR TABLET INTO A WEATHER STATION

With their array of sensors and GPS connectivity, smartphones and tablets are brilliant devices for tracking and reporting the weather. Some even have built-in barometers (www.snipca.com/14921).

Free app WeatherSignal (Android www.snipca.com/14918; iOS www.snipca.com/14919) takes advantage of these features by logging the weather conditions where you are, then submitting the data to its crowd-sourced weather map. So you not only get your own barometer, but also contribute valuable weather data to the scientific community.

To view detailed weather information such as winds, pressure and humidity, it's worth forking out £1.99 for WeatherGeek Pro 2 (www.snipca.com/14922, iOS only). The app gives you access to the same numerical weather models used by professional meteorologists, including the European ECMWF Model (www.ecmwf.int). You can draw or write notes on the animated maps with your finger, and they look fantastic on the iPad's Retina Display.

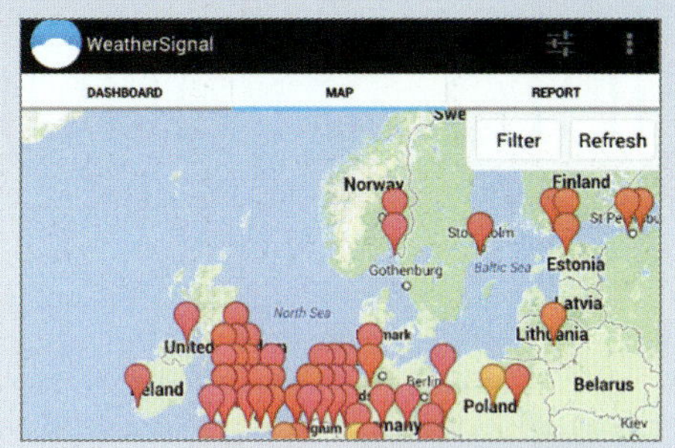

Use your tablet to help create a huge crowd-sourced weather map with WeatherSignal

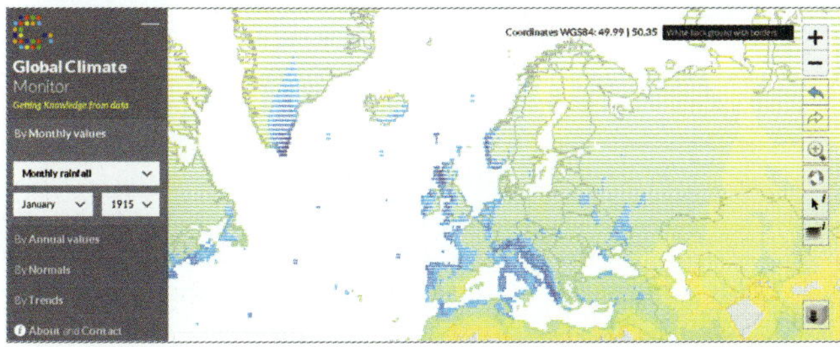

Compare today's weather with that of a century ago using the Global Climate Monitor

To see the progress of the tasks you've assigned your PC, open BOINC, click View, Advanced View, then click the Tasks tab. As well as listing its projects, BOINC also visualises your PC's calculations on a globe. To see this, go to the Tasks tab, click 'climateprediction.net' in the list, then 'Show graphics'. You'll see an image of the Earth (see screenshot bottom right) showing the climate conditions worked out so far by your PC, and based on the data provided by Climate Prediction.

You can even set this globe as your screensaver. Right-click your Desktop, click Personalize, then Screen Saver at the bottom right. In the new window, click the 'Screen saver' dropdown menu and select BOINC.

Monitor historical weather patterns

Were your childhood summers really sunnier and the winters more snowy? Put your rose-tinted memory to the test by checking what the weather really was like at specific times since the dawn of the 20th century.

The UK Met Office (www.metoffice.gov.uk) has a vast database of records on the UK climate, including average temperatures, extreme weather events and anomalies. The site's monthly climate anomaly records (www.snipca.com/14932) date back to 1919, so you can check the weather in the month and year you were born and see how it compares with today. The page also features summaries of UK climate by region and national weather extremes in the UK.

The Met Office's 'Past weather events' records (www.snipca.com/14933) only go back as far as 1990, but they're still fascinating. Click a year to discover the most significant UK weather events in that year, including storms, floods and record temperatures – for example temperatures in August 1990 reached over 35 degrees Celsius in many parts of the UK. All the records are free to access.

For a world-wide perspective, use the free Global Climate Monitor site (www.globalclimatemonitor.org) to analyse global monthly temperatures and rainfall, dating all the way back to January 1901. Everything is presented in a clear, colour-coded map, so you can see which parts of the world have warmed (and cooled) the most since the start of the 20th century (see screenshot above left).

Watch weather webcams around the world

Do you ever torture yourself by checking the weather in warmer parts of the world while we're in the middle of a thoroughly miserable winter? If so, you should bookmark websites that show weather-monitoring webcam footage uploaded by people all over the world.

The best of these is Weather Underground's Weather Webcams Directory (www.snipca.com/14909). The site features nearly 20,000 webcams that can be viewed by anyone for free.

Some feeds are displayed as pictures that are updated every 15 minutes, others are time-lapses, and there are even live video streams. In the right-hand pane of the site you'll see an option to set up your own webcam to stream weather footage to the world, so other people can get a taste of our gloriously unpredictable British weather.

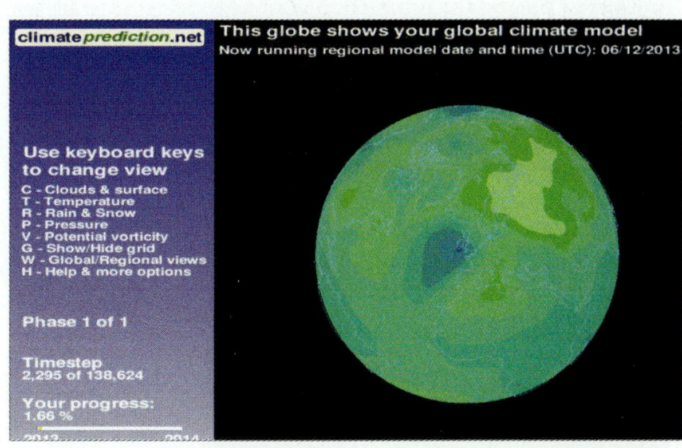

Use your PC to help the Climate Prediction project forecast the weather of the future

Turn your life story into an audiobook

Audacity is a free audio-editing program that lets you record a voiceover and embellish it with music and sound effects. Despite its overwhelming appearance, it's actually very simple to use. We'll show you how to record your life story, edit it, add an intro and background music, then save the file as an audiobook that your children and grandchildren will treasure. You can either use this Workshop to create one chapter of your life or to narrate your entire life story in one go.

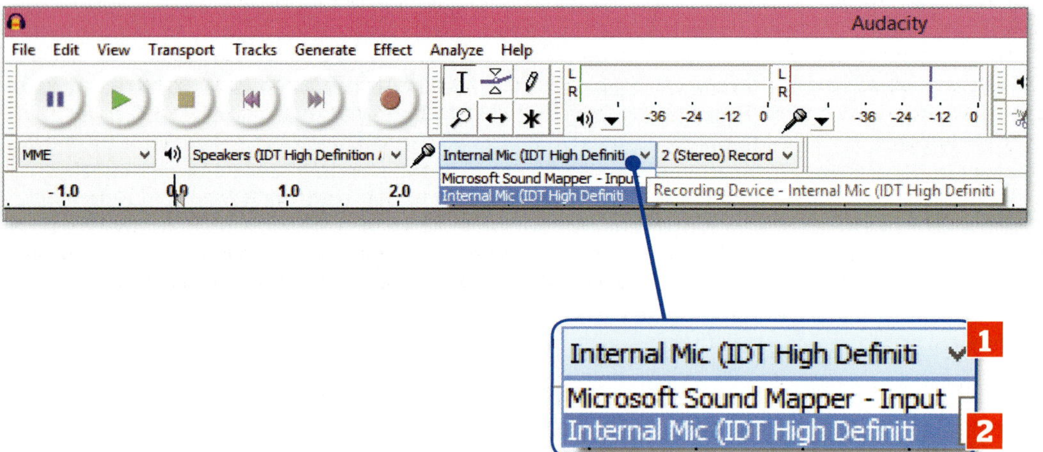

1 Go to www.snipca.com/14663 and click the 'Audacity 2.0.6 installer' link at the top. Click the setup file that downloads to your PC and follow the steps to install the program. Close the Help screen that pops up after it launches. Ensure you're in a quiet room while recording your voiceover. If you can, connect a microphone (mic) to your PC because your PC's built-in mic will pick up the ambient noises around you. Audacity will detect your mic **1**. If your PC has several mic options, use the dropdown menu **2** to select the one you want.

2 Create a test recording for about a minute to check that everything is okay. To begin recording, click the Record button (or press R on your keyboard) **1**, wait for five seconds and then start speaking (we'll explain why you need to wait in Step 5). You'll see waveforms (lines) appear as you speak, which represent your recording. To stop recording, click the Stop button **2** (or press the spacebar on your keyboard). To play back your recording, click the beginning of the waveform lines, then press Play **3** (or the spacebar). Hearing your recording back will give you an idea of whether you need to change your mic or move to a quieter room. Click anywhere on your recorded waveform then press Delete to delete this test recording.

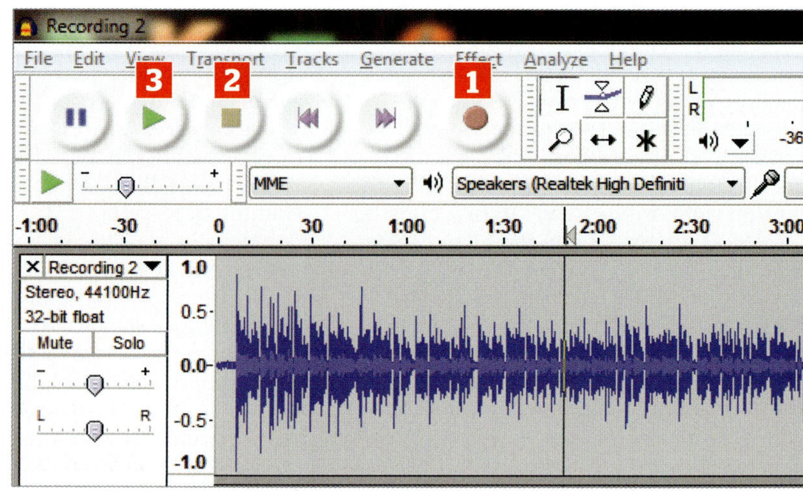

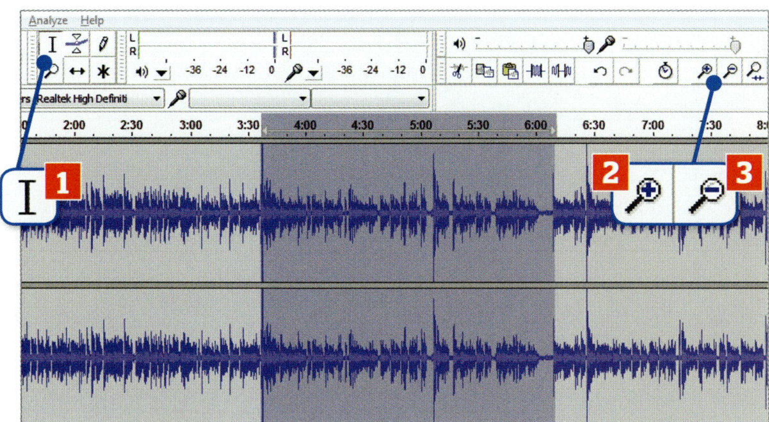

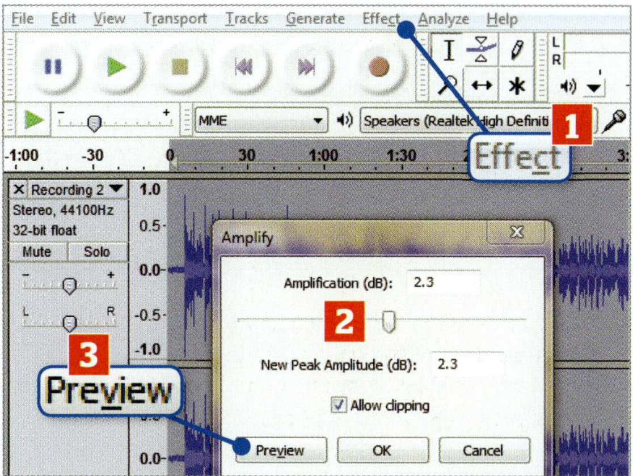

3 When you're ready to make your first recording, repeat Step 2. Record as much as you can in one go. Don't worry about any mistakes, repetitions or long pauses as we'll show you how to remove these in the next step. After you've finished, click the Selection Tool **1**, which is used to select any section of your file. To only play a section of a recording, highlight it and press the spacebar. Use the Zoom In **2** and Zoom Out **3** options at the top to zoom into a specific area of your recording and see it more clearly. You can also use the keyboard shortcut Ctrl+1 to zoom in and Ctrl+3 to zoom out.

4 Editing mistakes in Audacity is as easy as editing text in Word. Ensure that the Selection Tool is clicked, then highlight the section you want to delete (mistakes, long pauses, repetitions) and then press Delete on your keyboard. To undo a deletion, press Ctrl+Z. Audacity has tons of effects to make your audio sound better. For example, if you notice that your recording is too soft, press Ctrl+A to select your recording. Next, click Effect **1**, then Amplify. Now move the slider a fraction to the right **2** (moving it to the left makes it softer) and click Preview **3** to hear how a portion of your track will sound with the applied effect. If you like it, tick 'Allow clipping' then click OK to amplify the recording.

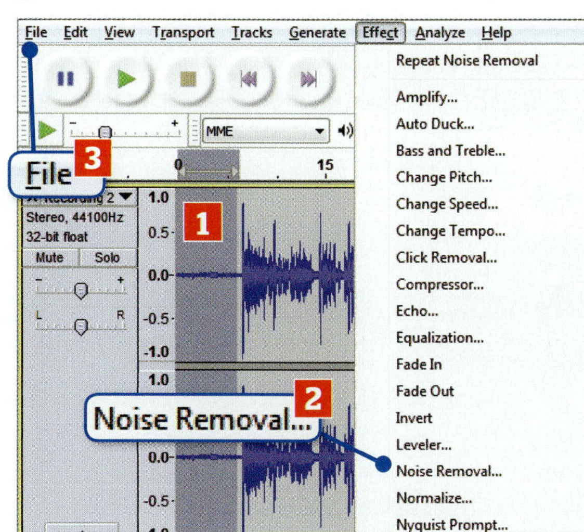

5 There will probably be background noise in your recording. Audacity has a brilliant built-in tool to minimise this. First, highlight the five seconds of static audio at the start of your recording **1**. Now click Effect, Noise Removal **2** and then click Noise Profile. This tells Audacity that it should detect that specific background noise throughout your audio and remove it. Next, select your entire recording by pressing Ctrl+A. Then click Effect, Noise Remove and OK to remove that background sound. We'll now save what we've done thus far as an Audacity file that we can edit later. Click File **3**, Save Project As, name your file and then click Save.

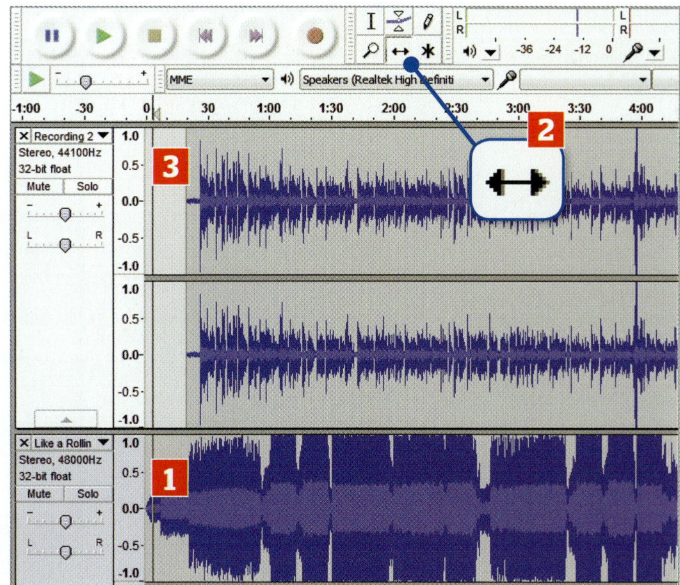

6 A great way to begin your audiobook is to fade in with a music track. Here, we're using the intro of Bob Dylan's Like a Rolling Stone. Open the folder containing that track on your PC and then drag and drop the track into Audacity. You'll see it loaded in a second waveform **1** at the bottom of your original recording. If you press Play at the start of your recording, both these tracks will play together. Because we only want the music to start, we'll use the Time Shift Tool **2**, which lets us move one track independently of the other. Click it, click your recording at the top and then move it to the right to add a blank space at the start of your recording **3**.

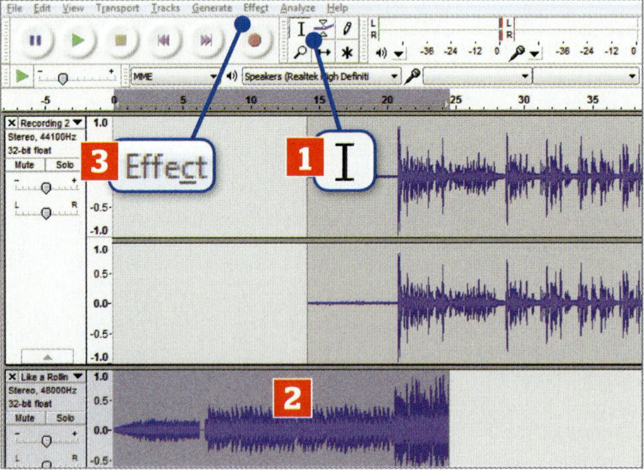

7 Now click the Selection Tool **1**, zoom into the start of your timeline then play your recording from the start by pressing the spacebar. You should only hear the music. Pause the track (by pressing the spacebar) and use the Time Shift Tool again to align your recording exactly where you want it to begin after the music intro. To add a Fade In effect to this intro (before your recording begins), click the Selection Tool, highlight the intro music **2**, click Effect **3**, then Fade In. Delete the rest of the track (see Step 4) so that the music doesn't conflict with your recording.

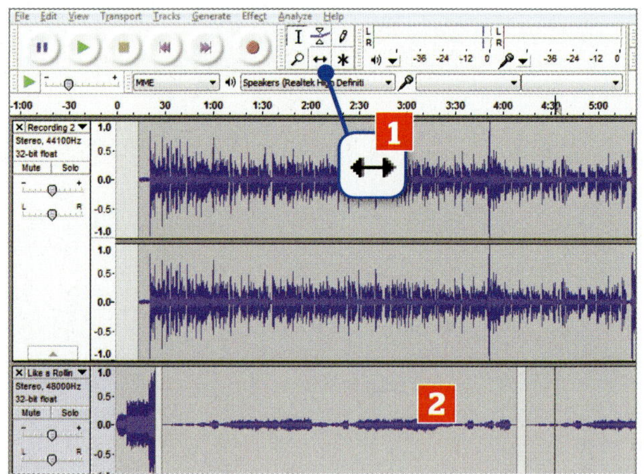

8 To keep your listener interested, you could use an instrumental backing track that compliments your recording. Use any instrumental track from your PC (you can also find and download royalty-free tracks from www.snipca.com/14669). Drop the track into Audacity and click OK. It'll appear as a third waveform. Click the Time Shift Tool **1**, then click the track and drag it from the third waveform to the second **2** (where your intro music is). If this backing track is not long enough, use the Selection Tool to highlight the entire track, press Ctrl+C (to copy it), then press Ctrl+V (to paste it). Join all these copies together using the Time Shift Tool.

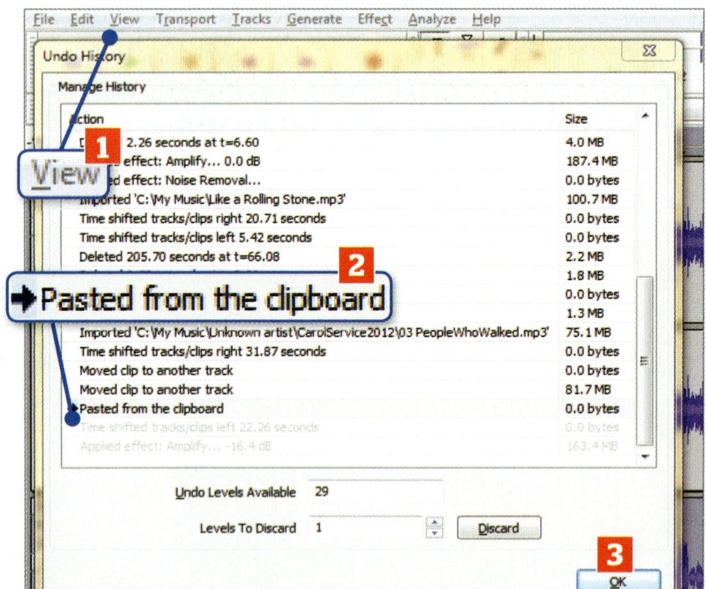

9 Make sure you divide up your audiobook into sections, each with its own intro and background music. You can also add sound effects (www.freesound.org is a good resource for free effects). For example, if you're describing your favourite beach holiday destination (or your honeymoon), you could use one of Freesound's wave effects. Don't worry about making mistakes as Audacity automatically saves all your changes to a History file that can be accessed by clicking View **1** and then History. Here you can jump to any past changes you've made by clicking it **2** and then clicking OK **3**.

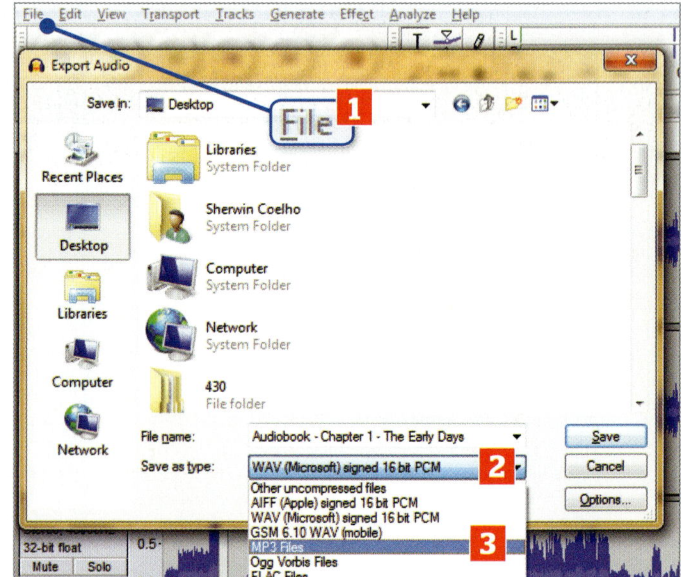

10 End your audiobook by adding some uplifting music. Add a fade-out effect by highlighting the last few seconds, then clicking Effect, Fade Out. To save your audiobook, click File **1** and then click Export Audio. By default, Audacity will save it as a WAV file **2**, which is a larger file format than MP3, with better sound quality. To save it as an MP3 instead, click the 'Save as type' and select that option in the dropdown menu **3**. Finally, name your track, navigate to where you want to save it, click Save and then OK on any confirmations that appear.

Chapter 7

Boost your web browser

Find out how to get the most from the piece of software we use more than any other

The web browser is the one piece of software we're guaranteed to use every day. Yet, most people tend to stick with the same web browser for years, maybe even venturing no further than the Internet Explorer browser that comes pre-installed with Windows. In this chapter we're going to open your eyes to some of the browser alternatives, and how you can get more from several of the most popular browsers, including Google Chrome and Mozilla Firefox. We'll also show you how to solve common problems, and warn you of the browser add-ons that you should stop using to make your internet sessions speedier and safer.

CONTENT

Browse the web with Vivaldi

When choosing a browser, most people tend to stick with the bigger names – Chrome, Firefox, Internet Explorer and Opera. Vivaldi stands out from the legions of lesser-known browsers because it has a recognised pedigree, coming as it does from a team headed by Jon S. Von Tetzchner, the co-founder of Opera. Vivaldi is a 'technical preview' rather than a finished browser, so some of its promised tools haven't yet materialised, but will be coming soon. Until that time, you may want to hold off using it as your main browser, although it's still worth taking for a spin. Vivaldi is based on Chromium, the open-source project on which Google's Chrome is built, so it's fast, stable and displays any web pages that Chrome does.

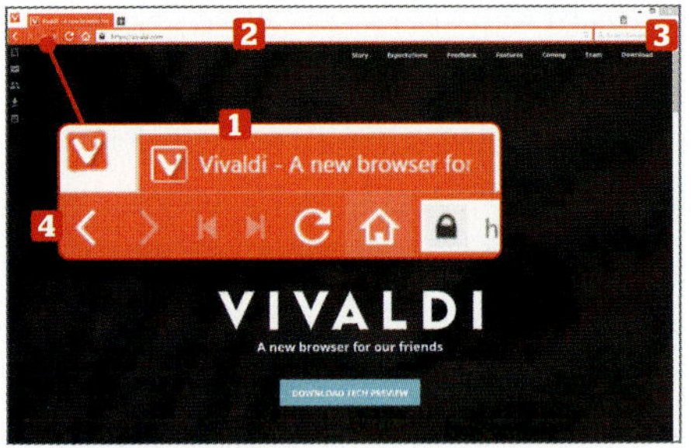

1 There are tabs along the top of the browser, **1** and separate boxes for address **2** and search. **3** Vivaldi installs Google as the default search engine. Navigation controls **4** are on the left of the address box. Despite being based on Chromium, like Google's Chrome, Vivaldi looks very different.

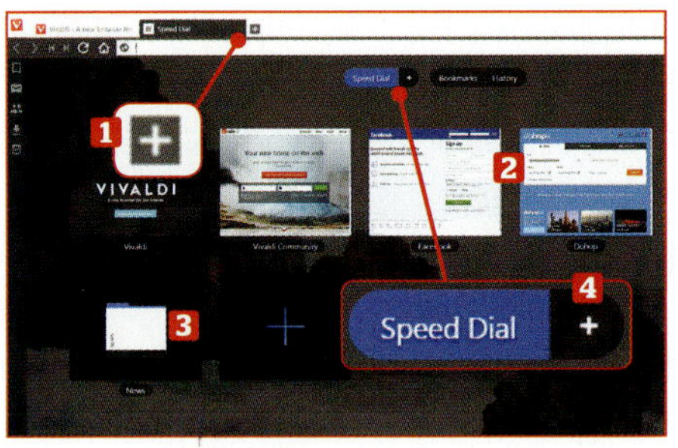

2 Click the plus sign **1** to open a new tab. This opens the Speed Dial page offering quick access to your favourite sites. Click a thumbnail to open its page. **2** You can reorder thumbnails by clicking and dragging, and drop them into folders. **3** Add a new Speed Dial page by clicking the plus button. **4**

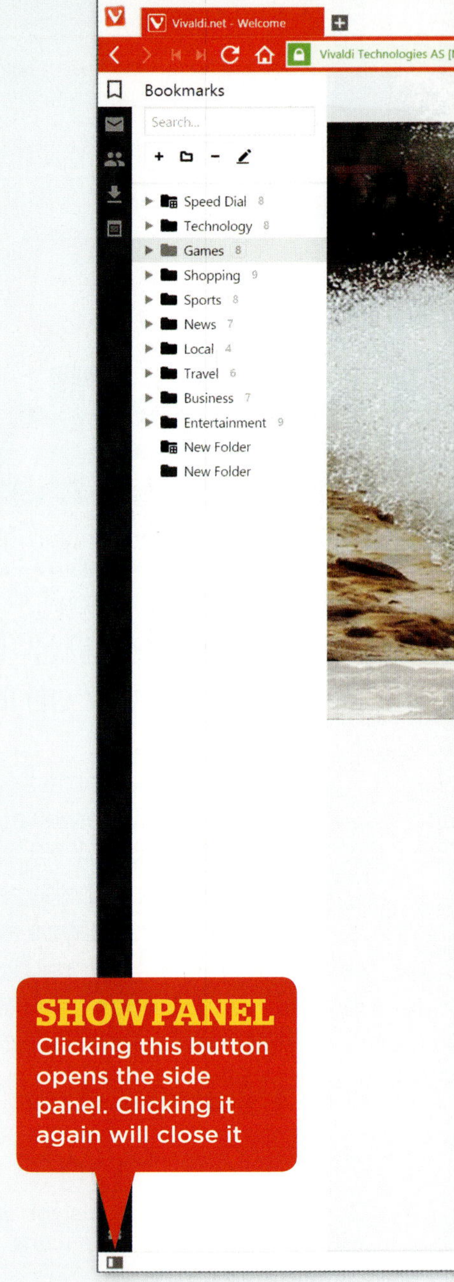

SHOWPANEL
Clicking this button opens the side panel. Clicking it again will close it

3 To add a bookmark to the Speed Dial, click the plus thumbnail (it will change to a cross) **1** and enter the URL of the site. **2** You can create a new folder here, too. **3** Click the Add button **4** and the site will be added to Speed Dial. After a few seconds, the thumbnail will be updated to show what the site looks like.

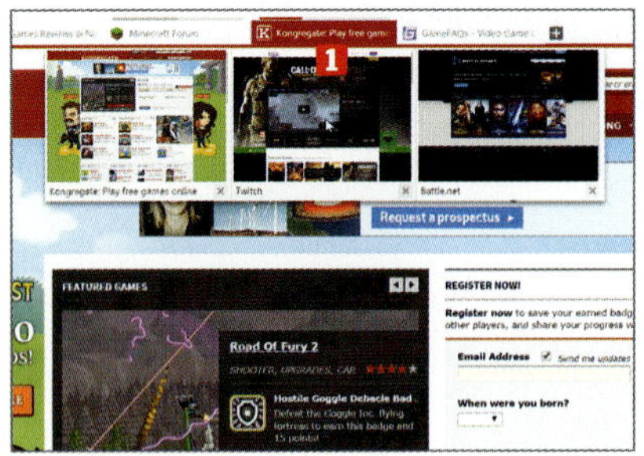

4 If you like having lots of tabs open at the same time, Vivaldi can help you manage them, without the top of the screen overflowing into a jumbled mess. Hover your mouse over any tab to see a thumbnail of the page. There's also a Tab Stacking feature. Drag and drop tabs on top of each other to create a stack. **1**

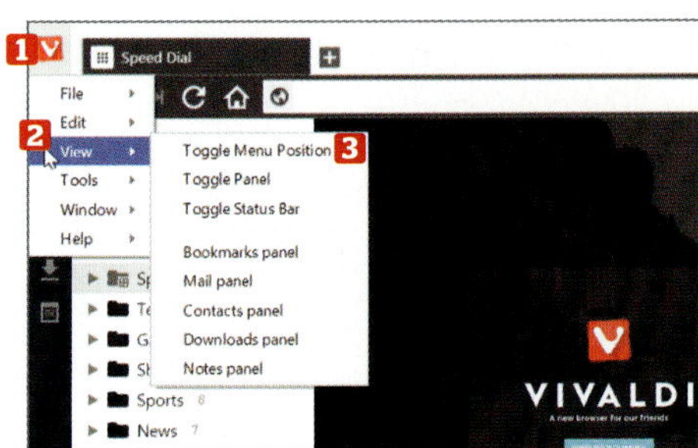

5 The Vivaldi button **1** displays the browser menu. You can access the File, Edit, View, Tools, Window and Help menus from here. **2** If you prefer to have the menu running across the top of the browser, go to View and select Toggle Menu Position. **3** You can also toggle the Panel and Status Bar on or off.

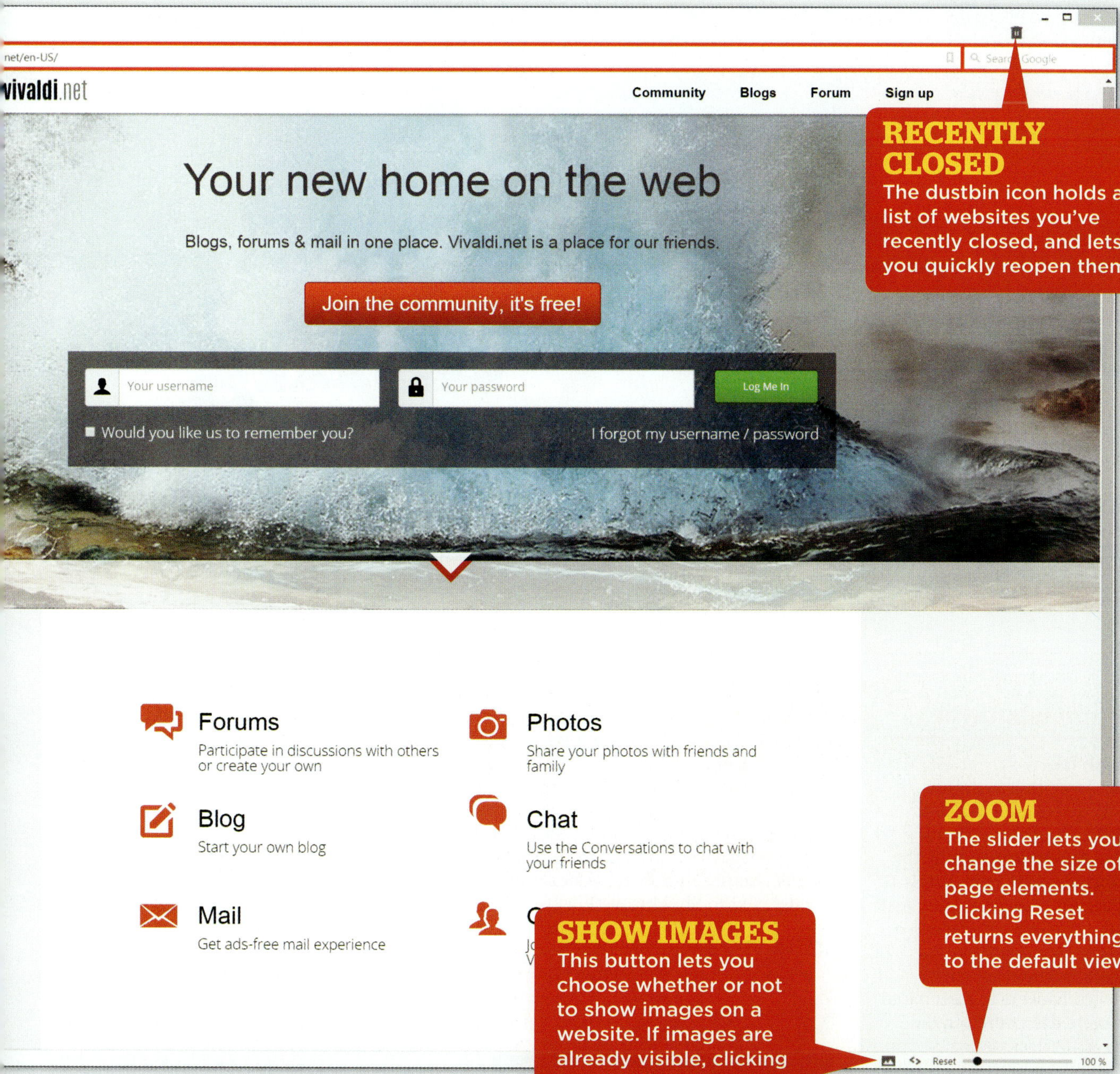

RECENTLY CLOSED

The dustbin icon holds a list of websites you've recently closed, and lets you quickly reopen them.

ZOOM

The slider lets you change the size of page elements. Clicking Reset returns everything to the default view

SHOW IMAGES

This button lets you choose whether or not to show images on a website. If images are already visible, clicking it will hide them

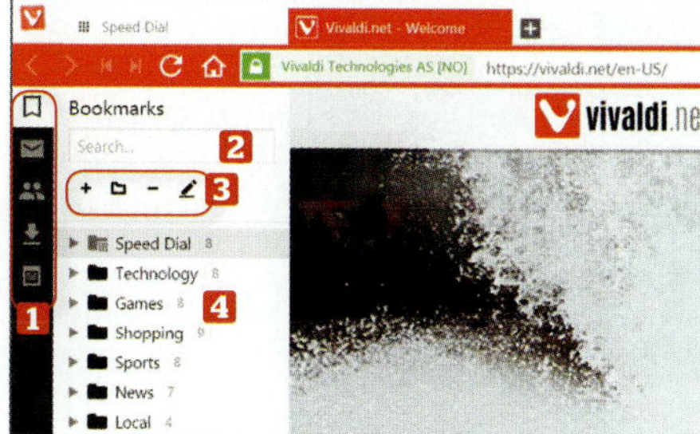

6 The side panel provides quick access to Bookmarks, Vivaldi Mail, Contacts, Downloads, and Notes. **1** You can search for bookmarks; **2** create new ones; add folders to store them in; and delete and edit them. **3** The browser comes with a selection of bookmarks organised into folders. **4**

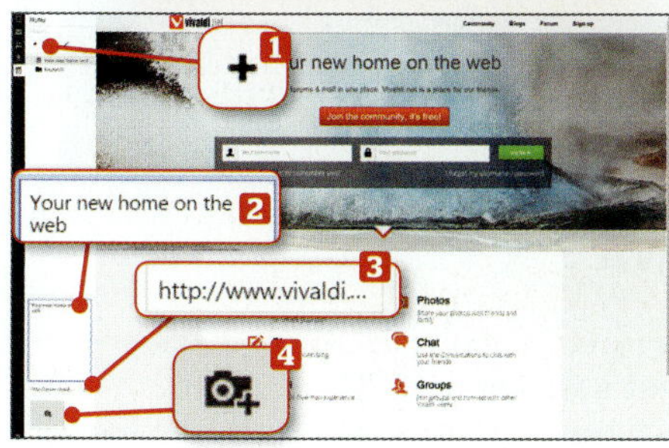

7 The Notes section provides a place to jot down information for later reference as you browse the internet. Click the plus sign **1** to create a new note, and type or paste content into it. **2** You can add and open a web address. **3** Click the camera icon **4** to take and add a screenshot of the current site.

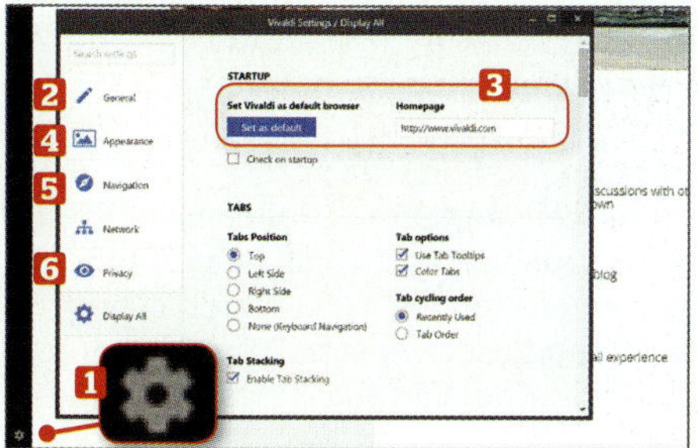

8 The cog button **1** opens the Settings. General **2** lets you make Vivaldi the default browser and set a homepage. **3** You can change how tabs, panels and menus look and work under Appearance; **4** change keyboard shortcuts under Navigation **5** and manage cookies and passwords under Privacy. **6**

Browser tools you should STOP using

Outdated plug-ins and add-ons compromise the security and stability of Chrome and Firefox. Find out why and how you should remove them from your browsers

FLASH
get.adobe.com/flashplayer

What's wrong with it?
Barely a week goes by without another security flaw being discovered in Flash, which leaves Adobe doing more patching than a patchwork-quilt factory. In 2012, the company had to introduce its own 'Patch Tuesday'-style monthly security update just to fix frequent vulnerabilities in Flash. And earlier this year, three serious 'zero-day exploits' (previously unknown security holes), which allowed hackers to infect your PC with Trojans, were discovered in the space of a month (bit.ly/flash369).

Add to this the well-known performance problems – such as Flash crashing and taking your browser with it – and it's clear why you should opt out of this buggy old plug-in.

What can I use instead?
A lot of web content that once used Flash, such as videos, games and animations, is now rendered in HTML5, which is built into all modern browsers. YouTube recently announced that it was ditching Flash for HTML5, and Mozilla is developing a tool called Shumway that converts Flash content into HTML5. Test Shumway by installing the add-on and trying the demos at mozilla.github.io/shumway.

How do I remove it?
Sadly, as some sites still use Flash, including BBC News, if you remove it, you won't be able to see certain content. Instead, you should disable the plug-in and choose whether or not to run it when you encounter Flash. To do this in Chrome, go to Settings, 'Show advanced settings', Privacy and click 'Content settings'. Scroll down to Plug-ins, select 'Click to play' and click Finished. In Firefox, go to Tools, Add-ons, Plugins and select 'Ask to Activate' next to Shockwave Flash.

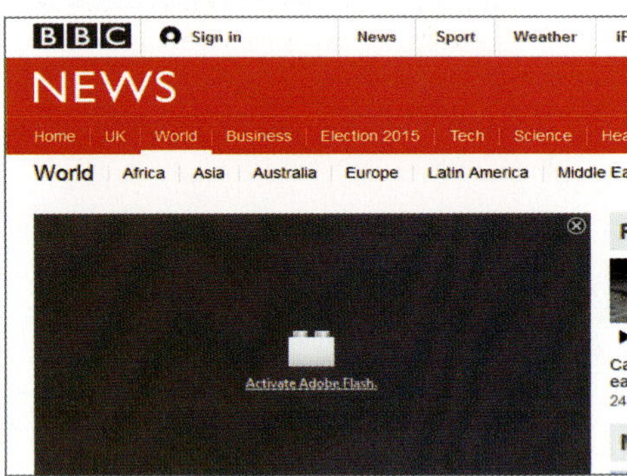

JAVA
www.java.com

What's wrong with it?
Once regarded as a "key building block of the web", Java has long served its purpose and, like Flash, its security vulnerabilities now make it more of a hindrance than a help. A few years ago, there was a significant increase in the number of malicious attacks targeting Java, and Oracle (the company that owns Java) was slow to patch known flaws. This led to Mozilla blocking Java in Firefox, and for security experts such as Graham Cluley to recommend that users disable the plug-in immediately (bit.ly/javaflaw369). Java has never really recovered from this bad publicity, and remains neglected by Oracle.

What can I use instead?
Nothing, and generally you shouldn't need to unless you're visiting a particularly old website or using a program that's based on Java (which will run separately from your browser). One place you'll use it without realising is on your Android phone, because Google's mobile operating system was written in the Java programming language, as are most Android apps.

How do I remove it?
As with Flash, you can choose to run Java only when you need it, but it's best to disable it altogether. In Firefox, go to Tools, Addons, Plugins and choose 'Never activate' next to the Java entries; and in

How to turn off Java in your browser - and why you should do it now

Join thousands of others, and sign up for Naked Security's newsletter

you@example.com Do it!

Don't show me this again

by Graham Cluley on August 30, 2012 | 182 Comments
FILED UNDER: Featured, Java, Malware, Vulnerability

Do you still have Java turned on in your web browser?

If your answer is "Yes" or "I'm not sure" then it's time to take action.

Right now, cybercriminals are aware and exploiting serious security flaws in Java that could lead to your computer becoming infected by malware.

And the worst news is that Oracle (who has known about the zero-day vulnerabilities since April) doesn't plan to issue a patch for the problem until October. (**Update:** Oracle has now issued a patch - but you should still consider whether you really want to run Java or not in your browser).

Chrome, type chrome:plugins into the address bar, press Enter and disable Java from there.

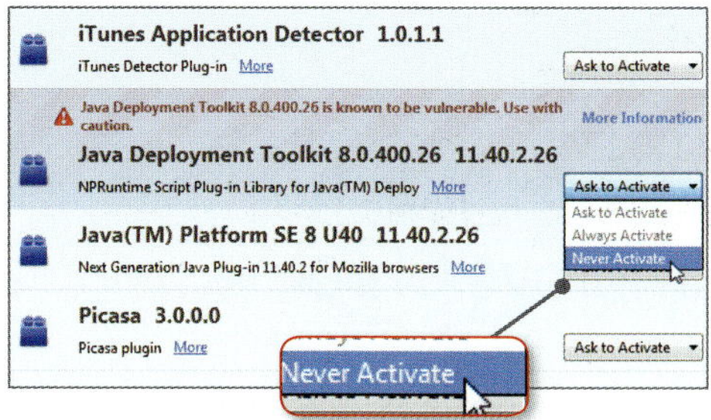

SILVERLIGHT
www.microsoft.com/silverlight

What's wrong with it?

Once touted as Microsoft's more versatile alternative to Flash, Silverlight unfortunately replicated some of the same problems as Adobe's plug-in, being slow to load, prone to crash and delivering less than perfect video playback. However, that hasn't stopped many big names from using Silverlight, including Netflix (until 2013), Amazon (for Prime Instant Video) and, of course, Microsoft itself, including in Bing Maps. But with the last new version released four years ago and Windows 8 supposed to herald a new "plug-in free" era, it seems that Silverlight is on its way out.

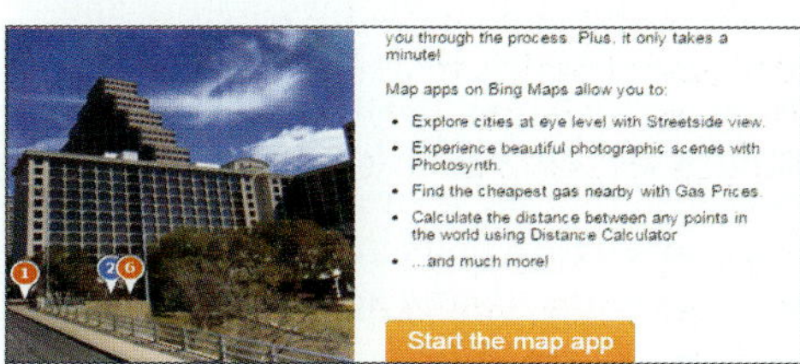

What can I use instead?

Like Flash, Silverlight is gradually being phased out in favour of HTML5, with reports suggesting that Microsoft will drop support altogether by 2021. This means that you're less likely to need the plug-in than a few years ago.

How do I remove it?

You can either run Silverlight only when you need it by choosing 'Click to play' or 'Ask to Activate', or disable it altogether, on your browser's Plug-ins page. Alternatively, you can choose precisely which sites can display Silverlight content. Type Silverlight into your Start menu or screen, press Enter, then click the Permissions tab and click Allow or Deny for all listed sites.

HOVERZOOM
hoverzoom.net

What's wrong with it?

With more than 1.3 million users, the image-enlargement tool Hover Zoom is probably the most popular Chrome extension to turn to the dark side. As it states on its page on the Chrome Web Store, you're now required to grant the extension permission "to collect browsing activity to be used internally and shared with third parties", which should immediately set alarm bells ringing. Hover Zoom is regarded as adware by the security tool Extension Defender (www.extensiondefender.com), because the data it collects (albeit anonymously) can be used to target you with ads.

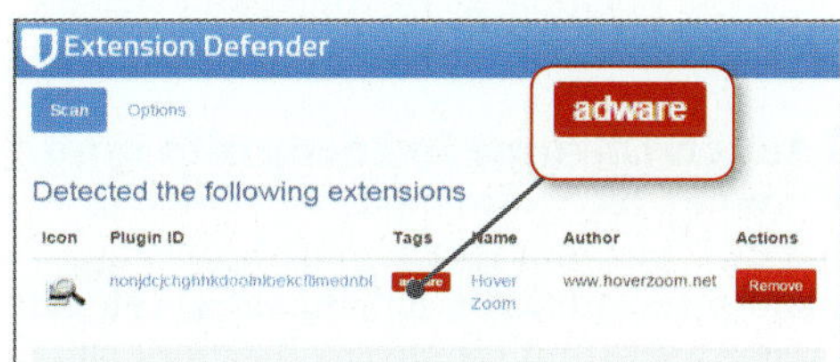

What can I use instead?

If you find Hover Zoom useful but don't like the idea of being spied on, you can stop it collecting data by going into the add-on's Options and deselecting the option 'Enable anonymous usage statistics'. If you still don't trust it, switch to Hover Zoom+ (bit.ly/hoverzoomplus369), which proudly proclaims itself to be a "spyware-free version of Hover Zoom" and works in exactly the same way.

How do I remove it?

It's easy to get rid of Hover Zoom, and it won't leave any traces of adware behind. Just right-click its icon on the toolbar and select 'Remove from Chrome'. Alternatively, click the menu button, choose 'More tools', Extensions, then scroll down to the Hover Zoom entry and click the dustbin icon next to it.

SITEADVISOR
www.siteadvisor.com

What's wrong with it?

There once was a time when McAfee SiteAdvisor was an essential security tool, but it now feels like a bloated memory guzzler that slows down your browser and displays scary red warning messages on perfectly safe sites. McAfee clearly thinks SiteAdvisor is past it, too, because it recently renamed the add-on WebAdvisor and gave it a new look that ditches the cumbersome old toolbar. However, at the time of writing, the transition was still in progress,

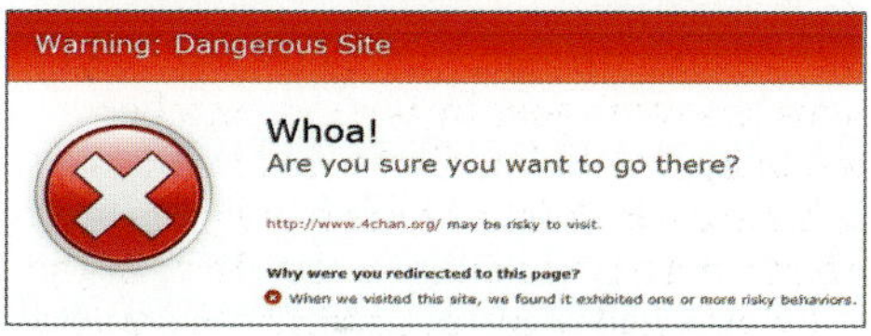

meaning that SiteAdvisor is still widely available across the web.

What can I use instead?

There are several good alternatives, which work in a similar way but are less heavy-handed and don't patronise you with warnings saying: "Whoa! Are you sure you want to go there?". The best is probably WOT (Web of Trust, www.mywot.com), which is available for Chrome, Firefox and Internet Explorer, and protects you from scams, untrustworthy links and dodgy stores, as rated by its community. We also like Bitdefender's TrafficLight tool (bit.ly/traffic369), which scans links for malware (even ones posted on social networks), trackers and phishing attacks, and forewarns you before you click them.

How do I remove it?

As well as disabling or removing the SiteAdvisor add-on in your browser, and resetting your search engine, you should uninstall it through the Control Panel in Windows. You may need to restart your PC to complete the removal.

Hack your Browser

You use a browser every time you go online, but are you getting the most out of it? Here are 27 top tips, tricks and add-ons to improve Chrome, Firefox, IE, Opera, and more

Most people browse the web without giving too much thought to the software that makes it possible. Web browsers are designed to display content and let you navigate a site as quickly and seamlessly as possible. You can customise your browser by installing add-ons to provide extra tools and features, and improve performance, but there are also lots of hidden and little-known tweaks you can use to improve upon the basic browser package..
Over the following five pages, we'll show you the best ways to get the most from a wide variety of web browsers, including adding a superior bookmarks manager to Chrome, checking for malicious web links in Firefox, accessing experimental features in the next version of Internet Explorer and blocking annoying adverts in Opera.

HACK CHROME

Access experimental features

Google groups all its experimental features in a single page. To view them, type chrome:flags into the address bar and hit Enter. Google warns that these experiments "may bite" and also change, break, or disappear at any time. Current experiments include enabling fast closing of tabs and windows, forcing hardware acceleration, displaying a frame-rate counter and turning on automatic spelling correction.

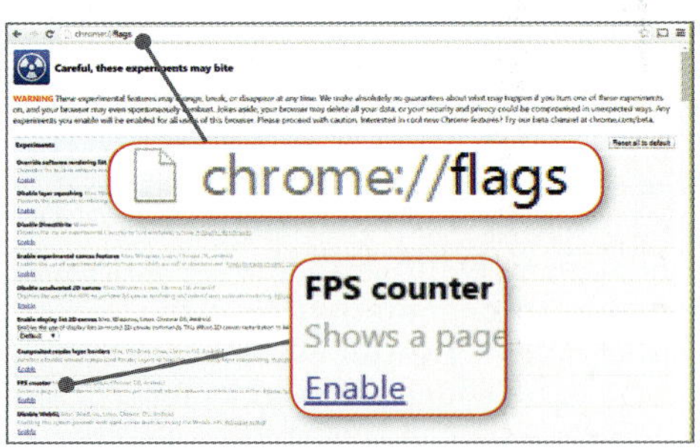

Get a better bookmarks manager

Chrome's bookmarks manager is a little on the basic side, so if you want a better way to manage your favourite sites, try Google's Bookmark Manager (bit.ly/googlebm363). The add-on displays your bookmarks as colourful tiles, and you can add an image and a note when you bookmark future sites. You can also organise bookmarks by topic, and share collections with friends.

Launch Chrome in Incognito mode

Chrome's Incognito mode can come in handy if you don't want your browsing history recorded for certain sites. You can create a shortcut for Incognito mode on your Desktop. Navigate to Chrome's installation directory

C:\Program Files (x86)\Google\Chrome\Application

then right-click Chrome.exe and select Send To, Desktop. Right-click the new shortcut on the Desktop and select Properties. At the end of the Target field, add a space after the quote and type -incognito. Apply and OK it.

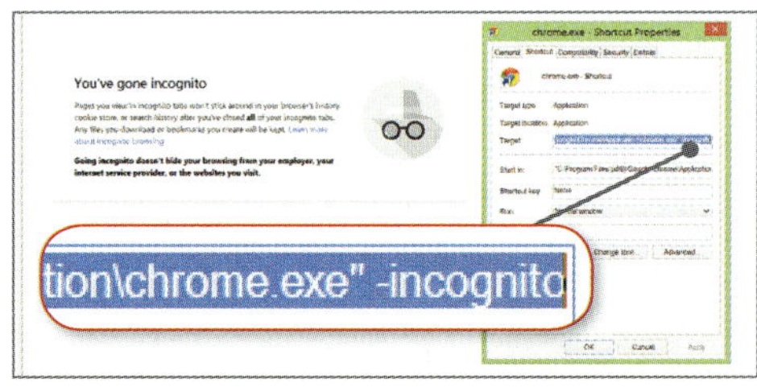

Re-enable plug-ins blocked by Google

Last year, Google began blocking most NPAPI (Netscape Plugin Application Programming Interface) plug-ins in Chrome. It's doing this for stability and security reasons, but it's frustrating if you want to run a plug-in such as Silverlight or Java and are happy to take responsibility for your actions. Until September 2015, you can still activate these plug-ins via the address bar, and Google has added an override that lets you re-enable NPAPI support. You can access it by typing chrome:flags/#enable-npapi into the address bar, and clicking Enable in the Enable NPAPI box. After September, NPAPI plug-ins will be permanently blocked.

Use Chrome for notes

If you want to copy content from one or more websites to use later, you don't need

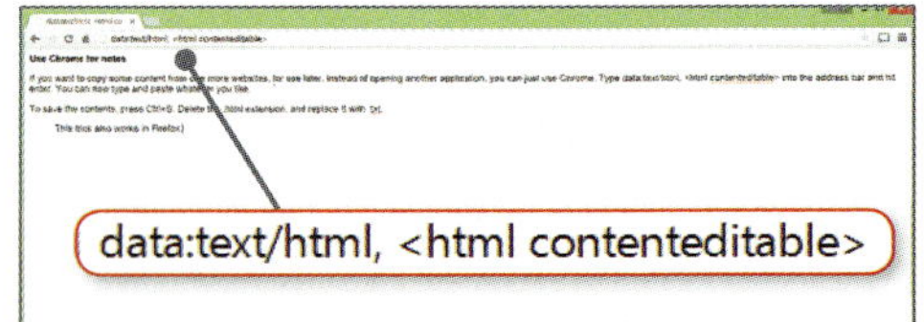

to open another application such as Notepad or Word – you can just use Chrome. Type data:text/html, <html contenteditable> into the address bar and hit Enter. You can now type and paste whatever you like in that tab, keeping it safe for future reference. To save the contents, press Ctrl+S. In the Save dialogue box, replace the file's '.html' extension with '.txt'. This trick also works in Firefox.

Download PDF files directly

When you click a PDF link in Chrome, the file will display in your browser. If you'd rather download the PDF – so you can view it in a different program or share it – just disable the built-in viewer. Type chrome:plugins into the address bar and hit Enter. Find the entry for the Chrome PDF Viewer and disable it.

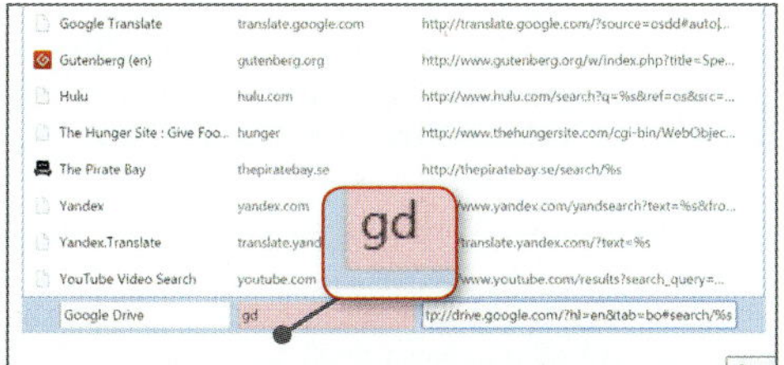

Search Google Drive in Chrome

You can use Chrome to search for files stored in Google Drive by adding a dedicated search engine to the browser. Click the menu button and go to Settings. Under Search, click 'Manage search engines', scroll down and type Google Drive in the 'Add a new search engine' box. Enter a keyword, such as 'gd' and in the URL box, type http://drive.google.com/?hl=en&tab=bo#search/%s. Click Done. When you want to look for files in Google Drive, type gd into the search bar and hit the Tab key. Then type some or all of the filename to find an item.

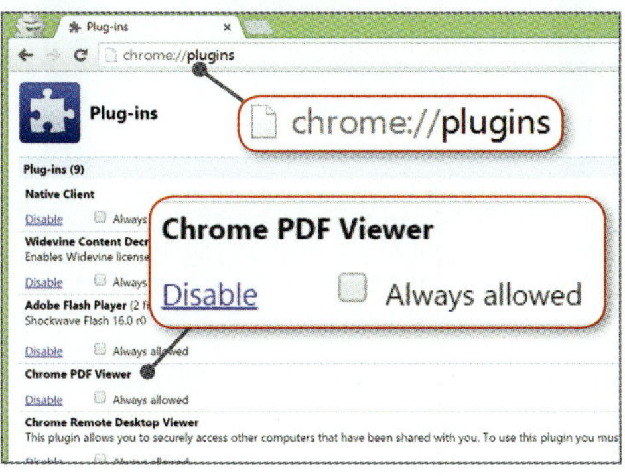

Print wirelessly

You can use Chrome to send content to any printer wirelessly, including non-wireless models. Click the Menu button in the browser and select Settings. Click the 'Show advanced settings' link at the

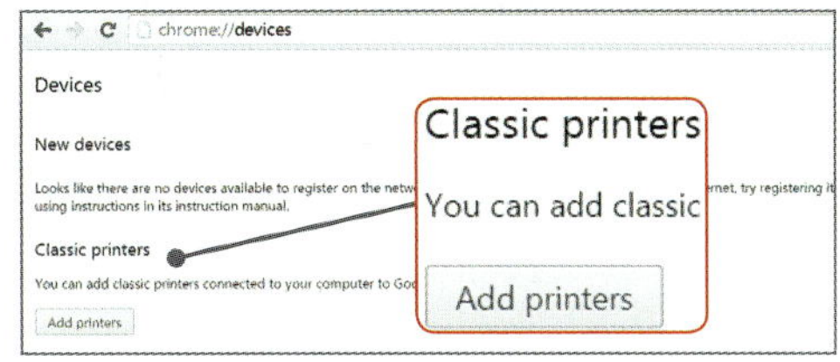

bottom, then scroll down to Google Cloud Print. Click the Manage button, then click 'Add printers' on the Devices screen to display a list of all the available printers on your network. Select the one you want and click 'Add printer(s)'. Now, open a web page or Google Doc in any Chrome browser on any device on your network (you'll need to be signed into your Google account). When you hit Print, your printer should be listed.

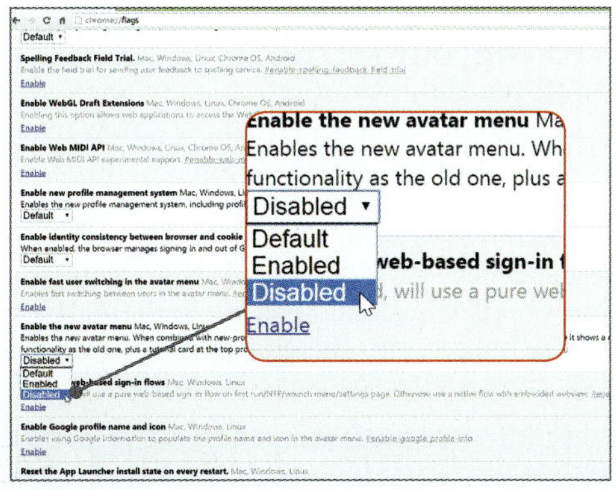

Disable Chrome's New User menu

Chrome lets you create profiles for multiple users, which is handy if you share your computer. However, Chrome lets you manage these profiles by adding a menu in the top-right corner, which may not be to everyone's taste. Fortunately, it's easily disabled. Type chrome:flags into the address bar, hit Enter and locate 'Enable new profile management system'. Change this to Disabled, then restart Chrome.

If you still want to be able to switch between users, you may prefer the old version of the New User menu. Search for 'Enable the new avatar menu' on the chrome:flags page and disable that instead, then restart Chrome.

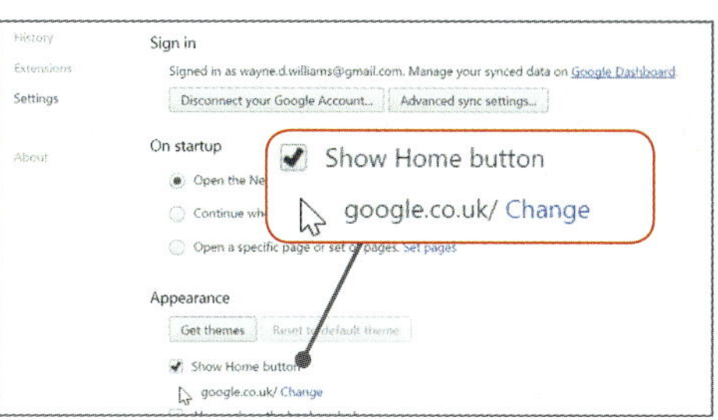

Add a Home button to Chrome

Clicking the Home button in your browser takes you straight to the default homepage. It's a useful feature, but Chrome has it disabled by default. To reinstate the Home button (it appears between Reload and the address bar), click the Menu button, open Settings and, under Appearance, tick 'Show Home button'. This brings up an option to change your homepage; just click the Change link and choose either 'Use the New Tab page' or enter the URL of the homepage you want in the 'Open this page:' box.

Speed up browsing with Data Compression Proxy

Chrome on Android lets you use a data-compression proxy to save bandwidth and speed up browsing. The recently updated Data Compression Proxy (bit.ly/chromedcp363) add-on for Chrome also offers ad-blocking; statistics that show what difference the add-on is making (if any); and the ability to add sites to a bypass list, so they load as normal without using the proxy.

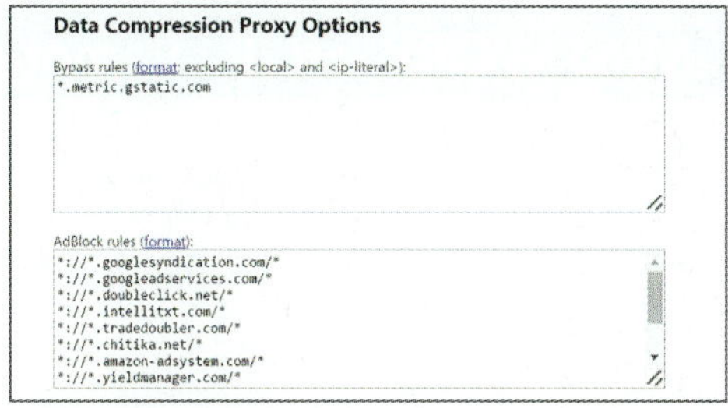

Use Chrome to remotely access your home PC

Chrome Remote Desktop (bit.ly/chromerd363) offers a simple way of accessing another computer over the internet. There are apps available for Android (bit.ly/chromerd android363) and iOS (bit.ly/chromerdios 363). Install the add-on in Chrome on your devices and follow our Mini Workshop on p124.

HACK FIREFOX

Hide your location

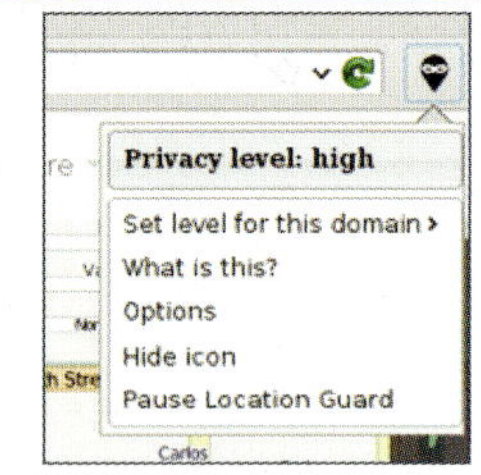

Websites sometimes want to know where you're browsing from, which is fine for certain sites – Google Maps, for example – but you probably don't want to share your exact location with every site you visit. The Location Guard add-on for Firefox (bit.ly/locguard363) disguises your location by adding confusing information (called "noise"). When you visit a site that wants to know where you are, the Location Guard button appears. Just click it to set one of three privacy levels, or to turn it off.

Get alerted when web pages update

Not all websites offer an RSS feed and it can be tiresome to have to keep refreshing a page if you're waiting for new content to appear. Install the Update Scanner (bit.ly/updatescan363) add-on, tell it which websites to monitor and it will run in the background, checking for updates.

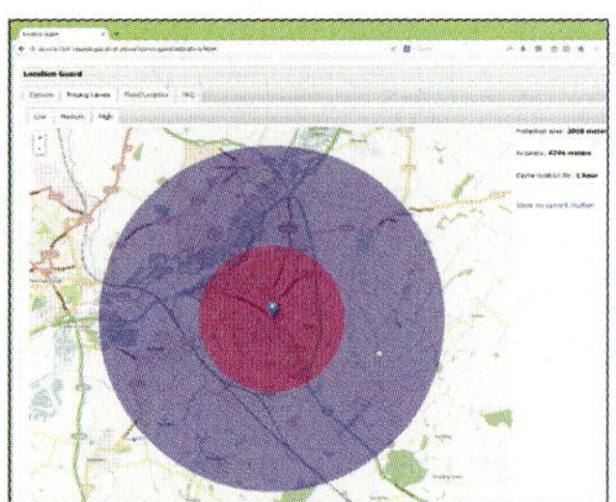

When it detects a change, it will notify you in a pop-up. Our Mini Workshop on the right shows you how to use it.

Move the toolbar to the bottom

Browsers place the menu bar at the top of the screen, but you can move it to the bottom if you want to. Install the Bottom UI extension in Firefox (bit.ly/bottomui363) and the top section of the browser, complete with address bar and open tabs, will appear at the bottom. It takes a while to get used to, but it works well. You don't have to restart Firefox for it to take effect.

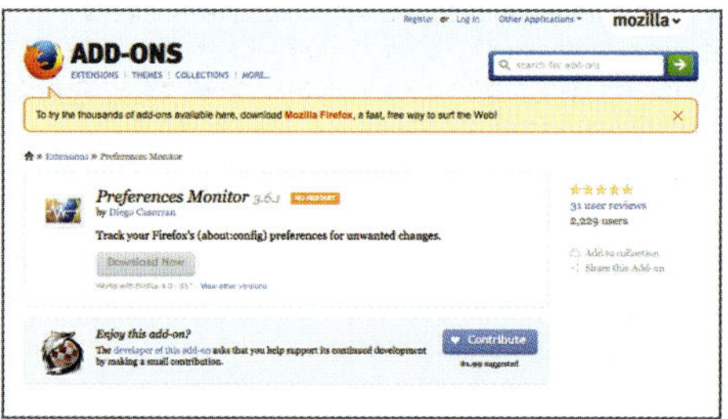

Protect your settings

Firefox is highly configurable but once you've got it set up exactly how you want it, the last thing you need is an extension or toolbar making unexpected changes. Preferences Monitor (bit.ly/prefmon363) keeps an eye on any changes that occur to browser settings, and can undo them. If you're happy with the changes being made, you can tell the add-on to allow them.

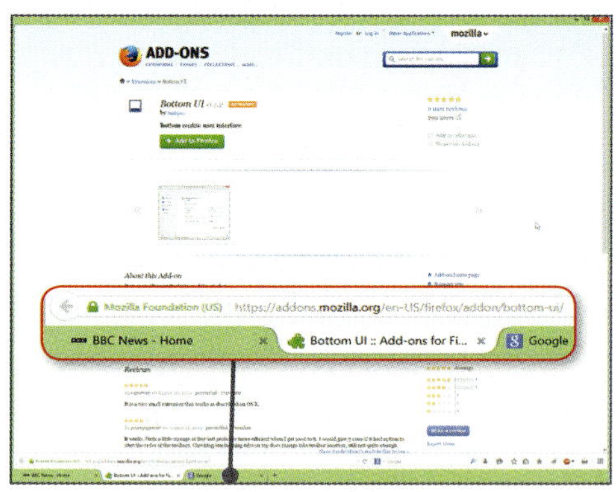

Check links for malware

If you're worried that a link on a web page might lead to a malicious site, install the Security Plus (bit.ly/secplus363) add-on. When you right-click a potentially suspicious link and select 'Scan file for viruses, or all kinds of malware', it will use the excellent VirusTotal service to check the link using 64 different anti-virus products. It then displays the results of the scan at the bottom of the page.

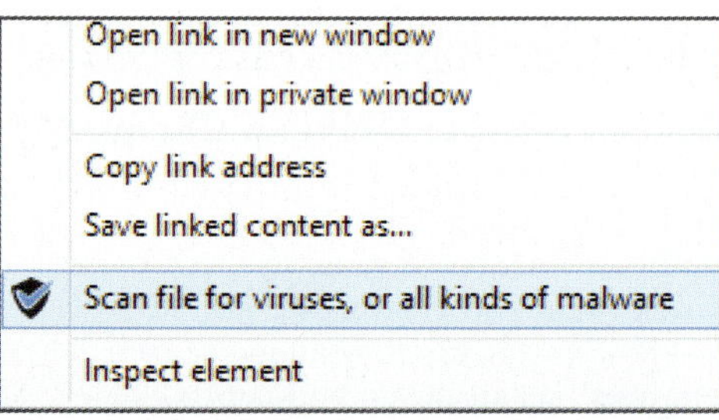

MINI WORKSHOP | Remotely access your PC from an iPad

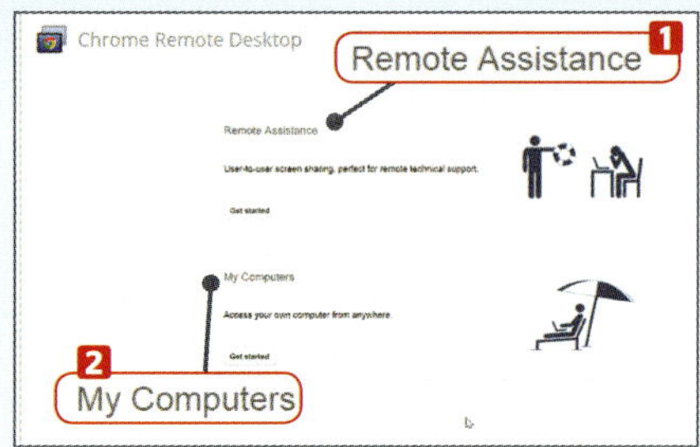

1 Install the Chrome Remote Desktop add-on (bit.ly/chromerd363) on your desktop PC and launch it. You'll be prompted to grant extended access permissions to your computer. Once that's done, you'll be given the option of connecting to someone else's computer (to provide remote support) **1** or your own, from anywhere. **2**

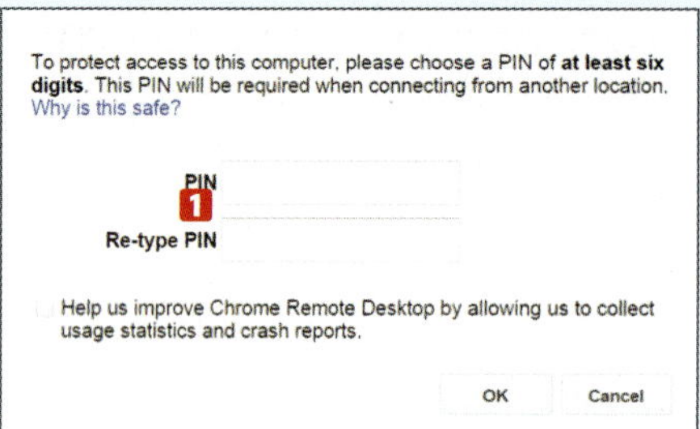

2 Select the option to access your computers and click 'Enable remote connections'. The Host installer will download. Run this and click OK. You will now need to enter a PIN **1** of at least six digits. Once you've confirmed your account and PIN, you're all set. Install the Chrome Remote Desktop app on your iPad (bit.ly/chromerdios363).

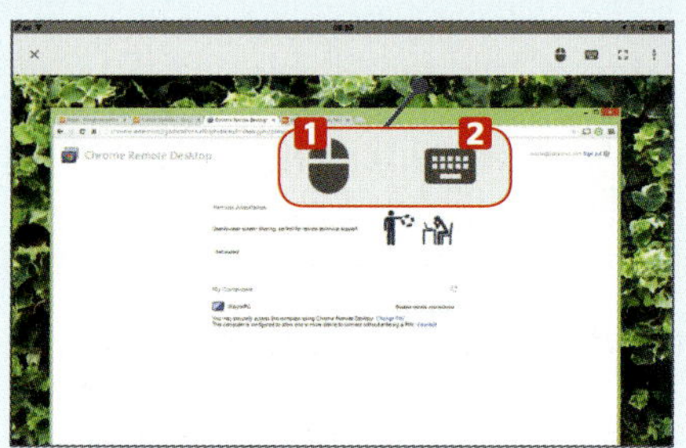

3 Launch the app and sign in with the same Google account you used on your PC. Tap your computer name and enter the PIN you set up earlier. Click Connect, and you'll be able to see and control your PC. Click the mouse button **1** to toggle the cursor on or off. Tap the button for the virtual keyboard **2** to open it.

MINI WORKSHOP | Get website update alerts from Firefox

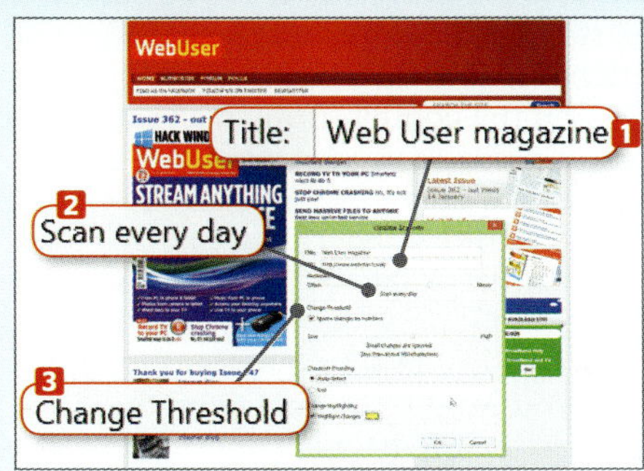

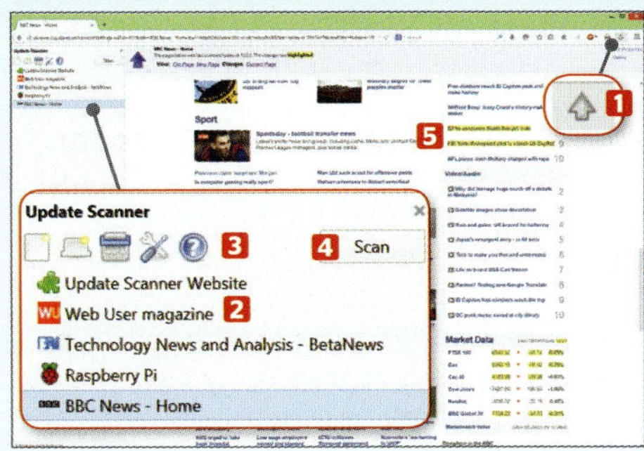

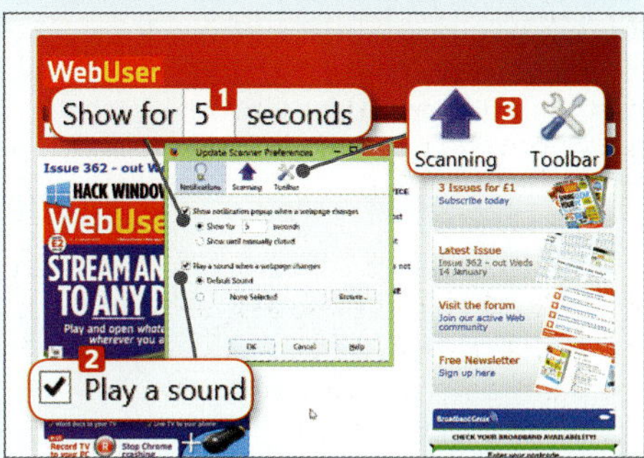

1 Install the Update Scanner (bit.ly/updatescan363) and go to one of your favourite sites. Right-click it and select 'Scan Page for Updates'. In the window that opens, enter a name for the site, **1** then set how often to check for changes **2** and how major you want the changes to be. **3** Click OK.

2 Click the Update Scanner button in the browser **1** to open the sidebar. This shows the sites you're watching. **2** The buttons along the top **3** let you create a new entry, show all changed pages in new tabs, delete entries and update preferences. Click Scan **4** to check for updates now. Changes on a page are highlighted. **5**

3 When a page is updated, a notification will pop up near the System Tray. Right-click the browser button and select Preferences to configure the settings. You can change how long the pop-up alert is shown for **1** and whether you want the add-on to play a sound. **2** There are also settings for Scanning and Toolbar. **3**

HACK INTERNET EXPLORER

Hide the address bar

The Modern UI version of Internet Explorer in Windows 8 displays the address bar at the bottom of the screen. You can hide this if you wish, so it only

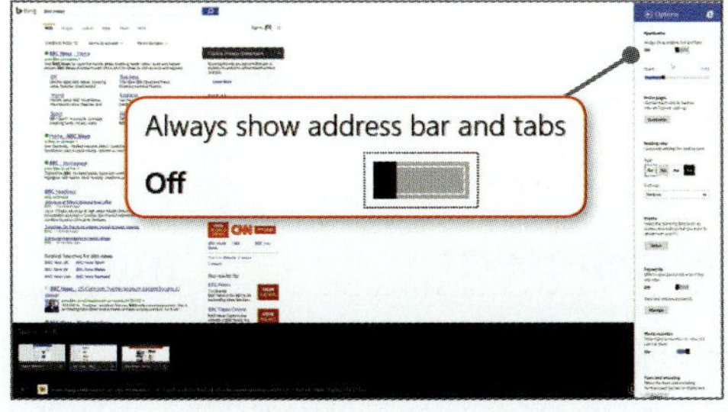

pops into view when required. Go to Settings, Options and set the address bar visibility to Off. You can view the bar by moving your mouse to the bottom of the browser or swiping upwards on a touchscreen.

Enable experimental features

Chrome, Firefox and Opera all offer the ability to turn on experimental features. However, with Internet Explorer, you need to be running the future version found in the most recent preview build of Windows 10. If you are, just type about:flags into the address bar, hit enter and an Experimental Features page will open in a new tab.

There are currently three features

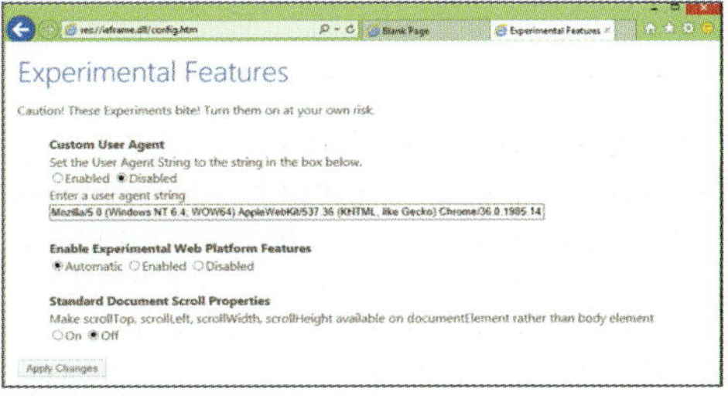

being offered – Custom User Agent, which lets IE pretend to websites it's a different browser; Enable Experimental Web Platforms Features, which activates the new browser engine; and Standard Document Scroll Properties, which changes the behaviour of scroll functions. You'll need to restart Internet Explorer before the changes will be applied.

Get back the Modern UI version of Internet Explorer

Windows 8 offers two versions of Internet Explorer – full-screen Modern UI and Desktop. If the Modern UI version vanishes it's because another browser has been set as the default. To undo this, go to the Start screen and type PC Settings. Launch PC Settings from the results, and click 'Search and apps'. Click Defaults and change the browser to Internet Explorer. It will now open in full-screen again.

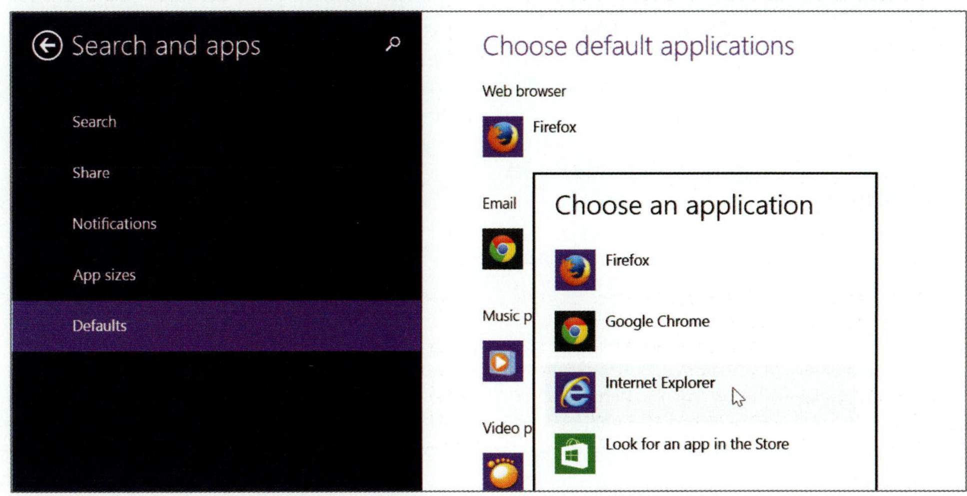

HACK OPERA

Install Chrome extensions in Opera

There are thousands of add-ons for Google's Chrome browser, and any of the ones available from the Chrome Web

Store can be directly installed in Opera using the Download Chrome Extension (bit.ly/downchromeex363). However, this only works with Chrome extensions, not web apps.

Block adverts

If you find your browsing experience is being ruined by adverts, you could use Adguard (bit.ly/adguard363) to remove them. It's an excellent ad blocker for Opera that can remove all types of advertising from the web. It can sometimes be a little too aggressive with what it removes, but you can easily tweak the settings to stop it blocking specific items.

Stop web pages automatically playing content

Websites that automatically start playing audio or video when you visit them can be really annoying, especially if you have a lot of tabs open and can't tell which one is the source of the racket. Most browsers now add a speaker symbol to indicate a tab that's making noise, so you can at least quickly locate and close the offending page.

To stop the content from even starting to play automatically in Opera, press Ctrl+F12 to open the Settings and click the Websites link. Under Plug-ins, tick the 'Click to play' option. This means that content will only start playing when you click it. You can set exceptions for any sites you want to exempt from this rule, such as the BBC, which doesn't host any of those auto-playing adverts.

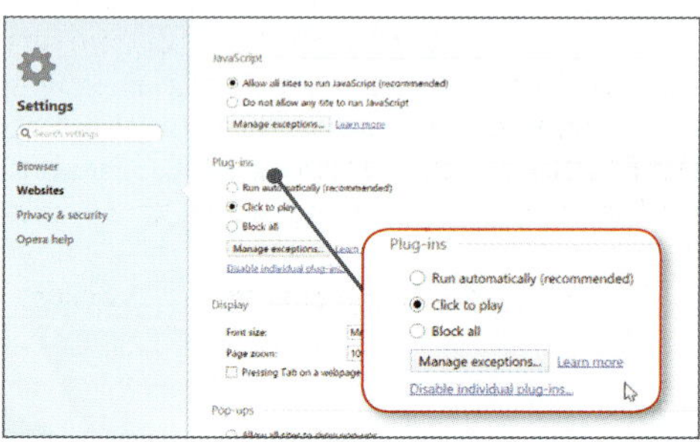

HACK OTHER BROWSERS

Speed up browsing in Pale Moon

The Pale Moon browser, which is based on Firefox, offers prefetching. This means that the browser predicts web pages that you may want to click, and prepares cached pages in readiness. The result is that pages load more quickly, although you should be aware that it will also increase bandwidth usage. Prefetching is not enabled by default, so if you want to enable it, type about:config into the address bar and hit Enter. Search for 'network.prefetch-next' and set the parameter to 'true'. To disable prefetching, repeat the process but set the parameter to False.

Use Firefox Compatibility Mode in Pale Moon

Pale Moon used to identify itself to websites as Firefox, which meant that any pages you visited would appear as they do in Mozilla's browser. That's no longer the case in the latest version, and this can cause problems on some websites that don't recognise Pale Moon, but the browser's Firefox Compatibility Mode solves the problem. You can access it by going to Options, and clicking the Advanced button. Firefox Compatibility will be listed at the bottom of the General tab. It should be enabled by default.

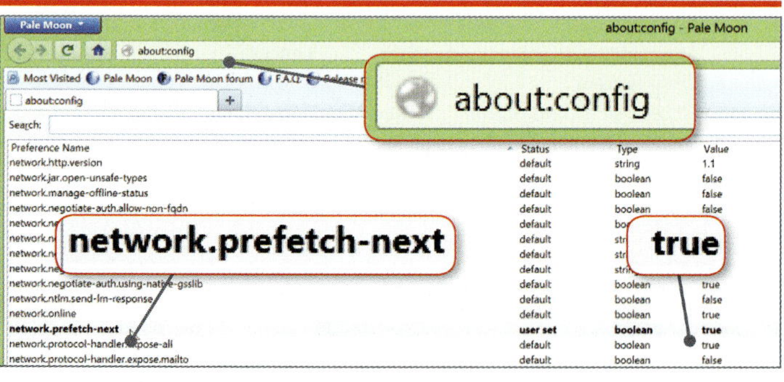

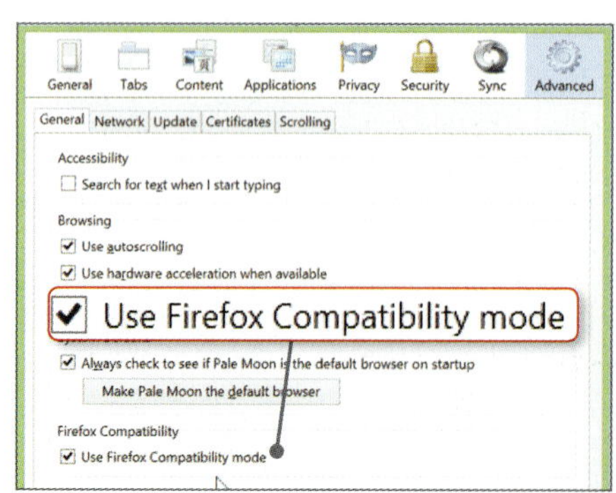

Install user scripts in Maxthon

Greasemonkey (bit.ly/greasemonkey363) is a powerful add-on for Firefox that lets you customise web pages as you browse by installing scripts that change how your favourite sites look and behave. You can get the same functionality and benefits in Maxthon by installing Violentmonkey (bit.ly/violentmonkey363). Once it's installed you'll need to add some scripts.

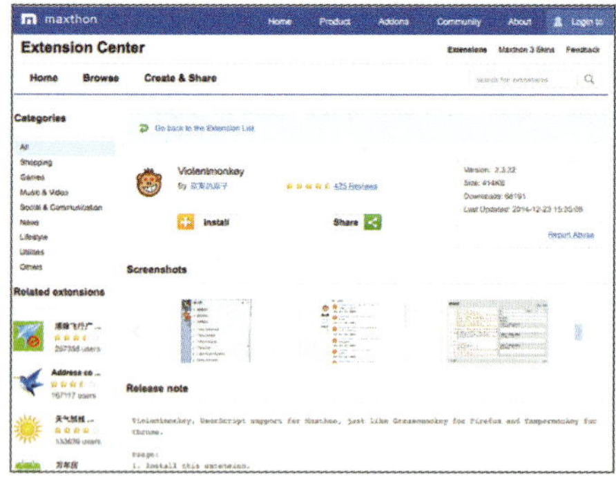

Private file sharing

www.snipca.com/14994 **What you need:** Windows 7 or 8

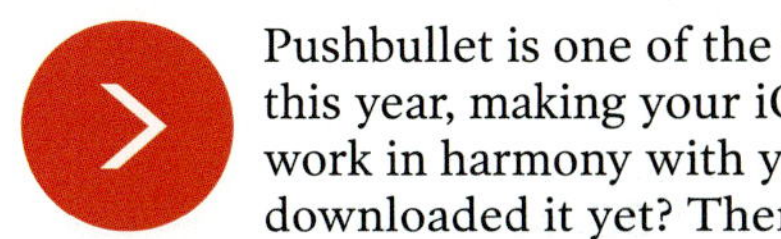

Pushbullet is one of the best apps we've come across this year, making your iOS or Android smartphone work in harmony with your Windows PC. Haven't downloaded it yet? Then you'd better do it now.

Pushbullet lets you send messages, photos, files and web links for free between all your devices that have Pushbullet installed, and to any of your Pushbullet contacts. It's party trick is letting you read and reply to mobile text messages on your PC.

Everything you send and receive is stored securely in your Pushbullet account on your PC, tablet, browser (Chrome, Firefox or Internet Explorer) and wherever else you use it. We still can't believe it's free.

The Windows program, which is described as 'beta' but seems very stable to us, has been updated with a Notifications tab where you can see a list of all your recent incoming 'pushes'. It also includes 'Universal copy & paste' for copying text from your PC to your tablet (the Pushbullet blog explains all: www.snipca.com/14995) and adds a Pushbullet option to the right-click menu so you can push photos, documents and other files to your friends or devices without opening the program or site. Another new feature, Channels, lets you sign up to notification news feeds (www.pushbullet.com/channels).

To download Pushbullet, go to the link above and click 'Windows (beta)', then run the installer. There's no adware to opt out of, but the installer does force your PC to restart, which was annoying for us because we were writing this at the time!

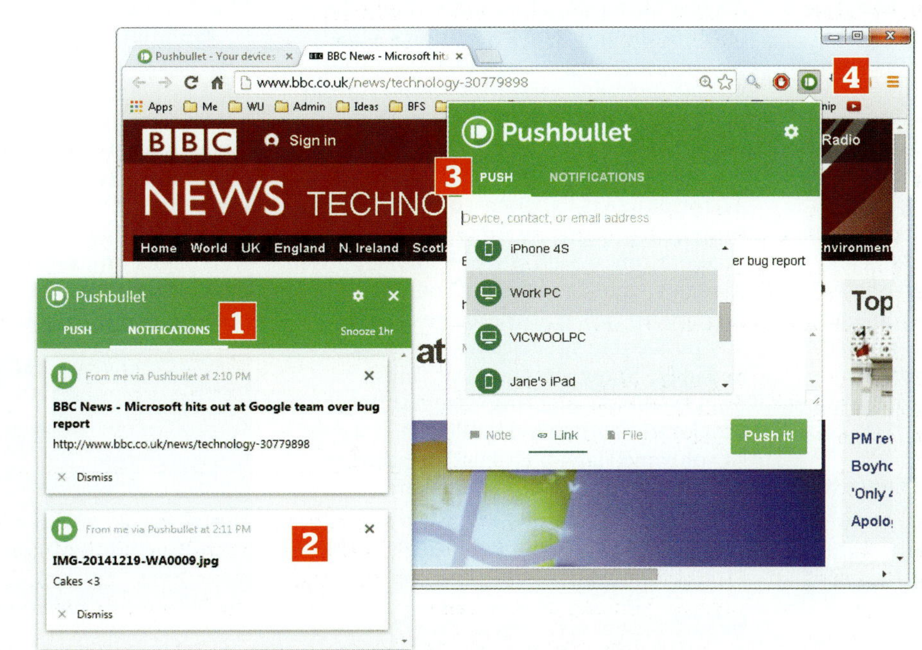

1 Pushbullet now includes a Notifications tab containing all your incoming messages, file shares and link shares. Notifications also appear at the bottom-left of your Desktop.

2 There are no previews in the Windows version of Pushbullet; you have to click a link or file name (a photo, for example) to view the contents. The browser and mobile versions do include previews.

3 To send ('push') a message, link, photo or other file, click Push and click Note, Link or File. Select a device or recipient (or 'All of my devices'), then click 'Push it!' to send it securely.

4 The Pushbullet browser extension lets you 'push' the current web page to your PC and other destinations with one click. Here, we chose our own PC, and the link arrived instantly.

Solve all your Chrome problems

If you've been having trouble with Chrome recently, you're not the only one. Here we reveal the most common complaints with Google's browser and explain how to fix them

WHY is Chrome so slow?

Chrome used to be renowned for its speedy start-up and lightning-fast loading of web pages, but judging from on our own recent experience and feedback from others, this is no longer the case. However, when we tested our version of the browser (Chrome 40) using the online benchmarking tools Browserscope (www.browserscope.org) and Peacekeeper (peacekeeper.futuremark.com), the results found it to be speedier than ever and faster than rival browsers such as Firefox and Internet Explorer. This suggests that there's nothing wrong with Chrome itself, but that the way it interacts with other elements may be slowing it down.

Often the cause is a wayward add-on,

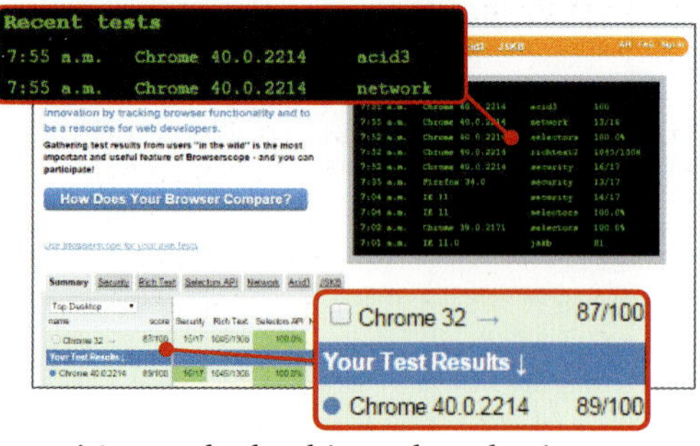

so it's worth checking what else is running each time you launch the browser. Open Chrome's Task Manager by pressing Shift+Esc and you'll see a list of all running processes, including tabs and extensions. Check to see if any of the latter is using an excessive amount of memory and, if so, select the greedy add-on and click End Process. If it's not an important extension, uninstall it altogether via Chrome's Extensions page. You can use One-Click Extensions Manager (bit.ly/oneclick362) to instantly disable (and re-enable) individual add-ons or all of them in one go. Adblock Plus (adblockplus.org) is a notorious resource hog, so consider switching to the similar but more lightweight uBlock (github.com/gorhill/uBlock) instead.

Another possible cause of 'laggy' performance is Chrome's use of GPU (graphics processing unit) hardware acceleration, which is ironically supposed to make pages load faster. You can try turning off this feature to see if there's any noticeable speed boost by going to Settings, 'Show advanced settings', System and deselecting 'Use hardware acceleration when available'. Next, type <t>chrome:flags</t> into the address bar, find the entry 'Override software rendering list' and click Enable. Click Relaunch Now and hopefully there should be an improvement in performance.

WHY does Chrome keep crashing?

One of the most common causes of crashes in Chrome is Adobe Flash, which can prevent some pages from loading properly and lead to the 'He's dead, Jim' or 'Aw snap' error message. The easiest solution to Flash problems is to type <t>chrome://plugins</t> into the address bar and click the Details link on the right. Disabling one of the two Shockwave Flash options should solve the problem. If one of the entries is already disabled and the other enabled, try reversing them. The downside to this method is that you won't be able to view Flash content such as videos and games, so you might want to try the less restrictive approach of running plug-ins such as Flash manually rather than automatically. Go to Settings, 'Show advanced settings', Privacy and click 'Content settings'. Scroll down to Plug-ins, select 'Click to play' and click Finished. This will block Flash content on web pages unless you click the Play button to run it, and hopefully prevent the browser from crashing.

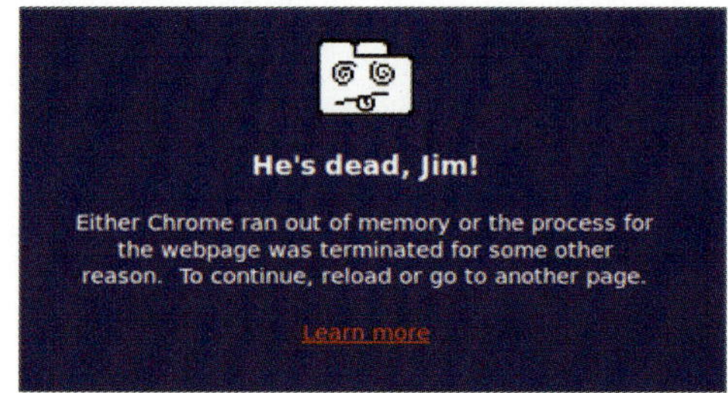

If this doesn't work, you can try to find out what else is causing the crash. Type <t>chrome: conflicts</t> into the address bar, press Enter and look for details of any 'modules' that are conflicting with Chrome. If everything is fine, you should see the message 'No conflicts detected'; if not, try updating or uninstalling the module responsible for the conflict.

[conflicts – zoom 'No conflicts']

If Chrome crashes as soon as you open

it, the cause is probably a corrupt user profile, so it's worth creating a new one to see if the problem persists. Make sure the browser is fully closed by right-clicking the taskbar and launching the Task Manager. Look for any instances of Chrome.exe running under the Processes tab, then select them and click End Process. Next, press the Windows key+R to open the Run box, type <t> %LOCALAPPDATA%\Google\Chrome\ User Data\</t> and press Enter. Locate the Default folder and give it a new name, such as Backup Default. Launch Chrome and a new Default folder will be created automatically.

WHY isn't Chrome syncing?

One of Chrome's best features is the ability to sync your bookmarks, extensions and other settings, so you can access them from any installation of the browser, which makes it very frustrating when it stops working. Fortunately, the problem can usually be solved simply by disconnecting your Google account in Chrome's Settings, restarting the browser and signing in again. Click 'Advanced sync settings' and ensure that all the options you want to sync are selected.

If Chrome is syncing old data, but isn't updating to include new bookmarks you've added or extensions you've installed, go to your sync dashboard at www.google.com/settings/chrome/sync where you'll see a summary of all your synced data. Click the 'Stop and Clear' button below this to stop syncing the listed items and start afresh. Don't worry - this won't delete any locally stored data in your browser.

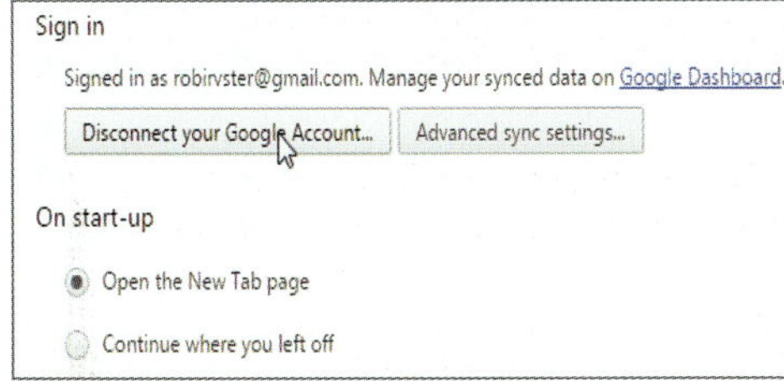

WHY does the virus scan keep failing?

If you see the message 'Virus scan failed' when you try to download a file, the first thing to do is scan your PC for malware that may be causing the problem, using

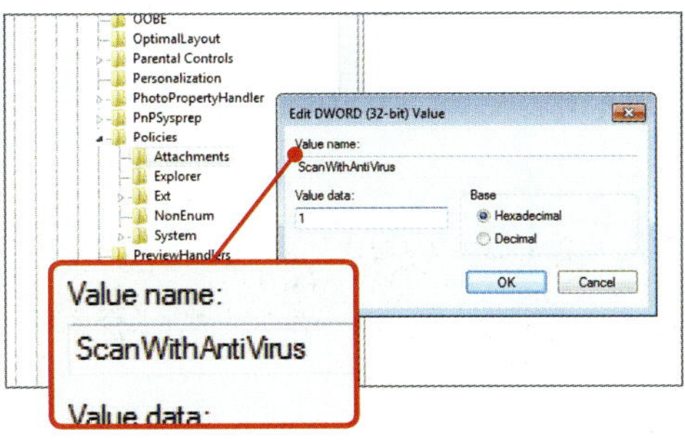

your anti-virus program or a free security tool such as Malwarebytes Anti-Malware (www.malwarebytes.org). Once you've detected and removed any threats, you can tweak the Registry to disable the automatic scanning of downloads. Press the Windows key+R, type <t>regedit</t> and press Enter. Navigate to HKEY_LOCAL_MACHINE\SOFTWARE\Microsoft\Windows\CurrentVersion\Policies\Attachments, double-click the value ScanWithAntivirus on the right and change the value data from '3' to '1' (you can change it back to turn the feature back on).

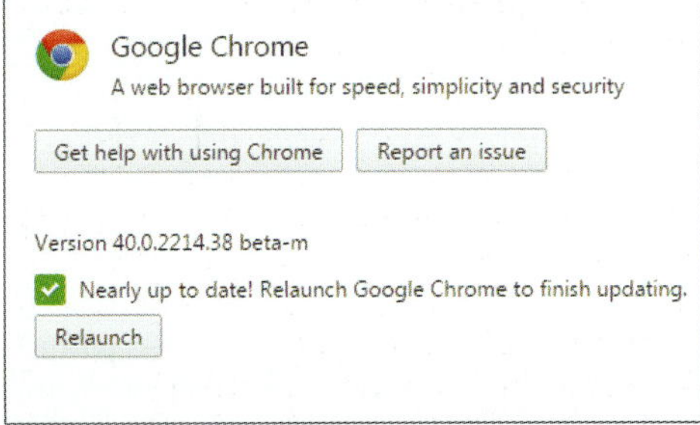

WHY isn't Chrome updating?

Chrome is set to update automatically, as soon as a new version becomes available, but occasionally this will stop working and you'll see the error message: 'Update failed (error: 7)'. This advises you to change a setting in the Group Policy Editor but this feature isn't accessible in home versions of Windows. Instead, you can solve the problem using a quick Registry tweak. Navigate to the key HKEY_LOCAL_MACHINE\SOFTWARE\Policies\Google\Update\, and delete the values Update{8A69D345-D564-463C-AFF1-A69D9E530F96} and Update{8BA986DA-5100-405E-AA35-86F34A02ACBF}. Restart Chrome, go to About Chrome and the browser should update without any problems.

WHY has Chrome changed my homepage?

If Chrome has changed your default start page or search engine, or added an unwanted toolbar, it's probably due to an unwanted program on your computer. You can fix the problem by downloading and running the Software Removal Tool (www.google.com/chrome/srt). This performs a 'factory reset' of Chrome by restoring the browser's original settings, including your start page and search engine, and removes programs that affect its behaviour.

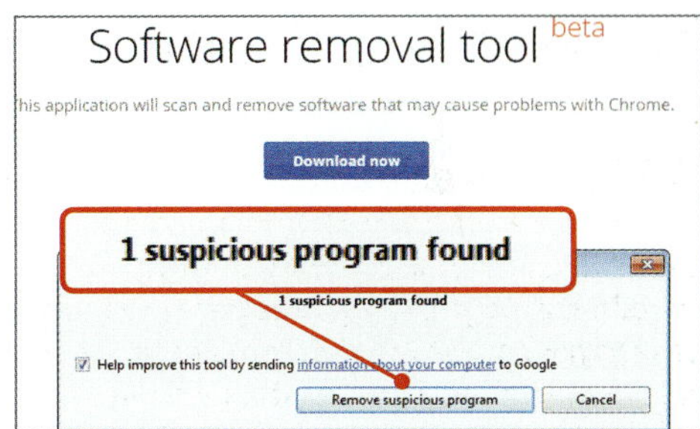

WHY does Chrome take ages to load pages?

If Chrome is taking a long time to load a website, it may be configured to access pages through a web proxy. If so, you'll see a "Resolving proxy" message appears in the bottom-left corner of the browser. To fix the problem, go to Settings, 'Show advanced settings', Network and click 'Change proxy settings' to open the Internet Properties box. Click LAN settings and deselect the option 'Automatically detect settings'. It's also possible that a corrupted cookie could be preventing Chrome from loading a page. You can clear your cookies by clicking 'Content data' on the Settings page, selecting 'All cookies and site data' and clicking Remove all.

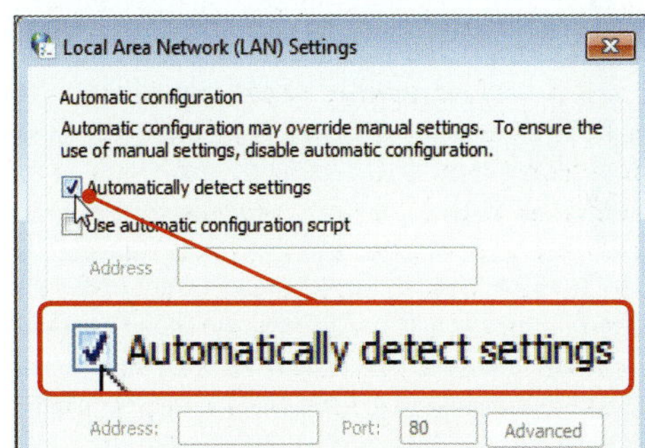

Block unwanted web content in Firefox

EXPERT TIP

If you'd like to use Policeman to block an advert but you're not sure of the ad's source, try right-clicking it in Firefox and selecting This Frame, then View Frame Source (this option is not always available). A page will open that may determine the URL of the advert. You can then use Policeman to block requests to this domain.

Do you ever wish you could prevent certain types of content from appearing on the websites you visit every day? Perhaps one of your favourite sites is plagued by ads, or your slow internet connection means that pages with lots of images take forever to load? Using the new Firefox add-on Policeman, you can make your browsing experience faster and safer, while preserving the layout of websites as the designers intended. Policeman is a powerful and flexible add-on that lets you set up temporary or persistent rules to control the types of content that Firefox will accept or reject. In this Workshop, we show you how to get to grips with Policeman so that you can filter specific elements by category, and learn how to reject or accept them by creating your own rules. Whether you want to block all external scripts from loading on a site or stop images from a specific domain, Policeman is the perfect tool for the job.

Policeman: bit.ly/policeman358 | 20 mins | Firefox

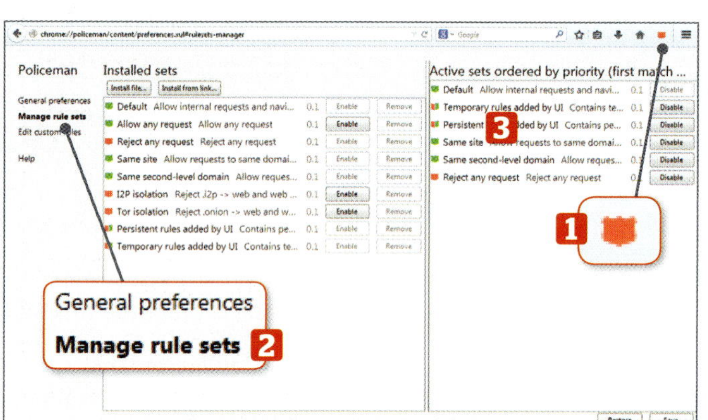

1 Visit bit.ly/policeman358 and install the Policeman add-on. A red icon shaped like a US police badge appears on your Firefox toolbar. **1** Click it and select Preferences, then 'Manage rule sets'. **2** The right-hand window shows your default-activated rule sets, listed in order of priority. **3**

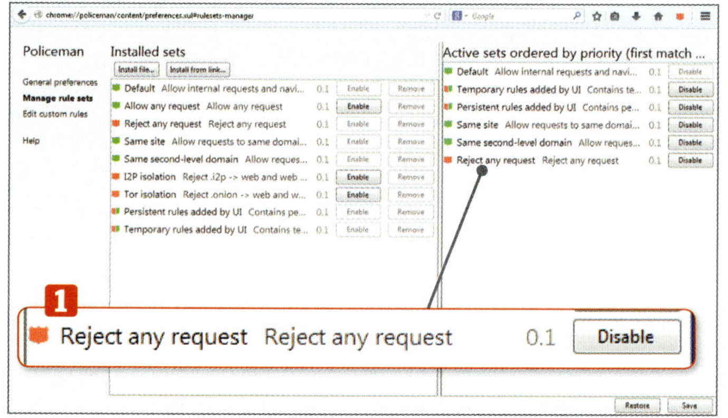

2 'Reject any request' **1** blocks requests that aren't approved by the rule sets above. By default, requests to domains other than the one you've visited will be blocked. To allow all requests and block only ones specified with custom rules, click Disable. **2** This will make 'Allow any request' appear.

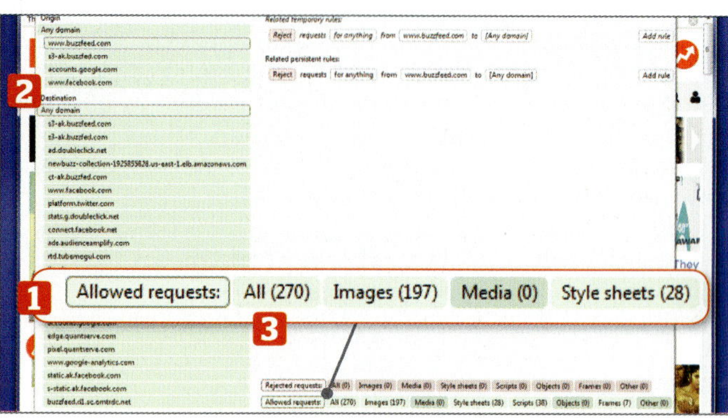

3 Click Save, visit a website you want to block requests from and click the Policeman icon. A breakdown shows the number of different types of 'Allowed requests'. **1** Clicking an origin or destination domain **2** filters the requests relating to it. Click All **3** to see them listed.

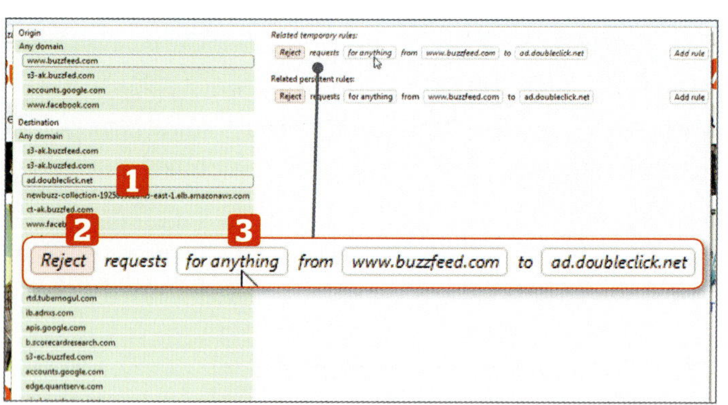

4 Click any destination domain you don't trust. **1** The rules at the top of the window will be updated to block any requests to that domain. **2** Click 'for anything' **3** repeatedly if you'd prefer the add-on to only block requests for images, music and video, style sheets or scripts to that domain.

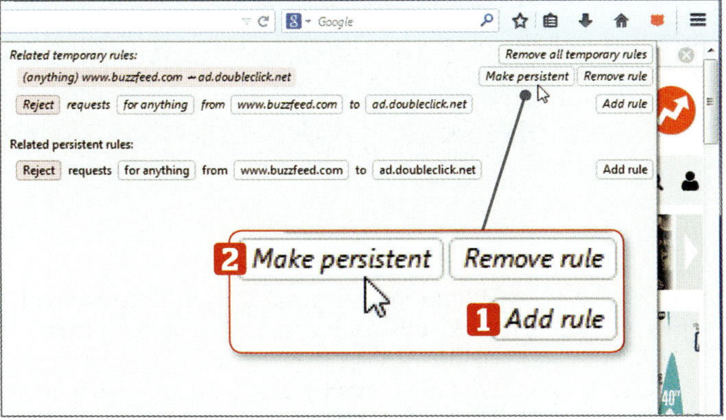

5 To add a rule temporarily, click 'Add rule' next to the appropriate entry. 1 Bear in mind that temporary rules only exist until the end of your session, so if you want to make the change permanent, you'll need to click 'Make persistent' 2 next to it.

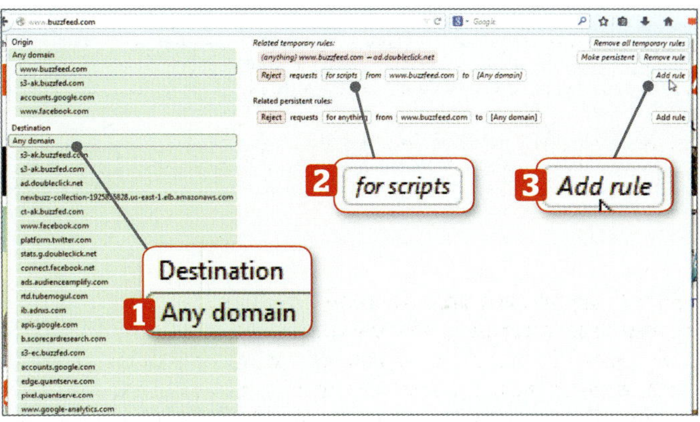

6 To block a type of request, regardless of its destination domain, leave 'Any domain' selected in this section. 1 Click the 'for anything' box to cycle through the options until you find the request type you want to block, such as 'for frames' or 'for scripts'. 2 Click 'Add rule'. 3

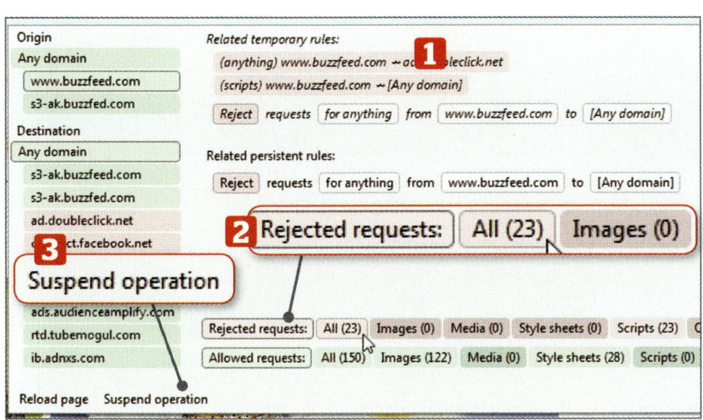

7 When you next load a page, Policeman will automatically apply any custom rules you've created. Open the add-on's pop-up window to see a summary of your applied rules 1 and a breakdown of 'Rejected requests'. 2 Click 'Suspend operation' 3 to toggle Policeman on and off.

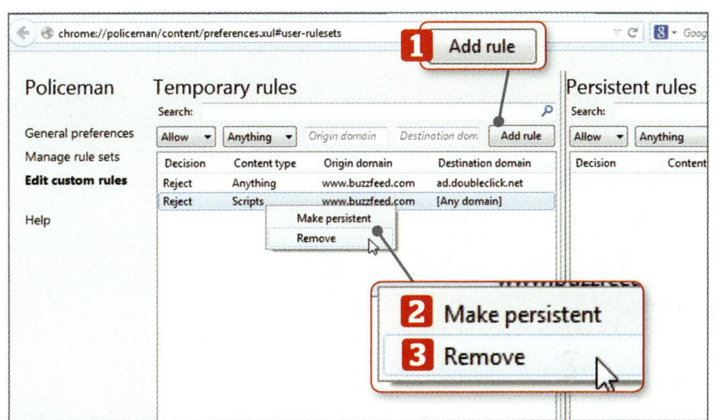

8 To manage your rules, click Preferences. The 'Edit custom rules' page will load. To create a rule manually, type the appropriate information into the boxes and click 'Add rule'. 1 Right-click a temporary rule and select 'Make persistent' 2 to add it permanently or Remove 3 to delete it.

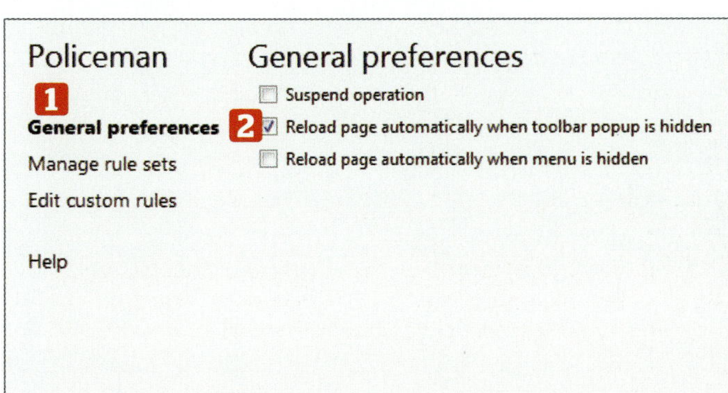

9 You can also click 'General preferences' to suspend Policeman from blocking requests. 1 Tick 'Reload page automatically when toolbar popup is hidden' 2 to prompt the add-on to automatically reload a page after you add a custom rule, so you can see if it's had the desired effect.

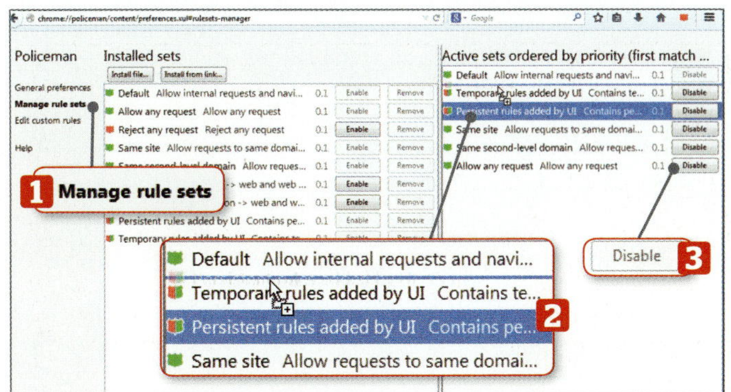

10 Once you've set up some of your own rules, revisit the 'Manage rule sets' page 1 to reorder the priority by dragging and dropping rules to a new position. 2 We think the default set-up works well, but you can also disable a rule set altogether by clicking Disable. 3

Chapter 8

Free software secrets

We show you where to find the very best free software, and how to (legally) avoid paying for apps you might otherwise stump up for

This whole MagBook has been devoted to free software. In this final chapter, we countdown 10 of our favourite freebies across different categories of software, and also give you our favourite alternative if the top pick doesn't float your boat. There are even mimi-tutorials to show you how to get the most from some of our picks. We also show you how you can avoid paying for commercial applications, without resorting to illegal software piracy. We'll reveal where to find sites offering free deals on software, how to get cutting-edge packages without paying, and much more.

CONTENT

Best free software

Give your PC a boost by installing some useful new software. We pick our 10 favourite new programs that you can download and start using today

There are so many new programs released each month that it's tough to know what to download and what to ignore.

You don't want to miss new free software that makes your PC faster, safer and more versatile; but neither do you want to waste time installing rubbish tools that don't do what they claim and fill your hard drive with junk.

To help you make the most of your PC and the web, we've chosen 10 of the most promising new programs and significantly updated versions of existing tools, as well as recommending some great alternatives.

The programs we've picked cover everything from optimising and protecting your PC to organising and converting your files, and they are all completely free and clean of malware. Hopefully, our choices – and alternatives for each category – will make your download decisions easier and will prove as rewarding to you as they have been for us.

System tool

Advanced SystemCare 8 Free

bit.ly/advanced360

Min requirements: Windows XP/Vista/7/8+

File size: 41.2MB

Why you'll love it

With a promise of '10 major improvements', the new version of Advanced SystemCare can fix PC problems, free up space on your hard drive and boost system performance in a single click. Click the Scan button to make the powerful optimisation suite run through a series of tasks including spyware removal, registry fix, privacy sweep, junk files clean-up, internet boost and shortcuts fix. You can choose which of the available options to include or select the whole lot, and the various modules can be accessed directly through the Toolbox tab.

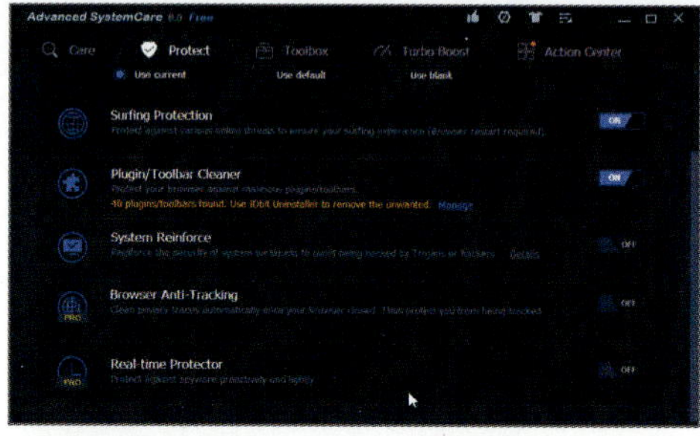

Additionally, Advanced SystemCare offers a useful Turbo Boost function to speed up your system, and a Protect tab with options to keep your PC safe from malware and dubious websites. There's also a plug-in/toolbar cleaner to remove unwanted junk from your browser.

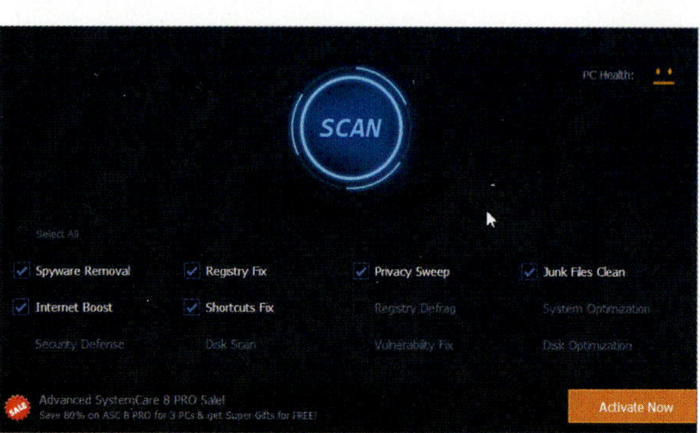

The latest version adds some interesting new features, such as the inclusion of IObit Uninstaller 4, which lets you remove batches of unwanted programs and apps in one go. There's a new software updater, too, to ensure you always have the latest and most secure versions of programs.

What's the catch?

Advanced SystemCare adds iobit.com to your browser bookmarks during installation, unless you deselect this option. It's annoying that some of the features shown are only available in the paid-for Pro edition or can only be accessed by installing additional IObit software, and that you have to upgrade to get some basic features, such as Registry and disk cleaners.

Try this instead

Synei System Utilities 2
www.synei.com

This powerful PC-optimisation suite offers both a 1-Click Maintenance mode and a selection of individual tools to perform actions such as tuning up your computer, defragging your hard drive and speeding up your browser.

System tool

Panda Free Antivirus 2015
www.cloudantivirus.com

Min requirements: Windows XP/Vista/7/8+
File size: 1.3MB (installer)

Why you'll love it
A lot of anti-virus programs are bloated resource hogs, packed with features you simply don't need. Panda Free Antivirus is lightweight and simple, and this 2015 edition has sensibly resisted the urge to start weighing the software down with unnecessary features. If your computer is getting on a bit, this is a great solution because Panda Free Antivirus will keep you safe without slowing down your system like some security software does.

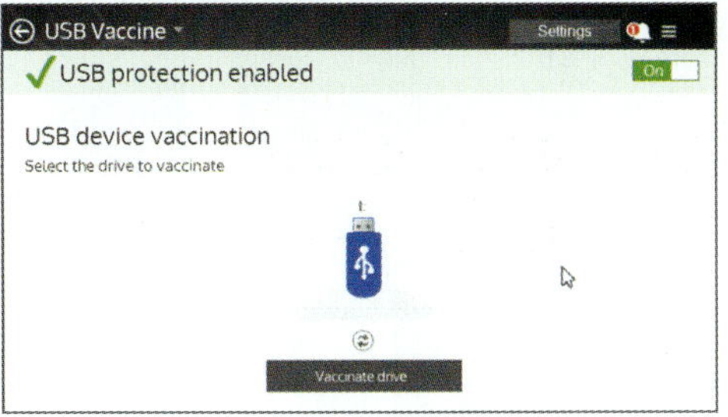

It pulls its virus definitions directly from the cloud, rather than downloading them, which saves time and means your protection is always up to date.

The latest version's interface is heavily influenced by Windows 8, with colourful tiles that you can reorder by clicking and dragging. Unwanted tiles are easily removed, and you can also add new ones, and arrange everything over three screens.

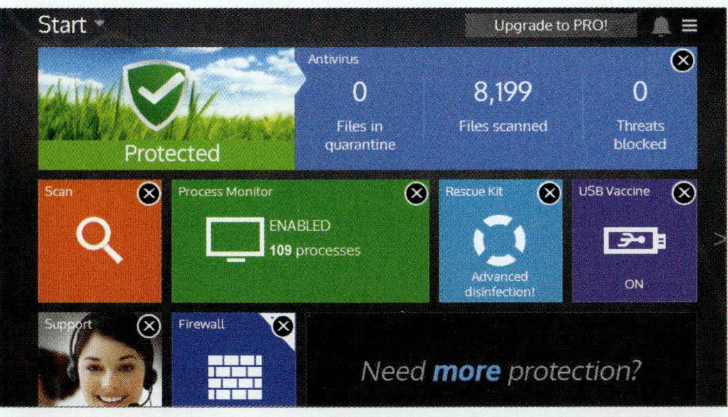

Useful tools in Panda Free Antivirus include an on-demand scanner, process monitor, USB vaccine and rescue kit. Although it seems pretty basic, especially when compared to other free anti-virus programs, don't worry that it won't keep you safe. The software's new XMT (Extreme Malware Terminator) Smart Engineering engine is actually very powerful, and in independent tests conducted by AV Comparatives (www.av-comparatives.org), Panda Free Antivirus regularly rates as one of the top choices.

What's the catch?
When you install the software, it will also offer to install the Panda Security Toolbar in your browser; change your default search provider to Yahoo; and set your homepage to MyStart. Happily, all three options are easily deselected, so make sure you don't skip past them.

Try this instead

Avast Free Antivirus 2015
www.avast.com

The biggest change to the latest version of this powerful free security tool is the addition of a Home Network Security Scanner that protects your Wi-Fi from threats. See our Workshop on page 54 to find out how to use this new feature.

MINI WORKSHOP | Monitor background processes using Panda Free Antivirus

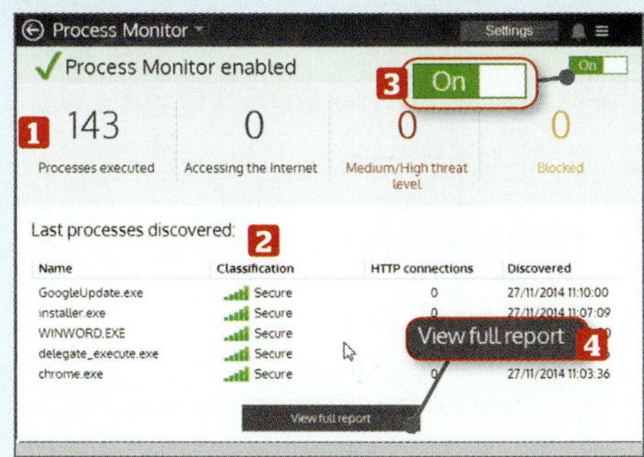

1 Process Monitor tracks system processes, so you'll be alerted if something misbehaves. Click the Process Monitor tile to open its page. You'll see an overview **1** and a list of processes. **2** You can toggle the monitor on or off. **3** To see all running processes, click View Full Report. **4**

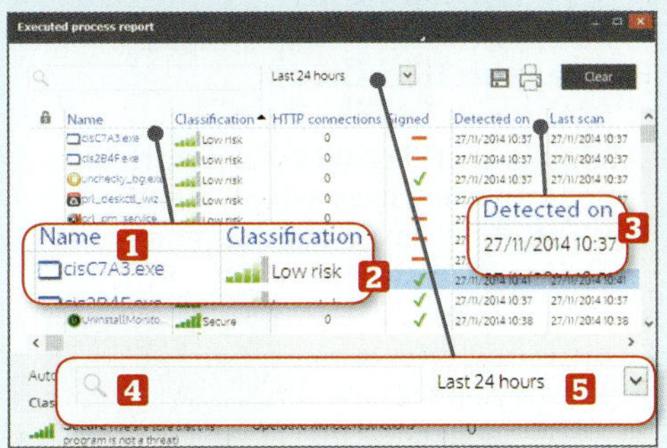

2 The full list of running processes will be displayed. You can browse the list or sort the contents by various criteria including name, **1** classification (whether they are secure or risky) **2** and detection date. **3** You can also search for a process by name **4** and filter the list by time period. **5**

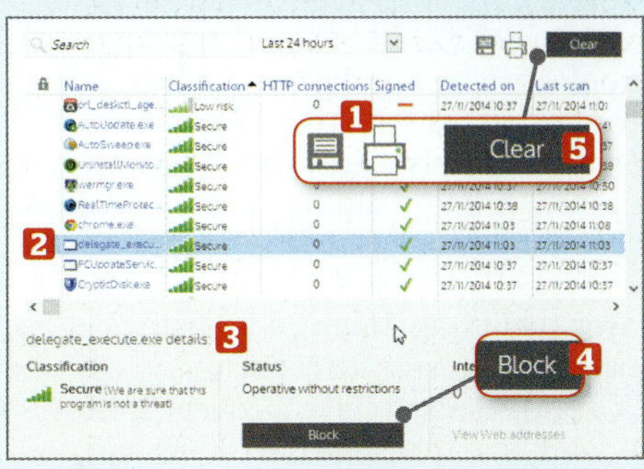

3 The list can be saved or printed **1** for later use (which could come in handy for troubleshooting problems). Select a process **2** to view its details. **3** If you think it might be malicious, you can block it (send it to quarantine). **4** Click the Clear button **5** to wipe the list.

Ebook manger

Calibre

calibre-ebook.com

Min requirements: Windows XP/Vista/7/8+, Mac OS X or Linux

File size: 65.4MB

Why you'll love it

If you enjoy reading ebooks on your computer, then Calibre is an essential tool for managing your collection. It is constantly being tweaked to make it even more useful and can handle most ebook formats. it comes with a built-in viewer and support for all the most popular e-readers, including the Kindle and the Kobo.

You can easily add books to your library, revise the information about them and filter them by various criteria, including title, author, language, format, publisher and rating. Calibre can instantly convert ebooks from one format to another, and you can edit the look and content of books in EPUB and AZW3 (Kindle) formats. You can also compare two books side by side, which is handy if you want to see the differences between converted versions or different editions.

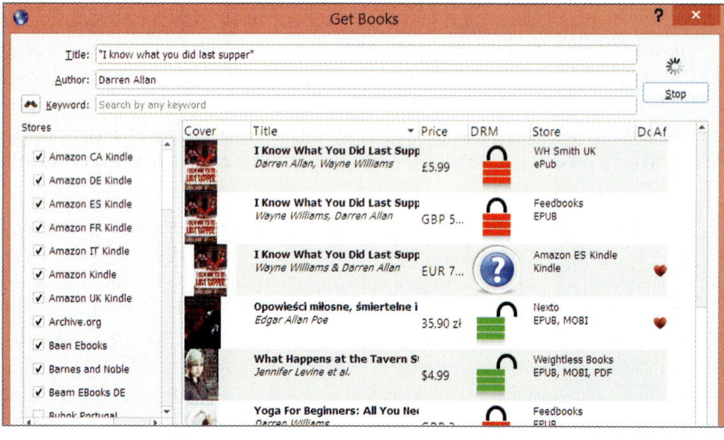

Books can be purchased directly in the program from a selection of retailers, including Smashwords, and stored and accessed online. Calibre's library contains more than 3,800 DRM-free books (drmfree.calibre-ebook.com), spanning genres including Biography, Historical Fiction and Horror/Paranormal.

If a book doesn't have a cover, Calibre can fetch one for you from the web or randomly generate a design. The program is being actively developed, which means you get regular updates that often include additional features and improvements, alongside the usual round of security and bug fixes.

What's the catch?

Calibres' book conversion can be slightly hit and miss, its interface could be more polished and it can be rather confusing at times, but these are minor issues rather than major problems, and shouldn't spoil your enjoyment of the program.

Try this instead

Amazon Kindle

bit.ly/kindle360

Why bother buying a Kindle when you can use Amazon's excellent software to download and read ebooks on your PC? We love that installing the Kindle app on your phone or tablet lets you sync to the furthest page read, so you can pick up where you left off on any of your devices.

MINI WORKSHOP
Convert and edit ebooks using Calibre

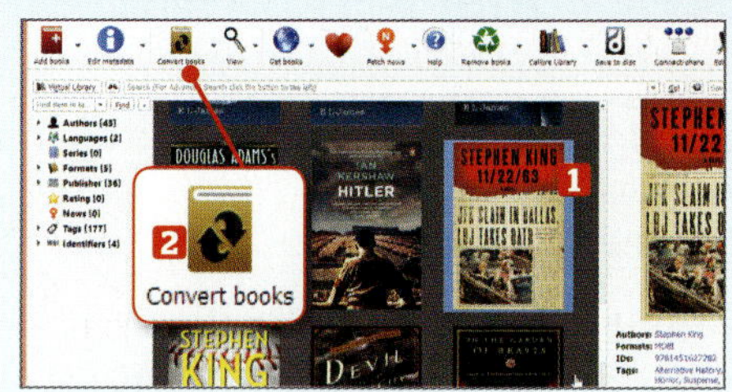

1 Calibre's ebook-conversion process is relatively straightforward. Select a book in your library **1** and click the 'Convert books' button. **2** The arrow to the right of the button will let you convert books individually or batch convert them. You can also create a catalogue of books.

2 The conversion window shows the book format **1** and lets you choose what to convert it to. **2** You can tweak the metadata and various elements, such as the look and feel, **3** and table of contents. **4** Click OK **5** to start the conversion.

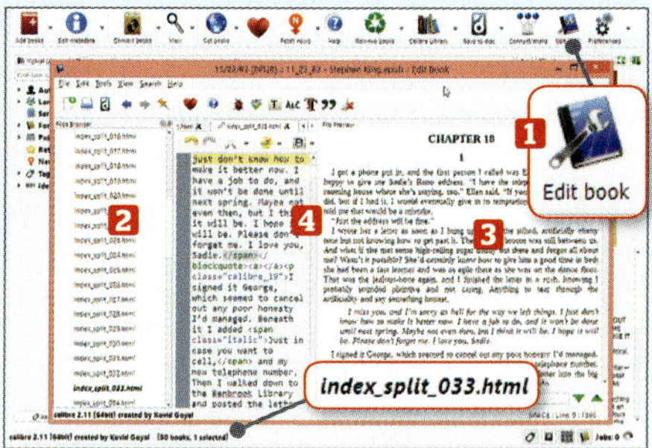

3 To edit a book's contents, select a title in either EPUB or AZW3 format and click the 'Edit book' button. **1** A new window will open. Double-click any of the pages listed in the left sidebar **2** to get a preview. **3** You can make changes to the book by editing the HTML. **4**

System cleaner

CCleaner 5
www.piriform.com/ccleaner

Min requirements: Windows XP/Vista/7/8+ or Mac OS X
File size: 4.9MB

Why you'll love it

CCleaner is a hugely popular clean-up tool, and deservedly so. As well as removing junk files from your PC, which frees up space, it offers lots of useful additional options to tidy the Registry,

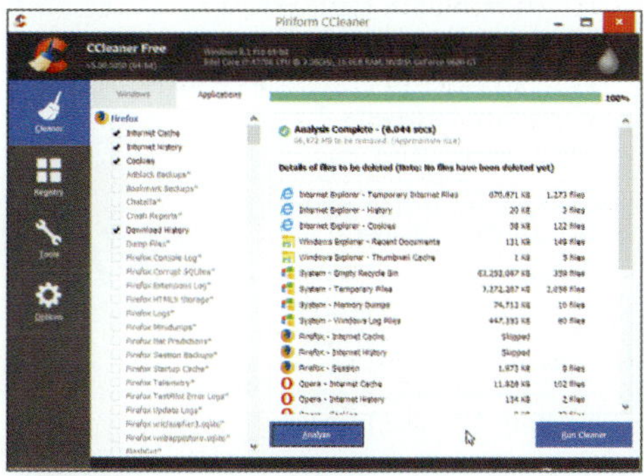

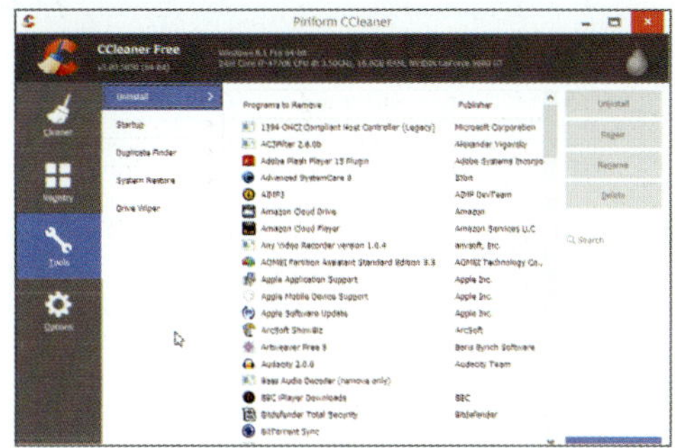

uninstall programs, streamline start-up, find duplicate files, manage System Restore and wipe free space on a drive to prevent deleted files from being recovered. Version 5 sports a flatter, more modern look; adds improved support for cleaning Chrome; lets you manage installed plug-ins; and improves its detection of start-up items.

The updated program detects and deletes junk files faster, thanks to changes in its internal architecture, and also offers optimised builds for Windows 8+ and Windows 10 Technical Preview.

What's the catch?

Originally, it seemed there was nothing massively different about this release. Then Piriform added a new Disk Analyzer tool which lets you see which files and folders are taking up the most space on your hard drive. However, it's not as advanced as some of the disk space utilities we've seen.

Try this instead

Clean Master for PC
bit.ly/clean360

The new PC version of the popular Android app is a worthy rival to CCleaner, with an attractive interface and lots of useful tools. We like that it gives you a precise breakdown of the space you'll reclaim by deleting specific types of file.

Document organiser

Rummage
getrummage.com

Min requirements: Windows XP/Vista/7/8+
File size: 7.7MB

Why you'll love it

If you have a lot of documents on your PC – Word files, spreadsheets, PDFs and so on – finding a specific one can be difficult, especially if you can't remember what it's called and can only recall a few details from its contents. Rummage makes it easy to track down any document whether it's stored on your hard drive or in a cloud storage service such as Google Drive, OneDrive or Dropbox. Once installed, you can add some folders (if you keep documents in places other than the default Windows location) and link your online accounts. Rummage will then get to work indexing your documents. This can take a (very)

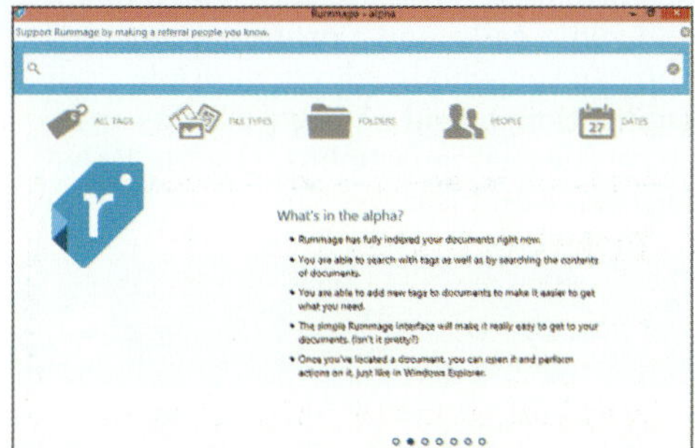

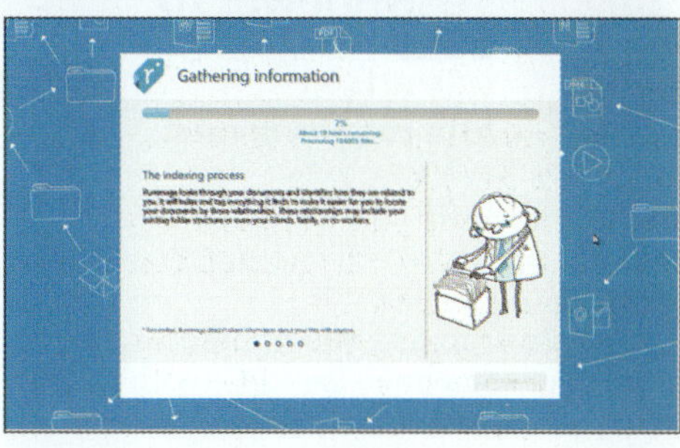

long time, so you'll need to be patient. Once the indexing is complete, you can search for files by name or content, and add tags to documents.

What's the catch?

The current release of Rummage is a an early build so a lot of planned features – such as automatically tracking new, moved, renamed and deleted documents – weren't available at press time.

Try this instead

Everything
www.voidtools.com

This tiny tool finds files and folders on your PC instantly. It's much faster than Rummage at indexing the contents of your hard drive, but doesn't have its advanced features.

Anti-malware

Malwarebytes Anti-Rootkit BETA

www.malwarebytes.org/antirootkit

Min requirements: Windows XP/Vista/7/8+
File size: 15.7MB

Why you'll love it

Rootkits are able to hide running processes, Registry data and even files and folders, cloaking them with a digital shroud of invisibility. Malware hidden in this way is much harder to detect and remove. Thankfully, the new Malwarebytes Anti-Rootkit identifies

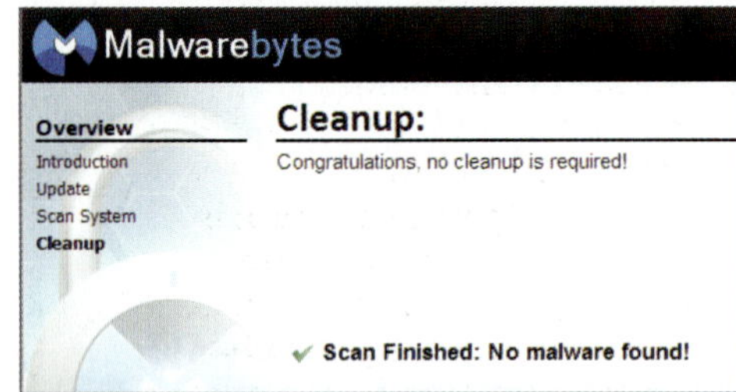

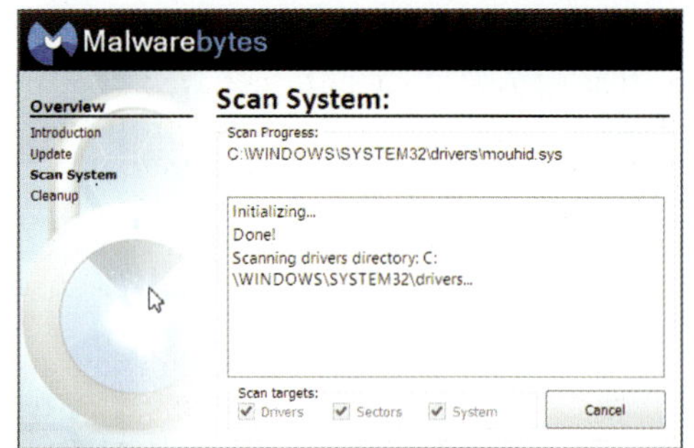

threats that other, similar programs miss, including the nastiest, most deeply embedded rootkits. It then attempts to repair any damage they might have caused.

The program is very easy to use; you just click your way through the wizard-based interface, choose which areas to target (Drivers, Sectors, and/or System) and click Scan. When the process is complete, you'll either receive a message stating that your system is all clear or be given the option to clean up any malware the tool has found.

What's the catch?

Because this is a beta release, you may encounter bugs and other minor problems. It's a very simple program, so there are no advanced options or settings, which may be disappointing for anyone who wants greater control over what it does.

Try this instead

McAfee RootkitRemover
bit.ly/mcafeerootkit360

McAfee Rootkit Remover tool is specifically designed to tackle complex rootkits and associated malware. Currently, it can detect and remove the ZeroAccess, Necurs and TDSS families of rootkit, but it hasn't been updated since June.

Remote-access tool

TeamViewer 10 beta

www.teamviewer.com

Min requirements: Windows XP/Vista/7/8+
File size: 7.5MB

Why you'll love it

TeamViewer 10 lets you remotely take control of someone else's PC (with their permission, of course!) so you can fix problems, show them how to perform a specific task, copy files between systems, and even host virtual meetings. The software is entirely free for personal and non-commercial use (it costs from £439 for businesses) and setting it up is very simple – install it on your main system and then install (or just run it) on the remote computer. Connections are made by entering a unique ID and password at both ends.

The latest version of TeamViewer has a new, modern design and improves performance. You can enjoy video chats and audio calls, add a profile picture (so you can see who is who in multiple connections), find nearby contacts and share files using Dropbox, Google Drive, OneDrive and Box.

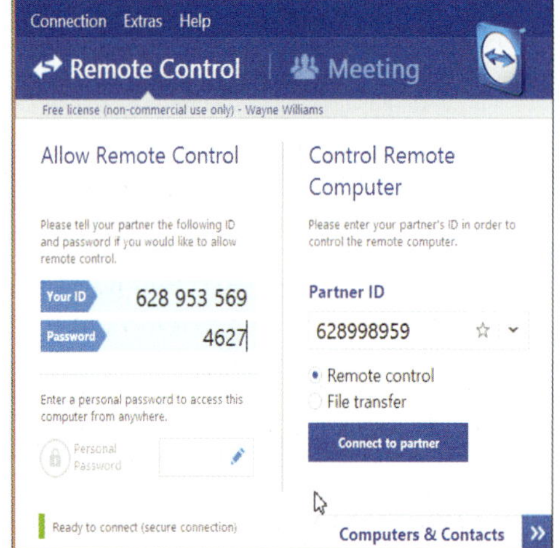

What's the catch?

TeamViewer is aimed primarily at businesses (who have to pay for a licence), so it's packed with features that home users don't need, which can make it appear overly complicated.

Try this instead

Chrome Remote Desktop
bit.ly/chrome360

Install this extension in your version of Chrome and that of a friend, and you can share your Desktops, view and control the other person's screen and fix problems remotely. Compared to TeamViewer, it's very basic, but it's also easier to use.

Secure messenger

BitTorrent Bleep
labs.bittorrent.com/bleep

Min requirements: Windows 7/8+ or Mac OS X
File size: 21.8MB

Why you'll love it

Following Edward Snowden's revelations about the US and UK governments spying on their citizens, along with a host of security breaches in 2014, you might be concerned that snoopers are listening in to your online conversations. BitTorrent Bleep is a peer-to-peer chat tool that lets you securely communicate with friends by text or voice. All messages are fully encrypted and only ever stored directly on your PC, Mac or Android phone. No personally identifiable information is required to use it, and BitTorrent doesn't know who is calling who, or even when communications take place.

You'll be prompted to create an account to use Bleep, which you do by entering an email address or phone number. If you prefer, you can skip this step and use the software incognito, which will allow you to chat with friends. However, they won't be able to search for you.

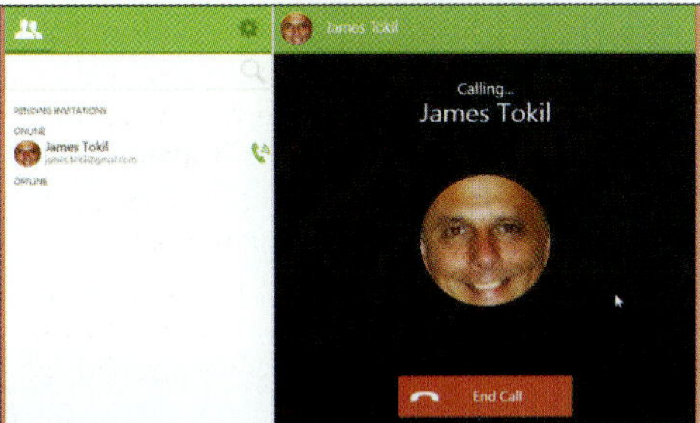

What's the catch?

If the other person you're communicating with isn't online, any messages you send won't be delivered until you're both connected. Offline message sending is set to be improved in future releases. Bleep is currently still an alpha release so it's a little buggy and we've found it often crashes.

Try this instead

Cryptocat
crypto.cat

This simple but powerful tool keeps your communication private by encrypting your messaging. It works with Firefox, Chrome, Opera and Safari; is compatible with Facebook Messenger; and lets you share photos and videos privately.

Media converter

Icecream Media Converter
icecreamapps.com

Min requirements: Windows XP/Vista/7/8+
File size: 30.9MB

Why you'll love it

There are lots of programs you can use to convert audio and video files from one format to another, but Icecream Media Converter is impressively fast, supports a wide range of formats and delivers excellent results.

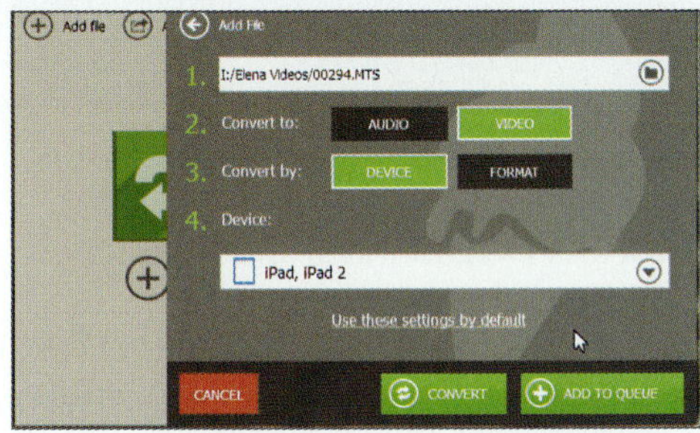

The program couldn't be simpler to use. Just drag your files onto the interface; choose whether you want to convert the media file to audio or video; then opt to convert by device or format. Pick the output type in the drop-down menu, then convert the file or add it to a queue. You can stop the conversion process at any time if you need to add extra files. You can also convert web content (such as YouTube videos) by pasting in the URL. Your conversion preferences can be saved as defaults.

What's the catch?

It offers a long list of devices you can convert to, but it's missing a few recent options, such as the iPhone 6/6 Plus. Sorting the device list into categories would make it easier to browse.

Try this instead

Freemake Video Converter and Audio Converter
www.freemake.com

We've long been fans of Freemake's free tools (but not their bundled extras), which are easy to use; compatible with a wide range of media formats; and can convert large and multiple files in a matter of seconds.

WILL BUNDLED 'CRAPWARE' GET WORSE?

Why do developers bundle software with third-party tools?
Some companies pay handsomely for their programs to be bundled with other software – anything from a few thousand dollars to $100,000 (£63,900) or more, depending on the number of downloads and installs. This makes it a lucrative option for software developers who may be struggling to make money from their work.

Are there different forms of crapware?
Some programs automatically install alongside the actual software you want unless you deselect them, and use underhand tricks, such as making the Decline button appear greyed out, to fool you into thinking you can't reject them. The worst are programs installed without your knowledge, which you then have to uninstall (often with great difficulty). Crapware frequently makes unwanted changes, such as switching your browser's homepage and default search engine.

Doesn't bundling junk hurt a developer's reputation?
Yes, but for many developers, the financial rewards make it worthwhile. Companies that provide crapware want their products on as many machines as possible, because it's often how they make their money. For example, the Ask search engine bundles its browser toolbar with lots of programs (such as the Java updater) and changes your default search option to Ask.com. The company makes its money from advertising, so it needs as many people as possible to run searches through its website.

How else can developers earn money?
They can sell their products, ask for donations, offer paid-for premium versions and include adverts in the products or on the download site. But these methods may not be as lucrative.

How do you avoid installing crapware?
Always choose the Custom option when installing software so you can reject any hidden extras. You can also install Unchecky (unchecky.com), a brilliant free program that stops you accidentally installing bundled adware and toolbars by automatically spotting and rejected unwelcome "offers".

Media centre

KODi
kodi.tv

Min requirements: Windows XP/Vista/7/8+. Mac OS X or Linux
File size: 67.4MB

Why you'll love it

Kodi is the new name for the popular XBMC media player and entertainment hub (which, in turn, was originally called the Xbox Media Center). It can be run on any operating system and lets you organise and play music and video files from local and networked storage media,

and stream content from the internet. If you have a TV tuner installed, you can use it as a PVR, to watch and record live television.

What's particularly great about Kodi is its support for third-party add-ons, so you can add lots of new features to the software, including YouTube and 4oD. You can browse and install available add-ons through the application itself, or on the Kodi website.

What's the catch?

Kodi is currently only a beta, so you may encounter bugs and other problems when using the software. If you do run into trouble, there is a stable version of XBMC you can download from the site.

Try this instead

MediaPortal
www.team-mediaportal.com
This program is an attractive alternative to Kodi that can play music, videos, DVDs, Blu-rays and live radio, and display photos and weather reports. It can also stream and record live television if you have a TV tuner installed.

Download paid-for software for free

The best programs and apps come at a price – most of the time. We reveal our favourite secrets for getting paid-for software for free

Discover freebies and offers before they expire

Get a paid-for program for free every day

The name of 'Giveaway of the Day' (GotD, www.giveawayoftheday.com) is itself a bit of a giveaway. This free website gives away a different paid-for program, for free, every day. It also archives the programs so you can download previously featured software at its full price.

Go to the GotD homepage and you'll see today's offer, with a ticker telling you how many hours and minutes are left until it expires. On the day we're writing this, the giveaway is InstantPhotoSketch Pro 2.0, a powerful but easy tool for transforming your digital photos with pencil and brush filters. It would normally set you back $39.95 (£26.50, www.snipca.com/15090) but, for one day only, it's completely free – only via the GotD website.

Click the yellow 'Proceed to download page' button to see a page with more information about the day's freebie, including user ratings and comments, system requirements, file size and a link to its publisher's website. Then click the blue 'Download [program name] now' link, save the ZIP file to your Desktop and extract its contents. Run the setup file, then run the licence-activation file to unlock the program's full version. Instructions are in 'Readme.txt'.

We visited a lot of 'deal of the day' websites when researching this feature, and most are ugly as sin. GotD is the exception that proves the rule, with a clean simplicity that makes it a pleasure to browse. It does include a couple of adverts unless you block them using an extension

Download a paid-for program free every day from 'Giveaway of the Day' – and see the giveaways you missed

like Adblock Plus (https://adblockplus.org), but it's extremely restrained compared with similar sites.

Scroll down the homepage to browse recent giveaways, which include EaseUS Partition Manager Pro (normally $39.95/£26.50, www.snipca.com/15088) and Aiseesoft Total Video Converter (normally $45/£30, www.snipca.com/15089).

What's the catch?

You have to act fast. The free program must be installed and registered within its 24-hour window. This isn't midnight to midnight, but 8am to 8pm UK time – because GotD is based in US (PST time). If you download the installer file (usually EXE or ZIP), but don't get round to installing it before the deadline, its licence will expire and it won't work.

Once you've installed your freebie, you won't get free technical support or upgrades to subsequent versions of the program. If you uninstall it, you can't re-install it for free.

As with all installable software, you must be vigilant during setup and make sure to choose a Custom option if offered, and opt out of added extras such as search toolbars. Our InstantPhotoSketch setup wizard didn't offer any unwanted extras at all, but the activation file did. To avoid the extra, click Close when you see a window that says 'Successfully activated', and don't click Install Software Informer.

Get a paid-for app for free every day

'Giveaway of the Day' also runs sites for Android (www.snipca.com/15096) and iPhone (www.snipca.com/15097; most apps also work on iPad, as you'll discover when you click 'Get the App'). These GotD sites are freebie-finders rather than freebie-hosts. They sniff out price-drops on the Google Play Store and Apple's App Store, list them all with ratings and comments, then link you to the relevant download pages. GotD has an Android app (www.snipca.com/15104) that lists current Play Store offers and lets you install apps from the Play Store with one tap.

Our favourite source of free apps, however, is the free online service AppGratis (http://appgratis.com). The first thing you see when you visit the site is a pop-up window. This would normally infuriate us, but we rather like this pop-up because it's your gateway to the free, unmissable, daily AppGratis newsletter.

Tick one or more of the boxes according to the devices you have (Android, iPhone and/or iPad), make sure the dropdown menus are set to English and UK, then enter your email address and click the green 'Sign up here' button. Now, every morning, you'll get a separate email for each of your chosen app platforms, with a link to download a paid-for app for free from the Play Store or the App Store. The email also contains a brief review of the app and an unrelated joke, video or piece of trivia to brighten your morning. It's much more likeable than it sounds.

More importantly, the savings can really add up, especially for iPad and iPhone apps, which were significantly more expensive than Android apps even before Apple whacked up their prices.

Even better, once you've installed an app during its freebie period, you will continue to get free updates after it goes back to being paid-for. You can even uninstall it from your tablet or phone to free up space

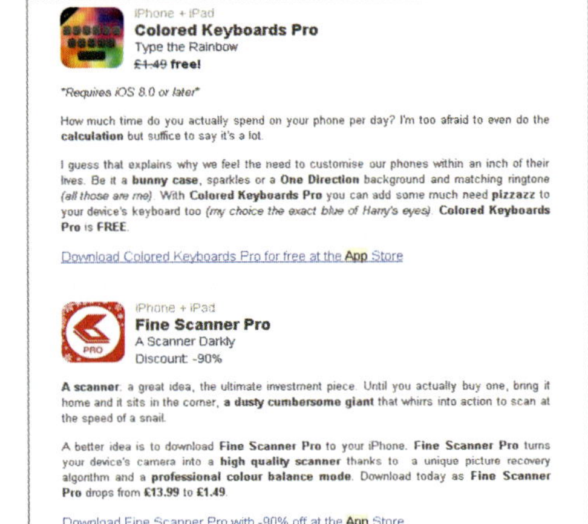

Get a paid-for iPad, iPhone and Android app for free every day via the AppGratis newsletters

and re-install it again later via your Google or Apple account.

There's also an AppGratis Android app (www.snipca.com/15105) that sends you daily freebie notifications and lets you download free apps safely via the Play Store. There used to be an AppGratis iOS app, too, and it was even more useful than the Android app, with huge savings to be made. But Apple kicked AppGratis out of the App Store in 2013 (see box below), so if you have an iPad or iPhone you'll have to rely on the daily newsletter for your freebie notifications.

Amazon's new Appstore (www.snipca.com/15121) is also worth a look if you're on Android. It doesn't link you to the Play Store; instead, you install apps by first installing the Amazon Appstore app (www.snipca.com/15120). Once you've installed the app, it offers one paid-for app for free every day.

What's the catch?

You've probably worked that out already. Most of these freebies are for Android only. Android apps are cheaper anyway (actually, they're usually free) so you simply don't stand to save as much money by getting these apps for free.

Apple hasn't quite managed to stamp out attempts to save people money. The AppGratis website and newsletter are still full of free iOS apps that would normally set you back a few pounds. We hope they continue going strong for a long time, despite Apple's best efforts.

WHY DID APPLE TRY TO KILL APPGRATIS?

The AppGratis story is really a story about Apple's prices. Have a seat and let's begin.

In 2008, French engineer Simon Dawlat created AppGratis for iOS and Android. The app scoured Google's Play Store and Apple's App Store for time-limited free offers, notified you, and let you tap a button to download the freebie instantly from the Play Store or App Store. Dawlat also struck deals with app developers to offer their wares free for limited periods.

AppGratis was free to use, quick, easy and saved you money. It was the perfect app. On Android, it still is the perfect app.

In April 2013, Dawlat was on a plane to Brazil when Apple announced it was kicking AppGratis out of the App Store – in other words, making it impossible to download or update on an iPad or iPhone. The move could have destroyed Dawlat's business overnight. When he landed in Brazil, he found so many concerned messages awaiting him that he thought a family member had died.

Dawlat quickly published his thoughts on the matter, along with the correspondence he'd received from Apple. You can still read it on the AppGratis blog (www.snipca.com/15106).

AppGratis is still going, of course, but the iOS app had been the main way its users – 12 million of them on iPhone alone – saved money. Which is why Apple didn't like it.

Since ousting AppGratis, Apple has been busy cracking down on other third-party attempts to compromise its income. Its operating systems have always been well protected, with Mac OS X and iOS both using sandbox technology to ensure apps can't be installed from outside the App Store. This structure also keeps out system tools such as battery-monitors and file managers; prevents sharing between apps; ties iOS users to iTunes, and gives Apple complete control over pricing.

That's either good business sense or sheer greed. People seem to be voting with their feet. iOS had a big head start on Android, but Android overtook it in June 2012 – and Google's platform has since forged ahead, far and fast. No-one can say why for sure, but we'll hazard a guess that cheap apps and a versatile, open platform make Android far more attractive.

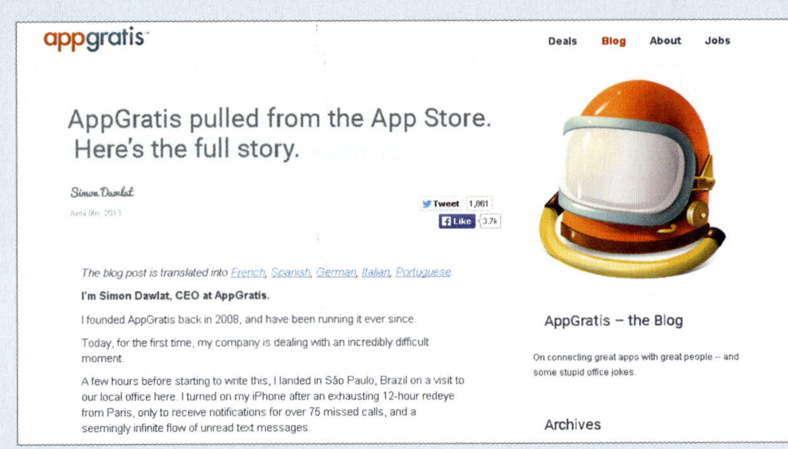

Apple kicked AppGratis out of the App Store in 2013, leaving 12 million iPhone users without their daily freebie

Be first to know about software freebies and offers

Deal-finding website HotUKDeals (HUKD, www.hotukdeals.com) looks cluttered at first glance. But look closer and you'll notice there are no adverts (unusually, HUKD looks exactly the same whether you enable or disable your ad-blocker), no dollar signs (it's a proper UK website) and a wealth of useful information, all extremely well organised.

HUKD doesn't sell anything, it just finds it. If a program, app or anything else catches your eye in the list of offers, click Get Deal, then complete your purchase on the third-party website, which opens in a new tab. For example, in our screenshot (right) we clicked Get Deal on the Windows 8.1 app Plex, so the relevant page of the Windows Store is open in the next tab at the top.

The offers go far beyond software. HUKD helps you save on gadgets, DVDs, computer games, toys, gifts, days out and even loo roll. If you're not interested in groceries, go to the HUKD Blogs menu at the right of the page and click the middle icon ('Mobot'). Now you'll see a list of tech offers, including cut-price tablets (loads of them), PCs and phones as well as software and games.

To save the hassle of visiting the site every day, sign up for the daily newsletter by typing your email address in the box above HKUD Blogs. You don't have to sign up with HUKD.

Money Saving Expert (MSE, www.moneysavingexpert.com) is worth a visit, too, and also has an email newsletter with the latest deals. Its remit is much broader than HUKD, so you have to look harder for the tech offers. But dig around and you'll find deals, tips and tools for saving money on your broadband, phone contract, photo printing and more, plus free online tools such as the Local eBay Deals Mapper, which rounds up the best eBay bargains in your area (www.snipca.com/15129).

HotUKDeals looks daunting but it's surprisingly easy to navigate. Click the 'Mobot' icon to filter tech deals, and type your email to get the daily newsletter

What's the catch?

The offers on these sites are cheap but not usually free. Still, a bargain is a bargain, and these sites are so good at finding them that they're somewhat addictive.

Our main problem with MSE is a side-effect of its size. Its unending menus and forum threads (www.snipca.com/15130) are intimidating, and even if you use the search box you have to wade through loads of results to find what you're after. To fit everything in, the site uses tiny text, so it's hard to read unless you zoom in – which prevents you seeing the whole page.

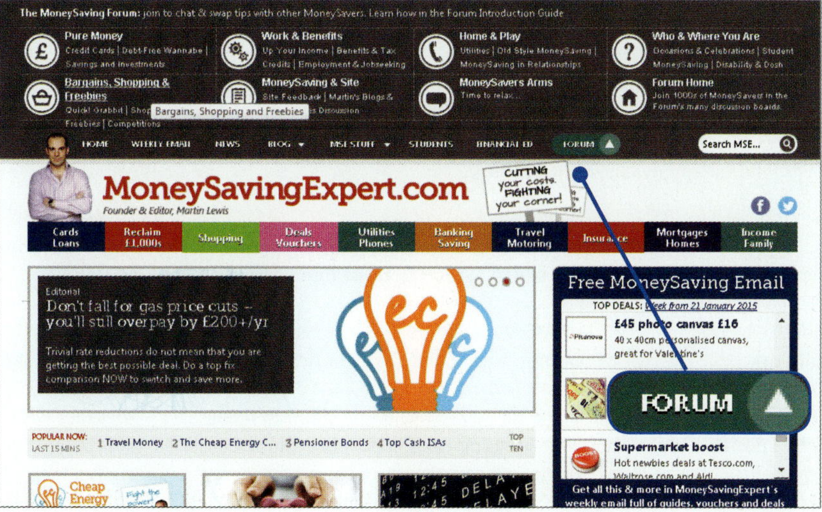

MoneySavingExpert.com has some great software deals if you dig deep – especially in its forum

Buy a cheap program, get an expensive program free

If you're a regular HUKD or MSE visitor you'll know the name TrialPay. This service is a kind of digital version of 'buy one get one free', but instead you buy one cheap product and get one expensive product free. Sounds like a good deal to us.

TrialPay's website (www.trialpay.com) is for business clients and doesn't include a menu of its current offers, which seems a bit daft. To find these deals, you have to go looking for them – and hope you find them before they expire.

You could search Google (type the name of a program, plus 'trialpay'), but most links will be expired offers. Instead, browse for current TrialPay offers on HUKD or MSE, and check 24Hsoftware.com (www.snipca.com/15132), which currently links to free offers for Able Photo Resizer (normally $15, or £10) and WinZip Pro (normally £42.95). A few deals on 24Hsoftware.com had expired when we checked them, so it's hit-and-miss, but still worth a look.

We clicked the Able Photo Resizer link on 24Hsoftware.com and it took us to a web page hosted by TrialPay (check that 'trialpay.com' is part of the URL). Here's where you complete your side of the deal by entering your name and email address. Keep 'Let me know about other special offers' ticked to receive the TrialPay offers newsletter, then click Continue. On the next page ('Complete 1 offer'), choose a cheap product or sign up for an online service. Finally, TrialPay will send you an email containing a licence number for the program's full version. Keep the licence number safe in case you ever need to re-install the program.

Most TrialPay offers are for US products, so the prices you see on the offer page are given in dollars. However, all the 'Complete 1 offer' prices are in pounds, so there are no international payment fees to pay. Click 'Learn more' next to any item in the 'Complete 1 offer' list to visit its third-party website (most are UK-based) and decide whether or not to complete the deal.

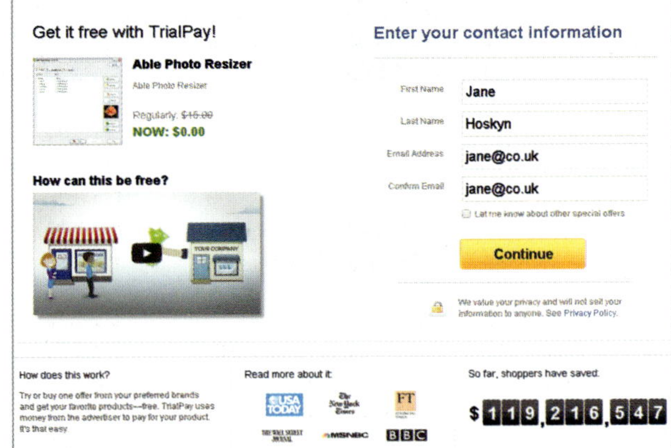

Fill in your details and buy a cheap item to get a paid-for program free using TrialPay

What's the catch?

We don't like handing over our name, email address and payment details to any company, let alone a company with the words 'trial' and 'pay' in its name. It just feels dodgy. But TrialPay is a legitimate company, and these are legitimate deals – just be aware they're in it to make money too.

A more worrying criticism of TrialPay is unreliability. When we researched people's experiences, we found a few forum posts complaining that the promised licence numbers never turned up. The problem was usually fixed after a stern email to TrialPay, but that shouldn't be necessary. You kept your side of the deal, so TrialPay should keep its side, no ifs or buts.

The deals, by the way, are TrialPay's responsibility. For example, if you were promised a licence for WinZip and it hasn't arrived, contact TrialPay, not WinZip. TrialPay is actually very strict with the companies it strikes deals with (its legal terms make heavy reading: www.snipca.com/15134), and they do want these offers to work as promised.
To contact Customer Support, use the secure form (with hideous captcha, sorry) at www.snipca.com/15135.

CAN YOU HACK 30-DAY SOFTWARE TRIALS TO LAST FOREVER?

It's possible. Like using torrents to get paid-for software free, trial-hacking breaks licensing rules – but people do it, and there's information about it all over the internet. Hackers aren't very good at keeping secrets, you see. They show off about their dubious labours on websites, forums and even YouTube, where you'll find videos like 'How to Crack Any Software' (www.snipca.com/15062).

In short, the process involves tricking an installed program into thinking it's at the start of its 30-day run instead of the end. Every month, the user "rewinds" the program's internal clock.

One of the most popular tools that's used (well, abused) for this purpose is RunAsDate (www.snipca.com/15069). This free portable tool lets you set different times and dates for different programs on your PC, for perfectly legitimate reasons, without affecting your system clock.

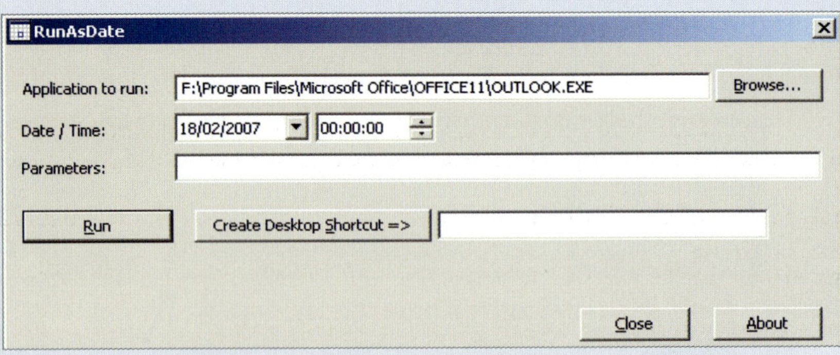

You can use RunAsDate to change a program's internal clock – a trick that some people have tried to use to extend trials of free software

RunAsDate is easy to use and made by one of our most trusted independent developers, Nir Sofer (aka NirSoft, www.nirsoft.net). Sofer really doesn't want you to use his program to break software licensing rules. Just below the screenshot on the download page you'll see an 'Important Notice!!' (big red letters), where Nir says he gets many emails from users who complain RunAsDate "doesn't work" – because they can't get it to unlock all the trial versions they throw at it. He stresses the tool is not designed for such law-breaking, and reminds users that many trial programs are set to automatically block unauthorised changes to the time or date.

More ambitious software-hackers have found ways to get around this by reverse engineering trial programs using tools like OllyDbg (www.ollydbg.de), which lets you take a program apart and put it back together with extra features (say, a permanent licence) and without unwanted features (say, limited trials). OllyDbg is not easy to use – which is why it's best left to amateur programmers, ideally those with honest intentions.

Get old and new software for free

Download future programs while they're free

Paid-for programs were free once, before they grew up and started asking everyone for money. To get this youthful software while it's still free, you have to know where to find it, and sometimes persuade its creator to let you download it – and here's where we can help you.

First, check the excellent website Betabound (www.betabound.com). Scroll down the homepage to see current betas, or click Beta Types at the top-left and browse categories including Windows Betas and iOS App Betas. If a project catches your eye, click Beta Test Now to visit its creator's site in a new tab, where you may have to fill in your name and email address before you can download anything.

If a project is described as 'early access', it's in pre-beta stage and its developer is still seeking funding. You can still download the software or test it online, and you can offer feedback, but you may need to pay a donation (still much cheaper than waiting for the finished product).

Betabound's categories also include Steam Early Access (beta games) and Backer Reward Betas (crowdfunded projects), but they were both empty when we visited them. Never mind – go to Steam (http://store.steampowered.com) and Kickstarter (www.kickstarter.com) instead, where you'll find free betas (even alphas, which are basically betas of betas) and crowdsourced software aplenty.

Simulators, puzzles and other games are far more likely to be released for beta-testing than big-name software. Steam is almost entirely devoted to games, and new titles appear every day. By the way, if you're a fan of simulators, don't forget to check out page 102 for our pick of several great plane, train and space sims.

What's the catch?

By definition, betas aren't ready. This means they're often buggy and require lots of updates, so you'll need to keep checking its website for the latest version.

Many betas are only available to a certain number of people, and the best projects fill up fast. Last July, BlackBerry's beta of 'BBM for Windows Phone' launched and expired within a few hours. So if you have a favourite brand or product, join its mailing list and follow it on social-networking sites. Microsoft distributes betas via its Google+ Community page (www.snipca.com/15136), as does CCleaner's maker Piriform (www.snipca.com/15137). Search for your favourite product on Google+ Communities (https://plus.google.com/communities) or browse the beta Communities at www.snipca.com/15138.

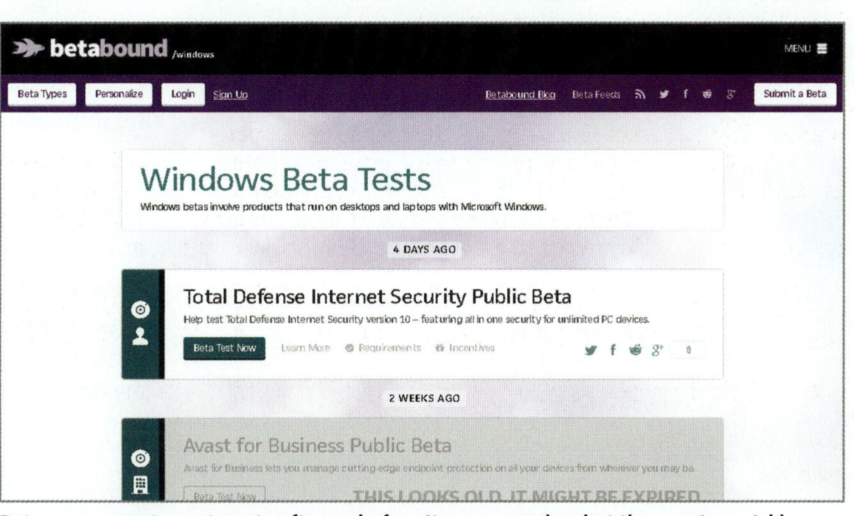

Betas are a great way to get software before it goes on sale – but they expire quickly

Download old versions of programs

As we mentioned in our Music and Video chapter, The Internet Archive (https://archive.org) lets you download classic films and TV shows for free. Here's even better news: you can download classic video games and software for free, too, including old versions of software that now costs money.

Click Software in the row of links at the top (or go straight to the page: www.snipca.com/15139), then settle down for a leisurely browse. This site is definitely not designed for the glance-and-grab approach to downloading software – and we mean that as a compliment. It's a wonderful place to spend an afternoon, a week or more.

It's easy to get carried away playing free Amiga-era games in the site's Old School Emulation Center (www.snipca.com/15140) or browsing the tens of thousands of free programs in the Open Source Software Collection (www.snipca.com/15141), but the real money-saving action is in the Shareware CD Archive (www.snipca.com/15142), a vast collection of downloadable software donated by Internet Archive users over two decades. Fancy turning the clock back with a free download of Microsoft Windows NT Server 4? You can (www.snipca.com/15143). Click the tiny 'CD/DVD' link on the left to download an ISO ('disc image') file containing the entire operating system, licence key included.

Everything on the Internet Archive is free to download or view online, but you'll see an appeal for donations at the top, just like on Wikipedia. If you can spare a couple of pounds to keep this incredible resource alive, you'll be helping to make the internet a better place.

What's the catch?

Old software is no longer supported or patched by developers, so they may not work as expected, and some versions may even have security flaws that could make you unsafe if you run it while you're connected to the internet.

If you want to squeeze more life out of an old software CD rather than shelling out for an upgrade, or you fancy trying some ISO files downloaded from the Internet Archive, run them in a partition or use a virtual PC program such as VirtualBox (see page 62), which is free (www.virtualbox.org).

Software directory